D0979870

HOW TO BE FUNNY ON PURPOSE

JOKES HUMOR COMEDY

CREATING
AND
CONSUMING HUMOR

Edgar E. Willis

With a chapter about humor on the Internet
by Richard L. Weaver II

How to be Funny On Purpose

Library and Archives Canada Cataloguing in Publication

Willis, Edgar E., 1913-
How to be funny on purpose / Edgar E. Willis.

Includes bibliographical references and index.
ISBN 0-9737545-3-2

1. American wit and humor--History and criticism.   I. Title.

PS430.W54 2005   C817.009   C2005-903887-X

This edition published by Cybercom Publishing
835 York Mills Rd., # 1135
Toronto, Ontario Canada M3B 1Y2
E-mail: benh@cybercominc.net

Cover, layout and text design: Tim Harrison
Cover illustration: Richard L. Weaver II and Anthony Weaver

Printed and bound in the United States of America and London, England.

This book is dedicated to:

my wife Zella (better known to me as Buster) who had the patience to decipher my penciled hieroglyphics, the skills required to turn them into an impeccably typed and edited manuscript, and the grace to laugh out loud on occasion at the jokes she was transcribing.

Special acknowledgments to:

Bentley Harrison, Tim Harrison, Richard L. Weaver II, and Anthony Weaver, who saw promise in my book and possessed the knowledge, the drive, and the perseverance needed to bring it before an audience.

The hundreds of funny people whose wit and humor have enriched my life through many decades, and whose jokes provided most of the raw material from which this book emerged.

Praise for How to be Funny on Purpose

"As an international lawyer, I believe that greater use of humor, as thoughtfully and entertainingly analyzed in this book, could do a lot to improve our relations with peoples and governments in other countries. And speaking of governments, the excellent chapter on political humor in the United States should be required reading for our current legislators who seem to have gotten themselves bogged down in acrimony and partisanship."

Mark Sandstrom,
Attorney, Washington, D.C.

"While reading How to be Funny on Purpose, I found myself acutely aware of humor in my personal and professional life. I found humor in the State Senate hearing room, in my refrigerator, and at the doctor's office. The book is also true to its title. Once I became aware of the opportunities, I found myself creating spontaneous jokes . . . much to the dismay of my family. Since reading the book, I now have the resources and tools to add humor to my public speaking engagements."

Becky Spencer,
Vice President of Child Care,
YMCA and JCC of Greater Toledo

"Few authors make use of such rich and wonderfully humorous examples to illustrate major concepts. Willis puts humor front and center in the human communication process---helping all of us to appreciate how we might enrich our lives (and the lives of others) through the art of telling jokes."

Pam Shockley-Zalabak,
Chancellor and Professor of Communications,
University of Colorado at Colorado Springs

"Warning-Do not read this book in bed----your laughter may awaken those around you! Edgar Willis lures you into learning how to create and tell good stories while he tickles your funny bone. He makes learning about humor a fun experience by 'practicing what he preaches' (or should I say teaches?). The laughter lasts throughout the book. A great book for anyone who does public speaking or who just loves good jokes."

Shirley Allen
Toronto, Ontario, Canada

"This book is a treasure trove of fascinating reading for anyone who takes special delight in humor and enjoys a good joke. Professor Willis provides an esoteric, but very readable analysis of why we laugh at jokes and why something is funny. He takes us into the realm of analysis, and he makes us understand how humor is deeply entrenched in our basic humanity.

After reading his analysis of why a particular joke is funny and works well as a joke, it seems almost transparent and obvious. He makes particularly effective reference to very well known jokes and lines from famous comedic personalities known to all of us, and this certainly further enhances the readability of this book."

William C. Orr, Ph.D.
President and CEO
Lynn Health Science Institute
Clinical Professor of Medicine
Oklahoma University Health Sciences Center

If you want to learn how to enliven your public speaking with humor, or upgrade your current results, "How to be Funny on Purpose" is just the book you need. It explains what makes a joke funny, gives you resources to mine, steps to follow in custom tailoring material, and examples galore. Even if you are afraid that you have no sense of humor, the reading will teach you to laugh - and enjoy it."

John C. Bryan,
President, BWB Consultants Ltd.,
Toronto, Ontario, Canada

"Dr. Willis is rib-ticklingly funny! It is a joy to read. His anecdotes cover a wide range of topics and styles. He teaches his reader how to create good stories that are short, pithy and witty. This book is a tremendous asset for anyone who wishes to communicate more effectively; it provides a wealth of information presented in a very humorous fashion. He is a master craftsman. "How to be Funny on Purpose" is a model of 'Edu-tainment'."

Rev. Kenneth Allen, Ph.D.
Retired clergyman and psychotherapist,
Toronto, Ontario, Canada

4b

Table of Contents

Why Read This Book?

Books and articles dealing with humor number in the many thousands, yet few of the authors responsible for this vast outpouring of words have attempted to explain how to create an original joke. Most of those who have tried tend only to nibble around the edges of the subject. One author, for example, counseled aspiring joke makers to roll ideas through their heads. That is good advice as far as it goes, but it leaves most of the process in a condition of fuzzy vagueness. This book provides a systematic description of the steps to follow in creating a joke from the time a beginning idea first flits into your mind to the moment a finished product emerges—fully realized, original, and funny.

I suspect that many of you are wondering at this point why you should be interested in learning how to construct your own jokes. Professional humorists need that ability, of course. It scarcely needs saying that to survive in the competitive world of comedy, you must be able to create new jokes bearing an individual personal stamp and do it on a regular basis. But most of you, I'm sure, are not thinking of becoming stand-up comedians, cartoonists, humorous essayists, or some other career that confronts you with the constant challenge of making people laugh. Why then should you learn how to create jokes?

Professional humorists are not the only ones, however, who benefit from being funny. People who can make their relatives and friends laugh at regular intervals become especially valued and sought-after companions. By inserting a joke into a sermon, a preacher can jar open the eyes of a nodding church goer, a teacher can add zest to a geometry lesson by embellishing it at times with humor, a lecturer can enliven, freshen, and add warmth and humanness to a speech or presentation, an office-seeker may even win votes with a joke if it is appropriate to the occasion and adroitly presented.

I sense another question. Why do I have to invent my own jokes to accomplish these purposes? Can't I just use a joke I've heard or read somewhere or seen on the Internet? The answer: Of course you can. In fact, most of the jokes we tell come from sources other than ourselves. Some people even acquire reputations as celebrated wits without ever giving birth

6

to a joke of their own.

In the light of these facts, you may well wonder whether there is anything at all that a person with no intention of becoming a professional joke maker can gain from learning how to produce original humor. I can think of at least three benefits. One is that a joke you invent can be tailored to fit precisely the situation you aim to illustrate. A second is that when listeners realize that the joke they are laughing at is one you made up, they may well respond with expressions of delighted surprise and looks reflecting newly felt respect and admiration. Their laughter is also likely to become far more exuberant than it would to recycled material, which, some in the group may have already heard. There is a third benefit. The deep feeling of satisfaction one always feels at making an audience laugh is transformed into a state of bliss bordering on the exquisite when that result is accomplished with a witticism you have invented.

You should not assume that the instruction in this book describes a method for turning out jokes automatically. No such system exists nor can it ever exist. To be funny one must possess some measure of creative spark, the ability to detect the quaint, the off-center, and the absurd in life. This book can help develop and nourish that talent. For those who yearn to become practitioners in the world of comedy, it can help build the foundation needed to get started. Others with the more modest goal of enlivening a speech, a lesson, or a conversation with wit of their own, can benefit from the practical guidance it provides.

Some of the information may be familiar to you, but you will also find yourself being taken down paths you have never before explored. You will be introduced to new and innovative terms which define concepts that are also new. You will discover that skill in making connections is at the heart of the joke-making process. You will find that unless listeners connect the ideas you present to ideas of their own, your joke will collapse like a punctured balloon. You will even learn there are things you can do to nudge your creative machinery into action when you lack even the faintest glimmer of a beginning idea.

But when I wrote this book, I had more in mind than the needs and interests of people who long to become creators of humor. As much as anything else, it is aimed at those who think of themselves simply as consumers of humor. And doesn't that include almost everyone? The actress Julia Roberts is reputed to have said, "Ask to see a person who doesn't like to laugh and I'll show you a person with a toe tag."

This book offers a feast of jokes, hundreds of them; there's even one in the index. With perhaps one or two exceptions, all were included for the specific purpose of illustrating an essential element in the art of joke making. That doesn't mean you are forbidden to enjoy them for their own sake. Each joke appears in an informative context. Among the things that may be explained are the circumstances that produced it, the technique or principle underlying its construction, or the role the audience played in bringing it to fruition. Even had you encountered these jokes without this surrounding context, I think most of them would have made you laugh. But now, armed with new and revelatory information, you will laugh harder because you know why you are laughing.

In a sense this book performs the same kind of function as courses in art and music appreciation. A teacher who draws attention to the delicate interplay of light and shade in a painting or identifies the recurrent themes in a symphony can materially enhance the understanding and enjoyment of a viewer or listener. In the same way this book can sharpen and heighten the enjoyment of consumers of humor by leading them into recognizing such factors as the flash of wit that became the joke's core idea, the masterly way the humorist aligned its elements, or the subtle means through which consumers were guided into making the required connection without its being made explicit. They will also experience the deep personal satisfaction that comes from seeing the point to the joke on their own.

Other material broadens these understandings. The first chapter catalogues the benefits that being funny can confer. The second journeys back to the misty beginnings of human history to show that men and women have always been preoccupied with humor. A legendary figure name Palamedes, a character in Homer's *Odyssey,* is reputed to have invented the first joke some 3000 years ago. Since then such transcendent thinkers as Plato, Aristotle, Cicero, Thomas Hobbes, Immanuel Kant, and Arthur Koestler have grappled with the intriguing mystery of what it is that makes people laugh. Their theories and speculations provide the foundation upon which my own approach is based.

The third chapter deals with humor created when people misspeak, fail to detect double meanings lurking behind ostensibly innocuous words, or become the victim of an unexpected configuration of circumstances and, thus, stumble into being funny without intending to be. Such mishaps are highly relevant to our subject because we guffaw at the hilarious and sometimes embarrassing eruptions caused by accidental humor for the same reasons that we laugh at carefully planned and rehearsed jokes.

The chapters following the five chapters devoted to explaining the mechanics of joke making deal with further facets of the subject. In Chapter nine I take the possibly presumptuous step of advancing a set of criteria for distinguishing good jokes from bad ones. In Chapter ten I discuss the difficulties arising when a joke designed to make an audience laugh suddenly whips around and nips you. Humor seen as being improper or inappropriate can sometimes fatally damage a career. Deciding whether to tell a certain joke is often a perplexing problem. I offer some criteria for determining which way to go. The final chapter describes practical ideas for using the Internet to locate a joke that fits a particular person or situation or to find material that can set you on the path to developing a joke of your own.

References to the giants of humor appear throughout the book. Mark Twain looms large. For those who are sufficiently mature, mentions of luminaries of the recent past like Robert Benchley, Jack Benny, Fred Allen, and Victor Borge should evoke warm memories of their droll and inimitable approaches to life's absurdities. Such contemporary comedians and humorists as Dave Barry, Jerry Seinfeld, David Letterman, Jay Leno, and Jon Stewart are also bountifully represented.

Those of you who like to tell jokes may find some gems to add to your repertory. Even those of you who recoil in horror from the mere thought of telling a joke may find that a particular joke strikes a chord. You suddenly experience an impelling urge to pass it on. If you still feel timid, you may benefit from reading a section of the book that details some rules for telling jokes effectively. Emboldened, you take the plunge. Astonishingly, you hear laughter. No sound is more addictive. A warning is in order. It may start you down the path that will lead you into becoming a habitual joke teller.

In fact, your addiction may become so serious that you begin to wonder whether inventing a joke or two of your own is beyond your reach. One day an idea floats into your mind. You nurse and develop it and eventually a full-fledged joke emerges. You try it out and once more you hear laughter. Again you are caught. No longer will you be a mere consumer of other people's humor. Now you will not only sit at the table, but you will be a contributor to the feast as well.

Edgar W. Willis

Chapter 1
Why Be Funny?

*Humor is a presence in the world
- like grace - and shines on everybody.*
                                      Garrison Keillor

S ome people would find the question that heads this chapter—"Why be funny?"— easy to answer. They make a living from inventing and purveying humor. If asked to name them, we would probably think first of performers like Jay Leno, David Letterman, Mike Myers, and Robin Williams. They are paid handsomely for their appearances on television and in movies and have acquired the kind of fame that makes them recognizable wherever they go. They also earn a less obvious reward—the exquisite pleasure one feels at making an audience laugh. Few other accomplishments evoke a feeling so intense and so satisfying.

The stars of comedy aren't the only ones who work in the humor industry, of course. Most of them don't get as rich or famous as the performers who deliver the funny lines, but if they are good at what they do, they can count on earning a living and, in some cases, a very good one. Some become minor celebrities, directors and writers are examples, and in the print field humorous essayists like Dave Barry have attained some measure of fame. On the other hand, most of us would probably have trouble naming the creators of our favorite comic strips, but a few have escaped anonymity. The comic strip *Peanuts* made the late Charles Schulz a national figure. Others who create humor attract no public notice at all. The contributions of writers to a comedian's monologues are seldom, if ever, acknowledged. The witty people who think up funny ideas for greeting cards—The Hallmark Company employs fifteen of them—work in complete obscurity.

Can any of these people share in the satisfaction that comes from making people laugh? TV and movie writers certainly can. When they hear a studio or theater audience roar with laughter at a joke they have created, they must feel a burst of pride. Gaining this reward is probably most difficult for those whose humor reaches consumers through the print media. I suspect, however, that when comic-strip artists or cartoonists come up with a particularly good gag, they experience a kind of vicarious enjoyment as they visualize an audience of readers laughing at it.

Clearly the financial and psychological rewards earned by people in the humor field vary greatly, depending on the kind of function performed. Some are quite routine. But many workers are confronted by exciting and testing challenges each day they come to work. Meeting them successfully can provide them with satisfying and fulfilling careers.

What if you have no thought of entering the comedy profession in any way whatsoever, will being funny bring you any special rewards? Obviously, it won't fatten your bank account or make your name a byword. You can count on one benefit enjoyed by professionals, however—the pleasure that comes from making people laugh. Your audience doesn't have to be large to gain that benefit. The sight of one set of eyes crinkling with amusement or the sound of a single explosive guffaw incited by something you have said can be enough to produce a feeling of immense satisfaction.

You can also take pleasure in the fact that you have made some contribution to brightening up the world around you. It would be a dreary place indeed if no one ever laughed. The evangelist Billy Graham summed up what humor can do in these words: "Humor helps us to overlook the unbecoming, understand the unconventional, tolerate the unpleasant, overcome the unexpected, and outlast the unbearable."

Being funny can also provide you with some significant personal benefits. It can turn you into a person who is fun to be with, one who can enliven a workplace or add zest to a social gathering. It can add sparkle to your teaching and writing, it can make you a more attractive and effective speaker, it can help you cheer up those who are buffeted by life.

What kind of humor will you dispense? Most of it, I presume, will consist of jokes other people have invented. Something will happen and it will remind you of a funny story you have heard or read somewhere. Because such material is likely to be your main source of humor, you may ask why you should read a book whose main purpose is to show you how to invent and construct your own jokes.

In answering that question, let me begin by saying there is nothing wrong with telling jokes you have picked up elsewhere. Indeed, by using other people's humor, some jokesters have built reputations as inimitable wits without ever devising a single joke of their own. Nevertheless coming up on occasion with a witticism you have invented adds an ingredient of special value to your humor. Because it springs directly out of the situation in which you find yourself, it is likely to be more timely and relevant than someone else's joke. Your listeners, recognizing that your humor is original, will respond with a greater surge of admiration and appreciation than they would to a story they may have heard before. Your inward smile of satisfaction will be greater because your wit has been responsible for the joke, not your memory.

Learning how to invent and construct your own jokes can also make you a better consumer of other people's humor. Having been through the process of creating jokes yourself, you will more quickly recognize and savor the skill required to arrange various ingredients into a combination that provokes laughter. That in turn will burnish and enhance your own sense of humor. Few attributes are more valued, both by those who possess it and by those who benefit from it. In fact, one of the greatest insults a person can suffer is to be reproved with the line, "Don't you have a sense of humor?"

For those of you thinking about becoming professional humorists being able to invent and construct your own jokes is absolutely crucial. No comedian can expect to forge a career simply by using material other people have created. It is true that most comedians who present their own program do maintain a corps of writers to help them prepare materials. In the beginning of their careers, however, they had to depend on their own resources. And even when they reach the stage where they employ writing staffs, they will have to provide direction and guidance. The jokes their writers create should bear their stamp and reflect their style. Audiences must be able to believe that they are products of the comedian's own wit.

Making a Living With Humor

One point seems obvious. The challenge the professional faces in being funny is far greater than that confronting the amateur. Telling a joke that falls flat can be embarrassing to those for whom humor is only a sideline, but it is not a disaster. Too many failed jokes, on the other hand, can end the career of an aspiring professional. Magazine editors, TV executives, the managers of comedy clubs are quick to reject the offerings of humorists who cannot arouse chuckles on a regular basis. Sometimes audiences almost seem to dare a comedian to make them laugh. Being funny in such circumstances is a profoundly difficult task. It requires the possession of certain special qualities. Reviewing the careers of people who have won success in the comedy field, we can discern certain characteristics that distinguish them from ordinary mortals.

First, professional humorists see what is going on around them from a slightly different angle than the rest of us do. Gary Larson, creator of the cartoon series *The Far Side,* seemed to view life through a distorted lens, which gave his humor a quality best described as weird. He is no longer producing new cartoons, but many have been re-published, and some are re-appearing in a line of greeting cards. The monologist Steven Wright, whose expressionless face and monotone delivery set him apart from other stand-up comedians, also takes us down quirky byways the ordinary person seldom travels. There was a unique twist to Phyllis Diller's impish perspective on life, and to Joan Rivers's view of the world.

Second, most professional humorists seem to have a natural, inborn talent for creating humor. Jokes bubble out of them like water out of a spring. They appear to grasp intuitively what they must do to lead an audience into arriving at an idea which they merely suggest. In many instances they cannot keep from being funny even when a situation calls for seriousness.

Often the talent for creating jokes shows up early in life. Jay Leno was producing full-fledged jokes when he was in the fourth grade and Woody Allen as a fifth grader was writing compositions so droll his teacher regularly read them to the other teachers. Allen began earning money as a writer of comedy material while he was still a teenager.

Third, professional humorists have the ability to produce humor in a never-ending flood. Each of the monologues Jay Leno delivers on the *Tonight* show contains 15 to 20 jokes. He and his writers face the enormous task of preparing new jokes night after night and week after week. Moreover, the ones you hear from him and other night-show hosts are only a tiny sampling of the jokes they actually create. Bill Scheft, while a member of David Letterman's writing team, put together something like 30 jokes per show from which Letterman chose only two or three for his monologue. Scheft's column for *Sports Illustrated* presents more than 20 satirical comments on sports events every week. One can suppose that he composes a number of paragraphs that he, or his editor, decide not to use.

Through their long careers, Bob Hope and Milton Berle and their writers each produced something like six million jokes. Steve Allen said in his book, *How to be Funny*, that he kept creating jokes even when he wasn't consciously working at it. Something like 10 to 12 of them sprang into his mind every day. He was so sure of his talent for inventing humor that he would sometimes go on the air without preparing a script ahead of time.

Fourth, professional humorists have the capacity to keep going in the face of rejection. A Jay Leno or a David Letterman did not win the spotlight overnight. Leno began his career as a comedian when he was nineteen. Many years went by, however, before a cruel and indifferent world finally recognized his talent. Along the way to the top his career was marked by buoyant ups and shattering downs. But he had the grit and determination to keep going despite the blows that struck him. David Letterman, who was the host of a late-night show on NBC, confidently expected to replace Johnny Carson on the *Tonight* program when Carson retired. Shockingly, NBC gave the plum assignment to Jay Leno. Despite his overwhelming disappointment, Letterman persevered and was soon selected by CBS to head its *Late Show*. In the years that followed he was afforded the unique challenge of competing directly with the man NBC had chosen over him.

The world of comedy is a harsh and demanding place where only the funniest and most persistent can survive. If you are thinking of entering it, you should conduct a searching examination of your potential. Do your talents and outlook on life measure up to some degree to the criteria I have just described? If you decide you possess what is required, at least in embryo, your next step is to nurture and develop your inborn abilities. The guidance in joke making provided in this book can set you on the right track. By learning what the components of a joke are and the process involved in creating one, you can bring into focus whatever intuitive feel for humor you may possess.

Next, you should seek out opportunities to practice the craft of humor. Doing so can accomplish a double function. First, it can give you a chance to measure audience response to your humor and thus help you determine whether you have the skills that justify persevering. Second, the experience will guide you into improving and polishing your presentations.

What opportunities are available? University students sometimes publish humor magazines. A number of successful professionals gained early experience by writing for them. Conan O'Brien's service on the *Harvard Lampoon* in the middle 1980s became a stepping stone into the professional world of comedy. His career began with stints as a writer for *Saturday Night Live* and *The Simpsons* and reached an early peak with his selection by NBC to occupy the host's chair vacated by David Letterman when he moved to CBS. Later NBC designated him the successor to Jay Leno as host of the *Tonight* show. Other *Lampoon* alumni have also done well in the comedy field. At one time half the writers of *The Simpsons* were Harvard graduates.

A church social event can provide you with a chance to try out jokes. If you participate in a public-speaking activity such as a Toastmasters club, you can make a comedy monologue one of your presentations. Inserting your own jokes into speeches you are invited to give to service clubs or other groups is another way of testing your skill as a joke maker.

If your goal is to become a stand-up comedian, you can begin by entering amateur competitions. If that experience indicates that you have a genuine comedic talent, you should try next for employment in low-echelon comedy clubs, then move on to bigger clubs, particularly those located in such centers of the entertainment industry as New York and Los Angeles. Producers of comedy shows scout them regularly to find new talent. Bookers for the *Tonight* show, for example, found both Jay Leno and David Letterman in that way. The rest, as we might say, is history.

One factor that has played a significant role in advancing the careers of many comedians is a strong writing talent. As we have already noted, Conan O'Brien was making a living as a writer of comedy material before NBC suddenly plucked him from obscurity to make him the host of its late-night talk show, despite his total lack of performing experience. Woody Allen began his career by writing jokes for other people. His next step was to perform the material himself as a stand-up comedian. Progression into the movies followed where he displayed a many-faceted talent as a writer, director, and performer. Along the way he wrote Broadway plays and humorous essays and stories for such magazines as *The New Yorker* and *The New Republic*.

The sketch series, *The Show of Shows*, one of the programs that caused critics to call the period in which it was broadcast the golden age of television, had a number of future Broadway television and movie luminaries on its writing staff. One was Neil Simon whose success as a writer of Broadway comedies is now legendary. Another was Mel Brooks who progressed to writing, directing, and performing in such movie comedies as *Blazing Saddles* and *Young Frankenstein*. More recently he wrote and produced the resounding Broadway hit *The Producers*. Carl Reiner, who both wrote and performed for *The Show of Shows*, went on to write for the movies and to create and write situation comedies for television. One of his series, *The Dick Van Dyke Show*, is now considered a classic of the genre.

Experience as a comedy performer in one medium is good preparation for successful appearances in another. The career of Woody Allen illustrates this point as does that of Robin Williams, who made his first big splash as an actor in the situation comedy *Mork and Mindy*. Before too long he had become a major motion-picture star. The sketch series *Saturday Night Live* gave a host of future film stars their first national exposure as comedians, among them Chevy Chase, John Belushi, Billy Crystal, Eddie Murphy, Dan Ackroyd, and Bill Murray.

The Amateur Humorist

Earlier in this chapter I noted that while professional humorists must rely almost exclusively on material they or their writers turn out, amateurs may use funny items they find elsewhere, along with any witticisms they happen to insert. Using humorous material other people have created is obviously less challenging than originating one's own jokes. Still, some people do it better than others. One necessity is to be alert to the humor around you—in books, magazines, newspapers, television, even the jokes your friends tell. Having a good memory is an obvious asset, but if you are in a field where a regular use of humor may be in order—teaching and preaching come immediately to mind—you should back up your memory by developing an organized system for keeping track of what you find. Filing it under topics related to the ideas you are likely to deal with helps guide you to relevant jokes and sayings when a particular need arises. When that well runs dry, you can turn to compilations of jokes and humorous sayings, many of which classify their contents under topical headings.

One resource you should not overlook in carrying out both the task of finding specific material and of organizing what you have in a meaningful way is your computer. It can provide you with access to the Internet, which teems with a limitless supply of jokes of all kinds. If you have a particular topic in mind, you can almost certainly find jokes related to it. Your computer can also provide you with efficient techniques for organizing the material you already have.

Indeed, your computer can help you be funny in so many significant ways that I have asked an expert in the field, Richard L. Weaver II, to describe the resources it offers and the methods you can use to take advantage of them. His suggestions appear as the final chapter of this book.

Another way in which amateur humorists differ from professionals is that making people laugh is often only a means of attaining another more important goal. The primary aim of people who write advertising copy, for example, is to persuade potential consumers to buy a certain product. Sometimes they employ humor, hoping it will help them achieve that objective. For professional humorists, in contrast, evoking laughter from audiences is their only purpose.

What kind of goals can humor help us attain and in what sorts of situations is its use most likely to be effective? Will it help people advance their careers and in what fields can we expect its use to be most beneficial? What are the specific ways in which it might lead to the betterment of society?

Humor in Explaining and Persuading

In communicating with other people two types of goals predominate. In most instances the aim is either to make some idea, concept, or process clear or to persuade others to accept an idea or undertake a certain course of action. Teachers, for example, are primarily dedicated to developing understandings in their students. The usual aim of politicians, on the other hand, is to persuade their colleagues or their constituents to act in a certain way. In many instances communicators are interested in achieving both clarification and persuasion. Can humor help explain a concept or promote the acceptance of a persuasive argument?

A great deal of research has been carried out to find an answer to that question and to related ones. Few clear-cut answers have emerged. In some instances the findings have been in conflict. That such research has produced equivocal results is not surprising. Designing a study that reveals what happens inside a person's head as the result of hearing a joke is one of the most difficult challenges a researcher can face. We do not need experimental studies, however, to arrive at some of the answers we seek. We can reach certain conclusions simply by observing how audiences react to humor. It is clear that being funny can help explainers and persuaders in a number of ways.

One obvious benefit is that humor captures the attention of an audience. It would be difficult to think of anything more important to a speaker or writer. If you don't catch the attention of your audience, you accomplish nothing. The playwright Herb Gardner summed up the point by saying, "Once you get people laughing, they're listening, and you can tell them almost anything."

Even neophyte speakers seem to sense intuitively that humor gets them the ears of their audience, and so they scramble around to find something funny to use as an opener. That is a commendable move, but a word of warning is in order. The humor should be relevant to the subject of the talk. At its best it should provide a direct lead into what is said next. Too many times speakers simply tack on a joke at the beginning of their speeches and then depart completely from whatever ideas it may have aroused to talk about something else. If a joke fails to connect with what comes next, it may do more harm than good. Listeners may be thrown off course and some time may go by before they get back on.

Julius A Stratton, a former president of M.I.T., who had been appointed the chairman of the Ford Foundation, was asked to give a speech about what he would try to accomplish in his new position. He began by saying, "Now that I have changed from academic robes to foundation garments...." In every way it was an admirable opener. First of all it was funny. Second, it was completely pertinent to the job transition he had just made. Finally, it was obviously the product of his own wit. That gave his joke extra impact.

Donald Strobe for many years was the senior minister of the First United Methodist Church in Ann Arbor, Michigan. A distinguishing feature of his sermons was his skillful use of humor. It added sparkle and interest, but even more important, it always illuminated and supported a point he was making. A story he told in one of his sermons shows how adroit he was in using humor to introduce his ideas.

The story concerned a mother who took her children to a farm where animals could be seen and petted, and in the case of Millie, the resident elephant, even ridden. The mother left her red Volkswagen beetle in the parking lot, but when she came back, she found to her dismay that the hood had been smashed in. It turned out that Millie had gotten loose, and mistaking the little red VW for the red tub she had been taught to sit on in the circus, had planted her huge bulk on it. Assured by the manager that the farm would pay to repair the damage, the mother set out for the airport where she was scheduled to pick up her husband. On the way she ran into a line of cars backed up by an automobile accident. Already late, she decided to avoid the obstruction by scooting down the shoulder. A policeman saw her damaged vehicle go by and thinking it had been involved in the accident, went after her with his siren screaming. On pulling her over, he accused her of leaving the scene of the accident. "I wasn't in the accident," she said vehemently.

"Then how did your car get damaged?" he asked.

"An elephant sat on it," she replied.

At that point the policeman reached for his breathalyzer.

Dr. Strobe then made the point from which his sermon was to evolve. "Obviously that woman and her car were in the wrong place at the wrong time." He might have added, "Twice."

In using humor in his sermons, Dr. Strobe was firmly within the tradition established by the founders of the Jewish and Christian religions. The Talmud advises teachers to "begin a lesson with a humorous illustration." Dr. Strobe in another of his memorable sermons pointed out that the Bible itself uses humor to enliven its teachings, but sometimes it is difficult to recognize because times and cultures have changed so radically since the Biblical era.

He cited as an example the promise made to Abraham and his wife Sarah that they would have a son despite their advanced age. The Israelites probably found that idea pretty funny. Sarah did, for Genesis 18:12 tells us that on hearing the promise, she "laughed to herself, saying 'After I have grown old, and my husband is old, shall I have pleasure?'" Their continuing amusement at this improbable event is reflected in the name they gave their son—Isaac—which in Hebrew means "laughter."

To most of us a camel is an odd looking animal. Someone once said that it was obviously designed by a committee. It was apparently odd looking to the people of Jesus's time also. Dr. Strobe believes that Jesus took advantage of the amused reaction people have to the appearance of a camel when he told his disciples in an instance recorded in Matthew 19:24 that "it is easier for a camel to go through the eye of a needle than for a rich man to enter the kingdom of God." We can see the disciples smiling as they visualized a camel trying to squeeze through a needle's eye. Besides amusing them, His humor also softened the harshness of what was an unpalatable precept. Jesus used the camel figure in another of his messages and again it might have tempered to some degree the hostility his reproof would arouse. In Matthew 23:23-24 we read that he rebuked the scribes and Pharisees by saying, "Woe to you, scribes and Pharisees, (for)...straining out a gnat and swallowing a camel."

Some groups have made the evoking of laughter a central part of their religious observances. One called the "Fellowship of Merry Christians," based in Kalamazoo, Michigan, publishes a bimonthly newsletter called *The Joyful Noiseletter*. Its editor, Cal Samra, said, "We feel there's too much solemnity and dourness about religion.... We're trying to capture both the joy and humor of early Christians." Crossing denominational lines, the group includes Protestants, Roman Catholics, and Eastern Orthodox, many of them clergy. In churches in Toronto, Canada, and London, England, parishioners often participate in spontaneous laughing sessions which may go on for more than half an hour. The pastor of the Toronto church called the experience "a gusher of the Holy Spirit" and others characterized it as "a very refreshing event."

In the public-speaking area, humor may reduce the hostility an audience sometimes feels toward a speaker. Henry W. Grady was a Southern statesman of the nineteenth century who took on the daunting responsibility of persuading an audience of Northerners that the South, which had fought to preserve secession and slavery, now supported union and freedom. At the time of his speech, the passions aroused by the Civil War still ran high. Grady began his argument bravely, but after a little while he stepped back to concede that his ideas were his own and he might be mistaken. To show how mistakes can happen, he told about a preacher who began reading from the Bible without realizing that some of the pages were stuck together. The scripture came out this way:

> "Noah took upon himself a wife, who was...one hundred and forty cubits long, forty cubits wide, built of gopher wood, and covered with pitch inside and out."

Blinking, the minister rescued himself by commenting that the passage certainly proved that "we are fearfully and wonderfully made."

We can speculate that Grady's humor helped win him a more willing and indulgent hearing than he might otherwise have received.

Surveys have shown that making a public speech is one of the most frightening experiences the average person can undergo. At least that was the case with a young woman whose trembling voice and shaking hands betrayed an acute case of nerves. Jittery speakers make audiences feel uncomfortable. They may become so concerned with the speaker's well being that they stop listening to what is being said. Recognizing the problem, the young woman decided to use humor to help settle down both herself and her listeners. "I'm going to get through this," she assured them and then added, "The butterflies are still zinging around, but now they're flying in formation." The ensuing laugh would probably relax everyone and thus enhance both the speaker's performance and the attention the audience would pay to her words.

Her humor gave her another advantage. It helped humanize her. Writers need that benefit even more than speakers. Their personalities are obviously more remote and less defined than those of people who address audiences in person. Hedley Donovan, a former editor-in-chief of *Time*, Inc., said at the beginning of his autobiography, *Right Places, Right Times*, that he had spent 40 years in journalism, "not counting my paper route." That little whimsical touch helped make him a real person for me, particularly since I also delivered papers in my younger years.

Humor helped me visualize another writer peering out from behind the printed word. In an article about ethics and journalism published in *The New Republic*, Weston Kosova apparently could not resist the impulse to interrupt a serious discussion of an important subject with a little joke. It popped up, unexpectedly and delightfully in the middle of a hypothetical question he had introduced: "Suppose I'm reporting a story about Senator X (not his real name)." I could see a little smile playing around Mr. Kosova's lips as he inserted his quirky little caveat.

Among the most anonymous of writers are the copy editors who compose newspaper headlines. It is easy to believe they are produced automatically by faceless machines. Occasionally, however, a touch of humor reveals the existence of a real person behind the words.

LAWMAKERS SKIRT NEPOTISM LAW
WITH RELATIVE EASE

LOW ON C-NOTES SEATTLE SYMPHONY
PLEADS FOR HELPING HAND

BEACHGOERS RELIEVED
TO GET MORE RESTROOMS

At times, of course, headline writers are funny without meaning to be, as we shall see in Chapter 3.

The anonymous writers of the copy news anchors read on television also show at times that they are people who like to laugh. Some years ago a story came into the NBC newsroom stating that because the Washington Zoo had failed to achieve a successful mating of the two pandas it owned, it was about to resort to artificial insemination. When a writer saw the names of the two pandas, his or her eyes obviously lit up. The story read by the news anchor ended with this dazzling bit of word play: "Shing Shing may have had his last fling with Ling Ling." The noted news personality, John Chancellor, scheduled to follow the story with commentary, came on the screen laughing uproariously.

A writer assigned to prepare graphic material for a TV broadcast of a football game between Notre Dame and the University of Michigan displayed a puckish turn of mind similar to that of the NBC news writer. The name of the Notre Dame quarterback was Ron Powlus. One of the Michigan running backs, a player of African descent, had a name that would put even the most experienced announcer to the supreme test—Tshimonga Biakabutuka. During a break in the action, this graphic appeared on the screen:

PRONUNCIATION GUIDE
Ron Powlus
Pronounced: Paw-lus
Tshimonga Biakabutuka
Pronounced: Touchdown Tim

If humor can do nothing else for explainers and persuaders, it can at least make what their audiences hear and read more enjoyable. I know that I remember with special warmth the teachers who enlivened their lessons with humor. One teacher who uses humor regularly to add sparkle to his lectures and articles is distinguished economist Lester Thurow. He is convinced that an idea encapsulated in a joke is not only more fun to listen to but is also one students are likely to remember.

A book I value highly is *The Careful Writer* by Theodore M. Bernstein, who served as an assistant editor for the *New York Times* and wrote a number of books and a syndicated newspaper column on language use. He has steered me away (I hope) from the more egregious infelicities. He has also made me laugh. His book is a delight to read because he regularly inserted diverting turns of phrase and quizzical comments into his instruction. The following exemplify his inimitable touch:

Defining a word, he said, "*Gender* is a grammatical term, denoting (in English) whether words pertaining to a noun or pronoun are classed as masculine, feminine, or neuter. It is not a substitute for *sex* (but, then, what is?)."

Rebuking Webster III, a dictionary he believed had gone astray with its advice on capitalization, he said: "For some obscure, almost masochistic, reason that dictionary bound itself into a no-capital straitjacket. It capitalizes no word (except God) but tells us that such terms as 'january,' 'new york,' and 'saint andrew; are *usu cap*. *Usu cap*? They are *alw cap*."

In a segment about an unfortunate metaphor, he quoted the following from a news story, "Although identified mainly with the Yiddish Art Theater, which was a Mecca for Jewish theatergoers on New York's Lower East Side"...Bernstein then added, "For Jews a Mecca yet!"

Don Fleming, the director of a training center for disturbed children, frequently lectures to parents about the problems of raising children. His topic is serious but he has fun dealing with it. His slightly mocking comments often bring grins to his grim-faced listeners. Of the parent who threatens a child by saying, "One more time and you're going to get it," Fleming remarked, "The trouble is kids through thousands of years have never found out what 'it' is." He called the kind of look which parents apparently hope will drill a hole through the head of a recalcitrant child the "Laser Beam Look." He is often refreshingly blunt. In discussing a tyke who specialized in taking kitchen appliances apart, he said, "That's the kind of child I call an interesting, funny, exciting, pain-in-the-ass kid." In another instance he remarked, "There are two areas we can't control: what comes out of their mouths and what comes out of other parts of their bodies."

Humor may even be a positive factor in sports education. James Fallows, writing in *The Atlantic* about taking lessons at two tennis schools, noted that the director of one of them, Vic Braden "has a relentlessly jokey manner." The slogan of his school is "Laugh and Win." He even eased the pain of paying for the course by making a game of collecting the tuition fees.

A type of persuasion to which most of us are subjected unremittingly is advertising. Can humor help motivate consumers to buy a certain product? Apparently many manufacturers think so, for it is estimated that one third of radio and TV commercials now incorporate some kind of humorous element. Advertisers see humor performing a number of helpful functions: it catches and holds attention; it makes a particular message stand out from the some 100,000 commercials an average American family sees every year; it reduces the hostility some people feel toward commercials; and it promotes the imprinting of product names and qualities on the minds of potential buyers.

Some years ago the deft use of humor in a series of TV commercials pushed Miller's Lite Beer to the forefront in the competition for a major share of the newly emerging market for light beer. The commercials showed individuals and groups arguing about whether the phrase "Tastes great" or the phrase "Less filling" was the better description of the beer's most attractive attribute. So indelibly were those phrases fixed in the people's minds that if the people at one end of a football stadium shouted "Tastes great" the people at the other end could be counted on to respond with "Less filling." In more recent times, the maker of Bud Light has turned to humor in its TV advertising. At the same time, the Miller company, evidently believing that at least temporarily humor has had its day, is using more sedate and conventional approaches.

The use of humor is by no means restricted to the United States. Some of the funniest commercials come from other nations. A few venture into areas that probably would be taboo in our country. An Australian commercial provides an example. Made for a manufacturer of sunglasses, it showed a couple embracing on a beach in the glare of a brilliant sun. As the passion index mounted the young woman interrupted to ask, "Do you have protection?"

"Of course," the young man replied," and pulled out a pair of sunglasses.

Humor is also used in print advertising, although not as often as in the broadcast media. Sometimes its use comes unexpectedly. The De Beer's Diamond Company generally seems content to arouse consumer desire simply by showing its products glistening seductively against a dark background. In one instance, however, it made a surprising move away from that austere approach. The advertisement featured the usual display of

25

diamonds, but at the bottom were three fortune cookies. Peeking out from one of them was this message: "She who is given diamonds is one fortunate cookie." I could almost see the normally somber faces of the company's executives breaking into tiny smiles as they authorized this deviation from their customary staid and conservative style.

Unexpected also was a venture into humor by a university. Usually the advertisements of educational institutions take the solemn and dignified approach. Adelphi University broke with that tradition in a series of print advertisements. One began as follows:

THIS IS
THE THIRD AD
IN ADELPHI
UNIVERSITY'S
NEW ADVERTISING
CAMPAIGN.
(AND JUDGING FROM
THE REACTION
TO THE FIRST TWO
IT COULD BE THE LAST.)

A printed advertisement that caught my eye because of the subtlety and irony of its humor was sponsored by the Areti Company, merchandisers of champagne and other wine products. The top one-third of the page was occupied with this headline:

THE EIGHTIES ARE OVER;
AN ERA OF AVARICE,
EXCESS, AND RECKLESS
SPENDING IS FINISHED.
[TO CELEBRATE, MAY WE SUGGEST
A $150 BOTTLE OF CHAMPAGNE?]

The rest of the advertisement explained why the superior quality of the company's Salon champagne made it cheap at that price.

Humor and Politics

Should politicians try to be funny? Will it help attain their primary goal of election or re-election? Centuries ago the philosopher Erasmus said, "Many times what cannot be refuted by arguments can be parried by laughter." While he was president, Ronald Reagan demonstrated over and over again how effective laughter can be in turning back criticism. A prime example of his skill in using humor occurred during his campaign for re-election in 1984. Lots of jokes were being made about his age, and when his performance in the first televised debate with his much younger opponent, Walter Mondale, was halting and ineffective, some began to wonder whether he was now too old for the office. Reagan countered this looming threat to his re-election with a joke. It turned his age from a disadvantage into an advantage. When one of the reporters raised the age issue during his second debate with Mondale, Reagan replied:

I want you to know that I will not make age an issue in this campaign. I am not going to exploit for political purposes, my opponent's youth and inexperience.

The audience in the studio greeted this sally with an uproarious laugh and even Walter Mondale could not keep from responding with a smile, albeit a somewhat rueful one. From that moment on Reagan's age vanished as an issue in the campaign.

During Reagan's presidency it was persistently rumored that he took naps in the afternoon and sometimes even fell asleep during cabinet meetings. Reagan didn't deny the accusation. Instead he used it as a jumping off point for jokes of his own. In one instance he said, "I'm concerned about what's happening to government, and it's caused me many a sleepless afternoon." At another time he was reputed to have said to one of his aides, "If a crisis develops, don't hesitate to wake me up even if I'm in a cabinet meeting." This self-deprecatory humor was a major weapon in helping to disarm his critics. Reagan's effective use of humor moved Robert Orben, a professional humorist, to comment that for presidents these days, "Humor has become very nearly a mandatory requirement." He added that "Because it can be a powerful weapon, a president who ignores the potential of humor does so at his own risk. Peggy Noonan, a speech writer for Presidents Reagan and the first President Bush, expressed a similar sentiment in her book *What I Saw at the Revolution:* "If a Presidential candidate is lacking in humor, don't vote for him. He lacks the Presidential sensibility, and he'll never succeed with Congress or rally the will of the people."

Of the presidents in recent times who served before Reagan, the one most noted for his wit was John Kennedy. Like Reagan, he was an expert at defusing criticism by turning it back on himself. To the charge that his family's wealth was buying him the presidency, Kennedy said that his father had instructed him as follows: "Don't buy one vote more than necessary. I'll be damned if I'll pay for a landslide." When the appointment of his brother as attorney general made him vulnerable to charges of nepotism, he responded, "I see nothing wrong with giving Robert some legal experience before he goes out to practice law." Kennedy was the first president to permit live broadcasts of his press conferences. His witty asides made them lively occasions, and the fact that they were heard at the very moment he uttered them gave them added impact. The self-deprecatory note predominated. Told by a reporter that the Republican National Committee had passed a resolution denouncing his administration as a failure, Kennedy commented, "I presume it passed unanimously." When asked how he had become a war hero, Kennedy replied, "They sank the boat."

The second President George Bush similarly made fun of himself when he addressed the yearly dinner of the White House Correspondent's Association in April, 2004. He began by reminding his audience that he had caused a public clamor by insisting that his vice president Dick Cheney accompany him when he answered the questions of the commission investigating the 9/11 disaster. Next he commented on the difficulty he had experienced in a recent press conference when he was asked to describe the greatest mistake he had made as president. He concluded forcefully by saying, "From now on I'm going to take Dick Cheney to all my press conferences, too."

Besides helping to disarm critics, humor can make a politician a more attractive figure. On this point the columnist and TV personality Mark Shields said, "Humor works. It says 'I'm not pompous, I'm not pretentious. I'm one of you.'" Hugh Sidey, writing in *Time* magazine, called Kennedy's humor "the trait that helped lift him on the way up and gave him special luster when he got to the top."

Reagan and Kennedy were not the only presidents who were funny, of course. Not much of the humor of our early presidents has come down to us, but the examples we know about suggest that they also made jokes on occasion. One is attributed to our second president, John Adams. Looking at the dour expression his portraits show, we might wonder whether he ever smiled. One episode indicates, however, that he had a well-developed sense of humor. During his campaign for re-election in 1800, he was accused of sending his vice-presidential running mate, General Charles Pinckney, to England to procure four pretty girls as mistresses, two for Adams and two for Pinckney. On hearing the story, Adams reputedly chuckled and said, "If this be true, General Pinckney kept them all for himself and cheated me out of my two."

Of the presidents of the nineteenth century the one who used humor the most was Abraham Lincoln. One historian has said that he joked more than any other president before or since. The device he used most often was the humorous story. There were few situations he could not embellish with a fitting anecdote. He also had a ready wit and was not above resorting to a pun on occasion. Hearing that the brother of one of his chief political opponents, Stephen Douglas, had gotten into trouble by peeping over transoms to watch women disrobing, Lincoln commented: "The cad should be elevated to the peerage."

Who was the funniest president of them all? James Dodson, writing in the September, 1987, issue of *Yankee* magazine, made a surprising choice. He gave the honor to Calvin Coolidge. Yet this was the president his contemporaries called "Silent Cal." Could such a person have been our funniest president? Dodson speculates that his remarks may have been too terse and subtle for people to recognize the humor in them.

A few examples illustrate his laconic style. When he was asked why he didn't run for re-election in 1928, he answered, "There's no room for advancement." That joke has been used by countless comedians ever since. A young woman sitting next to him at a dinner tried to coax him into becoming more voluble by telling him, "I've made a bet, Mr. President, that I can get more than two words out of you."

"You lose," said Coolidge.

After attending a conference which focused on international affairs, Coolidge was asked whether he had anything to say on the subject. "No," Coolidge replied, "and don't quote me on that."

Perhaps the best known anecdote illustrating Coolidge's stinginess with words concerns a reputed interchange he had with his wife. Because Mrs. Coolidge was not feeling well, Coolidge went to church alone. When he returned home, his wife asked what the minister had preached about.

"Sin," the president replied.

"What did he say about it?" Mrs. Coolidge asked.

"He was against it," Coolidge answered.

Another anecdote, and a rather surprising one considering the mores of the period, involved the Coolidge's visit to a farm. Apparently undeterred by the inhibitions of her time, Mrs. Coolidge pulled a farm hand aside to inquire whether roosters copulated more than once a day.

"Oh yes," the embarrassed farm hand replied. "Dozens of times a day."

"Tell that to Mr. Coolidge," she suggested.

On getting the message, Coolidge asked the farm hand whether the rooster's activity was concentrated on one hen.

"Oh, no sir," the farm hand replied, "It's a different hen every time."

"Tell that to Mrs. Coolidge," the president said.

Coolidge, like Reagan after him, enjoyed taking an afternoon nap. He responded to the joshing that practice invited the same way Reagan did—by making fun of himself. "My naps are in the national interest," he commented. "I can't make any disastrous decisions while I'm asleep."

The humor of Franklin Roosevelt was delicate at times and robust at others. Its delicacy was illustrated in the way he responded to a charge that he had used a naval ship to transport his dog, Fala. "Your accusation has sent Fala into a deep depression," he said with mock concern. The issue washed away in a wave of public laughter. The robustness of his humor was exemplified by a rhetorical device he used in one of his campaign speeches. He turned the last names of three of his political opponents, Joseph Martin, Bruce Barton, and Hamilton Fish, into a catchy refrain—"Martin, Barton, and Fish." Each time he repeated it, the laughter of his audience grew louder, and as he neared the end of his speech, his listeners were chanting "Martin, Barton, and Fish" along with him.

The term that best sums up the humor of Harry Truman is "saltiness." That characteristic is illustrated by a story which involved his wife, Bess. The two were showing some friends from Missouri the White House rose garden when Truman noticed that a number of the bushes looked a little frail. "Bess," he said, "I think they need manure."

Later one of the women in the group complained to Mrs. Truman about his language. "Bess, the President of our country shouldn't say 'manure'; he should say 'fertilizer'."

"Dearie," replied Mrs. Truman, "Do you have any idea how long it took me to get him to say 'manure'?"

In addition to being salty, Truman's language was often blunt and direct. In responding to Republican attacks on Washington bureaucrats, he said, "You know what a bureaucrat is? A bureaucrat is a Democrat with a job a Republican wants." He was fond of quoting Mark Twain's admonition: "Always do right. It will please some people and astonish the rest." That saying became a guideline for his own personal conduct.

Other presidents showed flashes of humor but none have become noted for their wit. Bon mots flowed rarely from Dwight Eisenhower. When Gerald Ford stumbled down some steps while descending from an airplane, he became known more for the jokes he inspired rather than for those he invented. Jimmy Carter's attempts at humor were often forced and artificial. One of his comments is worth recalling, however. After he had gone through a period of public abuse, he won renewed favor by helping bring about the Camp David peace agreements between Israel and Egypt. Shortly after the agreements were completed, he was greeted by a cheering crowd.

Afterwards Carter commented wryly, "That's the first time for a long time that people waved at me with all four fingers."

The first President Bush was not noted for the humor he created nor was Bill Clinton, his successor in the office. Clinton, however, could deliver jokes provided him by comedy writers like Jay Leno with professional flair. The speeches he gave at the yearly dinners of the White House Correspondents' Association were high points of the occasions. The second President George Bush presumably employed comedy writers to create the jokes he put into his speeches to the same group, but his delivery of them lacked the panache displayed by Clinton. He had a gift, however, for making audiences laugh with off-the-cuff remarks. In contrast, John Kerry, his opponent in the 2004 presidential election, conspicuously lacked that gift. Joe Klein, a *Time* magazine columnist, said that he had never seen Kerry experience one moment of spontaneous humor and further described his attempts to tell jokes as "ghastly." Writing in *The Atlantic*, Joshua Green referred to Kerry as "humor-impaired."

A number of former presidents were noted, not for their humor, but for their lack of it. Most of Richard Nixon's public utterances were consistently solemn and unremittingly earnest. An exception, perhaps, was his famous "Checkers" speech, which is credited with saving his candidacy for the vice presidency in 1952. It was marked by some lighter touches. One commentator speculated that had he been able to take the same approach during the Watergate crisis, he might have survived it. I suspect, however, that no joke could have washed away a scandal so deep and corrosive, and it might well have exacerbated it. As we shall see in Chapter 10, a joke can sometimes boomerang and bite you. Even that great quipster Ronald Reagan, probably wisely, made few if any jokes about his own great crisis, the Iran-contra scandal.

Perhaps the soberest president of all was Herbert Hoover. The historian James Free can recall only one try Hoover made at being funny. It came in a speech he gave just after his defeat by Franklin Roosevelt in the 1932 election. He said he had made a scientific analysis of the election results and had come to the conclusion that "I lost the election because I didn't have enough votes on my side," Perhaps it's just as well that he refrained from making any more jokes.

A number of unsuccessful candidates for the presidential office also made their mark as humorists. Among them was Adlai Stevenson who lost to Dwight Eisenhower both in 1952 and 1956. Typical of his inimitable touch was a remark he made on TV just after the returns following his first run for the presidency had indicated conclusively that he had lost the election. "I'm too old to cry, but it hurts too much to laugh."

George McGovern, the Democrat who opposed Richard Nixon in 1972, was not funny most of the time, but a rueful comment he made shortly after his defeat deserves mention. Reflecting on the chaotic campaign he had conducted, he said, "For years I wanted to run for the presidency in the worst way—and I sure did."

Most noted as a wit among the also-rans is Robert Dole who opposed Bill Clinton in 1996. The news commentator, Mark Shields, remarked that Dole was the most spontaneously humorous man ever to run for president. Two comments he made before becoming a presidential candidate illustrates his style.

On learning during the Watergate investigation that President Nixon had taped all of the conversations taking place in the Oval Office, Dole remarked, "Thank goodness when I was there I only nodded."

When his wife Elizabeth was appointed president of the American Red Cross, Dole remarked, "You never know how much blood you're going to give during the night."

Another way presidential candidates have used humor to make themselves better liked is to appear on comedy programs and late-night talk shows hosted by comedians. It seems difficult to believe, but the generally reserved Richard Nixon appeared on the *Laugh-In* show in 1968, at the height of his campaign against Hubert Humphrey, to utter a phrase often heard on the program—"Sock it to me!" Both George W. Bush and Al Gore were guests on *Saturday Night Live* during the 2000 race for the presidency. In 2004 virtually all of the presidential candidates subjected themselves to the sometimes barbed questions of such late-night luminaries as David Letterman, and on Letterman, they were usually inveighed into participating in his Top Ten routine. On the Jay Leno program, John Kerry made a supreme effort to humanize himself by coming out from the wings riding a motorcycle.

Humor in Everyday Life

Humor can not only make politicians more attractive, but, as I pointed out earlier in this chapter, it can perform the same service for ordinary mortals. People who can respond to a happening with a joke they have heard or wit of their own add zest and interest to an occasion. A man who can draw from a woman the comment, "He's a really funny guy" is likely to make better progress than a rival who is consistently serious. Surveys show that women rate a sense of humor as one of a man's most desirable attributes.

Sometimes, of course, our goal in being funny has nothing to do with advancing a cause of our own, but has the charitable aim of simply making people feel better.

Using Humor to Brighten the Environment. A joke can turn a world that is often gloomy and dismal into a somewhat more enjoyable place. One route some have taken to achieve that goal is to make humor part of the environment. A family living in my neighborhood, for example, maintains a bulletin board on their lawn on which they post jokes and funny sayings. When I take a walk, I make a point of going by their house to see their latest item. Usually it gives me a refreshing laugh. One I remember is the following:

I'm lost and I've gone to look for myself. If I get back before I return, ask me to wait.

Other jokes I've seen on that bulletin board have also made their way into this book.

The church I attend in Ann Arbor must deal with a problem many downtown churches face. Interlopers often clog its parking lot, making it impossible for parishioners with permits to find places for their cars. Most churches post a sign warning trespassers that their cars may be ticketed or towed away, a threat, incidentally, that is seldom carried out. A former pastor of my church, O. Carroll Arnold, added a little whimsy to the warning. The sign he composed read as follows:

PERMIT PARKING ONLY
FIRST BAPTIST CHURCH
We forgive those
Who trespass against us,
—but we also tow them.
THANKS FOR YOUR COOPERATION

Whether his message was more effective in discouraging interlopers than a straight-line warning would have been, is impossible to know, but I'm sure it drew appreciative smiles from those who passed by. A dentist, annoyed by trespassers who used a parking lot meant for patients, similarly matched the sign he composed to the kind of enterprise he operated. It read:

PATIENT PARKING ONLY
ALL OTHERS WILL BE PAINFULLY EXTRACTED

A bakery I patronize brightens the environment around it with a sign I always find amusing. What particularly tickles me, I think, is the touch of arrogance in the admonition:

GET YOUR BUNS IN HERE

Road repairs that tie up traffic rarely make us smile. One anonymous contractor, however, managed to use visual humor to reduce the irritation motorists always feel at such times. For several months a six-mile section of Highway 23 between Ann Arbor, Michigan, and Toledo, Ohio, was reduced to one lane while the pavement was being repaired. At the beginning of the single-lane section, the contractor posted a sign reading, "Six Miles to Go" and next to it put a face wearing a deep frown. At each mile interval thereafter, he posted other notices informing drivers how far the single-lane section still had to go and each time included a face. As the miles melted away, the frown gradually turned into a grin. By the time the "One Mile to Go" marker was reached, the face was lit up with a gloriously happy smile. My own smile grew broader along with it, and I'm sure that of other motorists did too.

<u>Using Humor to Relieve Tension</u>. The poet Langston Hughes once said, "Like a welcome summer rain, humor may suddenly cleanse and cool the earth, the air, and you." People sometimes get into situations in which they eminently need cooling. I saw humor accomplish that purpose during one of the hearings conducted by the Senate Banking Committee into the real estate investments made by Bill Clinton and his wife Hillary in the Whitewater area of Arkansas. The witness was former Senator Lloyd Bentsen, who at the time of the hearing was serving the Clinton administration as Secretary of the Treasury. He was being assailed by Senator Alfonse D'Amato of New York for alleged ethical lapses of Treasury employees. Just as tempers were about to reach the boiling point, Bentsen broke the tension by commenting, "This isn't the only bad day I've had recently. Awhile ago a man on an elevator recognized me as a former senator. I admitted I had been one. After a long pause, he asked, 'Whatever happened to you?'"

Even the waspish D'Amato broke into a laugh.

Humor can also defuse potentially explosive private confrontations. A friend of mine was called by a *Reader's Digest* representative requesting payment of a bill he had already taken care of. When the conversation became a little edgy, my friend asked if he might speak to Carol Slater, whose name he had seen in the company's advertising. The representative explained that there was no Carol Slater. The name was fictional. "Hmm," my friend replied. "I wonder if she knows Betty Crocker over at General Mills?" The *Reader's Digest* representative began to laugh, the tension dissolved, and the two settled their dispute amicably.

Humor is particularly effective in relieving the strains of family life. Christopher Peterson, a professor of psychology at the University of

Michigan, said that, "In a family if humor is never displayed, what's lost is a sense of pleasure and resilience to stress. When humor is there it dissolves boundaries and brings people closer." When a child does something wrong, humor can be used both to indicate that a certain type of behavior is unacceptable and at the same time reassure the child that forgiveness will follow. Professor Peterson illustrates that thought with an anecdote about a mother whose son broke a valuable dish. Instead of upbraiding him, she used the humor of exaggeration by saying quietly, "Now we're all going to gather around and watch you break every other dish in the house."

Bob Talbert reflected the same point of view in a column he wrote for the *Detroit Free Press*:

"I can't imagine a home without laughter, a world so devoid of humor that there's never a chuckle or laugh.... It's the fuel for the warmth we share and the switch for the light we shine. Laughter leads us, kneads us and sometimes helps bleed us of torments and woes."

One reason humor should be an element in every household is that children love it. Research shows that they laugh much more than adults. An average child laughs three times as much as an average adult. They make jokes among themselves, and they particularly enjoy jokes which make them the target. In addition to relieving stress, humor can stretch children's minds, for getting the point to a joke requires connecting one idea with another. Because jokes often deal with the ironies and contradictions of life, they also can help children develop a sophisticated and balanced outlook, thus starting them on the road to maturity.

<u>Humor in the Workplace</u>. Should people laugh at work? Some employers obviously think it makes them better employees, for they have taken steps toward making humor a regular part of the working experience. One company keeps a bulletin board posted with cartoons and funny sayings. It also takes note of special events in employees' lives by arranging celebrations featuring laugh-inducing games. One of them challenged contestants to match baby pictures to the corresponding adult. The Kodak Company even established a "humor" room. To get people in the right mood, it hung pictures of comedians like Groucho Marx and Charlie Chaplin on the walls.

A bank manager used humor to alleviate the stress employees experienced when they encountered difficult customers. His ploy was to institute a "Worst Customer of the Week" contest. The employees who came up with the best story about a customer's perverse intransigence won a prize. The result was that instead of trying to avoid difficult people, the tellers vied among themselves to attract them to their windows.

A touch of humor can often brighten up routine communications among fellow workers. An example was a report a policeman made after being sent to extricate a woman who had fallen into a large plant outside a restaurant. His report was terse and to the point. "Woman in restaurant planter retrieved. She was potted."

A number of researchers have carried out studies designed to measure the effects of using humor in the workplace. Some of the results are surprising. A study carried out at the University of Maryland found that humor can even sharpen thinking and increase productivity. The study required students to attach a candle to a wall fixture in such a way that it did not drip wax on the floor when lighted. Before the exercise half the students watched a comic film and the other half an educational film. There was an astonishing difference in the two groups' success. Those who watched the comic film were three times as successful in solving the problem as the other group. The result led the researchers to theorize that people in a good mood are better able to react creatively to an intellectual challenge than their less ebullient colleagues.

Other research demonstrates that humor in the workplace makes communication easier, helps to resolve conflicts, and enhances bonding among fellow workers. A study reported to the American Psychological Association indicated that the feeling of having fun at work contributes even more to a worker's effectiveness than overall job satisfaction.

Humor can also be beneficial in promoting the careers of those who dispense it. A recent survey asked the executive officers of 100 of the nation's largest corporations whether people with a sense of humor did better, the same, or worse than those who possessed little or no sense of humor. Eighty-four percent of those who responded thought that employees with a sense of humor did a better job. The fact that some companies include an item on their job application forms measuring a prospective employee's sense of humor indicates the importance they place on this factor.

The emphasis on lightening up the workplace with laughter has given rise to a new type of professional, one who provides businesses, hospitals, churches, schools, and governmental units with advice about what kinds of humor techniques work and how to introduce them. One is Paul McGhee who has written scholarly books and articles on the origins of humor and its effects. A technique he uses to seize audience attention is to bounce a tennis ball limply on the meeting-room floor. "Some days are tough," he comments. Then he throws down another ball that merely thuds and dies.

"And some days it doesn't matter what you do," he adds. "That's when a sense of humor will help you survive.... Humor gives you bounce-back ability."

<u>Making Life Bearable With Humor</u>. It is not just in the workplace that serious and sometimes overwhelming problems arise, of course. The American writer Henry Thoreau once said, "Most men lead lives of quiet desperation." We might add to that, "and women, too." One of the great benefits of humor is that it can help us bear up under the terrible burdens that life sometimes imposes. Abraham Lincoln, torn apart by the horrible carnage his effort to preserve the union was costing, said, "I laugh that I may not weep." Art Buchwald, a humorist whose columns at one time appeared twice a week in more than 500 newspapers, revealed in his autobiography, *Leaving Home*, that he had long suffered from depression caused by a painful childhood. Because his father was too poor to provide for him and his three sisters during his early years, he was forced into a series of foster homes, an experience that left him hurt and miserable. "Laughter was the weapon I used for survival," Buchwald wrote.

Former vice-president Al Gore once surprised *Newsweek* journalist Howard Fineman with his answer to the question: "What's the most significant thing the public hasn't realized about you?" Gore responded, "Probably the importance I place on humor. It helps almost everything in life to be able to laugh at the absurd parts of it or the ironic parts of it, and I do that a lot. That doesn't come through as much in public as it does in private." One can hope that he was able to laugh when he received a half a million more popular votes than George W. Bush in their contest for the presidency in 2000, but lost the election when Bush won in the Electoral College by a majority of four.

Have you noticed how much laughing there is before and after funerals? Sometimes jokes are even told during the service itself. Is humor in such a situation appropriate? Two professors, James Alfred Jones of the University of Illinois, Chicago, and James Vincent, a communications professor at the Moody Bible Institute, conducted research to find an answer to that question. They concluded that some humor, particularly the kind that reveals the humanity of the person whose life is being celebrated, is entirely proper. The mourners may not laugh, but many of them, the researchers say, "Will chuckle in their souls." That reaction is a natural and healing release from the pain caused by the death of loved ones.

The blow death delivers is even harsher when it comes by a family member's own hand. the comedian Joan Rivers went through that crushing experience when her husband took his own life. For months she could not even bring herself to speak his name. She finally managed to do so only by taking refuge from her ravaged feelings in a joke. "Edgar," she said, "asked to be cremated and have his ashes scattered in the Neiman-Marcus Department store. That way he knew I'd be visiting him regularly."

Illness can sometimes make life almost unbearable. A diagnosis of AIDS, despite the discovery of treatments that slow its advance, still confronts many of its victims with what they see as a death sentence. Can humor help in such desperate circumstances? The playwright Paul Rudnick obviously thinks it can, for he wrote a comedy about people afflicted with AIDS, which was produced in New York. His play, entitled *Jeffrey*, showed people suffering from AIDS reacting to various situations in odd and funny ways, just as ordinary people do. Rudnick noted that the AIDS victims in his audiences often reacted with uproarious laughter to what was happening on the stage. One reason for their response, he feels, is that "they are so sick of being treated merely as sick."

A diagnosis of breast cancer not only raises the specter of untimely death, but it can also shatter a woman's self image. Despondency is an almost inevitable result. Humor can help people deal with it. A self-help group made light of their plight, for example, by calling their organization, "Bosom Buddies." Linda Ellerbee, the journalist who underwent a double mastectomy, took refuge in laughter when she endured an experience most women would find crushing. The prosthesis she had attached while she went in swimming came loose and migrated to her back. "How can you not laugh at such a thing?" she asked. "Either you laugh or you cry your eyes out."

The humorist, Erma Bombeck, had funny thoughts even at the moment she was told she had a malignant tumor in her breast. "Humor had been such an important part of my life," she explained, "that it kicked in automatically. I thought of thousands of luncheons and dinners I had attended where they slapped a name tag on my left bosom. I always smiled and said, 'Now what shall we name the other one?' That would no longer be a problem." Her jokes helped her survive her ordeal with her psyche intact, and they also helped smooth out the rocky road her family had to travel.

Jokes help make intolerable conditions tolerable when disaster strikes. Funny stories even came out of the Dust Bowl of the 1930s when the lack of rain in some parts of Oklahoma ravaged the lives of thousands. One told of a man who was so overcome when he was hit on the head by a raindrop that a neighbor had to throw two buckets of sand in his face to revive him. Another described how a motorist came upon a ten-gallon hat lying on a sand drift. Picking it up he saw a head sticking out of the sand.

"Can I give you a ride to town?" he asked the head.

"No thanks," the head replied. "I'm on a horse."

In 1976 the collapse of the great Teton Dam in Idaho caused a flood which washed away many homes. Gathered safely on high ground, the flood's victims watched their homes go floating by. "Here comes the Jones' house," someone shouted.

"And there's the Jorgensen's right behind it," another added.

Said a voice from the back, "I see the Jorgensens are still trying to keep up with the Joneses."

It would be difficult to think of an experience more devastating than that suffered by the men who were taken hostage in Beirut during the 1980s. Two of them, Father Jenco and David Jacobsen, said after their release that humor helped them maintain their sanity during their years of captivity. They joked, for example, about the terrible food they were given. A dish labeled "chicken," which might possibly have had a chicken stroll through it at one time or another, they called "Hint of Chicken." Sometimes their guards asked what they could get for them. Since even their simplest requests were seldom granted, they usually responded in unison with the same answer, "A taxi."

In recent years budget cuts have forced university administrators to carry out the painful duty of reducing or eliminating programs to which some faculty members had devoted most of their professional lives. One such administrator was Billy Frye who served as Vice President for Academic Affairs at the University of Michigan during a period of economic stringency. When he began the distasteful task of downsizing some of the university's programs, faculty members affected by his actions naturally responded with cries of anguish. There was nothing he could do to wish away the budget constraints that had made the cutbacks necessary. No matter what decisions he made, some people were bound to suffer. The best he could do was attempt to soothe the wounds with the healing balm of humor. In a speech he made to members of the faculty, he said:

> I have sometimes felt in these past several years that my role as academic vice-president could best be likened to the keeper of the Biblical zoo. When asked how in literal fulfillment of the Biblical prophecy, he managed to get the lion and the lamb to lie down peaceably together, the keeper confessed, "Every morning I put in a fresh lamb."

Humor also can help one bear the pangs inflicted by the minor jabs of fate. Max Eastman, who wrote two outstanding books about the nature of humor, saw it as "the most adroit and exquisite device by which our nerves outwit the stings...and paltry bitterness of life." Or as Mort Walker, the cartoonist who draws the *Beetle Bailey* comic strip, put it, "Laughter is the brush that sweeps away the cobwebs of the heart."

Humor helped me laugh at a minor cobweb that once developed in my life. As a naval officer in World War II, I was in Philadelphia for a time waiting for my ship to be made ready for sea when my wife in Detroit notified me that the baby we had been expecting was about to arrive. Since I was simply standing by with the rest of the crew, it seemed to me that my services could be spared for a brief period while I went home to be present for the big event. Nevertheless the captain denied my request for leave. When the Executive Officer who reported the decision to me saw my crestfallen face, he helped me laugh it away by saying, "Remember, Mr. Willis, you had to be there when the keel was laid, but you don't have to be there for the launching."

It is not just the people who are struck by the hammer blows of fate who endure pain of course. It reaches out to afflict their family and friends. Sometimes even strangers suffer. That is particularly true of members of the medical profession. When they fail to cure an illness or save a life, even when the victims are known to them only as patients, they often feel great distress. Humor can help them too.

David Rock, a nurse at the Henry Ford Hospital in Detroit, wrote an article for a medical journal with a somewhat startling title, "I'm Sorry I Laughed When Your Father Died." He explained that he was suffering the pain of losing a patient when someone told a joke. It's feebleness scarcely deserved any response at all and yet "I laughed like a jackass, decorum forgotten" until he looked up to see the daughter of the dead patient looking at him with tears streaming from her eyes. "My laughter was inappropriate in that instance," he said, "but nonetheless it was a necessity. Confronting death as frequently as we do in hospitals causes us to weight the scales with sorrow. We are left to search out our own sources of counterbalancing....The most universal, inexpensive, legal, and portable source is laughter." I mentioned Rock's article to my minister's wife, Cindy Lambrides, who serves as a counselor in the emergency room of an Ann Arbor hospital. Her task is to help people cope with the devastating shock caused by the sudden and unexpected loss of loved ones. It turned out that she had read the article. "David Rock spoke for all of us who work with people suffering with pain or overwhelming grief," she told me. "Laughter is an absolute essential in relieving the stress we experience."

Once I was able to provide the medicine of laughter for a physician. My wife had a hip operation and while I was visiting her in the hospital, our family doctor came in. It was clear from the expression on his face that he was undergoing a particularly stressful day. Knowing that I sometimes lectured on humor, he asked if I could tell him a good joke. Fortunately, I was able to think of one about his own profession. It concerned a doctor who had failed to find the cause of a health problem a patient had described. Several months later the patient came in to see him about the same symptoms. This time the doctor was more successful in arriving at a diagnosis. "Weren't you in here about a year ago complaining about this same condition," he asked. "That's true," the patient replied. "Well," said the doctor with a touch of triumph in his voice, "You've got it again!" Our doctor went away laughing. In that particular instance, I felt I was the one who had administered the treatment.

Humor and Health

Thus far we have seen how humor can lighten the load when our burdens become too oppressive. In this section we take that idea a step further. Can humor actually help cure illnesses and promote health?

The theory that humor can have a beneficial influence on health is not new. In Proverbs 17:22 we read that "A merry heart doeth good like a medicine but a broken spirit drieth the bones." In our day the idea that humor can have a curative effect received its greatest impetus when Norman Cousins, a former editor of the *Saturday Review*, published an article in a medical journal which told how laughter had helped him recover from a crippling disease. When the medicine prescribed by his doctors failed to alleviate the near paralysis he was experiencing, he decided to apply his own treatment. He persuaded his nurses to read him humor columns and tell him jokes, and he made arrangements to see funny movies.

Cousins recovered from his illness and the key, he believed, was the treatment laughter had provided. He wrote, "I made the joyous discovery that ten minutes of genuine belly laughter had an anesthetic effect and would give me at least two hours of pain-free sleep." He expanded his article into a book, *Anatomy of an Illness*, and he later wrote a second one on the same subject, *The Healing Heart*, which described how a partnership with his doctor helped him recover from a heart attack. The UCLA School of Medicine recognized the contribution he made to the medical field by appointing him a researcher in the biochemistry of emotions and a professor of medical humanities.

What laughter does, Cousins said, is get patients into a frame of mind that makes them better recipients for other kinds of remedies. Few physicians would dispute the argument that a happy, optimistic patient contends with illness better than one with a negative attitude. Research has supported that conclusion. Studies carried out at UCLA, in which Norman Cousins participated, found that the symptoms of cancer patients tend to worsen at the time the disease is diagnosed because of the fear prompted by the dreaded label "cancer." It seems reasonable to suppose that replacing that fear with an optimistic outlook can alleviate the symptoms.

Other researchers have found that in addition to aiding a patient psychologically, laughter can also promote actual physiological improvement. William Fry of Stanford University discovered that laughter has the same beneficial influence as moderate exercise. By inducing a feeling of relaxation and lowering blood pressure, it produces an effect comparable to that attained by jogging. That last conclusion had a somewhat ironic effect on one reader of *Newsweek*, which published a report of Dr. Fry's research. Mary M. Reffenback wrote a letter to the editor which read: "It ain't fair! After 15 years of jogging I find...that my friends who laughed at me have derived as much benefit from their laughter as I have from my sweaty aching body. Geez!"

Other researchers have found that laughter can aid digestion and release endorphins which act in the body as natural pain killers. It can also fight off infection by enhancing the distribution in the body of white blood cells and other immune agents. Jeffrey Goldstein, a psychologist at Temple University, has gone so far as to suggest that laughter may increase longevity by reducing stress and hypertension. The editors of the University of California *Wellness Letter* reflected that idea when they ended an article about the effect of laughter on health with the comment: "Those who laugh—last."

In obvious recognition of the beneficial effect of laughter, some hospitals have engaged humor educators to advise them on how to introduce humor into their patients' lives in an organized way. One of those experts is Steve Allen, Jr. He knows about health, for he is a family physician who practices in upstate New York, and he knows about humor, for he is the son of the late Steve Allen, the TV and radio comedian. One of the younger Allen's principal techniques for making patients laugh is teaching them how to juggle. In his private sessions with patients, he also tells them jokes. On one occasion they brought a patient into such a state of relaxation that she drummed up the nerve to tell him he had his shirt on backwards. They both had a healthful laugh together.

St. Joseph Mercy Hospital in Ypsilanti, Michigan, set up a humor cart which carries such items as funny books, cartoons, and games to patients' rooms. At Johns Hopkin's Hospital patients can watch a closed-circuit TV channel specializing in presenting comedy programs. At Wilcox Memorial Hospital in Lihue, Hawaii, professional comedians donate time to make video tapes for showing to patients and at St. Joseph Mercy Hospital in Houston, the nuns are instructed to tell each patient a funny story every day.

Deborah Leiber, who founded a national organization called "Nurses for Laughter" dresses up in a clown costume when she gives children a shot. Her attire deflects their attention from the threatening needle in her hand, and before they have a chance to cry, the treatment has been completed.

Sometimes the most troublesome and grumpiest of patients can be helped with laughter. Patty Wooten, a California nurse who runs humor seminars for medical professionals, tells about one patient who kept calling nurses with her buzzer. A nurse who had been summoned so many times she had lost count, finally responded with a sharp "What's wrong this time?"

"It's my dinner," the patient complained. "This is a *bad* potato."

At that point the nurse decided to replace her frown with a smile. She picked up the potato in one hand and gave it a sound spanking with the other, reprimanding it at the same time with "You're a bad potato. Bad! Bad! Bad!" The dour-faced patient burst into laughter and for a time there were no more buzzes.

Taking Advantage of Humor's Indirectness

Sometimes we want to make a statement about a person or a situation that stated openly might be impolitic, unduly hurtful, embarrassing, or even risky. Using humor to get the point out can soften the edge. The reason is that the conclusion a joke aims for is never stated explicitly. Rather, it takes form in the minds of listeners as the result of ideas suggested by the joke teller. This indirectness reduces the jolt. Further, it places the responsibility for reaching the conclusion implied by the joke on the listeners and thus removes from the teller the onus for making what might be a shocking statement if said openly.

An example from the political realm illustrates how the process works. John Connally was the Democratic governor of Texas when John Kennedy was president and rode with him on his fateful trip through Dallas on November 22, 1963. Later, Connally made a highly publicized switch from the Democratic to the Republican party. Since he had been steadily growing more conservative, the impulse of his colleagues might have been to mutter,

"Good riddance." A Democrat named Frank Mankiewics managed to suggest that idea somewhat more gently by using humor. His comment was:

"When John Connally left the Democratic party for the Republican Party, he raised the intellectual level of both parties."

That bit of humor cloaks a very nasty insult, to wit: "John Connally is stupider than Democrats but brighter than Republicans." Saying so bluntly would have been grossly offensive. Furthermore, no one would have laughed. Implication helped take the sting out of the insult, and laughter added a further soothing touch. Even John Connally might have grinned a little on hearing it.

An old, old story about Julius Caesar shows how humor can modify the risk that complete candor might entail.

While Caesar was conducting his campaign in Gaul, he noticed that one of his soldiers strongly resembled him. Deciding to have a little fun, Caesar asked, "Was your mother ever in my father's court?" Apparently unable to hold back, the soldier replied, "No, but my father was."

Had that soldier stated openly what his remark insinuated, he probably would have experienced a swift passage from this life. We can hope that this turning of the tables earned Caesar's admiration rather than his vengeance.

The Canadian writer, Robertson Davies, once said, "The love of truth lies at the root of much humor." The problem is that the truth is sometimes unpalatable. The indirect approach of humor helps to soften its impact. We love our children, for example, but they sometimes try our patience. That idea is implicit in Ralph Waldo Emerson's comment, "There was never a child so lovely but his mother was glad to get him asleep." A sometimes irritating propensity of the very young is summed up in the statement, "You can always tell a home with a five-year old in it. You have to wash the soap before you use it." Equally irritating is a habit associated with adolescent females. A father of several daughters referred to it by saying, "It's been a long time since I picked up a telephone that wasn't warm." Harry Truman suggested the impossibility of controlling children's behavior when he commented, "I have found the best way to give advice to your children is to find out what they want to do and then advise them to do it." Monta Crane approached that idea from a slightly different angle. "There are three ways to get things done: Do it yourself, employ someone, or forbid your children to do it." A cartoon in the *Frank and Ernest* comic strip series poked fun at the difficulty efforts to protect our children sometimes cause. It showed a pharmacist handing a bottle of medicine to a senior citizen with this

WILLIS - How to be Funny on Purpose

instruction: "Take one of these every four hours or as often as you can get the cap off."

The irritations we have just been considering constitute only slight annoyances, of course. In many instances the realities of life are much harsher. Our society is still riddled with injustice and prejudice, for example. Humor can be a subtle but powerful instrument for bringing us face to face with our sometimes unpleasant selves. And that is what it should do. As John Lahr writing in *The New Yorker* said:

"All genuine comedy is politically incorrect: challenging assumptions, testing limits, crossing boundaries, disabusing the public of its most firmly held beliefs."

Groucho Marx was once refused membership in a California beach club because he was Jewish. He did not carry out a direct assault on its anti-Semitism. Instead, he used the subtle indirectness of humor to ridicule the club's racist policy. In a letter he wrote to the club's directors, Marx asked: "Since my daughter is only half Jewish, could she go into the water up to her knees?"

A Black man who lived in the South at the time drinking fountains were labeled "For Whites" and "For Colored" used the same delicate tactic Marx had used to take aim at the policy of segregation. A policeman stopped him for going through a red light. Recognizing that a traffic ticket was inevitable, he seized the opportunity to make a point.

"It's this way, officer. I saw the White folks going through the green
light, and I just thought the red light must be for us Black folks."
We can almost see him blinking his eyes innocently as he made his statement. In his small way he had helped edge his listener closer to what E. B. White called "the big, hot fire which is truth."

Sometimes indirectness is in order because stating the truth openly would be indelicate or shocking. A mother was taken aback when her daughter showed up wearing a bikini she thought was dangerously skimpy. She didn't want to be explicit about what might happen, but she got her point across by saying, "If I'd worn a bathing suit like that when I was your age, you'd be four years older than you are now."

There is a story about two maiden ladies who shared a house for many years. The two stayed as far away from men as they could, believing that awful things might happen if they let them get too close. For the same reason, they kept their female cat penned up inside the house. Then came a day when a man did get close enough to one of the ladies to propose marriage. She promptly accepted. On her honeymoon she wanted to communicate a message to her former companion which she could never have brought herself to say openly. She made her point by using the indirectness of humor. Her postcard had just four words on it.

"Let the cat out."

Earlier I alluded to the fact that the indirectness of humor requires audiences to become partners in reaching conclusions. That point deserves emphasis because it is a chief reason for being funny. It is not just that a joke makes people laugh. It also forces them to think by requiring them to connect one idea with another. The involvement of the audience made necessary by humor's indirectness constitutes one of its greatest strengths.

A couple of examples illustrate the process. In one of his books the novelist Peter De Vries wanted to communicate the idea that the moral climate of our country has changed since the nineteenth century. He could simply have stated that fact straight out, but his comment would probably have drawn no more than a "Ho-hum" from his readers. By using the indirectness of humor he made them his associates in reaching that conclusion and, incidentally, made them laugh. His line read:

"A hundred years ago Hester Prynne of *The Scarlet Letter* was given an 'A' for adultery. Today she should rate no better than a 'C+.'"

Kin Hubbard was a humorist who under the pen name of Abe Martin wrote short pithy paragraphs for the *Indianapolis News*, items that made its readers howl with laughter and at the same time invited them to draw conclusions about the foibles of our personal lives and the blemishes of society as a whole. The examples below show him taking aim at both types of targets.

Mr. an' Mrs. Lettie Plum, married in June, couldn' git ther car out o' garage last evenin' so they had to go to bed hungry.

Now an' then an innocent man is sent t' th' legislature.

Indirectness has another advantage. Often it can convey a rich and complex thought more effectively and efficiently than an explicit statement. Consider the following story.

A traveler in Massachusetts asked an old gentleman sitting in front of a store, "Does it matter which road I take to Boston?"

The old gentleman removed his pipe from his lips, thought for a moment, and then replied, "Not to me it don't."

Think of all the images that brief anecdote evokes. We see crustiness and taciturnity of manner; we observe a style of speech that is crisp and laconic, we recognize an attitude that says you go your way and I'll go mine; and we construct a clear, vivid, mental picture of the whole event taking place. One brief funny line calls up an entire New England character in full and rich detail.

Chapter 2
What is Funniness?

A comedian is a person who says things funny and a humorist is a person who says funny things..
Russell Baker

W hat makes us laugh? Why is it that regularly throughout our lives our eyes suddenly crinkle, our facial muscles contract, our diaphragms undergo spasmodic convulsions, and our mouths open to emit hoarse, animal-like sounds or inane cackles?   Usually the phenomenon we call laughter bursts forth because we have perceived something funny in what has been said, written, or done. Sometimes there are other causes. Exposure to nitrous oxide, commonly known as laughing gas, can start us giggling. Tickling can have the same effect. Strangely enough, fear, nervous tension, or embarrassment can make us laugh. At times the mere sight or sound of other people laughing can set us off. So can the simple pleasure of being with people we like and whose company we enjoy. The principal cause of laughter, however, and the one we are mainly interested in, is the sudden perception of something funny.

Answering our question that way, of course, merely substitutes one puzzle for another. Now we must define what funniness is. Great thinkers have grappled with that problem down through the centuries, among them Aristotle, Immanuel Kant, and Sigmund Freud. Despite their efforts and those of many other notable theorists, a definition has remained tantalizingly elusive. *The New Yorker* writer E. B. White compared funniness to a bubble which disappears with a sudden poof if you poke at it. Some who have thought about it have seemed at times to throw up their hands in defeat and admit that a definition is impossible. The actor and comedian Billy Crystal seemed to be among them when he said: "There's no explaining why something is funny. It just is." The celebrated Canadian humorist Stephen Leacock began his book on *Humor* by saying: "Men are said to laugh because the story is funny, and the story is known to be funny because the men laugh at it." The Australian psychologist D. H. Monro resorted to the same type of circular reasoning when he said, "We laugh because we have seen something laughable." This initial defeatist stance did not stop either man from advancing their own hypotheses, however.

Most theorists about the nature of funniness have been based on observation and speculation. Few of the philosophers and thinkers who originated them tested the validity of their conclusions by conducting controlled experiments. Even the experimental studies that have been done usually did not attack the key question of defining the essence of funniness. Most dealt instead with such auxiliary questions as determining whether the use of humor can persuade an audience to act in a certain way or grasp the meaning of a concept. As I noted in the previous chapter, carrying out experiments in these areas is so difficult that arriving at clear-cut answers is almost impossible. The same is true of studies designed to explore the nature of funniness itself.

The experiments of two psychologists illustrate the problems of carrying out research on humor. Norman Holland, author of the book *Laughing*, reported a study whose purpose was to measure the relative funniness of various jokes by recording the amount of laughter they evoked. An immediate problem was to assign a value to various types of responses. Did a loud guffaw from one listener constitute a greater reaction than muted "heh-hehs" from several? There was no obvious answer to that question.

The British psychologist Michael Mulkay once set out to record the number of times he laughed or smiled during an eight-hour period. The problem was that when he became aware of an impending smile and prepared to record it, his scientific purpose negated the impact of whatever it was that had amused him, and the smile never materialized. In the end he abandoned his experiment before the eight hours had run their course.

Does the fact that theories about the nature of funniness are based mainly on speculation mean that we should disregard them? Not at all. For one thing, doing so would leave us without much left to go on. For another, we can comfort ourselves with the thought that many of humankind's most insightful ideas have come from people who did no more than sit on a rock or in an armchair and think them up.

To cover all the theories that have been expounded from the time of Aristotle on would take the rest of this book and many volumes more. To narrow the focus, I have concentrated on those theories that have a direct application to the task of joke making. They provide guidance, for example, about what to put into a joke and how to mold and shape it to attain the maximum effect.

I suspect that this talk about theories has caused the eyes of some of you to glaze over, and you may be muttering to yourself, "Now comes the heavy stuff." I cannot deny that some of what has been written about humor has a fairly ponderous tone. A paragraph from a scholarly paper on humor, cited by Norman Holland in his book *Laughing*, illustrates this tendency. Holland remarked that it provides an example of the "strange dialect" in which researchers often write. He did not identify the author.

> Experiments now in progress hope to establish whether fewer than three dimensions of value normative anti-conformity suffice to generate incongruity humor, and whether the minimum number of required dimensions anti-conformed to depends upon if the norms violated represent ego-involving values or non-ego-involving beliefs.

Resisting the temptation to use such language must be difficult, for later in his book Holland wrote a paragraph of his own that may well carry the general reader into a verbal thicket almost as impenetrable as the one he satirized.

> Identity theory says the "I" of "I know" knows within an identity that is itself something known and relative to the knower. Thus identity decenters our knowing, indeed our very selves.

That paragraph illustrates the point that much current writing about humor is meant for special audiences. What Holland said probably would be clear to those familiar with the identity theory to which he refers. In the same way John Allen Paulos must have been aiming at an audience whose grasp of mathematics is somewhat firmer than mine when he wrote his book *Mathematics and Humor*. I should modify this comment by saying that some of what he wrote is eminently clear and readable. In the early pages of his book he provided an excellent review of the main theories of humor and the way they developed. He also summed up the qualities characteristic of effective humor in an admirably lucid way: He noted them as "cleverness and economy, playfulness, combinational ingenuity, and logic." When he went on to say that we find these same qualities in good mathematics, I must admit that he moved somewhat beyond my reach. I also lack the background to appreciate his comment that the proof of a geometrical theorem is equivalent to the punch line of a joke. And when he converts jokes into algebraic equations and geometrical figures, I find myself completely out of my depth. Mathematicians, I am sure, would find them intriguing and insightful.

Another who compared mathematics and humor was the German philosopher Arthur Schopenhauer. He once said, "We laugh at the angle between a circle and its tangent." Mathematicians may find that juxtaposition funny. I'm afraid it doesn't even make me smile.

I believe that the theories I review will be meaningful and clear to a general audience. True, some of the language used to describe them has a musty, archaic flavor. That is not surprising considering that a number of them were conceived hundreds, even thousands, of years ago. But though the words may be quaint at times, I think you will find the ideas they express easy to grasp.

You may still wonder whether covering them is worth the bother. I think it is because these theories provide the foundation from which our current understanding of the nature of funniness has evolved. In learning about them, you will discover that the methods and techniques of creating humor, described later in this book, did not suddenly materialize out of thin air. They have deep roots, and this chapter describes what those roots are.

One thing you will note as you read the next few pages is that opinions about the nature of funniness are not necessarily unanimous. Theorists sometimes disagree with one another. One factor that promotes disagreement is the attempt by some to trace all laughter to a single cause. Those who make this attempt tend to differ about what that elemental cause is. Others see laughter as a phenomenon brought about by a number of different stimuli and are content to describe one cause of merriment without trying to make it a part of an all-encompassing theory.

From all that has been written or said, three main theories about the nature of funniness have emerged—the superiority theory, the incongruity theory, and the surprise theory. Other ideas have also appeared. Though they have not attained the status of a central theory, many of them complement what the principal theorists have said. As I do with the main theories, I concentrate on the complementary ideas that bear directly on the process of joke making.

The Superiority Theory

In 1651 the English philosopher Thomas Hobbes published a work entitled the *Leviathan* which contained one of the most celebrated comments ever made about the cause of laughter.

Sudden glory is the passion which maketh those grimaces called laughter, and is caused either by some sudden act of their own that pleaseth them; or by apprehension of some deformed thing in another, by comparison whereof they suddenly applaud themselves.

When Hobbes used the term "sudden glory," he was clearly referring to what we might call a feeling of superiority. He saw it as being induced by two different kinds of developments. One is the carrying out of some act that infuses us with a pleasant sense of personal achievement. Having the perspicacity to see the point to a joke is just such an act, and, as I argue in Chapter 4, it is one of the reasons we laugh. The other kind of development that makes us feel superior is the perception that in some way we are better than someone else. That feeling, as Hobbes says in another section of this treatise, can arise when we detect "some eminency in ourselves by comparison with the infirmity of others."

Shortly after the publication of Hobbes's work, the English essayist Joseph Addison carried that last idea one step further by suggesting that we can enhance our feeling of superiority by not only perceiving a defect in someone else, but by ridiculing it as well. In one of his essays we find this passage:

> Everyone diverts himself with some Person or other that is below him in Point of Understanding and Triumph, in the Superiority of his Genius, whilst he has such Objects of Derision before his eyes.

In our own day, commentators on humor emphasize the significance of a superiority feeling in producing laughter. The film director Marcel Pagnol made the point this way: "Laughter is a song of triumph. It expresses the laughter's sudden discovery of his own momentary superiority over the person he laughs at." The psychologist Albert Rapp went so far as to argue that a feeling of superiority is not just the cause of some laughter; it is the cause of all laughter. In his book, *The Origins of Wit and Humor*, he wrote, "The single source from which all modern forms of wit and humor have developed is the roar of triumph in an ancient jungle duel." He commented further that "Laughter was born out of hostility....All the current types of wit and humor retain evidence of this hostile origin." Another psychologist, Donald Hayworth, added an interesting sidebar to Rapp's theory. In his view the victor's laughter was not just an expression of triumph. It also notified his supporters that the threat had been dealt with and the danger was over.

As humankind developed, softening influences made physical combat between individuals less common. According to Rapp, that did not eliminate the possibility of engaging in a contest whose victorious outcome could generate a feeling of superiority. Instead of using fists and clubs to defeat opponents, combatants made words their weapons. What had been a physical contest became a duel of wits. Turning the tables on an antagonist with a clever quip could produce the same feeling of superiority experienced by knocking someone down with a club.

As this change came and certain types of humor like riddles, conundrums, puns, and jokes developed, the door opened to another type of triumph. Persons who saw through a riddle, detected the double meaning of a pun, or got the point to a joke would experience a flush of pleasure at their own perceptiveness. A feeling of superiority would follow and then a laugh. Norman Holland supports that concept with the comment that one result of seeing through a joke is a feeling of exuberance and triumph.

Another facet of the superiority theory of crucial importance to joke makers is the fact that the feeling of superiority incited by victory is not limited to the people who actually win. Their immediate family and their supporters experience it also, but it can extend beyond them. Even strangers can savor it. All of us tend to identify with winners and to share vicariously the sense of superiority they feel.

Albert Rapp points out that it is not even necessary to witness a triumph in its entirety for us to visualize ourselves as winners. The sight of someone falling down can make us laugh. The reason, according to Rapp, is that the primitive impulses of our caveman ancestors suddenly engulf us. A potential opponent is down. Victory is imminent. That delectable anticipation calls forth a laugh of triumph. Being able to suggest a victory by revealing only one of its parts is obviously a tremendous boon to joke makers.

That a feeling of superiority creates funniness and therefore generates laughter has been noted down through the centuries. Aristotle observed that some people seem to take pleasure in the misfortunes of others. In the Roman period Cicero saw humor as a weapon, advising orators to provoke audiences into laughing at their opponents because it confounds, hampers, and frightens them. Sigmund Freud commented on the aggressive tendency in jokes, and the novelist and philosopher, Arthur Koestler remarked that "the emotional climate of humor is aggressive and malicious." Al Capp, whose comic strip *Li'l Abner* made millions of newspaper readers laugh, said that "all comedy is based on man's inhumanity to man."

A point springing from all this is that much humor, if taken seriously, would be unpleasant. Putting someone down, even though it is done only in a figurative sense, is not an exercise in niceness. Artistotle called humor "educational insolence." Max Eastman, who wrote two books on humor, said that "In every case in which a man laughs humorously there is...the possibility of tears." Or as the humorist Jim Filling put it, "It always hurts a bit when you hit your funny bone." All of this seems to suggest that to be funny, you need to be insensitive to human misery. Indeed, the French philosopher Henri Bergson said that a humorist must experience "a certain anesthesia of the heart."

Two things help soften the callousness of the humor of disparagement. First, it often deals with trivial matters. Aristotle conceded that laughter is incited by some blunder or ugliness, but added that it does not cause great pain or disaster. Second, even when the insults, if taken seriously, could be deeply hurtful, their impact is modified by the manner in which they are delivered. In essence humorists let us know that they don't mean all they say. They are just having fun.

That humor must be playful to be truly effective is one of the main points made by Max Eastman in his book *Enjoyment of Laughter*. He considered this point so important, in fact, that he opened his book by emphasizing it, "The First Law of humor," he said, "is that things can be funny only when we are in fun." How an attitude of playfulness can take the sting out of the most outrageous insult is illustrated by the performances of the comedian Don Rickles. The remarks he directed at members of his night-club audiences, if taken literally, were often grossly offensive. Instead of clobbering him, however, they laughed because they knew he was just being playful. The same attitude prevails at celebrity roasts. Their targets are subjected to the most scurrilous insults their friends can contrive, yet instead of flushing with anger, they laugh uproariously. The playful mood has negated the nastiness.

Though most philosophers agree that a feeling of superiority can incite laughter, few join Albert Rapp in seeing it as the single source from which all funniness springs. They list a superiority feeling as one of the causes of laughter, not the only one. Max Eastman refused to go even that far. He came close to rejecting the superiority theory in its entirety. He wrote at one point that it is possible "to dismiss from the topic of laughter at the outset the topic of scorn." The laughter ascribed by other authorities to a feeling of superiority, he argued, is actually caused by other stimuli.

One reason some tend to shy away from the superiority theory is that acceptance of the meanness it involves makes them feel uncomfortable. It can also be argued that being offensive is incompatible with the pleasant feeling funniness is presumed to produce. Some salve their queasiness by pointing out that offensive humor confers some benefits on society. The early Greeks saw the laughter it provoked as a way of correcting excessive behavior. Much the same thought came from the nineteenth-century English critic George Meredith who held that ridicule acts as a sort of social corrective which helps to restrain those who "wax out of proportion." Often they are people who occupy positions of great authority. As a writer identified only as Taki remarked in *Esquire*, "Humor is a reminder that no matter how high the throne one sits on, one sits on one's bottom." Mary Douglas said in an essay on jokes that all jokes have a subversive effect on the dominant structure of society." The French playwright Moliére extended their influence even further. "Comedies," he said, "render agreeably on the stage the faults of all mankind." George Bernard Shaw, as we might expect him to, chose a somewhat different target. He saw the function of comedy as the destruction of old-fashioned morals.

Kenneth Burke, who has made notable contributions to the study of rhetoric, found another kind of value in aggressive humor. He saw it "not so much a glorifying of the self as a minimizing of the stresses menacing the self." Seeing ridicule as an agent of defense obviously makes it more palatable than viewing it merely as a means of inflating one's ego.

The Incongruity Theory

Another cause of laughter, noted by many writers on the subject, is the sudden perception of an incongruity. One of the first to recognize the critical role it plays in creating funniness was the Scottish poet and philosopher James Beattie. In an essay on laughter published in 1776, he said that "Laughter arises from the view of two or more inconsistent, unsuitable, or incongruous parts or circumstances." Beattie apparently saw incongruity as just one cause of laughter, not the only cause. Others, however, argue that the funniness of everything we laugh at is created by the existence of an incongruity. One of the firmest proponents of this theory was the German philosopher Arthur Schopenhauer. In 1818 he wrote, "The cause of laughter in every case is an incongruity between a concept and the real object." The Canadian humorist Stephen Leacock did not state this position quite so positively, but he obviously saw incongruity as a major element in everything that amuses us. He wrote, "Humor finds its basis in the incongruity of life itself." Another who considers incongruity the major element in the production of humor is the mathematician I referred to earlier, John Allen Paulos. He said: "A necessary ingredient of humor is that two or more incongruous ways of viewing something (a person, a sentence, a situation) be juxtaposed and compared." He added that incongruity involves unusualness, oddness, and inappropriateness. Examples of incongruity he cited are "expectation versus surprise, the mechanical versus the spiritual, superiority versus incompetence, balance versus exaggeration, and propriety versus vulgarity."

Another thought about the nature of incongruity came from Max Eastman. He said that it often arises "from a violation of the patterns with which we contemplate the world." To illustrate, he cited a scene in a Charlie Chaplin film in which Charlie tipped his hat to a cow he was about to milk.

Arthur Koestler in his 1964 book *The Act of Creation* attempted to identify the factors involved in all creative activity. One type of activity to which he devoted a great deal of attention was the production of humor. He identified one element in the process with a word he coined, "bisociation." He described it as "the perceiving of a situation or idea in two self-consistent but habitually incompatible frames of reference." What he seems to be referring to is an incongruity.

Incongruity also arises when something that appears to be completely logical when we first encounter it collapses all at once into absurdity. Jack Kroll, who wrote film and theater criticism for *Newsweek*, expressed that idea in somewhat earthy terms when he said that "Laughter is an orgasm triggered by the intercourse of reason with unreason." We can see how seeming logic is suddenly transformed into nonsense in the kind of statement Stephen Leacock called an Irish Bull. A good example is the querulous complaint, "And where will ye find a house built in our own times that has lasted as long as one of thim Norman castles?"

The poet Samuel Taylor Coleridge once said that in humor the little is made great and the great small. He obviously was referring to two other elements that create a perception of incongruity—exaggeration and understatement. In the following quatrain exaggeration is the element that makes it amusing.

So very deaf was my grandfather, Squeers,
That he had to wear lightning rods over his ears
To hear thunder, and oftentimes then
He was forced to request it to thunder again.

The line below which appeared in a newspaper report, illustrates a technique that lies at the other end of the spectrum from exaggeration—understatement.

A traveler would have missed the train yesterday had he not stepped
on a peach pit at the head of the stairs.

There is an obvious mismatch between the restrained and moderate tone of that sentence and the event it described. Visualizing it, we can see a man's feet suddenly going out from under him followed by a projectile-like descent down the stairs, ending in a bounce that catapulted him through the door of the train. The reporter's words in no way do justice to that tumultuous happening, and that's why they're funny.

Sometimes exaggeration and understatement are juxtaposed to produce a comic effect. The English humorist P. G. Wodehouse did this brilliantly in his short stories and books about Bertie Wooster and his valet, Jeeves. The two have radically different ways of expressing themselves. Bertie's language is marked by an extravagance that sometimes becomes nearly hysterical in its exaggeration. Jeeves in contrast is always cool, contained, and formal. *The New Yorker* critic Terrence Rafferty described the difference this way: "Bertie's words poured out in a raging flood of deranged hyperbole, Jeeves aimed with the utmost precision, in quick cooling jets of pure reason."

The Surprise Theory

A third way of creating funniness, according to a number of theorists, is to confront audiences with a surprise. The most frequently quoted expression of that idea came from the German philosopher Immanuel Kant. "Laughter is an affectation rising from a sudden transformation of strained expectation into nothing." The English philosopher Herbert Spencer said almost the same thing. "Laughter is the indication of an effort that suddenly encounters a void."

Some refuse to give the element of surprise a category of its own, but classify it instead as a type of incongruity. You may recall, for example, that John Allen Paulos put "expectation vs. surprise" in his list of various kinds of incongruities. That approach is not entirely unreasonable. Because a surprise disrupts the normal order of events by frustrating our expectation, we can think of it as an incongruity. We can turn this around, of course, by arguing that an incongruity constitutes a surprise because it confronts us with the unexpected.

That there is a close relationship between the concepts of incongruity and surprise cannot be denied. There is one factor, however, that justifies placing them in separate categories. That factor is emphasis. In some humorous material, the element we identify as incongruity seems to be the major provoker of laughter. It may surprise, too, but it owes most of its laugh-producing power to the incongruity we perceive. In other material just the reverse is true. Though it contains an incongruity, the dominant trigger of laughter is a surprise.

In the previous section we saw some examples of humor in which the emphasis was on incongruity. Let us look now at some material in which surprise is the dominant element. I found the first example in a column Goodman Ace wrote for the *Saturday Review*.

A mother barges into her son's bedroom and finds he's still in bed.
"Get up," she shouts at him, "You've got to go to school."
"I'm not going to school today," he responds obstinately.
"You have to go to school," she insists.
"I'm never going back there again, he answered. "They hit me. They throw things at me. They make fun of my clothes."
"There are two reasons you have to go to school," the mother replies firmly. "First, you're 42 years old, and second, you're the principal."

The whole situation is incongruous, of course. But I think there can be no question that what really makes us laugh is the surprise the story delivers at the end.

A scene in Charlie Chaplin's film *The Immigrant* provides another good example of surprise as the chief inducer of laughter. We see Charlie hanging over the rail of a ship jerking and twitching convulsively. His actions suggest that he is going through the final stages of sea sickness. His apparent retching goes on so long, in fact, that one begins to feel uncomfortable. Then suddenly he turns around and for the first time we see that he is holding a fishing line in his hands. At the end of it a fish squirms and flops. This sudden revelation of the real reason for his behavior is bound to draw an outburst of laughter from the audience.

In his book *Laughing*, the psychologist Norman Holland cited another example of surprise produced entirely by physical action. A group of college sophomores was invited to participate in a study ostensibly designed to measure their ability to lift a heavy weight. The object, however, was not heavy at all. It was made of rubber, but had been made up to look like steel. Misled by its appearance, the students lifted with all their strength. The result was that the object flew upward with a sudden whoosh. The response from the students in almost every case was a loud laugh.

The significant role surprise plays in making people laugh has long been recognized. Aristotle identified the main humorous element in a joke as a deceived expectation, and the Roman teacher of oratory Quintillian mentions it also. In our day Arthur Koestler discussed a specific kind of funny surprise in his book *The Act of Creation*. He said that we laugh when an event which we had previously believed to belong in one context suddenly is seen to belong in a different one. A letter to the editor of an Irish newspaper, quoted by *The New Republic's* film critic Stanley Kauffmann illustrates how funny a sudden shift in context can be. The writer leads readers into thinking he has one type of misdeed on his mind before suddenly revealing it is quite another.

> Sir—I was shocked by the language of Molly McAnailly Burke's piece on lesbian rockers, and your allowing it in a family newspaper. The offending phrase "five writhing beauties hot for each other" should be "five writhing beauties hot for one another," since *each other* applies only to two. This panting male cannot allow such looseness to go uncorrected.
> —Sean O'Brien, Rathfarnham, D14

A similar switch in context is exemplified by the following joke. The last line abruptly makes clear that the parties to the conversation view the situation in entirely different lights.

A man says to a woman while pouring her a drink, "Say when."

The woman replies, "Right after this drink."

Max Eastman also discussed surprise but under a different heading. In his books *The Sense of Humor* and *Enjoyment of Laughter* he devoted a good deal of space to describing what he called his "Disappointment Theory." He began by quoting the French philosopher Pascal's statement that "Nothing produces laughter more than a surprising disproportion between that which one expects and that which one sees." Eastman called the effect disappointment rather than surprise. The trouble with his term, as Albert Rapp pointed out, is that disappointment, associated as it is with defeat, failure, and frustration, is more likely to make us cry than laugh.

Complementary Theories and Considerations

A number of ideas provide adjuncts to the main theories in helping us understand the nature of the stimuli that evoke laughter. Sigmund Freud was the source of some of them. In his book *Jokes and Their Relation to the Unconscious*, he advanced the hypothesis that jokes provide a means of expressing the sexual and aggressive impulses we normally keep bottled up in our unconscious. In that sense a joke provides a disguise that shields us from public scorn when a primitive desire comes to the surface. It is a means of stating a thing indirectly, which good manners would ordinarily keep us from saying. (You will recall that in the previous chapter I mentioned that one of the advantages of using humor is its indirectness.) Freud commented further that being indirect makes us laugh for two reasons. First, it releases the tension caused by keeping basic urges hidden and suppressed. Second, breaking through a societal taboo produces a feeling of gratification that comes out as laughter.

Those familiar with Freud's work will recognize that his speculations about humor constitute a further aspect of his general theory that we suppress motives and desires society might frown on by relegating them to the unconscious. They escape that prison by showing up in dreams, by coming to the surface in the kind of mistake we call a Freudian slip, and by being disclosed in jokes.

Albert Rapp linked Freud's idea that laughter comes when we defy a societal taboo with a joke to his theory that the source of all funniness is the feeling of superiority one experiences in achieving a victory. In the case of a joke that releases a suppressed desire, the triumph is over the forces and restrictions that work to keep it hidden.

Another trigger of laughter, according to Max Eastman, is satisfaction. In both of his books on humor, he placed great emphasis on it. Earlier we noted his belief that the comic involves a kind of disappointment, and satisfaction, he felt, is necessary to redeem it. He cited as an example of such redemption a clown whose antics presumably aroused the ire of someone in the audience, who begins throwing apples at him. The thrower, of course, is an accomplice of the clown. The viewers, in Eastman's view, expect the clown to be hit, but he manages to avoid the flying apples by catching them or ducking at the last moment. The satisfaction of seeing this "exhibition of nimble dexterity," as Eastman described it, redeems the disappointment the viewers felt when their expectation of seeing an apple bounce off the clown's noggin was not realized. As a result the audience's expectation changes. Now they look forward to a continued demonstration of his agility. Then another reversal takes place. The clown stumbles and an apple hits his forehead and splatters into bits. His failure to avoid it confronts the audience with a second disappointment. It is quickly redeemed, however, by the satisfaction arising from seeing the realization of their original expectation that he would be hit. As Eastman put it, this story provides an illustration of two disappointments and two redeeming satisfactions.

A number of theorists and practicing comedians have noted that an important factor in determining the effectiveness of humor is the nature of the audience. Some points seem self evident. The raucous laughter your jokes evoke from an audience made up of your friends may make you think you are ready to join David Letterman and Jay Leno in the pantheon of comedians. You will find that strangers subject you to a far sterner test. The time of day you perform also makes a difference. Early-morning listeners are likely to respond less effusively than those who hear you later in the day.

The psychologist Norman Holland pointed out that the size of an audience can also influence the effectiveness of humor. The larger it is the more vociferous the response is likely to be. You probably have had the experience of watching a film comedy in a nearly empty theater. I suspect you laughed very little. If you had seen the film with other people, some of what brought forth only tiny smiles might have evoked boisterous laughs. The responses of others builds up your response and you in turn build up theirs. That phenomenon is called social facilitation. It operates so powerfully that merely seeing or hearing others laugh can make you laugh also, even though nothing funny has been said or done. It is why canned laughter is such a common ingredient in television comedy shows.

Bob Hope found out how important audience size is early in his career as a radio comedian. Just before U. S. involvement in World War Two, his sponsor suggested that he originate one of his shows from an army camp. Reluctant at first to leave the comfortable environment of a radio studio, Hope finally agreed to try it on an experimental basis. The experience was a revelation. He found that even his weakest jokes brought waves of laughs from the soldiers massed in front of him. The most enthusiastic responses from his relatively small studio audiences had never matched the tumultuous reception he received. From then on he made regular visits to military installations all over the world. As one war followed another, he continued to make such visits. They made him a unique figure among American comedians.

The way an audience is arranged also can influence its response. The closer people sit together, the louder they laugh. When I'm scheduled to give a lecture on humor, I can scarcely repress a groan when I discover that I will be speaking in a restaurant setting. The space between the tables dampens the laughter. I find I get my best response when listeners are arranged in front of me in a conventional audience setting.

Types of Funniness

Thus far I have discussed funniness without defining some of the terms we associate with it. One of them is <u>humor</u>. You may well ask whether a definition is necessary. Doesn't everyone know what humor is? Not necessarily, because the word has two different meanings. Sometimes it is used as an all-encompassing term which denotes all the words, pictures, and acts that make us laugh. Stephen Leacock and Max Eastman used the word in that sense when they chose titles for books they wrote analyzing the various kinds of stimuli that evoke laughter. Leacock's title was *Humor: Its Theory and Technique*, Eastman's *The Sense of Humor*.

The term is also used in a more restricted way to designate a specific kind of funniness. Humor in this limited sense refers to material that is just one of the elements in the larger panoply of material referred to when humor is used in an overall way. In a sense it becomes a division of itself. It is obvious that when you use the word, you must be clear about which of these two meanings you have in mind.

Defining the meaning of humor in its umbrella sense is relatively easy. Defining its meaning when it is used to describe a particular category of funniness is considerably more difficult. One approach is to distinguish it from another form of funniness we call wit. How do the two differ?

One of the characteristics of humor, noted by many commentators, is that it tends to be kinder and gentler in its impact than wit. The English writer Thomas Carlyle said that, "the essence of humor is sensibility; warm, tender fellow feeling with all forms of existence...its essence is love." Albert Rapp struck a similar note with his comment that humor is "affectionate ridicule; humor pities what it smiles at; loves what it taunts." It has even been said that because humor is rarely malicious it can even be healing and rejuvenating in its effect.

Wit, on the other hand, is sharper and crueler in its impact. It tends to be aggressive and hostile, and can cut like a knife. The poet Louis Untermeyer put it this way, "Wit leaps out audaciously and wickedly." Max Eastman called it "a practical joke played on the mind."

Humor differs from wit in a second way. It tends to be slower and spun out, garnering laughs as it goes along. It may not arrive, in fact, at any particular point at all. Wit, in contrast, is "sudden and startling" as Untermeyer put it, and is much terser and succinct than humor. Its purpose is to make a point, and the laugh comes only when the point is revealed. Usually the journey to this destination is too quick to permit time for any laughs along the way. Peggy Noonan, a speech writer for presidents Ronald Reagan and the first George Bush, described an effect of this difference when she said: "Wit penetrates, humor envelops."

A third difference between humor and wit is that humor, as Carlyle said, springs from the heart whereas wit is intellectual by nature. Humor does not "assault the mind but laughs its way into the heart" remarked Louis Untermeyer. Wit, on the other hand, as Peggy Noonan remarked is "a function of verbal intelligence." Indeed, it often involves verbal sparring in which the weapons are words rather than fists. The effect of a reversal brought about by an ingenious turning of the tables can be as devastating as a physical blow. An interchange between a congressman and one of his constituents provides an example.

Constituent: I wouldn't vote for you if you were St. Peter.

Congressman: If I were St. Peter, you wouldn't be in my district.

Some analysts have discerned a fourth difference between humor and wit. In their view humor is more effective than wit in illuminating the truth and in exposing what is false and misleading. The writer Leo Rosten called humor "the affectionate communication of insight." Wit, on the other hand, intent as it often is on ridiculing something or someone, may actually mislead. It is also more superficial than humor. Dorothy Parker described the form of wit we know as the wisecrack as simple "calisthenics with words."

Thus far we have seen that the word "humor" is used in two ways: In one use it refers to funniness in general, in the other to a particular kind of funniness. It is also an important element in the familiar phrase *a sense of humor*. What do we mean by that term?

Generally, we use it to describe people who have the ability to see the funny side of life. Even though a situation may have its serious aspects, they can focus on what is amusing or diverting about it. Their response may consist of an intriguing or unexpected interpretation of what has occurred and in some instances it may take the form of a joke or a wry witticism. But even those who cannot create humor of their own are thought of as having a sense of humor if they respond positively to the jests of others. We are especially inclined to confer that accolade on those who laugh at the jokes we tell. On the other hand, if listeners fail to get the point, or seeing it, describe it as dumb or silly, we are likely to think of them as lacking a sense of humor.

As we noted in the previous chapter, a sense of humor is one of the most prized of human attributes. In assessing the qualities that make a person attractive, we usually put it at or near the top of the list. Just as we value it in others, so do we value it in ourselves. E. B. White said, "Whatever else an American believes or disbelieves about himself, he is absolutely sure he has a sense of humor."

The word humor, oddly enough, also appears in a phrase that denotes a decidedly unattractive characteristic. When people get up in the morning feeling grumpy and out of sorts, we describe them as being in a "bad humor." To understand why we use this word in such sharply contrasting ways, we have to go back to its origin. In Greek times humor referred to a bodily fluid. The Greeks speculated that four humors—blood, phlegm, yellow bile, and black bile—were important constituents of the human body. The disposition or mood of a person depended on which fluid dominated. When it was blood, for example, they felt happy and optimistic; black bile, in contrast, put them down in the dumps. Victorian ladies who fainted were sometimes said to be suffering from the "humors." As the centuries went by, humor tended to lose its connection with bodily fluids and came to refer most of the time to something comic or funny. When we describe someone as being in a bad humor, we are harking back, of course, to the original meaning of the word.

Let us look now at some other terms that appear regularly in the literature about humor. Two words closely allied in meaning to wit are *satire* and *sarcasm*. *Satire* refers to material that holds up to scorn and ridicule the follies and idiosyncrasies of humankind. Louis Untermeyer said that "satire is probing and critical; it cuts through pretension with quick, corrosive acid; its purpose is coldly destructive." The contemporary

63

journalist Molly Ivens remarked that "satire is traditionally the weapon of the powerless against the powerful." Politics and politicians are its most frequent targets. The monologues of Mark Russell, broadcast by PBS, are devoted almost entirely to political satire, and it appears regularly in the presentations of such talk-show hosts as Jay Leno and David Letterman.

James Thurber deftly summed up the contrasting meanings of wit, humor, and satire in this way:

The wit makes fun of other people.

The satirist makes fun of the world.

The humorist makes fun of himself.

Sarcasm is wit of the sharpest and cruelest kind. It is meant to wound its targets. In its original meaning the word meant "a tearing of the flesh." That better than anything suggests how savage its bite can be.

One of the most important terms for us is *joke*, for a major purpose of this book is to explain how this kind of funniness is created. Like many of the words we commonly use, it is not easy to define. Albert Rapp defined a joke as "a highly compressed short story with the requirement of a laughter-tripping ending." A joke, someone else said, presents a character or a problem and disposes of it all in one breath. Its major characteristics are crispness and suddenness. A joke also makes a point. It takes form in the listener's mind as the result of material the joke maker presents. Is a joke a form of wit or of humor, thinking of that word now in its subsidiary sense? Its terseness and its coalescing around a point definitely put the joke in the wit column. Humor, you recall, is often rambling and sometimes arrives at no point at all.

Sigmund Freud once said something about wit that admirably sums up the process involved in creating a joke. "The essence of wit lies in the neat and economical spanning of a gulf between different and alternative ideas." Carrying out this process is a delicate and difficult task. A joke is a fragile entity that can easily fall apart if the joke teller expresses the idea clumsily or fumbles the telling of it.

A form of humor closely allied to the joke is the riddle. It involves a duel of wits in which one of the participants asks a question deliberately designed to conceal the truth. The other participant wins the contest by seeing through the deception and coming up with the answer. The most celebrated riddle of all time was propounded by a legendary Greek monster called the Sphinx. She sat at the roadway near Thebes and asked this question of those who passed by:

It goes on four legs in the morning, two legs at noon, and three legs in the evening. What is it?

64

The Sphinx killed those who could not answer, and that included everyone until Oedipus came along. He correctly figured out that she was talking about a man—who crawls on all fours as an infant, walks erect as an adult, and must use a cane as an old man. The solving of the riddle so upset the Sphinx that she killed herself.

A form of riddle called the conundrum depends on a pun to confuse the listener. This makes it almost impossible for a listener to solve. The answer to a riddle, on the other hand, can be figured out by those who are adept at working their way through figurative language. The following illustrates the crucial role played by punning in the creation of a conundrum:

Why is a skunk the most generous of all animals?

Because he'd give you his last scent.

The close relationship of the conundrum to the joke is indicated by the fact that you can turn this conundrum into a joke simply by replacing the question-and-answer format with a conventional joke format.

Skunks are the most generous animals in the world because they'd give you their last scent.

Other forms of funniness we encounter at times are *caricature, parody*, and *burlesque*. *Caricature* is usually thought of as a visual form, but it can also be expressed in words. It makes fun of people by exaggerating their features or an idiosyncrasy of dress. Editorial cartoonists tended to give George W. Bush outsized ears while depicting his presidential opponent, John Kerry, with mountains of hair, capping an elongated, gaunt face. A *parody* is a form of humor that makes fun of a written work by exaggerating a characteristic of its style or by retaining the style by changing the words to create absurdities and surprises. *Burlesque* is somewhat more difficult to define. Stephen Leacock viewed it as a form of humor that went beyond the ridiculing of a particular author to making fun of a whole mode of writing. The authority on English usage, H. W. Fowler, saw burlesque in a somewhat different light. He differentiated between the three terms in the following way: "Action or acting are burlesqued, form and features are caricatured, and verbal expression is parodied."

A figure of speech that can sometimes be funny is *irony*. The word is even more difficult to define than burlesque. One reason is that it has a variety of meanings. It is sometimes used to refer to a technique employed by the philosopher Socrates. It was his practice to feign ignorance of a subject as a means of drawing those around him into a discussion. The contrast between his great wisdom and the ignorance of his audience constituted irony as the Greeks saw it.

The Greeks also used the word to refer to the difference between what an audience knew about the story of a drama and what its characters knew. In Greek times dramatists generally didn't invent stories of their own. Instead they dramatized legends and tales that were familiar to everyone. Audiences came to the theater knowing ahead of time what was going to happen in the play. The characters, on the other hand, learned about the developments only as the drama progressed. Audiences, for example, knew from the beginning that Oedipus had married his mother. Poor Oedipus didn't learn that terrible fact until the drama revealed it. The Greeks called this difference between the audience's knowledge and Oedipus's ignorance dramatic irony.

In our day the term has two principal meanings. First, a situation is deemed to be ironic when events take a turn that is the opposite of what one might expect. Irony also develops when one happening is inconsistent with other happenings in a situation. It is ironic, for example, when a fire station burns down or when a lecturer on temperance is arrested for drunk driving. In 1959 an actor was rejected for a part in a play for a reason that in the light of later developments proved to be ironic. The play was *The Best Man* by Gore Vidal. The actor was Ronald Reagan, and the role he was considered for was that of a candidate seeking to become President of the United States. The reason given for turning him down was that he lacked the "presidential look." An item which appeared in the British newspaper *The Guardian* illustrates how irony develops when one aspect of a situation is incompatible with other aspects. The item reported the holding of a medical conference on alcohol and related diseases. The agenda for one of the morning sessions was listed as follows:

9:15 Alcohol in the blood
10:15 Alcohol in the liver
11:15 Alcohol in the pancreas
12:15 Alcoholism
12:45 Bar opens

Second, a statement is said to be ironic when a word is given a meaning utterly different from the one it usually implies. In most cases we accomplish this transformation of meaning by the kind of emphasis we give the word. Thus, a wife whose husband has made a fool of himself at a party may say, "That was a fine performance you gave tonight." She doesn't mean it was fine, of course, she means it was disgusting.

Is irony funny? It may be at times. We may grin, for example, when we hear that the payday of postal workers was delayed because their checks were lost in the mail. We may also find that the conflict between the words people use and the meaning they intend sometimes elicits a smile. Most of the time, however, irony provokes philosophical reflection rather than amusement. And even when it does strike us as funny, it usually does not call forth a guffaw. Still, it does have a place in the array of humorous devices, but those who use it must tread carefully. Its implications can easily be misunderstood. Your words may be taken literally rather than in the ironic way you intended. Because irony is one of the most sophisticated forms of funniness, it can easily come to naught if its users bungle the delivery of its delicate nuances.

Before leaving this matter of definitions, a few words are in order about the terms I use to refer to the audiences of humor. They may receive it through their ears as listeners, through their eyes as readers, or as observers of drawings or amusing action. An all-purpose word that takes in all of them is recipients, but it has a somewhat formal tone so I have used it sparingly. The word audience has the same inclusive quality, but it suggests groups of people responding together to the same material, even though, technically speaking, an audience can consist of just one person. Whenever it seems appropriate, I have used that term. In some instances I distinguish among the various types of audiences as I did at the beginning of this paragraph. At other times, I simply refer to the recipients of humor as listeners even though they may include readers or observers.

Applying the Theories

In the chapters that follow, you will encounter again many of the ideas about funniness summed up in this chapter. In some instances the language used to describe them may be a little different. For example, I refer to self-satisfaction as one of the three major triggers of laughter rather than to a feeling of superiority. Self-satisfaction, I feel, is a broader, more inclusive term. I also introduce some new terms and concepts.

Because theorists sometimes disagree, I have had to make choices between conflicting theories. I mention only one of them at this point. I am convinced there is no single cause or source of everything that is funny. Laughter is an exceedingly complex phenomenon, and it is my belief that the stimuli inciting it are equally complex. The other choices I have made should become clear as you continue your reading.

You may wonder how I arrived at the methods and techniques for creating jokes which I describe later in this book. My major source of information was the multitude of jokes I have collected through the years. I examined them with two questions in mind. First, which jokes really made me laugh? Second, what was it about them that tickled my funny bone? At the forefront of my thoughts as I carried out this process were the theories about the nature of funniness, which I have just described. As my examination went on, I arrived at conclusions about the kind of content that can be counted on to provoke laughter. I also saw that a joke is made up of certain specific elements, and I formulated a process for bringing those elements into being. Most important of all, I recognized that both the joke teller and the listener have crucial responsibilities in making a joke work, and I arrived at conclusions about what those responsibilities are.

I did not rely entirely on my own judgment in drawing up my recommendations. During my lectures on humor, I observed the way people reacted to various kinds of jokes. I also seized on opportunities to test jokes in social situations. Sometimes my only reason for telling a certain joke was to find out what sort of laugh it would provoke. In a sense I was using my friends as guinea pigs without their knowing it. Their reward, I hope, was a laugh.

Most of the time we tell or create jokes with the specific intent of being funny. At times, however, we stumble into making people laugh without meaning to. As a prelude to describing the techniques for being funny on purpose, we look in the next chapter at some of the ways humor erupts unintentionally.

Chapter 3
Being Funny Without Meaning To Be

One of the best things people can have up their sleeves is a funny bone.
                    Richard L. Weaver II

It may seem odd to include a chapter on humor that occurs accidentally in a book designed to explain how to create it on purpose. One reason for doing so is that other people's missteps generate essentially the same kind of laugh-inciting circumstances and conditions that planned humor does. An analysis of unintentional humor can therefore point the way to techniques and principles that can be applied to producing it intentionally.

A second reason for discussing accidental humor is to help you avoid it. Unlike planned humor, unintentional humor usually works to the disadvantage of those who create it. If nothing else, it is often profoundly mortifying. Even more serious consequences may follow. The stumbles that evoke laughter may interfere with the clarity of communication. When you blunder into creating laughs, you are likely to divert your audience from the ideas you want it to grasp. Even more damaging, laughter erupting unexpectedly can cause you to lose control of a situation, and it may be some time before you can get back on course.

Describing the roots of unintentional humor cannot provide an absolute defense, for sometimes it creeps up on you so surreptitiously that it cannot be detected ahead of time. In some instances you may even know that a laugh you don't particularly want is coming, but can do nothing to avoid it. This discussion, however, can alert you to the kinds of quicksands lying in wait to trap the unwary and help you bypass most of them.

Turncoat Words

Among the principal prompters of unexpected laughter are turncoat words. They are words that seem innocuous when you decide to use them, but which flip around to betray you as a second meaning you hadn't noticed suddenly springs to the surface. It pushes your audience into thinking thoughts you hadn't planned on.

Were all words limited to just one meaning, the possibilities of provoking laughter would be enormously reduced. The pun, for example, which some have called the foundation stone of humor, could not exist without double-meaning words. People who create humor deliberately are keenly aware of both meanings, of course, and count on audiences recognizing them. Unintentional humorists, on the other hand, unmindful of a particular word's second meaning, sail blithely along until a burst of unexpected laughter signals its existence. If the second meaning is risqué or indelicate the laughter is likely to be even louder. As you realize what you have overlooked, your reaction may range from a rueful smile to a blush of acute embarrassment. In some cases you may never figure out why the audience laughed.

Almost all of us have been the victims at one time or another of turncoat words. An experience I had with one etched a scar on my psyche. In teaching a class about creating commercials, I was explaining that commercials gain effectiveness if selling appeals are presented in a climactic order. To illustrate I said, "Suppose you are emphasizing the features that make the car you are advertising particularly attractive looking. You might begin by mentioning the sporty wire wheels, move to the two-tone color design, then reach your climax on the foam-rubber cushions." There was a moment of dreadful silence before the class exploded into uncontrollable laughter.

Instantly aware of the import of my words, I waited with my face a bright red for the class to quiet down, but several attempts to resume my lecture were frustrated by a somewhat chubby young woman sitting in the front row. She obviously was trying desperately to regain control but despite her effort, her ample sides would start shaking, her eyes would crinkle, and before long she would collapse again into helpless laughter. Her outbursts naturally triggered further eruptions from the class. A full five minutes went by before I could resume my lecture.

That incident illustrates another point about laughter. It resounds more loudly when authority figures like university professors make fools of themselves. Those who blunder into suggesting sexual connotations in a religious context also invite greater reactions than would ordinarily result. A minister once preached a sermon on Jesus's parable about the five wise virgins who took along oil for their lamps and the five foolish virgins who forgot to. "Now," asked the minister, "Which would you rather be with, the five wise virgins in the light, or the five foolish virgins in the dark?" The laughter of the congregation indicated it hadn't quite got the message he was intending.

Another minister attending an out-of-town conference was asked how his church's program was being maintained in his absence. "My wife is back at home," he replied, "bravely carrying on with the deacons." It would take a great deal of self control to keep from laughing at that answer.

When notices in church bulletins inadvertently carry double-entendre implications, they also provoke a greater reaction than they would appearing elsewhere. We can speculate that parishioners laughed loudly when they saw this item in their church bulletin: "Both the north and south ends of the church will be used for Sunday morning services. Children will be baptized at both ends."

A former pastor of mine, Bob Wallace, produced another type of double

71

entendre in a notice he wrote for the church newsletter. Its purpose was to recruit volunteers to supervise homeless people who would be using the church as a sleeping area for a two-week period. His effort to explain that the volunteers must take turns at staying awake throughout the night came out this way: "You will trade off sleeping with the other volunteers." He then sank deeper into the quicksand by adding: "You will know what is expected of you."

That innocent appearing words can sometimes explode in one's face was a lesson learned by Walter Cronkite during one of his newscasts. He was reporting the activities of Lyndon Johnson during a crucial period in his presidency. Momentarily, it seemed, the crisis had eased, and Cronkite summed up by saying, "We understand the president has put on his pajamas and has gone to bed. We now switch to Nancy Dickerson who is covering him."

At times unintentional humor develops because an element in the total context is missing. A professor had asked a university librarian to notify him when Walter Lord's book about the *Titanic* disaster became available. Shortly thereafter the book was returned and that evening the librarian saw the professor in the university cafeteria. The startled diners heard her call out to him, "Come up to the library after you finish eating, and I'll give you *A Night to Remember*."

Words differ in the obviousness of their double meanings. Some are so subtle it is easy to see why they are overlooked. Certain words, on the other hand, flaunt danger signals so openly that anyone employing them should realize that careless usage can invite trouble. Ed Rollins, President Reagan's campaign manager in 1984, probably should have been alert to the image he was conjuring when he called the Democratic vice-presidential candidate, Geraldine Ferraro, "the biggest political bust of recent years."

Even commonplace words can sometimes whip around to nip you. A couple of television announcers found that out when they were describing a football game between Stanford and Army being played in a driving rain. The weather conditions made it necessary for a game official to dry off the football after every play. Noting that fact, one of the announcers added, "There are certainly a lot of wet balls out there." Unfortunately for them, they were on camera at the time, and it was immediately evident from their suddenly glassy eyes that both realized they had floundered into forbidden territory. Their desperate effort to maintain decorum was as entertaining a spectacle as I have ever seen on television.

A woman who made a similar faux pas in one of my public speaking classes seemed to be the victim of her own naiveté. She apparently failed to recognize that the topic she had chosen, "The Breeding of Canaries," simmered with double-entendre possibilities. Even more crucial, she appeared to be quite unaware that some members of the class might give a technical term she planned to use a meaning quite different from the one she intended. The critical moment arrived when she was describing how canary breeders arouse the interest of the female in the male's advances. "One thing they do," she explained, "is heighten natural coloring by painting the cock yellow," Instantly a wave of laughter engulfed her. Her eyes opened wide in utter puzzlement. I have the feeling that she hasn't figured out to this day what caused the outburst.

If innocence tripped my student up, how can one explain the obtuseness of a supposedly sophisticated office manager who became upset at the personal use some staff members were making of the copy machine assigned to the secretary? To put a stop to the practice, he posted this sign: "Employees are not to tamper with the secretary's reproductive equipment without my express permission."

Usually the person who stumbles into using a double-meaning word is the one embarrassed, but at times other people become the victims. During her stint as co-host of the *Today* show, Jane Pauley was confronted with a man who suffered from impotence. Carefully threading her way through the dangerous terrain, she asked him how the problem had affected him psychologically. "Well, you know how a man likes to be on top of the situation," he replied. Her guest seemed quite unaware of the implication he had created, but Jane was momentarily transfixed as she tried to force out her next question through rigid lips.

Words do not necessarily have to suggest a risqué connotation to cause merriment, of course. Many readers undoubtedly smiled when they saw this newspaper headline: "ZOO OPENING DELAYED BY WILDCAT STRIKE." The Maine Highway Commission once circulated a bumper sticker that reminded parents of an important responsibility by asking this question, "Have you belted your kids today?" A teacher who volunteered to give a course in English composition to a group of prison inmates found out that a word that would be completely innocuous in one setting can acquire a painful double meaning in another. He began his opening session with the assembled convicts by saying, "I think you all know what a sentence is." Bitter laughter followed.

Unwary copy editors frequently construct headlines whose double meanings go unperceived until readers see the headlines. The following are just a few of the many examples of such editorial mishaps available on the Internet:

RED TAPE HOLDS UP BRIDGE
POLICE BEGIN CAMPAIGN TO RUN DOWN JAY WALKERS
TEACHER STRIKES IDLE KIDS

Double meanings are often apparent to audiences as soon as the triggering word comes out. Other meanings are far more elusive because the thought processes required to make the connections are more subtle and complex. The reaction to such words is likely to be mixed. In a speech on humor, I sometimes quote an announcement which appeared in the *Wisconsin State Journal*. "The La Leche League will discuss breast feeding at two meetings, Tuesday on the West side and Thursday on the East side." Some laugh at it immediately, some laugh after an interval, and some never laugh at all. I suspect that husbands in the audience who may have to explain the cause of their merriment to their wives are likely to be met with this: "Well, that's the kind of a mind you have."

I once observed a similar mixed response in quite another setting. It occurred at a showing by a university cinema group of the 1930s movie classic, *Les Misérables*. A climactic moment occurs when Jean Valjean, carrying the unconscious body of Marius, his ward's loved one, escapes through the sewers of Paris from his relentless pursuer, Javert. When Marius revives, he greets his rescuer with these words: "I know what you must have gone through." A few students reacted with an uproarious laugh. The rest of the audience, caught up in the drama, were obviously bewildered by their outburst. I must admit, I was in that group until I finally made the connection.

Double meanings lurking undetected can sometimes turn an intended compliment into a veiled insult. The newly elected president of a Rotary Club was delegated to present a gift to the person he was succeeding. He did so with these words: "It's really not worth very much, but it shows what we think of you."

Ministers must grit their teeth at times at some of the comments parishioners make about their sermons. One lady who was obviously trying to be nice said this: "Well, you certainly know how to fill up the time." Another remarked in a kindly way, "We shouldn't make you preach so often." And what is one to make of this comment addressed to my own minister, George Lambrides: "Pastor, I want to tell you something about your preaching. Do you realize that each of your sermons is better than the next?" The implication seemed to be that as far as his sermons were concerned, it was all downhill from then on.

Ministers, of course, aren't the only victims of unintended insults. The wife of a former mayor of New York, John Lindsay, was giving a reception, and one of the persons she invited was Yogi Berra, whose misadventures with words have become legendary. The day was hot and Yogi showed up wearing a lime-green suit. Mrs. Lindsay greeted him with, "My you look cool today." Yogi, apparently attempting to be gallant, responded, "You don't look so hot yourself."

Even polished speakers can stumble in the same way. Everett Dirksen of Illinois, one of the most eloquent orators ever to grace the United States Senate, was once listening with annoyance to what he thought of as a petty attack on Clare Boothe Luce, who had been nominated for an ambassadorship. Finally he rose to his feet and with an angry shake of his leonine head thundered: "Why thresh old straw and beat an old bag of bones?" Guffaws from the gallery drowned out Dirksen's frantic attempt to rephrase his remark.

At times a seemingly innocuous remark apparently directed at no one in particular becomes by implication a gratuitous insult. An announcement made by a Rotary Club president just before introducing the speaker of the day acquired a painful pertinence. The president began by saying that the club's board of directors had just voted to increase the budget for visiting lecturers. "Which means," he went on happily, "that beginning next year we'll be able to afford a better class of lecturer." He then proceeded to introduce the current speaker apparently oblivious to the fact that he had just labeled him "inferior goods."

Humor is being used more and more these days to enhance the attractiveness and selling effectiveness of radio and TV advertising. Sometimes, however, humor creeps in unexpectedly because the copywriters fail to detect the double meanings hidden in their commercials. The people who produced the following radio commercials probably wished they had reviewed their copy more carefully.

> When I see a housewife who does her own cleaning and still has soft, pretty hands, I know she has been using her head.

> Try this remarkably effective cough syrup. We guarantee you'll never get any better.

> See Harry Applebaum for that new pair of pants, open Sundays and evenings for your convenience.

The writers of printed copy also fall victim at times to the ubiquitous double meaning. The editor of a department-store catalogue let this line get into print. "Designer gown, lovely with a low neckline for easy entertaining." This ad appeared in the classified section of a newspaper. "Free. Big brown dog. Eats almost anything. Loves kids."

A double entendre is occasionally communicated by something that happens rather than by something said or written. The classic example occurred on the *Tonight* show when Johnny Carson was the host. His guest was Ed Ames, the singer and actor, who was then appearing as a Native-American character in the TV series *Daniel Boone*. Johnny invited Ames to demonstrate his skill at throwing a tomahawk. Ames let the tomahawk fly at a cardboard cutout of a man provided as a target. It ended up in a highly suggestive upright position in the figure's mid-section. What was most hilarious about this unexpected result was Carson's handling of it. Only the knowing look in his eye revealed his recognition of the image that had been inadvertently created. Ed Ames, on the other hand, was convulsed with laughter. The participants were not embarrassed by this development, of course, for comedy was the aim of the program. In that sense the wayward tomahawk's unseemly landing point turned out to be a welcome diversion. So celebrated did this episode become that it was shown again and again on Johnny Carson's anniversary programs and was included in a video collection of the best moments from the *Tonight* show.

If double-meaning words can rear up to trip people whose familiarity with the English language is prolonged and deep, how much more likely are they to ensnare those for whom it is a foreign tongue. A sign in an Italian clothing show betrayed ignorance of the language's subtler meanings. "Dresses for Street Walking." A note appended to a restaurant menu in a Mexican hotel was obviously designed to allay some tourists' concerns. "All water served in this restaurant personally passed by the manager." Reassurance was also the aim of a sign posted at the baggage reception area of a Copenhagen airport: "We take your bags and send them in all directions."

Trouble can also erupt at times when English language words are translated into another language. On entering the Chinese market, the Kentucky Fried Chicken company found to its dismay that its slogan "finger licken' good" came out as "eat your fingers off" when rendered into Chinese. Even a name can hurt a product's sales. The Chevy Nova didn't sell well in Spanish-speaking countries because in Spanish *no va* means "it doesn't go."

Insidious Juxtapositions

Humor sometimes erupts unexpectedly because ideas, thoughts, or happenings that aren't funny when they occur separately become highly amusing when they occur together or follow one another in quick succession. In most cases the juxtaposition of the two elements takes place completely accidentally. A TV movie I once saw came to a commercial break with a mother crying piteously because her child had just been murdered. Her tear-streaked face was suddenly supplanted by a brightly smiling Cybill Shepherd saying, "It's not worth all the 'boo hooin'." I thought at first the story had abruptly gone off in another direction before realizing a commercial had interrupted it. Shepherd's words introduced a message detailing the virtues of a cosmetic. The clash between the two segments was both shocking and funny. Such jarring juxtapositions in network presentations are difficult to avoid because programs come from one source, commercials from another.

An accidental juxtaposition was also responsible for getting my father into trouble. He told me that as a young boy he was attending a Church of England service with his parents. The congregation had reached the part of the ritual that reads, "And we have left undone those things that we ought to have done" when he looked up to see that the woman in front of him had left the back of her dress unbuttoned. His shriek of laughter echoed throughout the church. That unfortunate conjunction of circumstances cost him a sound spanking after he returned home.

In another church service chance was also responsible for connecting two similarly incompatible elements. To the surprise of the congregation, the minister interrupted the order of worship to announce his resignation, saying that "The Lord Jesus has called me to another church." Unfortunately, he had failed to notice that the hymn the congregation was about to sing was "What a Friend We Have in Jesus."

There was a similar collision between a hymn and a minister's words when he announced "Today's final hymn will be number 312; 'Take Time to be Holy.'" He then added, "Because we're short of time, we'll sing only the first and last verses."

How laugh-producing juxtapositions can come out of nowhere is illustrated by an experience a college president had while he was conducting a faculty meeting. He was calling members of the administration staff forward to make reports. One of them, the Director of Admissions, was a pert young woman whose shapely form drew the appreciative glances of her male colleagues as she tapped her way to the platform in high heels. With a smile on her face, she reported that enrollment figures were on the upswing. As she made her way back to her seat, all eyes were again on her except those of the president who unfortunately was thinking only of the good news she had delivered. "I must say that figures like that really excite me," he commented.

The editors who arrange stories and photographs on newspaper pages sometimes fail to notice discordant juxtapositions between pictures and adjoining headlines as did one editor who put a story about a zoo featuring a picture of a monkey next to a headline announcing that a royal couple had had a bouncing baby boy. Intriguing connections between pictures and captions also can occur if writers are not attentive. Even a single headline can communicate an unlikely combination of ideas, as this one does: ROBBERS HOLD UP ALBERT'S HOSIERY. The writer of the following advertising blurb may have brought into focus a thought better left latent. "Our nylon stockings cost more, but they are best in the long run." This church notice in a newspaper probably caused some second takes. "Morning worship 10:30 A.M. Sermon topic: 'When the Wine Runs Out.' Followed by coffee."

Some of these juxtapositions might have been detected and eliminated if the people responsible for them had reviewed their work more carefully. In some instances, however, it is almost impossible to avoid communicating unintended meanings. For many years the signs designating the names of two intersecting streets in Ann Arbor, Michigan, did no more than identify a geographical location. Then along came the Watergate scandal, and all at once those same street signs were making a political statement. The names of the streets are Nixon and Bluett. At times a writer may sense potential trouble and still find that avoiding it is extremely difficult. What is an advertising copywriter to do, for example, when the TV movie of the week is entitled *Woman on the Run* and the sponsor is Phillips' Milk of Magnesia?

Concepts in Conflict

One of the reasons we laugh at some juxtapositions is that they present us with an incongruity. Clashing ideas, words, and images have significant laugh-producing capacity. Even concepts that simply fit together poorly can amuse us.

The disharmony of the elements in the following news report, for example, is likely to make our eyes crinkle with amusement: "Members of the Audubon Club heard a lecture on 'Bird Survival and the Wetlands' and then enjoyed a chicken dinner." A similar touch of discord is evident in this announcement: "The talk by the noted psychic Mrs. Foster has been cancelled due to unforeseen circumstances."

Unintentional incongruities are even more likely to occur in spoken language because words often burst out unplanned, and the speaker has no chance to review and correct them. Jerry Coleman, who became a sports broadcaster after his baseball career ended, described an exciting moment in a game this way: "He slides into second with a stand-up double." A Michigan legislator told his assembled colleagues, "The handicapped have made great strides in recent years." An editor, who felt that the writing in his newspaper was getting too predictable, exhorted his staff "to find some new clichés." The motion-picture producer Samuel Goldwyn rejected a proposal with these oft-quoted words: "Include me out." Another well-known "Goldwynism" is the instruction he gave to one of his writers: "Don't call the hero Joe. Every Tom, Dick, and Harry is called Joe."

An ill-advised choice of metaphor can sometimes create an inappropriate connection, as this newspaper headline does: BUDGET INCREASE GIVES DRUG PROGRAM A SHOT IN THE ARM. Representative Bob Jones had metaphor trouble when he introduced John Glenn during the former astronaut's run for the presidency in 1984. "If he can go to the moon or stay in orbit, then he is a man who truly has his feet on the ground." Besides mangling the metaphor, Jones was also wrong about Glenn's going to the moon.

Although inappropriateness is the hallmark of incongruity, words that fit a situation almost too well can seem out of place at times. That may have been true of a statement made by a Michigan Medical School dean in discussing the recruiting of new faculty. "We are looking for people at the cutting edge of the surgical field."

The ultimate incongruity is a statement that seems plausible at first, but which suddenly collapses into nonsense. Yogi Berra's well-known comment, "Nobody goes to that restaurant anymore: it's too crowded" is an example. We may nod affirmatively for a moment before realizing he has made no sense. Twisted logic of this type has come to be known as an Irish bull. Classic examples are the statement: Abstinence is a good thing, but it should always be practiced in moderation; the exasperated comment of a harried mother, "Lucky are the parents who have no children;" the reproof given to a delinquent churchgoer, "If you'd been in church this morning and seen the empty pews you would have been ashamed to be absent"; and the complaint of the man who said, "He kicked me in the belly when my back was turned." Former President Ronald Reagan may have betrayed his Irishness in a speech to the United Nations in which he said, "I believe that the future is far nearer than most of us would dare hope."

You don't have to be Irish, of course, to commit an Irish bull. A great many sentences containing dissonant ideas and images flow constantly from the lips of people of all lineages, among them the following: A mother insisted that her daughter wake her up as soon as she came in from a date,

"Because you know I can't sleep a wink until I know you're safely home." A man hoping to pass a physical examination for an insurance policy floundered into absurdity when he was asked the causes of his parents' deaths. "I'm not sure," he said, "but I know it was nothing serious." A mother admonishing her child for dangling dangerously from a tree, called out, "If you fall and break your leg, don't come running to me." When an adolescent youth came home from his first solo drive with a banged-up fender, his exasperated mother rebuked her husband with these words: "I told you to go with him the first time he drove alone." That is an Irish bull in its purest form. Equally pure is the comment of a woman who was extolling the virtues of the area to which she had just moved: "Everything is so close you can even walk to the car wash."

A question once asked of the movie actor Kirk Douglas was not quite an Irish bull, but it came close. Douglas told in his autobiography about picking up a hitchhiker. The young man snatched a glance at him as he settled into his seat, then turned back with an astonished second take, and blurted out, "Do you know who you are?" Douglas commented that the question may not be as nonsensical as it sounds, adding that it is one we might ask of a number of people, perhaps even of ourselves.

Oddly enough, a comment that is at the opposite pole from nonsense—one that states an undeniable fact in a clear and cogent way—may be amusing at times. No one can question the truth of these headlines: TESTER LINKS PYGMY DEFECT TO SHORTNESS and COLD WAVE CAUSED BY TEMPERATURES. The incongruity arises from the self-evident nature of the insights and the fact that someone found it necessary to state them. The humor quotient rises when people belabor the obvious in a manner suggesting they are revealing a great truth. Yogi Berra once said, "You can observe a lot just by watching." In a speech to young people the actress Brooke Shields included this thought: "Smoking can kill you, and if you've been killed, you've lost an important part of your life." When President Richard Nixon visited the Great Wall of China, he was asked to comment. His response was "This is certainly a great wall." President Calvin Coolidge once said, "When more and more people are thrown out of work, unemployment results." The sheer banality of those statements makes them funny. If they were made in a deeply solemn and earnest manner, as I suspect they were, they would be even funnier.

Mangled and Misplaced Words

Sometimes unexpected laughter bursts forth simply because speakers fail to get their words out properly. An English clergyman of the late nineteenth century actually became famous for his habit of interchanging the sounds and syllables of words. He was the Reverend William Spooner, who served as the warden of an Oxford University college. In a marriage service he announced that "It is kisstomary to cuss the bride," and in a sermon he referred to manual laborers as "noble tons of soil." His effort to make a graceful reference to Queen Victoria as the "Dear Old Queen" came out as the "Queer old dean." In addition to switching sounds, Reverend Spooner was also prone to getting the words in sentences in the wrong order. He is reputed to have said that "Work is the curse of the drinking classes." Those kinds of linguistic errors have come to be known as "spoonerisms."

Spoonerisms in our day are most likely to be noticed if they come from the lips of radio and television announcers. Their articulatory bungling gives us special pleasure because we expect them to be word perfect. One of the most celebrated mangling of sounds occurred in the early days of radio when an announcer named Harry von Zell turned the name of the president of that period, Herbert Hoover, into "Hubert Heever." A contemporary of von Zell, Andre Baruch, interchanged words in a Spooner-like manner when he opened a program thusly: "Good Ladies Evening and Gentlemen." The sports announcer Mel Allen once began a tobacco commercial with an enthusiastic "It's smipe poking time." I have not been immune to this virus. As the announcer of a university radio news show, I said "The sports menu next week will feature wrestling and boxling matches." On another occasion I substituted a "v" for an "s" in a key word with the result that I announced "Next week we prevent Dean Albertus Darnell speaking on the subject 'Is College Worthwhile?'".

Hubert Humphrey, who served the nation as senator and vice president, was noted for the effortless way in which he produced a constant stream of words. On at least one occasion, however, his normal fluency broke down. Humphrey was trying to pronounce the name of an area in Brooklyn known as Bedford Stuyvesant. First he called it "Styford Bevarant," then "Byford Stedevasant." At that point he gave up, saying, "Oh, you know what I mean." By an odd coincidence former president Jimmy Carter had similar difficulty when he referred to Hubert Humphrey at the 1980 Democratic convention. Apparently Carter was thinking about the British naval officer whose exploits are chronicled in a number of novels by C. S. Forester because the name of the former vice-president came out as "Hubert Horatio

Hornblower."

Ill-Chosen Words

Words do not necessarily have to be mispronounced to invite unexpected laughter. President Carter articulated the sounds of the name he mentioned acceptably: it was simply the wrong name. In the same way words that come out impeccably can still produce titters if they fail to fit a particular occasion, thought, or context. An example is a statement made by a former ambassador to the United Nations, Warren Austin, about the turmoil in the Middle East. He suggested that Jews and Arabs try to resolve their differences "in a true Christian spirit." Avoiding an error of that type requires close attention to the meanings and implications of the words used. The renowned baseball pitcher Dizzy Dean showed that his grasp of language was not quite as firm as his grasp of a baseball when a reporter asked him whether his injured toe had been fractured. "Fractured, hell," Dizzy replied. "The damn thing's broken." Ron Fairly, a baseball player who became a sports announcer, demonstrated a similar insensitivity to word meanings when he said, "Last night I neglected to mention something that bears repeating."

In more recent times our 43rd president, George W. Bush, has become noted for his misadventures with language. He read from a teleprompter quite smoothly, but when speaking in an ad-lib situation, he was prone to making several kinds of mistakes—choosing the wrong word or inventing one, failing to achieve agreement between subject and verb, miswording a common saying, or constructing a sentence whose meaning was effectively disguised. These errors came to be known as "Bushisms," and several books have been written to record them. Here are some examples:

Security is the essential roadblock to achieving the road map to peace.

They misunderestimated me.

What is your ambitions?

I know how hard it is to put food on your family.

I am the master of low expectations.

The power of ill-chosen words to create laughter is greatest if the incorrect word sounds very much like the one that should have been used. This type of mistake is also identified by a person's name, but in this instance it is that of a fictional person—Mrs. Malaprop—a character in Richard Sheridan's play, *The Rivals*. Thus "malapropism" joins "spoonerism" in our glossary of terms referring to linguistic errors. Best remembered of Mrs. Malaprop's slips is the statement that her niece is as "headstrong as an allegory on the banks of the Nile."

Sheridan, of course, deliberately caused Mrs. Malaprop to misuse language to make audiences laugh. In real life people stumble into the same kind of error. A legislator accused of misconduct inevitably reminds one of Mrs. Malaprop with his heated reply, "I deny the allegation and I defy the alligator." So too does the person who responded to a proposal with these words: "I'll have to regurgitate on that awhile." Chicago's former mayor, the first Richard Daley, like Mrs. Malaprop, missed the target just slightly when, in defending the actions of his police force, he said, "The policeman isn't there to create disorder. The policeman is there to preserve disorder." The writer of the following notice in a church bulletin was obviously reaching for the word "affiliated" but didn't quite make it. "The Outreach Committee has enlisted 25 members to make calls on people not afflicted with any church." Children often confuse one word with another. A little girl turned a line in a Stephen Foster song into "O Susanna, don't you cry for me. I'm goin' to Louisiana with a bandage on my knee."

Thinking of one word while trying to say another can lead one into trouble. A husband who had decided to stay home from work was accused by his wife at breakfast of neglecting his duties because he wanted to play golf. "Nothing could be further from my mind, he responded testily. Now, would you please pass the putter."

A sign posted by university students in a recreational area read, "No smoking, no drinking, and no profound language." At first glance it seems reasonable to assume the students had confused the words "profound" and "profane," but an intriguing thought arises. Is it possible that the sign said exactly what the students wanted it to say?

Malapropisms gain an extra fillip when the misuse of a word reveals a truth which correct usage would have kept hidden. A radio announcer might have been on target when he reported that a certain couple "will celebrate their fortieth year of holy deadlock." A father might unconsciously have revealed an uncomfortable truth in the answer he gave to his son, who had asked him what the word "a cappella" means. "It means," the father replied, "that the choir will sing without musical accomplishment." A notice in a church bulletin implied the existence of what might have been some legitimate concerns about the cooking competency of certain parishioners. In announcing that a cookbook was being compiled, the notice included the instruction that "In submitting your favorite recipe, please include an antidote relating to it."

The confusion of words in that example brings to mind a newspaper item that mixed them up in precisely the opposite way. It reported the death of a dog by poisoning and concluded, "The dog did not respond to the anecdote."

Metaphors sometimes fall apart because of malapropisms, as this one does. "That's the whole kettle of fish in a nutshell," and this, "It's a horse of a different feather." A Michigan legislator once denounced some impending legislation with these words: "We need this bill like a horse needs a fifth wheel." Another legislator warned a department head, "From now on I'm watching everything you do with a fine-tooth comb."

Akin to that error is the garbling of well-known sayings. "It takes two to tangle," is an example. A speaker responding to a questioner asking for more details about his proposal answered, "When we come to that bridge, we'll jump off it." Someone trying to quote George Santayana's comment that "Those who forget the past are condemned to repeat it," twisted it into "Those who cannot forget the past are condemned to remember it." The most notorious example of the conversion of meaning into nonsense was former Vice President Dan Quayle's version of the slogan used by the United Negro College Fund. "A mind is a terrible thing to waste," became in Quayle's words, "What a waste it is to lose one's mind." So celebrated has this misquotation become that the editors of *Bartlett's Familiar Quotations* included it in a new edition.

Old sayings also can lose their point if speakers leave out essential words. The writer John Keasler says that his grandmother had the habit of truncating proverbs. He describes her as saying with great earnestness, "You can't make a horse drink" or "a bird is worth two in the bush." Sometimes headline writers and sign makers, forced by space limitations to keep their messages as brief as possible, create both confusion and amusement. The following headline shows the effect of compression. POLICE SQUAD HELPS DOG BITE VICTIMS. This compressed notice posted on the Pennsylvania turnpike—CAUTION WHEN WET—always makes me smile. A sign being seen more and more these days is HANDICAPPED TOILETS. Would anyone really want to use one? James Thurber cited this statement by a landlady who was describing the facilities of her boarding house. "We can sleep twenty people, but we can only eat twelve." Perhaps she was being slightly over economical with words.

We can even find examples of accidental humor in the Bible caused by images created by the particular words the writer chose. In Chapter 7 of "The Song of Solomon," the writer extols the beauty of a "queenly maiden" by listing one by one the physical attributes that make her stunningly attractive. But when he describes her face in verse 4, one can't help speculating how the object of his flattery would react to this line: "Your nose is like a tower of Lebanon, overlooking Damascus."

Misplaced Phrases and Clauses

Phrases and clauses that appear in the wrong order can cause as much havoc as ill-chosen or misplaced single words. Readers undoubtedly blinked when a news item described a robber as "a five-foot ten-inch man with a heavy moustache weighing 155 to 160 pounds." A newspaper report summarizing the results of an explosion could be even more startling. "No one was injured in the blast, which was attributed to a build-up of gases by one town official." Puzzlement would probably be the main product of this item: "She rode 106 miles on a bicycle with 1400 other people." An invitation in a bulletin designed for visitors to Moscow presumably caused foreheads to furrow. "You are welcome to visit the cemetery where famous Russian composers, writers, and artists are buried daily except Sunday." A student misplaced a clause when he wrote in a history report, "Lincoln composed the Gettysburg Address while traveling from Washington to Gettysburg on the back of an envelope."

A father probably should have rethought his choice of words and the order in which he used them when he admonished his children to "Help your mother when she mops up the floor by mopping up the floor with her." That, one hopes, would not appeal to any suppressed desire, but this instruction in a bulletin for employees might. "Submit your expense reports promptly with the required receipts attached to your department head."

Pronouns that are unclear about the nouns they replace can magnify the muddling effect of misplaced phrases and clauses. The following news item might lead some readers into a wrong inference. "The Queen smashed a champagne bottle against the prow of the ship, and the crowd cheered as she slid majestically into the sea."

Treacherous Typos

Almost all of the errors discussed thus far were committed by those who originated the material. Sometimes, however, the blunder is the fault of someone else. An errant typist or a careless compositor can totally distort the message the writer meant to convey by dropping out letters, words, or punctuation marks. Adding or transposing them, or substituting one letter or word for another, also can mangle meaning. When that happens the writer is simply an innocent victim.

A transposition of letters by a church secretary must have startled members of the congregation. The title the minister submitted for his Sunday sermon was "Our God Reigns." It appeared in the church bulletin as "Our God Resigns." A superfluous comma abetted by an uncapitalized letter in the following school notice might have caused some pupils to celebrate a little too soon. "School will be dismissed for good, Friday." The substitution of one letter for another can turn the meaning of a sentence completely around. A reporter who described a charity organization as "not for profit" must have cringed at the thought of the irate telephone calls he was about to receive when it came out in the newspaper as "hot for profit."

Typos like other unintentional errors can sometimes reveal hidden truths or feelings. A church bulletin reported that the "Sunday School picnic was a hug success." Probably true. A notice at the bottom of a school program listing selections to be performed by pupils might have reflected the reactions of some mothers and fathers to the performances of their offspring. "Parents are encouraged to stay throughout the concert and not heave at the end of their child's performance." A secretary who left a letter out of a notice she typed for a church newsletter might have unconsciously revealed her own feelings about such affairs. "Scheduled for Friday night: A Pot uck."

Sometimes editors attempt to mitigate the effect of a typographical error by publishing a correction. When this effort goes awry, the waters they find themselves in are likely to get deeper. There are two oft-quoted examples. In the first instance a newspaper story described a man as a "defective in the police force." The corrected story identified him as "a detective in the police farce." In the second instance, the obituary of a war hero extolled him as a "bottle-scarred veteran." In the next issue of the newspaper there was an apology with the explanation that the newspaper meant to say that he was "a battle-scared veteran."

You can often blame someone else for typographical errors, but in some instances the writer may be responsible. That was the case with a retiring schoolteacher whose continual requests for a new chalkboard had long been denied. Just before she left school for the last time, she printed this message on the worn-out chalkboard: "Put a new broad in this classroom. This one has had it."

A peculiar typographical practice employed by the translators of the King James version of the Bible led to accidental humor. It was their custom to print in italics words that had no direct counterpart in the original material. Reading verse 27 of the 13th chapter of I Kings, you may well wonder who or what got saddled. "And he spake to his sons, saying, Saddle me the ass. And they saddled *him*."

Accidentally on Purpose

The expression "accidentally on purpose" describes occurrences that appear to happen without conscious intention, but which are really carried out deliberately. Some of the mistakes that seem to provoke laughter unintentionally fall in this category. Comedians realize that obvious premeditation and conscious artfulness tend to dampen the laugh response. By giving an off-the-cuff flavor to their jokes and repartee, they heighten the humorous effect. Some even go so far as to stimulate the mistakes ordinary people stumble into. Norm Crosby, a comedian who appeared several times on the *Ed Sullivan* and *Tonight* shows, made the intentional mangling of words one of his main comedy techniques. On a *Tonight* show he remarked that "Salt water cures you of your impunities" and then added, "I say this honestly without fear of contraception." The performer who called himself Professor Irwin Corey larded his pseudo-learned discussions of scientific topics with malapropisms and misused words. Two writers of the nineteenth century, whose nom de plumes were Josh Billings and Artemus Ward, seized on fractured spelling as a comedy technique and made it the main instrument for producing laughs. Billings's essay on "The Mule" begins, for example, "The mule is haf hoss, and haf jackass, then kums tu a full stop, natur diskovering her mistake."

Was the copywriter who wrote "Bargain in braille books. Must be seen to be appreciated," merely obtuse or a sly joker? It is difficult to believe that the pun in the following ad for an adult protective garment—"Don't let lack of bladder control dampen your day"—slipped through undetected. I suspect that bored headline writers sometimes enliven their workday by composing headlines that give the impression of being funny inadvertently. This may have been one of them—FIRE OFFICIALS GRILLED OVER FAULTY KEROSENE HEATERS—though one can't be sure. The injection of puns into some headlines, however, is obviously intentional. After President Bill Clinton presumably blocked traffic at a busy airport for about an hour while he had a $200 haircut, one headline read: CLINTON'S HAIRCUT SHEAR MADNESS.

Sometimes deliberately contrived humor is made to appear accidental by attributing it to someone with a reputation for being funny unintentionally. It is highly doubtful, for instance, that all of the scrambled expressions supposedly uttered by Reverend Spooner actually originated with him. Inventive minds have embellished his reputation with further examples. An admonition he supposedly addressed to a wayward student has a suspicious air of contrivance about it. "You have hissed all my mystery lectures, you have tasted the whole worm, and must leave by the first town drain." His statement that "Work is the curse of the drinking classes" has also been attributed to Oscar Wilde except that Wilde said "ruin" instead of "curse." If Wilde originated it, he used each word quite deliberately.

Stand-up comedians of today often make up funny statements and then put them in the mouths of politicians and other celebrities. At times it is difficult to distinguish between a legitimate quote and what is only a joke. Former Vice President Dan Quayle is a case in point. By committing a series of verbal blunders on his own, he established a foundation on which comedians gleefully built. There is no question, for instance, that he mangled the slogan of the United Negro College Fund, referred to earlier. And I know that he said in a television interview, "I stand behind all the misstatements I've made," because I heard him say it. I'm not convinced though, that he actually turned the name of the South Pacific island Pago Pago into "Pogo Pogo," as one comedian averred. And I'm sure he did not say what a comedian quoted him as saying after he returned from a trip to Latin America, "I'm glad I studied Latin in high school, because I could speak to the natives in their own tongue." A remark equally inane attributed to the first president George Bush is almost certainly the product of some inventive comedian's brain. "Dan Quayle will become president over my dead body."

Quayle provided such a rich lode of comedy material that it is likely none mourned his loss of the vice presidency more than stand-up comedians. Some seemed unwilling to let him slip quietly into oblivion. Four months after he retired from office, Jay Leno reported on the *Tonight* show that Quayle had inquired plaintively whether he would become the former president if something happened to George Bush.

Quayle probably resented the inventing of supposed blunders, for they further marred an image already damaged by the howlers he was responsible for. Some people, however, believe that verbal blunders can actually be beneficial. According to one of Samuel Goldwyn's biographers, Goldwyn added to the mistakes he had made on his own by commissioning writers to create new ones. Apparently he thought that publicity, no matter what its nature, was good for him. One of those invented "mistakes" may well have been Goldwyn's supposed comment that, "A verbal contract isn't worth the paper it's written on." One might also wonder whether the flood of nonsensical remarks attributed to Yogi Berra all came from him spontaneously or whether he or others have begun to contrive them deliberately.

One reason so much unintentional humor has survived is that individuals and organizations have collected choice examples and made them available to the public. Kermit Schafer has taken note of what he calls "bloopers" made by radio and television performers and published them in a number of books. Dick Clark and Ed McMahon carried on that tradition with their TV program *Bloopers and Practical Jokes*. Unintentional humor figures largely in two collections assembled by Richard Lederer in his books *Anguished English* and *Crazy English*.

A number of periodicals have also helped preserve prime examples of unintentional humor. *The New Yorker* uses mixed metaphors, errant headlines, and jumbled announcements as filler material. *The Reader's Digest* collects unintentional humor under several headings, among them, "Pardon, Your Slip is Showing," "Oops," and "Huh?" In a feature called "The Lower Case" the *Columbia Journalism Review* publishes examples of headlines gone astray and the sometimes hilarious juxtapositions of pictures and headlines. The comedian Jay Leno does the same thing at regular intervals on the *Tonight* show in his "Headlines" segment. He has also published the best examples in a number of books.

Chapter 4
The Master Key to
Creating Jokes

Comedy has an instant critic—laughter.
                                    Jackie Gleason

The renowned Canadian humorist Stephen Leacock was once asked how he managed to produce all of the funny material he brought to a grateful public in a steady stream of books, humorous essays, and lectures. He answered, "You just jot down ideas as they occur to you. The jotting presents no problem; it is the occurring that is difficult."

Leacock might have added that "occurring" is not likely to happen at all in a mind whose cognitive machinery is idling. Some sort of organized thinking is needed to produce jokes. There are times, of course, when they seem to pop into our minds without any conscious effort. But even jokes that appear to arise spontaneously are the product of a process. Without realizing it, we have been alert to detect connections between ideas. All at once they come together with an almost audible click and a joke erupts.

The Anatomy of a Joke

The distinguishing feature of a joke as a way of making people laugh is that it suggests a *point* which the audience must grasp if the joke is to work. Joke making is therefore a cooperative enterprise in which both the jokester and the audience have a part to play. If either one fails, no laugh results.

The ideas to which various jokes lead differ widely in their general nature. Among other things a joke may cause us to recall a fact or happening, it may spark the recollection of a personal experience or suggest a conclusion, it may lead to a philosophical reflection, or it may merely make us visualize something.

Jokes take different forms. The most common is a verbal expression of some type, either spoken or written. Pictures and drawings can also lead us to a point, either standing alone or reinforced by the kind of verbal expression we call a caption. Physical action can convey ideas on occasion. I suppose it is even possible to think of a situation where the dropping of one's pants can make a point.

As a first step toward learning how to create a joke, you must understand what its elements are. That means we must take scalpel in hand and do some dissecting. As our first specimen let us probe into a joke so old and familiar that I'm sure you've all heard it. "One man asks another, 'Who was that lady I saw you with last night?' The second man replies, 'That was no lady, that was my wife.'"

To most of us the lines I have quoted—the idea or ideas the joke teller presents to the listener—constitute the joke. But as I have just noted, to complete the joke, the listener must draw some kind of inference from what the joke teller has said. In this case it is rather an obvious one. The second man quoted in the joke has inadvertently insulted his wife by implying she's not a lady.

That point is so obvious, I can hear you muttering, "It scarcely needs saying." You are right, of course, and it must never be stated as part of the joke. It should come into existence only in the listener's mind. Different listeners if called to put it into words might not agree on what those words should be. Some jokes, in fact, may imply a certain idea to one person and quite a different one to another.

It follows from all this that a joke has two elements. One is the idea or ideas the joke teller says, writes, or draws in explicit form. We can call this part of the joke the *expressed* idea. The second element is the idea or ideas the listeners or readers draw out of what the joke teller has presented. We can call this part of the joke the *inferred* idea.

To provide another example of anatomical analysis, let us dissect a joke that is almost as famous as the one just quoted. It was presented as part of a program the comedian Jack Benny broadcast on radio, and according to legend it drew the longest laugh in radio history. Jack Benny was returning from a visit to a friend when he was accosted by a robber. "Your money or your life?" the robber asked fiercely. When Benny failed to respond after several seconds had gone by, the robber demanded even more fiercely, "Your money or your life?" Thus pressed, Benny finally said, "I'm thinking it over. I'm thinking it over."

We can discern in this joke the two elements I have described. The dialogue of the robber and Jack Benny constitutes the *expressed* idea of the joke. The thought one draws from it—that Jack Benny values his money over his own life—is the *inferred* idea. Incidentally, in the long run of the *Jack Benny Program* on both radio and television, the writers devised a great many different expressed ideas to suggest to audiences the same inferred idea—namely, that the character portrayed by Jack Benny was one of the stingiest men alive.

For our final dissection specimen, we focus on a joke of more recent vintage. It was included in a monologue Jay Leno presented during a *Tonight* show appearance. At one point he commented that "Some people in Washington, D.C. have tried to put together a Christmas crèche but have been unable to find either three wise men or a virgin." This statement, of course, is the expressed idea of the joke. It leads the audience into doing two things. First, it must conjure up the image of a crèche and visualize its components. Second, it must connect this picture to what Leno has said and pull out the inference that there is little wisdom in Washington and almost no women who have been sexually inactive. Together these two responses

93

make up the inferred idea.

The Role of the Audience

One lesson our dissection should have reinforced is that the audience is a vital cog in the process of creating a joke. It is not merely a passive recipient of the humor the joke teller dispenses. It must respond by doing something. That something is to draw out of what has been presented some kind of conclusion, recollection, reflection, or image. Moreover—and this is of crucial importance—the audience must be permitted to arrive at that inference entirely on its own if the joke is to achieve its maximum effect. If the audience is helped along the way, its laughter is likely to be diminished or extinguished altogether. And laughter, of course, is the oxygen that gives a joke its life.

Jay Leno might have added to his comment about the fruitless search for wise men and a virgin in Washington, D.C. something like—"Well, that shows that Washington is a place of silliness and sin." Doing so would have drained away most of the humor, for adding the comment makes it unnecessary for the audience to complete the joke. Audiences must be left free to participate in joke making by arriving at the appropriate inferences without being helped. That is true whether they are made up of one person listening to a friend's story, 300 people in a comedy club, or the millions tuned into a television program.

At the heart of the joke maker's craft is the technique of *indirection*. Bluntness or obviousness kills laughs. The joke teller must carry out the delicate maneuver of providing just enough information to enable the audience to grasp the point by itself without giving it away. All of the pieces are provided except one. The audience supplies that missing piece and thus completes the joke.

The importance of letting the audience supply the final element is illustrated by what happens when people fail to see the point to a joke and must have it explained to them. They may nod in understanding, but they seldom laugh. The reason is they have been denied the feeling of self satisfaction that comes from successfully meeting an intellectual challenge. Those who see through a joke feel good about their mental acumen. And people who feel good about themselves are inclined to laugh.

You may wonder at this point whether that is all there is to it. Is leading an audience into making an inference from clues you have provided enough to guarantee a laugh? In some cases that seems to be all that is needed. Most of the time, however, you need to do more than that. If you are to achieve a truly satisfactory reaction to your joke, you must use material in your expressed idea that will call forth an inferred idea possessing the power to generate laughs. It has that power if it produces certain kinds of effects in the audience. An analysis of what those effects are and the type of inferences that lead to them is the subject of our next two chapters. Before turning to them, however, we must think some more about the structure of a joke and the basic process of bringing it into being.

Getting a Joke Started

How does a joke begin? It may begin with anything—a comment made by a friend, an item you see in a newspaper, something you observe, a line in a book—the possibilities are endless. That's not very helpful, however, if you are sitting at a desk with a blank sheet of paper in front of you or at a computer with a blank screen, trying to invent a joke. You can't just sit there mentally inert hoping that some kind of useable idea will float into your mind. You must set out actively in search of one, and you must do so in an organized fashion.

There are two basic starting places for the construction of a joke. One is to think up the *inferred* idea—the thought you want your audience to draw out of what you say, write, or portray. To complete the joke you must now devise the *expressed* idea—the material that will lead the audience into making the desired inference.

The second place to start is the other way around with all or part of an expressed idea. You may have found an item in a newspaper, for example, that you think has possibilities. To complete the joke, you must now find another idea your listeners can connect with that item and present enough clues to lead them to it. Merely relating the item may be enough to identify the inferred idea for your audience. In many instances, however, you must add something else if your audience is to get the point of your joke. We can call this part of the expressed idea the *bridge* to the inferred idea. Sometimes constructing a bridge is not necessary at all; in other instances the step is essential.

We obviously need some examples to illustrate how the two starting points I have described actually work. Let us begin with jokes that get under way with the identification of an inferred idea. There is an old fable you are all familiar with that tells how a frog was turned into a prince by the kiss of a maid who loved him. Is there anything we can do to cause an audience to recall that story, thus making it the inferred idea of a joke? You may protest that even if we succeed, the idea is not likely to elicit laughter because it is touching rather than funny. Remember, however, that leading people into making an inference entirely on their own can, in and of itself, cause them to laugh. The improbability of the story, moreover, provides an opportunity to enhance the humorous effect with what has come to be recognized as a major inciter of laughter—the element of incongruity.

Two cartoons I have seen recently show that jokes can be created with the Frog and Prince story as the inferred idea. (As you may have suspected, I did not pluck it out of thin air.) One cartoon drawn by Nick Downes for *Diversion* magazine shows a wedding ceremony. The groom, wearing princely robes and a crown, is standing at the front of the church with his bride. The pews on the groom's side, in contrast, are filled with nothing but frogs. The cartoon does not even need a caption to lead the audience into making the proper connection.

The second cartoon took a different route to the same destination. Drawn by Bill Maul for the *National Enquirer*, it shows a man in royal robes sitting in front of a genealogical chart. His face is distraught and his shoulders are slumped, for pictured at the beginning of his ancestral line is the image of a frog. Beside him stands his wife, reproving him with these words, "I told you you'd regret getting all involved with this *Roots* business." This joke is somewhat more complicated because it requires the audience to make a connection not only with the Frog and Prince story, but also with the book and TV miniseries *Roots*, in which Alex Haley told us what he had learned about his slave ancestors.

The content of these cartoons constitutes the expressed ideas devised by their creators to call up the same inferred idea. Whether they actually began with the inferred idea, I have no way of knowing, of course, but it is certainly a likely starting point. Two other cartoons illustrate the same process. As with the first two, they point to the same inferred idea but use different ways to lead their readers into thinking of it. In this case their purpose is to induce readers into recalling the familiar rhyme about Humpty Dumpty and his great fall.

One cartoon, drawn by Gary Larson for his syndicated *Far Side* panel, shows three men struggling to reassemble a shattered Humpty Dumpty. In the background stand some horses. A fourth man is saying, "Ok, Ok, you guys have had your chance—the horses want another shot at it." That picture and caption will start the entire rhyme reverberating in most minds.

A drawing by Al Ross, a cartoonist for *The New Yorker*, demonstrates a second way of kindling the same recollection. It shows a father with a book entitled *Humpty-Dumpty* on his lap. He has just read the story to his young daughter, who is lying in bed about to go to sleep. Reflecting on what she has just heard, she comments, "Maybe they didn't try hard enough."

These are not the only jokes I have seen lately that have been inspired by the Humpty Dumpty rhyme. Gary Larson returned to it in a cartoon captioned "Humpty Dumpty's final days." It shows a waitress serving a very large omelette to a restaurant patron. And a *New Yorker* drawing by Michael Crawford presents another variation on the same motif. A large egg wearing a woman's hat enters a hospital and is greeted by a doctor. The caption reads: "You might want to sit down, Mrs. Dumpty." I have not seen any other cartoons or jokes that spring from the frog and prince story, but an advertisement in the *Ann Arbor News* required readers to call it up. The ad described a special service available in its classified section which provides a way for singles to make contact with one another. The lead into the advertisement was the sentence, "You won't have to kiss a lot of frogs."

Let us turn now to a joke that probably began at the other starting point—the finding of material that becomes part of the expressed idea. It was delivered by Andy Borowitz, a writer of humorous essays for *The New Yorker*. He also appears every Friday on CNN's *American Morning* program with two other people to comment on the news events of the week. Borowitz's particular function is to make the funny remarks. One of the items the panel discussed was the news that former President Bill Clinton's autobiography, *My Life*, was to be published the following month, June, 2004. The part of the story that attracted Borowitz's special attention was the fact that the book had taken much longer to complete than had been expected. Borowitz began his expressed idea by stating this fact. He then added this comment: "Writing the book probably took so long because Clinton and his editor couldn't agree on what the meaning of 'is' is." Most viewers would be instantly reminded of Bill Clinton's most notorious response when he was being questioned during the investigation of the Monica Lewinsky scandal.

Whether Andy Borowitz's route to his joke began with material that became part of the expressed idea, we have no way of knowing, of course. One thing I'm sure of is that he would not describe the steps in the terms I have used since they are my terms, not his. Indeed, it is quite possible that in constructing his joke he was not aware of going through any process at all. For people experienced in a craft, the consciousness of process tends to drain away as creative tasks are completed in an almost intuitive fashion, and often in an instant.

Jokes, however, do not usually jump full blown into beginners' minds. To repeat a point already made, they must develop a system for inventing them. The analyses of jokes created by professionals illustrate two different approaches. Let us see whether we can use the approaches just described to create jokes of our own, beginning with the approach that gets under way with the identification of an inferred idea.

I once saw a TV commercial featuring a woodpecker carrying on a search for insects in the way woodpeckers customarily do. Its beak rat-tat-tatted into the tree with such force that its whole body seemed to shake. It was an amusing sight but describing it does not constitute a joke because the picture alone doesn't lead to any thought the audience can draw out of it. What if we begin by deciding that the image of the woodpecker itself will be the inferred idea of the joke? Now we must invent an expressed idea that will lead an audience into calling it up. A joke told by the comedian Steven Wright during one of his stand-up routines suggests how that might be done. At one point he said, "Imagine if birds were tickled by feathers." Hearing it, an audience is almost bound to visualize a bird. In our case we must do more than that, however. It is not enough merely to lead an audience into conjuring up the picture of a generalized kind of bird. We must cause it to call up the image of a specific type of bird engaged in the sort of action that sets it apart from other birds. We might accomplish that purpose by saying, a la Steven Wright, "I've often wondered whether woodpeckers ever get headaches." Beginning with the identification of an inferred idea, we have now completed our joke by inventing an expressed idea that will spur an audience into calling it up.

There are many sources of inferred ideas. Earlier I described how a number of cartoonists had evoked recollections of the Frog and Prince story and the rhyme about Humpty Dumpty's great fall. Material of that type is available in abundance. As an example we might pull out of a multitude of possibilities the old saying, "When the cat's away, the mice will play" and make it the inferred idea of a joke we are about to invent. To complete the process we must create an expressed idea that will cause an audience to recollect the familiar maxim I have just quoted. One possibility is to communicate it in the form of a cartoon showing Mickey and Minnie Mouse at a piano playing a duet. The caption below would read, "Mr. and Mrs. Katz are away on vacation."

Let us shift gears now and try to begin the construction of a joke by identifying an expressed idea. In the first joke we created, we began by making the image of the woodpecker rat-tat-tatting into the tree the inferred idea. Can we turn the pattern around and make it the expressed idea instead? In taking that approach we must decide on the inferred idea we will prompt the audience into evoking. There seems to be an obvious candidate. It is the thought contained in the expressed idea of our first joke that a woodpecker's food-seeking technique may make it prone to getting headaches. The final challenge is to devise a bridge which will call that idea into being. The completed joke might consist of a cartoon made up of two panels. The first one shows the main element in the expressed idea, a woodpecker with its head vibrating furiously as it pecks into a tree. The second panel presents the bridge part of the expressed idea, a drawing showing the woodpecker standing in front of a medicine cabinet holding a bottle of pills saying, "I find that aspirin works best for me."

Thus, we have used the same basic material to create two different jokes. The first began with the identification of an inferred idea, the second with the identification of an element in an expressed idea. These two jokes also demonstrate that the same item of information can serve in two different roles.

Let us proceed now to invent a couple of other jokes that begin with the identification of a comment in an expressed idea. What can we do with the image of a bald eagle? (I seem to be on a bird binge.) Can we contrive a bridge that will lead an audience into inferring what kind of an eagle it is? How about showing two large birds engaged in conversation. The bridge is the caption beneath the drawing which has the first bird asking the second one. "Have you ever considered a feather transplant?" It would be an obtuse reader indeed who would not draw from all of this the inferred idea that the second bird is a bald eagle.

For a final example of jokes whose creation begins with the identification of an expressed idea, let's turn to a four-legged member of the animal kingdom for inspiration. A few years ago I was watching a football game between the University of Michigan and Purdue University when a rabbit suddenly appeared on the field and made several trips between the fifty-yard line and one of the goal lines before it finally left to pursue other interests. The incident was amusing in and of itself, but simply describing it does not constitute a joke. To turn it into one, we must do something that will lead an audience into recognizing some kind of point. One possibility is to induce the audience into recalling the score of the game, which happened to be 24 to 17 in Michigan's favor. To do this we need to do more than mention the rabbit's participation. We must think up a bridge that will point directly to the score. Our expressed idea, made up of the rabbit story and the bridge, might go something like this: "A rabbit took part in the football game between Michigan and Purdue. Purdue would have won if it could have counted the touchdowns the rabbit made."

Another possibility for an inferred idea is to lead the audience into focusing on the rabbit instead of on the score. When we think about rabbits

WILLIS - How to be Funny on Purpose

a certain type of activity usually comes to mind. To turn the joke in that direction, we need a different kind of bridge, of course. Our new version might read like this: "A rabbit took part in the football game between Michigan and Purdue today. Purdue scored two touchdowns, Michigan three, and the rabbit four. The rabbit would have scored five touchdowns if it hadn't stopped for a quick 'Wham bam, thank you ma'am,' on the twenty-yard line."

Making Connections

In the previous section we have seen that the invention of a joke can begin at two different points. It may be that an inferred idea first comes to mind. In other instances, it is the recognition of an expressed idea that gets the process of creation under way. Identifying these possible starting points has several advantages. It reinforces the fact that a joke is made up of two major components, and thus improves your grasp of its structure. It provides a way of getting started when inspiration fails. Most important of all, it brings into focus the principle that skill in getting an audience to make connections is more crucial to a joke maker's success than any other element. It is, in fact, the master key to creating jokes.

When a beginning thought comes into your mind, it may not be necessary to decide immediately whether it will become the expressed idea or the inferred idea of a joke. What you should do first is to roll it through your mind to see what other ideas it evokes. As this process continues, the structure of the joke will gradually emerge as the various elements fall into place. Along the way you will crystallize the thought you want your audience to draw out of the ideas you present. And you will make sure that those ideas lead inevitably to the inference you seek.

As we have already noted, the ideas that can get a joke started exist everywhere. Events reported by the news media provide starting points for most of the jokes delivered by the late-night comedians, Jay Leno, David Letterman, and Jon Stewart. Another rich source of material are works of literature. We have already seen how the Frog and Prince story and the Humpty Dumpty nursery rhyme inspired a number of cartoons. These are literary references almost everyone would recognize. Others would be familiar only to people with extensive literary backgrounds.

Jokes that make demanding challenges sometimes appear in surprising places. Getting the point to an entry in the *Eek and Meek* comic strip series required that readers recall a line from Shakespeare's *Merchant of Venice*. It shows a man looking at a sign in a restaurant window which reads

"Quality of Mercy Soup." When the man asks the waitress what kind of soup that is, she answers, "It's not strained."

An even more oblique reference to a Shakespearean line appeared in a movie review written by Stanley Kauffmann for *The New Republic*. Commenting that the performers in the film, which was intended to be a comedy, seemed to be having more fun than the viewers, Kauffmann went on to say that "the audience feels more grinned against than grinning." Readers familiar with Shakespeare's *King Lear* would relish the play on the line, "I am a man more sinned against then sinning."

Many other literary works have been referred to in jokes. An entry in the *Frank and Ernest* comic strip series led readers into recalling the main plot line of Oscar Wilde's novel *The Picture of Dorian Gray*. It shows a clerk in a photo-developing shop informing a man named Dorian Gray that his snapshots haven't turned out very well. Peter De Vries reminded readers of Victor Hugo's best known work when he wrote in his novel *Sauce for the Goose* that one of the characters was so ineffective in bed that he had become known as the *lay misérable*. In his novel *"Q" Clearance* Peter Benchley invited readers to make a connection with a Bible story when he noted that a character had named her parakeet Onan because "he spilleth his seed upon the ground."

Getting the point to a joke sometimes calls for geographical knowledge. Woody Allen's remark that "his girl friend was a streetwalker in Venice, but she drowned," is an example. The most famous account of African adventure and exploration gave rise to a somewhat grisly joke. A cannibal hands a bowl of soup to another cannibal. The second cannibal tastes it with the comment, "Dr. Livingstone, I presume." A specific fact about language can become the point to a joke as a story about an American woman traveling in Germany illustrates. She had become frustrated by her failure to break through the language barrier. One day going into a shop, she sneezed vociferously and a clerk called out, "Gesundheit!" "At last," she said gladly as she went up to him, "Someone who speaks English." Sometimes all a joke does is cause an audience to visualize something. Mark Twain did that with the line, "I washed my hands in the previously limpid water." Kin Hubbard's aim was also visualization when he wrote, "There's few funnier sights than a full set of whiskers in bed."

Some comedians find a rich mine of material in their own personal experiences. Jerry Seinfeld concentrated on the petty annoyances that crop up in carrying out such mundane activities as parking a car or standing in line for theater tickets. Louie Anderson told stories of his family life to prompt memories of similar experiences in his listeners' minds. In one instance Johnny Carson found the inspiration for a joke in a situation that was directly affecting him at the moment he told it. The Writers Guild had gone on strike and the writers who ordinarily helped him create jokes for the *Tonight* show were forbidden by union rules from writing anything. Carson explained the situation to his audience, complaining that it had forced him to prepare his material without any help. "My writers are walking a picket line outside the studio right now," he said, "and they're carrying signs." He paused and then added, "But the signs are all blank."

Comedians such as Jay Leno, David Letterman, Dennis Miller, and Mark Russell depend on their audiences' recalling events in the news, many of them involving the misfortunes and missteps of political leaders, particularly those who occupy the presidential office. While Ronald Reagan was president, the trait most frequently made fun of was his reputed inability to grasp or remember the facts of a situation. A drawing by the editorial cartoonist Jim Borgman shows him standing in the middle of an office occupied by his assistants asking "Have I said anything lately that I should know about?" The political satirist, Mark Russell, evoked the same idea with a joke he told during one of his public-television programs broadcast at the height of the Iran-Contra scandal. According to Russell, Reagan was informed that some of his assistants working in the basement of the White House had been carrying on illegal negotiations with Iran. Reagan, apparently astonished by the news, responded: "Do you mean to say there's a basement in the White House?"

In some instances presidents continue to be targets even after they leave government. In discussing Clinton's first visit to Japan, Jay Leno wondered whether Clinton would emulate his predecessor's last visit to that country in every respect, thus inviting his audience to recall that at a formal dinner the first President Bush had thrown up on the Japanese prime minister.

President Clinton's scandalous sexual behavior was the target of many of the jokes aimed at him. Among the gentler gibes were jokes making references to his apparent addiction to McDonald's hamburgers. A cartoonist brought this idiosyncrasy into readers' minds by showing the design of a space station Clinton had approved. It was dominated by a set of McDonald's golden arches.

Many of the jokes that targeted the second President Bush took as their starting point his difficulty pronouncing words. The word "nuclear" was always too much for him it seemed. A joke on the *Tonight* show took advantage of his pronunciation problems with the line: "Yesterday President George W. Bush was severely injured trying to pronounce the name of Arnold Schwarzenegger."

The list of topics to which jokes can refer could go on and on. That does not mean material is hanging on trees ready to fall into your lap. You must find and pluck it. But it is there waiting to be harvested by those perceptive enough to recognize its potential. Perceptiveness is certainly necessary. So is the perseverance that keeps you at the job of searching and sifting until ideas come together in your mind. Knowing how a joke is structured and familiarity with the kinds of ideas that incite laughter will also help. All that is not enough, of course. You must also bring to the process a quality no book of instruction can produce—the ability to invent a means of bringing into your listeners' minds in a subtle and indirect way the connecting idea you want them to grasp.

Levels of Difficulty

We all know that it is easier to get the point to some jokes than it is to others. Even small children are likely to understand the play on words in the comment a husband made after his wife served him a dinner of carrot salad, stew with carrots, and carrot cake: "You really got carrot away, didn't you?" Appreciating Steve Allen's remark on seeing a church fire, "Holy Smoke," requires a slightly higher level of sophistication. On still a higher level is the story about the man who turned up wearing one green sock and one red one. When someone said, "That's the strangest pair of socks I've ever seen," he replied, "Not too strange. I have pair just like them at home." Most young children would lack the mental agility to draw from this story the appropriate inference. The point to the advertisement for a talking parrot that included the warning "for mature audiences only," would probably be beyond them also and so would the idea implied in the response of a man who had been fined $500 for counterfeiting and forgery: "How do you want it, cash or check?"

The particular background of a listener is obviously of great significance in determining whether the point to a joke is easy or difficult to grasp. People with a general knowledge of literature would have no difficulty with the "Quality of Mercy Soup" and the "Dorian Gray" comic strips cited earlier. Detecting the wit in a note an agent sent to a client named Ishmael, however, would require somewhat more specialized knowledge—the exact way in which Herman Melville opened his novel *Moby Dick*. The agent's note read, "Don't call me, Ishmael. I'll call you."

I once saw a cartoon in *The New Yorker* which baffled me for some time. When I finally figured it out, I realized its point would probably have been clear immediately to workers in the building trades. Drawn by Jack

Zeigler, the cartoon shows two extension cords lying on the floor below a couple of electrical outlets in the wall. One of the extension cords has turned to the other with the comment: "The one on the left is cute." Not until I remembered that electricians and plumbers designate fixtures as male and female depending on their form did I get the point.

Besides background, mental agility is an important factor in determining whether a person will see through a joke. Appreciating the more subtle ones requires the ability to decipher cryptic insinuations. A reproof administered to George Bernard Shaw by a female friend might test those less mentally adroit than he. It seems that Shaw sometimes led young women on only to leave them stranded short of the final destination. One victim of that behavior rebuked him with an admirably delicate metaphor: "You had no right to write the preface if you were not going to write the book." In retrospect, the wording of her complaint had a peculiar aptness, for Shaw later became a noted writer of prefaces.

Walter Mondale, who served as vice president during Jimmy Carter's presidency, is noted for his subtle wit. So enigmatic are some of his quips that people who lack a certain degree of mental dexterity may be unable to grasp his allusions. An example is a remark he made while he and Carter were posing for pictures to be used in their 1980 re-election campaign. The photographer kept urging them to stand closer and after several admonitions along that line Mondale responded, "If we stand any closer, we'll carry California." Some in the group laughed. Jimmy Carter was not one of them. It wasn't that he disapproved of the joke. He simply failed to get the point. If you don't either, have someone from San Francisco explain it to you.

Matching the Joke to the Audience

It is obvious that if an audience fails to see the point to a joke, no matter how deft and meaningful it is, the joke maker has failed. Even as experienced a performer as Johnny Carson regularly ran into that difficulty. During one of his *Tonight* show monologues, he remarked that at Gettysburg Abraham Lincoln originated the phrase sometimes heard at Academy Awards presentations, "And now the envelope, please." Only a numbing silence followed. Apparently no one in the studio audience was familiar with the apocryphal story that Lincoln wrote the Gettysburg Address on the back of an envelope while riding in a train from Washington to the cemetery. A somewhat more surprising gap in audience knowledge caused another Carson joke to emerge stillborn. Referring to a *New York Times* report that sushi is going out of style, he complained that "this is happening just when I've learned to cook it." His audience stared blankly up at him. Carson seemed baffled by the lack of response. He had assumed that almost everyone would know that sushi is fish served raw.

Comedians who specialize in topical humor often become victims of deficiencies in audience knowledge. Even events and personalities featured prominently in news stories may not be known to some in the audiences. As the event and personality recede into the past, the danger of nonrecognition becomes greater. The following was a good joke for its time: "A blonde sitting at a bar confessed, 'I don't know how the Russians do it. When I drink vodka, I say yes to everything.'" Appreciating it fully, however, requires immersion in the atmosphere of the cold war when representatives of the Soviet Union were equally noted for drinking vodka and saying "nyet" at international conferences. Dimming recollections of the sugar-sweet image projected by Dinah Shore on television make it difficult to savor the wit in a comment Oscar Levant made about her. "I never watch Dinah Shore on TV. I have diabetes." Most people seeing the T-shirt inscription—"Will Rogers never met J. R." would recall the odious character portrayed by Larry Hagman on the TV series *Dallas*, but how many would remember that Will Rogers, who rose to prominence in the 1920s, once said, "I never met a man I didn't like"?

Some topical jokes do have lasting qualities. Vice presidents have been the targets of humorists from the beginning of our nation. So too have the houses of Congress. Edward Everett Hale, who served as chaplain of the Senate, was once asked whether he intended to pray for the Senate. "No," he replied. "I'll look at the Senate and then I'll pray for the country." In the same vein former President Theodore Roosevelt commented that "When they call the roll in the Senate, the senators don't know whether to answer 'Present' or 'Not guilty.'" Those remarks have such a contemporary ring to them we might well believe they were part of a monologue delivered by Jay Leno or David Letterman.

Sometimes people do get the point to jokes but only after they have taken time to figure them out. This delayed response can be as damaging to oral humorists as an audience's total failure to see through a joke. Comedians can't stand around and wait while listeners think about what they have just said.

I once had a professor who was noted for the subtlety of his wit. Eating lunch in the university cafeteria after one of his lectures, I would sometimes see a student sitting alone abruptly burst into laughter. I knew what had happened. The light had suddenly gone on. The professor, of course, was denied the pleasure of seeing the student laugh at one of his jokes. For him that was a minor problem, but for a stand-up comedian such a delayed reaction can be fatal.

Humorists whose work appears in print can give their audiences a little more time to figure out what they are driving at. There is danger, however, in being too enigmatic. Some readers may never get the point to the material at all, and some who might work it out in time, are unwilling to give it extended contemplation and move on impatiently to the next item.

There is no fool-proof way of ensuring that listeners or readers will get the point to your jokes. Some precautions, though, are obvious. It is clear that you must think carefully about the nature of your audience. Contributors to *The New Yorker* would submit cartoons quite different from those they would send to the *National Enquirer*. Most jokes tailored for a comedy-club audience would not fit people attending a church supper. Children laugh uproariously at jokes whose simple mindedness would probably alienate adults. I have lectured on humor to widely varying types of audiences, among them university students, lawyers, teachers, engineers, health specialists, senior citizens, and in one instance a group of cemetery operators. Some jokes worked well with all of them; some that went over with one group fell flat with another.

One thing I could always expect were surprises. Jokes I thought were surefire sometimes fizzled miserably, and comments I made only incidentally occasionally drew big laughs. The unpredictability of audiences is the reason producers of stage shows try them out elsewhere before taking them to Broadway. Even movie producers sometimes show preliminary cuts of their comedy films to get a measure of each gag's laugh potential. Comedians who produce jokes five nights a week on national television have no chance to try out material ahead of time, of course. Johnny Carson used to complain somewhat plaintively when a routine expired pitifully, "We can't test this material out on the road, you know." Performers who move from one comedy club to another can polish their material, but even then new audiences are likely to bring new surprises.

Is the solution to the problem using only those jokes you are sure the audience will understand? Most people know enough about golf, for example, to get the point to this joke: "I call my socks golf socks because they have 18 holes in them." Some in the audience may laugh, but more will probably groan. You are likely to get the same reaction with this remark about inflation: "Dimes have changed." In one of his *Tonight* show monologues Johnny Carson told about a seal who came into his Malibu home to sweep the floor and wash the dishes, "I call him my Good

Housekeeping seal," he said. The studio audience actually booed him.

The reason audiences grow hostile on hearing such jokes may be that they share Rodney Dangerfield's feeling that they aren't being shown enough respect. People like to be tested. Moreover, when they succeed in connecting complex ideas, they tend to guffaw much more loudly than when the joke is simplistic.

There is a line spoken by a character in a Peter De Vries novel which reads as follows: "Love is an art; I can feel my craft ebbing." I have sometimes used it in lectures to test the capacity of audiences to recognize an abstruse reference. Most people greet it with a tiny smile. Perhaps they have found some amusement in the idea of calling love-making a craft. On one occasion, however, a young woman positively exploded with laughter. Her reaction was so boisterous that everyone in the group turned to look at her. She had recognized a second level of meaning in the joke—a play on the name of the nineteenth century German neurologist Richard von Krafft-Ebing, who wrote a pioneering work on sex. The explosiveness of her reaction, I believe, was directly related to the consciousness of her own erudition. She had made a connection no one else had been able to make. Realizing how perspicacious she had been gave her a deep feeling of self-satisfaction. The greater that feeling is, the louder the laughter seems to be.

It is clear that joke makers tread a narrow line between creating jokes that are too simple and jokes that are too complex. Most of the time you want listeners or readers to get the point. But if you challenge them, as you must, you also face the inevitable fact that some jokes will slide over their heads. What can you do when that happens? When Johnny Carson ran into that problem, he sometimes told his listeners what the point was. No one laughed, of course, but at least he relieved their puzzlement. At other times, he turned the failure of the joke into another joke. It was often funnier than the one he had prepared.

Carson's successor, Jay Leno, frequently tries to forestall difficulty by describing the event his joke will refer to before he begins telling it. On other occasions he uses the Carson technique of explaining the point when the audience doesn't get it. The trouble with both techniques is that the comedian is making the connection the audience should have made. The result will be a dampened laugh or none at all. In most instances the best thing you can do when an audience fails to grasp the point is to heave an inward sigh, and move on to the next joke in the hope it will fare better.

Chapter 5
A Trigger of Laughter: Self Satisfaction

For me, being funny is the best revenge.
Art Buchwald

In describing the components of a joke—the expressed idea which you as the joke maker present and the inferred idea which your audience draws out of it—we have been concerned mainly with structure, what we might call the two-by-fours of a joke. Now we turn our attention to the kind of material you hang on those two-by-fours. The subject matter you choose can have a profound effect on your success as a joke maker.

One reason people laugh at a joke is that it produces a feeling of self satisfaction. As we learned in the previous chapter, the very process of joke making itself leads to the production of that effect. A well-constructed joke requires listeners to think of an idea which connects with one the joke maker has presented. When they complete the process successfully, they experience a pleasant sense of personal achievement, and feeling good about themselves, they laugh. Merely putting a joke together may be enough to generate the kind of laugh you want. To attain a full, ebullient response, however, you usually must supplement the effect produced by the structure of a joke by clothing its two-by-fours with material that has the power to trigger a laugh.

Several types of material have that power. One type has the same effect on listeners that seeing the point to a joke gives them. On hearing it, they experience a feeling of self satisfaction. Thus, the effect created by the joke-making process itself is directly intensified and augmented. In this chapter we consider through definition and illustration the kind of material that produces a sense of self satisfaction. In the next chapter we examine two other types of material that also have laugh-provoking power.

Winning and Self Satisfaction

Nothing is more likely to make a person feel superior than winning some kind of contest or confrontation. The resultant self satisfaction the person feels is so intense that the urge to laugh becomes almost irresistible. You recall from reading Chapter 2 that the psychologist Albert Rapp actually went so far as to speculate that all laughter began with the roar of triumph uttered by a caveman after victory in an ancient jungle duel. William Shakespeare struck the same note in his play *Othello* by having the title character remark, "They laugh that win."

To observe how laughter is generated by the self satisfaction that comes from winning, you have only to observe how football players behave when television permits you to visit the locker room of a winning team. The predominating ingredient in the bedlam you witness is the sound of laughter. The coach of a winning football team even laughs when his players douse him with a bucket of ice-cold Gatorade. The satisfaction that comes from winning is so strong it suppresses his reaction to what appears to be an unpleasant assault on his dignity.

A contest does not necessarily have to be physical to produce a feeling of self satisfaction, or course. Victory in a collision of minds can be as gratifying as victory in a collision of bodies. Turning the tables on someone who makes an insulting wisecrack about you by coming back with a rejoinder that is wittier and more pointed can send the same surge of satisfaction through you that winning a tennis match does.

You do not even need to have an actual antagonist to experience the thrill of victory. Perhaps, like me, you watch the TV game show *Jeopardy* on occasion and try to shout out the correct responses before the contestants in the studio do. In your mind you have converted them into your opponents, and when you get ahead of them, you probably accompany your response with a self-satisfied chuckle. In some instances your opponent may even be yourself. Children playing all by themselves have been seen to laugh uproariously after figuring out the correct answer to a puzzle.

It is not only the actual winners of a contest who feel satisfaction. Those who support them also experience it. They express their feelings in the same way the winners do—by laughing. You can see this response occurring by watching spectators file out of a football stadium at the end of a game. You can easily tell which team has won. The spectators wearing the colors of the winner are chattering and laughing; those wearing the colors of the loser are grim faced and silent.

The supporters of the winning team laugh because they identify with their team. Thus its triumph produces a deep sense of personal satisfaction even though they have done nothing to contribute to it. Their identification with their team may be so complete, in fact, that their legs move in unison with the leg of the place kicker as he tries to propel the ball between the goal posts, their shoulders hunch forward as their team tries to push the ball over the goal line. The ensuing triumph belongs almost as much to them as it does to the players who were actually responsible for it.

Put-Downs and Self Satisfaction

The fact that a feeling of triumph can be experienced vicariously is a tremendous boon to joke makers. They take advantage of it by manipulating their audiences into identifying with a winner. The winners they identify with in many instances are the joke makers themselves as they make fun of people, institutions, or ideas. By spouting derisive comments, they suggest the existence of a contest in which the target of their sarcasm becomes the loser. In some instances the winners may be characters who triumph in a battle of wits in the stories joke makers tell. Audiences tend to identify with the winners, whoever they may be, and thus they experience vicariously the triumph that produces a feeling of self satisfaction. The result is—they laugh. That is why so much humor involves a put-down. Even if audience members don't sense the existence of a contest, they still feel superior to the person who becomes the butt of a joke, and that too is a powerful generator of self satisfaction. They can even feel self satisfaction when the object of the ridicule is an idea or a happening, for they can tell themselves they wouldn't ever be responsible for committing any such foolishness. The power of the put-down to produce laughter is the reason the hosts of late-night talk shows spend so much of their time speaking derisively of political leaders, ridiculing members of various professions, particularly lawyers, or satirizing some aspect of our culture.

The Duel of Wits. The type of joke in which the existence of a contest is most evident is the duel of wits. It has two antagonists who clash with each other. The combat is incited when one of them makes a provocative statement which disparages the other. It ends when the target of the abuse takes those words and throws them back at the person who uttered them with a remark that is sharper and even more insulting. This turning of the tables is a distinguishing feature of the duel of wits and one that audiences especially savor.

Why, you may wonder, would the listeners to such a contest necessarily identify with the person who wins? When the joke begins, they are probably in a neutral position, supporting neither person. They often do not know the antagonists; in some instances they are not even named. Yet when the duel ends with a triumphant retort, they usually ally themselves with the person who made it. The main reason is that people like to be on the side of those who win. If all other factors are equal, if listeners have no bias one way or another, they are likely to end up on the side of the victor.

In constructing a duel of wits, you must do everything you can to intensify a feeling of identification. One of the most effective steps you can take is to make the winner someone with whom the audience will sympathize. Consider this classic duel of wits, for example:

> An old woman was walking down the road one day when she met a young man going the other way. "Good morning, Mother of Asses," he greeted her insolently.
>
> Affecting a gentle smile, the old woman replied, "Good morning, my son."

As soon as the young man utters his derogatory greeting, the sympathy of listeners is almost bound to go out to the old woman. Allying with her, they can take personal satisfaction in the deft and clever way in which she makes the young man the victim of his own impudence.

You can also enlist sympathy by making the winner of your duel of wits a mild-mannered person who manages to outdo an arrogant one. People are likely to identify themselves, for instance, with a New Englander who was listening patiently to a Texan as he boasted about the size of his ranch.

At one point the Texan asked condescendingly, "How big a place do you have?"

"Three hundred acres," the New Englander replied humbly.

"Is that right," the Texan responded, smacking his lips. "You know I can start driving across my place early in the morning and not be even half way across by noon."

"I know what you mean," the New Englander replied. "I had a car like that once."

Other types of individuals likely to draw sympathy are persons in service positions who strike back at patrons who subject them to demeaning treatment. An example was a pompous English duke who often made life miserable for the waiters in his London club. One of them finally retaliated but did so with such finesse that the duke would have difficulty defining the nature of any complaint he might wish to make. The episode began when the duke, annoyed that his wants were not being attended to promptly, called a waiter over and snarled at him, "Do you know who I am?"

Putting on his most polite manner, the waiter responded, "I do not sir, but I shall make inquiries and inform you directly."

Equally skillful was the way a waitress fended off a demeaning sexual overture by a boorish customer. He ordered half a dozen oysters and then accompanying his remark with a suggestive wink, said, "You know what they say about oysters, don't you sweetie? They make you sexy."

Keeping an absolutely straight face, she answered, "If that's your aim sir, I think you need many more than six."

Audiences are also likely to connect emotionally with those who succeed in putting down people who make life unnecessarily difficult. Airline personnel responsible for ticket matters are sometimes the targets of abuse from customers when flights are delayed or cancelled. As representatives of the airline, they are expected to stand quietly and take it. Sometimes, however, the vituperation becomes so extreme they are goaded into striking back. That happened to one reservations clerk whom a woman passenger seemed to be holding personally responsible for the fog that had delayed her flight. When her tirade ended with the statement—"The way you run an airline, a witch on a broom could get there faster"—the clerk couldn't resist taking advantage of the opening she had given him by replying:

"Madam, be my guest. Runaway D is open."

For the same reason that audiences would end up cheering that airline clerk, they would also applaud the film director Alfred Hitchcock for his neat put-down of an actress notorious for the problems she created on the set. On one occasion she kept delaying the production with complaints about the way she was being photographed. "You must be sure," she kept insisting, "to photograph me from my good side."

An exasperated Hitchcock finally burst out, "Madam, you are sitting on it."

Rude interruptions from patrons in nightclubs make life difficult for comedians who are trying to complete a monologue. The other customers usually smile with satisfaction when a witty comeback humbles the obstreperous patron. Groucho Marx once advised an obnoxious guest, "to bore a hole in yourself and let the sap run out." Henny Youngman said to one heckler, "You know I've been looking high and low for you, but I guess I didn't look low enough." And to another, "If I give you a going away present will you go away?" Perhaps the prize for nimbleness goes to a comedian named Jack Douglas whose response reflects the fact that most hecklers are awash with alcohol. To one tipsy patron he made this comment, "I know you're an alcoholic, but you're not being very anonymous."

At times people who dedicate themselves to promoting causes tend to make life difficult for other people because of the intensity with which they pursue their course, not permitting those around them to forget for a moment what they stand for. You can elicit laughter at times by making such people losers in a duel of wits. Most audiences, for example, are likely to ally themselves with a man whose behavior was unexpectedly questioned by a woman who apparently wore her feminist creed on her sleeve. In going into a building, he held the door open for her. "I hope you didn't do that just because I'm a lady," the woman said.

"Not at all," the man replied. "I did it because I'm a gentleman."

A problem with that story, as I'm sure some of you noticed, is that a true feminist would be unlikely to refer to herself as a lady. Changing the word to "woman," however, damages the contrast with the word "gentleman." Another version of the story has the woman saying, "I hope you didn't hold that door open for me because of my sex." The answer it draws from the man is somewhat ruder than the first one.

"I wasn't thinking of your sex. I was thinking of your age."

Sometimes the unreasonableness of people we view as authority figures creates difficulties for us. You can enlist the sympathy of an audience for someone who challenges such a person with an adroit response. Most of us, for example, are somewhat intimidated by doctors and even when they irritate us, we are disinclined to confront them. One person who apparently felt no such restraint, reacted to his surgeon's advice that he return to work by saying, "I don't think I'm quite ready for that yet."

"Nonsense," the surgeon said, "I had the same operation you had, and I went back to work in two days."

"Right," the patient replied, "but you had a different surgeon."

Automobile mechanics do not have quite the authority status of physicians, but they can also be intimidating on occasion. Most of us at one time or another have wished we could think of something that would gently prick a mechanic we think is trying to take advantage of us without creating an open wound. When a customer in a situation like that comes up with a rejoinder your listeners would like to have made themselves, you can be certain they will experience vicariously a feeling of victory. This next story provides an example of such a response.

After looking over a car, a mechanic said to the owner. "If I told you your transmission needed replacement, would you have enough money to pay for it?"

Fixing the mechanic with a level gaze, the owner asked, "If I didn't have the money to pay for it, would I need a new transmission?"

Many duels of wits have become enshrined in the lore of joke making because the person who struck the final telling blow is a historical figure. Your stories draw a greater response if the characters in them are people your listeners know, particularly if they are ones they admire and respect. An account of one of Abraham Lincoln's encounters with his political rival, Stephen Douglas, provides an illustration.

Douglas once made the comment that when he first met Lincoln, he was serving as a bartender. Lincoln admitted the truth of the charge but then added, "I have left my side of the counter, but Mr. Douglas still clings tenaciously to his."

Another American politician credited with a retort that turned the tables on a fellow congressman was Henry Clay, a legislative leader in the early years of our nation. Though less well-known than Lincoln, his name nevertheless would draw sufficient recognition to add an extra fillip to the following story:

Clay once interrupted a long-winded colleague by suggesting

that he had made his point and should relinquish the floor to others.

"You sir, speak for the moment," the congressman responded tartly. "I speak for posterity."

"You are right," Clay answered. "And apparently you are determined to speak until the arrival of your audience."

A British political leader, noted for the masterly way in which he turned back attacks made on him by rivals was Great Britain's wartime prime minister, Winston Churchill. His devastating wit won him many battles in the political arena, but he was not averse to using it to put down private individuals who dared to challenge him. Even when the victim of his clever ripostes was a woman, as in the case in the following story, audiences are likely to side with Churchill because of his reputation and the admiration they have for him.

Lady Astor, a redoubtable wit her self, once greeted Churchill by saying, "If you were my husband I'd put arsenic in your tea."

Churchill's instant response was, "If you were my wife, I'd drink it."

An exchange involving George Bernard Shaw provides another prime example of the duel of wits in which one of the antagonists adroitly turns an insult back on the one who delivered it. The victim in this case was Shaw's literary rival, G. K. Chesterton. Though they were great friends, the two were quite different both in their outlook on life and in their physical appearance. Shaw, a vegetarian, was thin to the point of scrawniness; Chesterton, a hearty eater of meat, was undeniably obese. This difference inspired one of their barbed exchanges.

"Looking at you, Shaw," Chesterton said, "people would think there was a famine in England."

Responding to his portly companion, Shaw observed, "And looking at you, Chesterton, people would think you were the cause of it."

Another instance in which Shaw demonstrated his skill in verbal battle occurred just after the first performance of his play *Arms and the Man*. In response to cries of "Author!" Shaw stepped from behind the curtain and bowed as a delighted audience gave him a standing ovation. But then a discordant "Boo!" from the gallery sounded above all the applause. Nodding in the direction from which the sole negative reaction had come, Shaw remarked dryly, "My dear fellow, I quite agree with you. But what are we two against so many?"

Most duels of wits take place orally, with the antagonists facing off in each other's presence. One of the most famous, however, was conducted by letter, and again one of the participants was George Bernard Shaw. His opponent was that other master of repartee, Winston Churchill.

Shaw once sent two tickets for his latest play to Churchill accompanied by a note which read: One ticket is for you, and one is for a friend—if you have one."

The next mail brought Churchill's reply, "I'm sorry I can't make the first performance, but I'd be happy to receive tickets for the second—if there is one."

In an earlier chapter, I noted that former senator and presidential aspirant Robert Dole is considered by many to be the greatest wit among contemporary politicians. At one time he too used a note to rebuff in a graceful way a constituent who had the temerity to criticize the way he conducted an aspect of his private life. When a photograph was published showing Dole helping his wife, Elizabeth, make up a bed, the constituent wrote to chide him for doing women's work. In his reply, Dole deftly turned the situation around by saying, "Buddy, you don't know the half of it. The only reason she was helping me was that the photographer was there."

There was even one instance in which a classroom chalkboard was the battleground for a duel of wits. A professor had left this message on the chalkboard: "Professor Brown will not meet his classes today." A mischievous student, finding himself alone in the classroom, picked up an eraser and eliminated the "c" from "classes." The professor happened to come by a few minutes later and observing the revision won the battle of the erasers by picking up one himself and deleting the "l."

Most of the encounters just cited were not invented by humorists but actually took place. This is not true, however, of all the duels of wits in which historical figures presumably participated. One of the techniques employed by joke makers to give their stories more impact is to put the clever lines they create into the mouths of people whom audiences will recognize. The exchange between Abraham Lincoln and Stephen Douglas probably occurred, but another example of Lincoln's wit, and one that is much better known, apparently originated with an anonymous joke maker. It seems that some hard-nosed foes of alcohol complained to Lincoln that his victorious general Ulysses S. Grant drank too much whiskey.

"I wonder if you could get me a few barrels of that same whiskey," Lincoln is said to have replied, "And I'll give it to my other generals."

Lincoln denied he ever made that statement, but it so perfectly reflects the wit he was famous for it is little wonder the story has been accepted as authentic.

Two British political leaders of the late nineteenth century have been credited with originating one of the most celebrated duels of wits ever recorded. They are William Gladstone, a member of the Liberal Party who served as prime minister, and his bitter rival, Benjamin Disraeli, who as the leader of the Conservative Party alternated with Gladstone as prime minister. During one of their heated confrontations, Gladstone is reputed to have shouted in exasperation, "Sir, you will either end up on the gallows or die of a venereal disease."

"That all depends," Disraeli is said to have shot back, "on whether I embrace your principles or your mistress."

It is highly doubtful that those two eminent Victorians ever spoke those words. They do not fit the character of either man. Unlike the Lincoln-Grant example, however, they were not invented by a joke maker and put into their mouths but probably originated with two other historical figures, John Wilkes, an eighteenth-century politician and journalist who made the winning retort, and the Earl of Sandwich. The exchange has also been attributed to two other British political figures, William Pitt and Robert Walpole. The problem the story teller faces is that none of these last four names is likely to mean much to the average listener. To give the story more interest, the lines were shifted to the much better known Gladstone and Disraeli. The practice of attributing jokes comedians invent to celebrities or of taking a smart rejoinder spoken by a relatively unknown individual and giving it to a more recognizable person still goes on today. As a result it is almost impossible to know at times whether the clever lines celebrities are supposed to have uttered were actually spoken by them, were stolen from lesser-known people, or were concocted by joke makers.

The duel of wits has been a framework for devising jokes which creators of humor have used productively down through the centuries. The major vehicle for bringing them to the public has been the drama. Four hundred years ago, William Shakespeare made intellectual confrontations the principal means of making audiences laugh in one of his most popular plays, *Much Ado About Nothing*. The antagonists in what Shakespeare called "a skirmish of wit" were a spirited young woman of the court named Beatrice and a nobleman named Benedict. Even after they discovered they loved each other, they continued to exchange pointed barbs. In 1993 movie goers could see the British star Emma Thompson, an Academy Award winner, and the director and actor Kenneth Branagh play the embattled lovers in a film version. Many other dramatists, among them George Bernard Shaw and Oscar Wilde, have infused their plays with clever retorts by characters who turn the tables on other characters, and in the television world today, duels of wits are often featured in the situation comedies that attract so many

118

viewers.

The Naked Put-Down. Many jokes that end with a disparaging remark about a person do not involve a duel of wits at all. There is only one participant not two, so there is no confrontation. The offensive comment erupts without any specific provocation, which means there is no turning of the tables as there is in the duel of wits. In some ways the target of the ridicule is no more than an innocent bystander. Thus all of the elements of battle so characteristic of the duel of wits are missing except the derisive remark. Yet audiences still laugh loudly at this type of joke.

One reason they laugh is that the naked put-down, though shorn of the paraphernalia of conflict, still suggests that a contest has taken place. To illustrate the point, let us consider a full-fledged duel of wits and then compare it with a naked put-down that uses the same type of culminating insult. Milton Berle once challenged an entertainer named Frank Fay to a duel of wits, intimating that his superior intellect would make him the winner. Fay politely declined the invitation, saying, "I never fight an unarmed man."

The story has all of the elements of a duel of wits—two antagonists confronting each other, a provocative challenge, and a clever rejoinder that turns the challenge back on the one who made it. Now compare it with one made by Tom Reed, a former Speaker of the House of Representatives, who was noted for the crushing one-liners with which he disparaged his legislative antagonists. Reed is said to have remarked of one such person, "With a few more brains he could be a half wit."

The insult is the same as the one delivered by Frank Fay, but it was uttered under different circumstances. It did not arise during a confrontation between two people, the comment was not specifically provoked, and it was directed not at the target of the derision but was made about him to other people. All that is left of the duel of wits is the final insult. Yet for listeners it alone is enough to carry an aura of victory. They fill in the framework of a duel of wits for themselves and thus take pleasure in what they see as the winner's clever rejoinder. Knowing that Reed made his remark about an actual opponent helps the process.

Winston Churchill once said of his political rival Clement Attlee, "He's a very modest man—and with good reason." This is another truncated duel of wits which would benefit from the audience's knowing that Churchill probably was hostile toward the man he had demeaned. After leading Great Britain to victory in World War II, Churchill undoubtedly believed that a grateful public would keep him in power as prime minister. In a stunning development the electorate replaced him with Clement Attlee. It would be easy for an audience to visualize Churchill's remark as the climactic element in a duel of wits between two bitter antagonists.

It is not necessary, however, that a naked put-down be aimed at a person its originator dislikes for an audience to think of it as the winning thrust in a duel of wits. Comedians who regularly insult a wide variety of people do not necessarily nurse any antagonism toward the targets of their ridicule. In fact they are often people they respect and admire. To use a third example of a "wit" joke, when one comedian says of another, "He thinks he's a wit, and he's half right," he isn't reflecting any particular animus, but is simply having fun. The audience in the same spirit of fun expands the remark into a duel of wits won by the comedian and experiences satisfaction by vicariously participating in the victory.

That a part can suggest the whole is demonstrated by what happens when we see someone with a black eye. Most of us are inclined to laugh. We do so because in our minds we envision a fight from which the person with the black eye has emerged an obvious loser. In our perverse way, we tend to ally ourselves with the winner, thus gaining a feeling of satisfaction.

Even if we do not expand a naked put-down into a full-fledged duel of wits, it still gives us the chance to feel superior to the person who is belittled. That feeling produces the sense of self satisfaction that incites laughter.

It has been estimated that ridicule, both the kind that is truly hostile and the kind that is friendly in tone, is the key element in seventy percent of all humor. One has only to watch a situation comedy or two to see how prevalent the insult is. A major aim of the characters, it seems, is to put one another down. In the same way stand-up comedians spend much of their time indulging in ridicule. The renowned political satirist Mort Sahl pinpointed the key role of the insult in his routines by asking at the end of his performances, "Is there anyone here I haven't offended?"

You would be a very unusual joke maker, indeed, if a large part of your material did not turn on some sort of derisive element. To avoid it would eliminate a major means of creating the self satisfaction in your listeners that leads to laughter.

Representatives of a large variety of occupations and professions have been the target at one time or another of the naked put-down. Certain groups, however, draw particular fire, and reviewing who they are may guide you into finding similar targets and concocting the deprecating statements that make audiences laugh.

One group comedians aim at regularly are politicians. Hosts of the late-night talk shows and such specialists in political satire as Mark Russell constantly make fun of them. This type of humor appears to be increasing. Much of it is cruel and in some instances it is grossly unfair. It can also influence the course of political events. Comedians played a major role in destroying the credibility of Richard Nixon during the Watergate scandal. Most prominent among his tormentors was Johnny Carson, who for an extended period included a Watergate joke or two in almost all of his *Tonight* show monologues. An example was his response to Nixon's claim that some of the recordings of oval office conversations were missing. Carson asked his audience whether they "would believe Moses if he had come down the mountain with only eight commandments?" Equally devastating were the impersonations of Nixon performed by David Frye and the barbs tossed by Mark Russell, among them his revision of the presidential song into "Bail to the Chief."

The multitude of jokes about the faux pas of Dan Quayle, vice president during the administration of the first George Bush, may have brought Quayle's political career to an end. The stories about his blunders, both real and manufactured, severely damaged his image. He was an object of ridicule, not only in night clubs and television shows, but in comic strips as well. In one of the *Frank and Ernest* comic-strip series, a man in a store looking for a costume to wear on Halloween, said to the clerk, "I want something real scary....Give me a Dan Quayle mask and a red telephone." Another strip in the same series showed a teacher telling his class, "Any child in this country can grow up to be president." One of the students responded, "and if you don't grow up, you can still be vice president." There is no other word to describe this kind of ridicule except "savage."

The many jokes about the difficulties the second President George Bush has had with language and pronunciation have probably tarnished to some extent the image he has tried to project of being a strong and capable leader. It is doubtful, however, that they will be the significant factor they apparently were in the case of Dan Quayle. The sexual misbehavior of Bill Clinton spawned countless jokes, but it was the behavior that damaged him, not the jokes.

The type of joke that ridicules politicians for defects of personality or appearance they cannot eliminate does seem to be a little unfair. Michael Dukakis and the first President George Bush tended by their very nature to be dull and uninspiring speakers. Even the noted newsman David Brinkley, whose comments were usually gentler in tone, made fun of their flat personalities when he appeared on the *Tonight* show during the 1988 presidential campaign. He remarked that "If either Dukakis or Bush tries to give a fireside chat, the fire will go out." And Dukakis surely is not responsible for his Greek ancestry and his shortness of stature. That did not prevent a humorist from saying of him, "Beware of Greeks wearing lifts."

One reason there are so many jokes about elected officials is that people tend to experience special satisfaction when those in power are ridiculed. Our behavior is almost perverse. We elevate individuals to high office and then do everything we can to puncture their authority. In Australia, this is known as the "tall poppy syndrome"—the tendency to cut down anyone superior. To show you how perverse the tendency is in Australia, some there have used it to explain why most politicians, some academics, and the occasional millionaire command a level of community admiration inferior to that of a toilet cleaner.

Being the butt of comedian's jokes is a price presidents and their appointees apparently must pay for holding office. Some humorists don't accept any blame for making fun of politicians. Will Rogers said for example, "I don't tell jokes. I just report the facts." That remark is reminiscent of one Harry Truman made in defending himself against the accusation that he was giving his opponents hell. "I don't give 'em hell," Truman retorted. "I just tell the truth, and they think it's hell."

Another group that regularly suffers the naked put-down includes writers, performers, directors, producers, and artists. The critics who launch the barbs sometimes seem more intent on devising clever ways of expressing ridicule than they are on producing reasoned evaluations. The targets have done nothing to deserve it unless the act of creating works that fall short of meeting their standards can be considered a provocation.

Some of the put-downs critics have produced are prime examples of the insulter's art. Eugene Field described the performance of a shaky actor in this way: "He played the king as if in constant fear that someone was about to play the ace." Mark Twain said of the novelist James Fenimore Cooper, "He saw life as through a glass eye, darkly." George Jean Nathan, a prominent drama critic of the 1920s, remarked of a production: "It is a play for the ages, the ages from five to ten." Dorothy Parker, a contemporary of Nathan, often expressed her disdain in language that matched his in terseness and pungency. She advised potential viewers of one play, "If you don't knit, bring a book." She even took aim at the usually admired Katherine Hepburn, remarking of her performance in *The Lake*, "She ran the gamut of emotions from A to B." Another critic disposed of an entire book with the comment, "You can find better writing on the side of a shredded wheat box." Ambrose Bierce rendered this stinging verdict in one of his reviews: "The covers of this book are too far apart." Equally dismissive was the remark of an art critic who said of a painting, "they couldn't find the artist so they hung the picture." One of the most elaborate insults directed at a stage production came from Percy Hammond, another drama critic of the 1920s. Concluding a review of a musical comedy, he said, "So far I have knocked everything except the chorus girls' knees, and nature anticipated me there."

Sometimes artistic creators are the victims of wit that originates with their own kind. The pianist Artur Schnabel was once asked to comment on a piano recital performed by a woman who possessed great technical skill but lacked emotional power. His wry reaction was, "Immaculate but no conception." Among stand-up comedians family members are favorite targets of naked put-downs. Insulting mothers-in-law is not as fashionable as it once was, but Henny Youngman could still get laughs by telling an audience, "I just came back from a pleasure trip. I drove my mother-in-law to the airport." Spouses seem to have taken their place as the main objects of ridicule. Most famous of all the spousal put-downs, I suppose, is that same Henny Youngman's "Take my wife...please." Alan King was another major player of this game and the comedian Marty Allen once said of his wife, "She looks as if she just stepped out of *Playboy*, at the publisher's request." There is even one example of a posthumous insult. The German poet Heinrich Heine apparently felt such animus for his wife that he chose to mock her from beyond the grave. He left his estate to her, but only on the condition that she remarry. He explained in his will that as a result, "there will be at least one man to regret my death."

Spousal insults are not one sided by any means. Many come from performers on the other side of the gender gap. Phyllis Diller said of the husband she called Fang, "He cut himself shaving this morning, and his eyes cleared up." In a dialogue with Johnny Carson, Joan Rivers said she once suffered from a skin disease. A dermatologist advised her it could be cured by having sex 300 times a year. When she told her husband, he said, "Put me down for two."

In thinking about people who are subjected to naked put-downs, we cannot overlook lawyers. The savage mockery of the assaults directed at them is exemplified by this remark: "Lawyers need have no fear of swimming in shark infested waters. Professional courtesy will protect them." The ridicule has become so unremitting that the President of the California Bar Association once plaintively begged for mercy, claiming that the constant flow of derisive comments was destroying the dignity and reputation of the profession. His plea seems to have had no effect on such comedians as Jay Leno who regularly includes barbs directed at lawyers in his *Tonight* show routines.

Doctors do not get into the line of fire quite so often, but they do not escape unscathed. Many of the stories cast aspersions on their healing powers, as the following story does. Its target is a rarity these days—a doctor who still makes house calls. A patient telephoned him one night and then apologized for asking him to make a long trip on a cold night. "No problem," the doctor said. "I have to visit another patient who lives near you so I'll just kill two birds with one stone." Incidentally, *The New Yorker* has collected cartoons that take aim at both doctors and lawyers and published them in separate compilations.

Every profession has been subjected to the comedian's rapier. If you enter the name of a profession into one of the Internet's search engines, you will discover it lists thousands of jokes, sometimes hundreds of thousands. I must confess, though, that I have yet to see what I would call a good joke about engineers. Maybe they lead more placid and uneventful lives than most professional people. (Perhaps this statement will bring me some.)

Ministers have not been spared. Jokes about plumbers abound. There are jokes about life insurance agents, this one, for example. An agent was trying to persuade a potential customer to invest in a life-insurance policy. When he found the prospect hesitant, he assured him there was no rush. "Why don't you sleep on it," he suggested, "and then call me in the morning. That is, if you wake up."

Officials who make calls in sports contests often have the acuteness of their vision brought into question. The football coach Bum Phillips, squirming under an unfavorable decision by a referee, told an assistant, "Take him a copy of the rules, and be sure it's in braille." A baseball player called out at home by an umpire named George Moriarty asked him how he spelled his name.

"M-O-R-I-A-R-T-Y," was the answer.

"Just as I thought," the player said. "Only one eye."

That story, incidentally, was told by Michael Moriarty, the TV and film actor, who is the umpire's grandson.

People who participate in sports contests are also the subjects of put-downs. Mark Russell crystallized one commonly heard aspersion about football players in a remark he made on a TV special. "I haven't hugged an illiterate today, but I did the next best thing. I shook hands with a college football player."

Sometimes the subject of a put-down is not an individual but an entire group of people. We usually think of this type of joke as ethnic. The English, the Scots, the Welsh, and the Northern Irish live together in what is apparently an uneasy union, for they constantly ridicule one another.

Among the notable insulters was the eighteenth-century writer Dr. Samuel Johnson. His principal target was the Scots, or the Scotch, as he called them. (A true Scot maintains that the word "scotch" refers to a drink not to a people.) Best known among Johnson's expressions of scorn is the comment that "Much may be made of a Scotchman if he be caught young." He also said that "The noblest prospect which a Scotchman ever sees is the highroad that leads him to England," and he referred to oats as "a grain which in England is generally given to horses but in Scotland supports the people." An anonymous writer also cast a barb in Scotland's direction when he defined the Scots as a people who "keep the Sabbath and anything else they can get their hands on."

The propensities of other inhabitants of the United Kingdom have also been pungently described. The Irish have been characterized as a people who "value peace and will fight anyone anywhere to maintain it," a Welshman as a person "who prays on his knees on Sunday and on his neighbors the rest of the week," and an Englishman as "a self-made man who worships his creator."

Similar rivalries exist in other parts of the British Commonwealth. In Canada the animosity between the French and the English has spawned countless ethnic jokes. Even places are made fun of at times. When I visited Australia, I learned that the cities of Melbourne and Sydney are envious competitors for national attention. As we were leaving Melbourne on a bus, our driver, a native of Sydney, commented "Your best look at Melbourne is in a rear-view mirror."

The United States, of course, has not been immune to this sort of rivalry. The following quatrain points a scornful finger at New Englanders:

You can always tell the Irish,
You can always tell the Dutch.
You can always tell a Yankee;
But you cannot tell him much.

Oscar Wilde took aim at the entire country when he said in his customary deft way, "Of course, America had often been discovered before Columbus, but it had always been hushed up."

The offensive remarks meted out by various nationalities and cultures often demonstrate a unique approach to the art of being insulting. According to the anthropologist Edgar Gregersen, the Japanese like to give them a vegetable flavor. If you irritate them you may be called a "horseradish rascal" or "an out-of-focus eggplant." Yiddish insults are often elaborate and sometimes funny. Examples are "go bother the bedbugs" and "you should grow like an onion with your head in the ground and your feet above."

Jokes that make fun of physical disabilities or disadvantages are less common than they used to be, but they still persist. Like other put-downs, much of their laugh-making effect comes from the superiority feeling arising from the realization that some people are less intelligent, physically adept, or good looking than we are. Members of primitive societies apparently laughed outright at the sight of malformed and handicapped people. Children in our time still do, but adults are usually more restrained, although in some contemporary cultures the misfortunes of others still cause outbursts of laughter. It has been reported that witnesses to executions in China have been seen laughing uproariously.

Gibes at physical disabilities though they may amuse some can hurt those who suffer them. Even so mild a comment as Dorothy Parker's couplet "Men seldom make passes at girls who wear glasses" may not be appreciated by women who must correct their vision problems with glasses. And the following joke, which appeared in a British magazine, is likely to provoke laughter except perhaps in those who are hard of hearing:

Two men with hearing problems were riding together on a train.

"Is this Wemsley," one asked as they came into a station.

"No it's Thursday," the other replied.

"So am I," said his companion. "Let's have a drink."

A joke of American origin uses the same technique to make fun of the deaf.

A young man with liberal leanings was arguing with his hard-of-hearing grandfather, a dedicated conservative, about the voting record of a particular senator.

"He's one of those damned liberals," the old man growled. "He's no damn good."

"I disagree," his grandson said. "He's a good man. In fact he's the son of a bishop."

The old man quickly countered, "They all are."

There was a time when comedians in vaudeville, in the movies, and even on radio made their audiences laugh by imitating stutterers. With the development of greater sensitivity in our society, the stuttering act has been put on the shelf, but the ridicule of stuttering still lingers in some jokes, as it does in this one:

A man and woman came independently to a golf course and applied to the manager for permission to play a round. When the manager discovered that they both stuttered, he decided it would be a good idea to have them play as a twosome. He brought them

126

together and asked them to introduce themselves.

"My n-n-name is P-P-Peter," the man said, "B-b-but I'm n-n-not a s-s-saint."

"My n-n-name is M-M-Mary," the woman replied, "B-b-but I'm n-n-not a v-v-very good player."

Neither old age nor extreme youth are generally thought of as a disability, but they are sometimes treated that way by joke makers. As far as old age is concerned, it is the tendency of very mature minds to lose their grip on facts that often becomes the focus of the joke, as the following story illustrates:

A venerable old gentleman, who had once served as a United States senator, boarded a train only to discover he had forgotten to bring his ticket. He was extremely flustered by his oversight, but the conductor, who knew him well, consoled him with these words, "It's all right, Senator. Just take your seat and ride along. You can bring the ticket with you the next time you ride the train."

"That's all very well for you to say," the Senator replied. "But without my ticket, how am I to know where to get off?"

Remembering names is a problem for many people but is especially difficult for those of advanced age. The next joke pokes fun at the handicap:

A guest in an elderly man's home congratulated him for always calling his wife by such endearing names as "honey," "sweetie," and "darling." When he had a chance, the elderly man whispered in his guest's ear, "I haven't been able to think of my wife's first name for ten years."

President Reagan, whose age was often the target of humorists' jokes, took them in good spirit and sometimes told jokes himself that focused on the frailties of senior citizens. Like the story just recounted, this one of Reagan's takes aim at the problems old people have with memory.

An elderly couple were getting ready for bed when the wife found she was suddenly hungry for ice cream, and there wasn't any in the house. "Would you go and get me some vanilla ice cream?" she asked her husband. "Oh, and get some chocolate sauce, too, and some cherries. I want a cherry on top."

Her husband assented and started to leave.

"Vanilla ice cream, chocolate sauce, and cherries," she repeated. "You'd better write it down, or you'll forget."

"I won't forget," he responded grumpily.

A few minutes later he came back and handed her a paper bag. She opened it and pulled out a ham sandwich. She took one look and said, "I told you to write it down. You forgot the mustard!"

Most of us love our children yet we often make fun of their innocence and naiveté, doing so in many instances in their presence, something we are not likely to do with adults. A little boy had been permitted to see a new baby who had just come into his home. When he was asked by a visiting relative whether it was a boy or a girl he replied: "I couldn't tell. It didn't have any clothes on." His ingenuous response was greeted by loud guffaws, and he heard it repeated a number of times to the relatives and friends who came in later.

<u>Mixed-Breed Put-Downs</u>. One type of joke falls somewhere between the duel of wits and the naked put-down. It is like the duel in that it involves two people in a dialogue that ends with a reproof or insult. It is unlike the duel, however, in that only one of the participants is adversarial in attitude. The other participant has no intention of trying to get the better of anyone. The affront comes in response to a comment or question that is completely innocuous and free of guile and that, in some instances, is intended as a compliment. The insult, therefore, like the naked put-down springs forth unprovoked.

The American painter James McNeill Whistler was noted not only for his innovative contributions as an artist, but also for his wit. His wry and subtle turn of mind is illustrated by a comment he made about flunking out of West Point. "If silicon had been a gas, I would have been a major general instead of an artist." During a stay in England, he came to know another of the great wits of his time, the Irish writer Oscar Wilde. They often engaged in dazzling repartee in which each tried to outdo the other. Oddly, however, the exchange that is best remembered did not involve a duel of wits at all. Rather, it exemplifies the mixed-breed put-down in which one was trying to be nice and the other decided to be nasty. The two were eating dinner together when Whistler made a particularly clever remark. Wilde responded with an admiring, "I wish I'd said that."

"Don't worry, Oscar," Whistler replied, "You will."

Members of the minority party in the House of Representatives were often the victims of unprovoked affronts during the two periods that Tom Reed served as Speaker. One of them was subjected to such treatment simply because his mind went blank just as he started a speak. To cover himself, he muttered, "I am thinking...I am thinking...."

The sharp-tongued Reed broke in at that moment, saying, "I hope no one will interrupt the gentleman's commendable innovation."

An entire choir, which presumably was simply trying to do its best, was once twitted with an elaborately worded gibe by its conductor, Thomas

Beecham, when its rendition of a Bach composition fell short of his expectations. He interrupted the rehearsal to say, "Ladies and gentlemen, if you will make a point of singing 'All We Like Sheep Have Gone Astray' with a little less self satisfaction, we shall meet the esthetical as well as the theological requirements."

People who in a friendly way try to make the acquaintance of celebrities sometimes meet with sharp rebuffs. It is said that as a youthful newcomer in the movie field, Ava Gardner went up to Bette Davis, by then a noted star, put out her hand and said "I'm Ava Gardner."

Looking at her imperiously, Davis replied, "I'm sure you are," and swept regally away.

Incidentally, this is another of those stories that has more than one set of characters. Davis's icy response has also been attributed to the British actor and writer Noel Coward, and the victim in his case was the American actor Chuck Connors.

Ranking high in sarcastic bite is a remark Groucho Marx made to someone for whom he apparently developed almost instant dislike. "I never forget a face, but I'll make an exception in your case."

People merely seeking guidance sometimes find they are the victims of individuals who get more satisfaction from delivering a clever put-down than they do from providing wise and caring counsel. A college student met that fate when he went to his adviser to explore his potential for becoming a physician. The professor took one look at the grades the student had earned in his chemistry courses and then said, "Young man, the only way you're going to get into medical school is as a cadaver."

Sometimes mere foolishness elicits a mocking response. That was the case with a man who requested a bank teller to cash a check for one cent. The teller gave him a curious look and then in a voice laden with feigned concern asked, "How would you like it, sir, heads or tails?"

A response that sounds sarcastic in some instances may be merely the product of innocent curiosity. The Roman Catholic prelate Bishop Fulton J. Sheen, who won fame in the early days of television as a speaker on religious themes, tells in his autobiography of one such incident. He was on his way to give a lecture in Philadelphia's Town Hall when he lost his way. Stopping a couple of boys to ask directions, he told them he was scheduled to speak on the topic, "How to Get to Heaven." One of the boys looked at him with undisguised astonishment in his eyes as he said, "Do you mean to say you're going to tell people how to get to heaven, and you can't find your way to Town Hall?"

There are even times when people belittle themselves, with the hope, perhaps, that the other person will buttress their ego with reassuring words, but find instead that they are the target of further belittlement. That happened to Michael DiSalle, who was appointed by President Harry Truman to be Director of the Office of Price Stabilization. Thanking the president for the honor, DiSalle, apparently trying to show a becoming modesty added, "Surely, there must be many people far more qualified than I for this responsibility."

"There are, Mike," Truman replied, "And don't think we haven't tried to get them."

That put-down had no real hostility in it. Some do, of course. I suspect that the exchanges Winston Churchill had with Lady Astor and George Bernard Shaw correctly reflected their true feelings. DiSalle and Truman, on the other hand, were close friends and whatever denigrating banter passed between them was part of a game.

The same was undoubtedly true of James Whistler and Oscar Wilde. Though they competed ferociously to come up with the final devastating riposte, their rivalry was obviously based on a foundation of mutual respect and admiration.

Reactions to Ridicule. One would expect that most victims of derisive humor would be resentful, especially when it focuses on an embarrassing frailty. That seems not to be the case in all instances. In fact, some people even seem to relish being made fun of. One reason may be that it puts them in the spotlight. Like Samuel Goldwyn, they apparently feel that any publicity is good publicity even if it consists of ridicule. That is why celebrities submit themselves to roasts in which their friends and colleagues make fun of their foibles and idiosyncrasies. The focus of one such event, in fact, was heard to complain because the ridicule wasn't savage enough. In many instances the objects of the taunts are the ones who laugh the loudest.

We can see the same phenomenon at work when patrons at a night club scream with laughter when a comedian makes fun of them. Don Rickles made a specialty of that kind of humor. Rather than resenting the barbs, his targets clamored for more.

A number of our presidents apparently did not resent the jokes made about their various foibles. Gerald Ford's stumbles down some airplane steps, as noted earlier in this book, led to a whole series of jokes about his reputed clumsiness. Of a forgiving nature, he invited a number of comedians who had made fun of him to a seminar on presidential humor, which he organized at his alma mater, the University of Michigan. Some of the barbs directed at Ronald Reagan were sharp, indeed, like the one that said he wanted memos kept to one page because reading longer ones made his lips tired. Instead of complaining, Reagan made fun of himself by expanding on some of the themes comedians had used. This exercise in self ridicule helped endear him to the public.

The quirks of delivery and language characteristics of the first President George Bush's speeches were imitated on *Saturday Night Live* by the comedian Dana Carvey. Frequently heard in his routines was a phrase Bush often used, "Wouldn't be prudent." The impersonations were unquestionably stinging caricatures of Bush's speaking style. Despite the assault on his dignity, he extended a cordial invitation to Carvey to be his guest at the White House.

The second President Bush has also been impersonated on television, particularly on the *Tonight* show. Steve Bridges, the actor who performs the impressions, so clearly resembles George W. Bush in voice and appearance that the first time I saw Jay Leno introduce him, I was beguiled into thinking that his guest was actually the President of the United States. Bridges is particularly adept at imitating the convulsive shaking of the shoulders that characterizes Bush's response to jokes. Bush seems willing to accept being made fun of as one of the prices he must pay for being president. Like Reagan, he occasionally engages in self-deprecatory humor, based at times on what comedians are saying about him.

Putting One's Self Down. A number of comedians do not limit themselves to making derisive comments about other people. They generate a feeling of superiority in their audiences by belittling themselves. The personal put-down was a major element in the comedy routines of Jack Benny. Through many years on the air, he consistently portrayed himself as one of the stingiest men on earth and regularly lampooned his sensitivity about his age and his thinning hair. Groucho Marx engaged in bitter self-deprecation when he said "I wouldn't belong to a club that would have me as a member." Tom Brokaw used exactly the same approach when in responding to a question from Jay Leno on the *Tonight* show about whether he might run for the presidency some day, he said, "I wouldn't want to live in a country where I was president." Phyllis Diller ridiculed her ungainly appearance and Joan Rivers emphasized her supposed lack of sexual attractiveness. She once described herself as a homely kid, adding "When the boys in the neighborhood played doctor, they made me the receptionist." In the same vein, Rodney Dangerfield, who constantly complains that he "gets no respect" once said that "If it weren't for pickpockets, I wouldn't have any sex life at all."

The verbal put-down is just one of the devices comedians use to disparage themselves. Some put the spotlight on what we might usually think of as physical disabilities. Ed Wynn, who came to prominence as a stage comedian in the 1920s and went on to star in radio and television, added to the inane impressions he made by exaggerating his natural lisp. The actors Andy Devine and Eddie Anderson, who played Rochester on the *Jack Benny Show*, made their raucous voices essential elements in their comedy personas. David Letterman made his gap-toothed grin a feature that elicits smiles and gives him identity.

Comedians have also used costumes to make themselves look ridiculous. Phyllis Diller purposely designed clothes that emphasized her skinny legs. The movie comedians Charlie Chaplin and Harry Langdon helped make themselves figures of fun by wearing jackets that were too small and shoes that were too big. Memorable in the TV shows starring Red Skelton were the outrageous hats he often wore.

Comedians are not the only people who have made us laugh by putting themselves down. The newscaster Connie Chung once described herself as "America's best known yellow journalist." Despite many years of brilliant service as a Detroit Tiger's short stop, Alan Trammell, who later became the team's manager, has remained an exceptionally modest person. He said at one time, "Fans keep pestering me for autographs. They bring me a baseball and ask me to see whether I can get Cecil Fielder to sign it." Fielder was one of the team's noted home-run hitters during Trammell's playing days.

A writer noted for his inability to spell had a bumper sticker made up which read: "Poor spellers of the world, untie."

Even politicians take part in the game of self disparagement. Abraham Lincoln sometimes drew attention to his gawky figure and homely face. When a political opponent accused him of being hypocritical, Lincoln responded by saying, "If I were two-faced would I be wearing this one?" The erstwhile presidential candidate Ross Perot on at least one occasion apparently joined comedians and cartoonists in making fun of his somewhat outsized ears. In one of the 1992 presidential debates, he responded to a question from the audience by saying, "I'm all ears." A burst of laughter followed. His response might have been unplanned, of course, but the glint I saw in his eyes suggested that he made it deliberately to provoke laughter.

Vice president Al Gore is another politician who has taken a taunt leveled at him by comedians and used it against himself. In an appearance on *Late Night with David Letterman* he mocked his own awkwardness of manner by saying, "You can always identify the vice president when he's surrounded by Secret Service agents. He's the stiff one." He also seized the opportunity to poke fun at his boss, Bill Clinton. Using Letterman's "Top Ten List" framework, Gore listed ten advantages of being vice president.

One of them was, "You get to eat all of the French fries the president doesn't get to."

Breaking Taboos and Self Satisfaction

Society surrounds us with taboos and restraints that put a limit on what we can say or do. We accept most of these controls willingly, recognizing that they serve everyone's best interest. Some of the less crucial ones, however, occasionally cause us to grind our teeth in frustration, and when we challenge them successfully, we experience a sense of gratification. Jokes that break through taboos can also induce this same kind of feeling in audiences. The mechanism is the same as the one operating when audiences share the feeling of superiority and victory that comes when someone triumphs in a duel of wits or belittles another person with a naked put-down.

One of society's longest standing taboos puts limits on the open discussion of subjects with sexual connotations. When comedians flout this taboo, audiences usually laugh. It is easy to conclude from this that talking about sex is, in and of itself, funny. It is not the topic per se, however, that causes audiences to laugh. It is the fact that discussing it violates a restraint. Participating vicariously in breaking the taboo, the audience experiences the self-satisfaction that generates laughter.

That it is the defiance of the restriction not the reference to sex that causes laughter can be shown by the fact that challenging other types of restraints can also make audiences laugh. Most people, for example, do not openly ridicule their employers unless they have another job firmly in hand, yet sometimes at company picnics or office parties just that sort of ridicule goes on. The occasion brings the bars temporarily down, and this breaking through repression causes the employees to laugh uproariously. The same phenomenon occurs when university students at end-of-term parties, their inhibitions temporarily loosened by the implicit permissiveness that comes into play on such occasions, make fun of their professors. I have never heard students laugh louder than the time one of them gave an impression of me at such a party, revealing, incidentally, idiosyncrasies of manner I didn't know I possessed.

Among the most rigid restrictions are those governing the behavior of military personnel. Bob Hope discovered in the many performances he gave at military bases that making fun of the authoritarian rule under which his listeners lived could provoke greater laughter than even jokes with a sexual connotation. Performing before an audience of naval recruits, for example, he referred to the boot camp at which they were stationed as "a concentration camp on our side." A burst of overwhelming laughter followed.

Sometimes using a single word not commonly heard in polite society can make an audience laugh. The word does not necessarily need a sexual connotation to have that effect. All that matters is that using it is generally forbidden. George Bernard Shaw found out during the first production of his play *Pygmalion* in 1915 how much effect a single word can have. In one scene the character Eliza responds to another character by saying "Not bloody likely" and in so doing spoke a word never before uttered on a British stage by a woman. The audience burst into laughter and went on laughing for so long that Shaw became worried that the rhythm of the drama was being disrupted.

I observed this same phenomena some thirty years ago during the production of a play on the University of Michigan campus. At intervals during the performance a character used the word shit which I, and presumably a young woman sitting across the aisle from me, had never heard from a stage before. Though the play was not a comedy but was, in fact, a tragedy of the starkest kind, each occurrence of the word caused the young woman to break into laughter so unrestrained that at times tears ran down her cheeks.

One factor affecting an audience response to the breaking of a taboo is the nature of the situation in which it occurs and the character of the person who does the breaking. The use of a forbidden word or the making of a sexual reference by one type of person in a certain situation may scarcely evoke any response at all, whereas the use of the same word or the making of the same reference by another type of person in a different situation may cause a thunderous reaction. In the case of Shaw's play it was the fact a woman spoke the naughty word that made the difference. A former pastor of mine, the Reverend Robert Wallace, discovered how much these factors can influence an audience's response when he told the following story during one of his sermons:

A little girl asked her grandmother how old she was. The grandmother answered tartly, "That's my business."

"Well, will you tell me how much you weigh?"

"That's also my business."

Some time later the grandmother's driver's license slipped out of her purse and fell to the floor. The little girl found it and holding it triumphantly in her hand, came up to her grandmother.

"Now I know you're 63 years old, and you weigh 145 pounds." The little girl paused briefly, and then added, "I also know you got an F in sex."

There was a moment of shocked silence in the sanctuary before the congregation exploded in laugher. The story would probably have drawn a response in any setting, for it has all the attributes of a good joke, but the fact that it came from a minister during a church service enormously magnified its effect.

I think that Reverend Wallace was surprised by the outsized reaction, but even had he anticipated it, I suspect he would have told the story anyway. This underlines the point that in recent years great changes have taken place in the public's attitude toward what is acceptable in language and subject matter. Nowhere is this more evident than in the entertainment industries. Considering the kinds of words heard in movies these days, it is difficult to believe that a 1951 movie, *The Moon is Blue*, was denied a seal of approval by the code authority of the motion-picture industry mainly because the word "virgin" appeared a number of times in the dialogue. The denial of the seal meant that many theaters would refuse to exhibit the picture. It is worth noting that the director, Otto Preminger, refused to cut the offending word, accepting the loss of revenue as a price he was willing to pay.

A further indication of the changing standards is that once squeaky clean comic strips are employing double entendre to gain laughs. An entry in the *Beetle Bailey* series showed the commanding general of Camp Swampy going up the steps to his office as he muttered to himself, "I need some time off." Entering the room where his two secretaries were working, he added, "I haven't had any in a long time"—the only words they heard. As he disappeared into his inner sanctum, one secretary asked the other, "What hasn't he had in a long time?" and the other responded, "I can think of a hundred possibilities."

The change in public attitudes about what is acceptable obviously affects the amount of self satisfaction comedians can produce in their audiences by breaking through restraints. The following joke, which originated in the days when milkmen delivered milk house-to-house from horse-drawn vehicles, would have been considered extremely daring for its time.

> Seeing a milkman on the street outside, a woman opened an upstairs window and called out, "Do you have the time?"
>
> "I have the time, madam," the milkman replied, "If I can get someone to hold the horses."

Today that joke would raise very few eyebrows. This means that comedians must go further than they once did to achieve the effect obtained by challenging taboos. Using the word "bloody" which sent the audience viewing Shaw's play *Pygmalion* into gales of laughter in 1915 would

135

scarcely cause a ripple today. That is why some comedians have increased the salaciousness of their material and pepper their monologues with obscene words.

We might note that comedians who rely too much on shocking their audiences to get laughs soon wear out their welcome. A succession of nothing more than four-letter words quickly becomes tiresome. The best comedians still challenge taboos as a way of making people laugh, but they do so subtly rather than explicitly. Moreover, they make the breaking of a taboo part of a fully developed joke with a funny point for the audience to detect and savor.

We might note further that despite the change in what is acceptable, one can still go too far. And lowering the bars has not made the decision about the topics one should treat any easier to reach. I'll have more to say on this subject in Chapter 10 where I take up the question, "Should I tell this joke?"

Chapter 6
Triggers of Laughter:
Incongruity and Surprise

Wit surprises, humor illuminates.

Eli Schleifer

In the previous chapter we examined one of the main triggers of laughter—self satisfaction. There are two other effects produced by jokes that can also trigger laughter. One is the perception by the audience that an incongruity exists in the material presented by the joke teller. The other is the feeling of surprise an audience experiences when the joke maker abruptly switches from one meaning to another or changes contexts.

Incongruity arises when the elements in a situation do not fit together, when words, for example, fail to match in tone the situation to which they are applied, or when ideas presented to an audience are so inconsistent they nullify each other. Other terms that suggest incongruity are inadequacy and inappropriateness. Surprise is somewhat easier to define. It occurs when audiences are confronted with the unexpected.

As we noted in Chapter 2, most jokes involving incongruity also deliver a surprise, and the reverse is also true. It appears, however, that in some jokes incongruity is the main provoker of laughter. In others surprise is primarily responsible. Consider the following quatrain:

Willie poisoned his father's tea;

Father died in agony.

Mother came and looked quite vexed:

"Really, Will," she said, "What next?"

The reaction of the mother to her son's deed is unquestionably surprising. What makes the quatrain so amusing, however, is the utter unsuitability of her response to the gravity of her son's deed. One would think he had merely tipped over a glass of milk. Incongruity appears to be the main trigger of laughter in this instance.

Other jokes, in contrast, make surprise the principal comic element. Here is an example:

An airline pilot was asked by a doctor during a medical examination, "When did you have your last sex experience?"

The pilot replied, "1999."

"So long ago? the astonished doctor asked.

The pilot took a look at his watch and said, "Well, it's only 23:10 now."

An incongruity is involved in this joke also—the clash produced by thinking of 1999 as a year and then realizing it refers to the time—but the main reason we laugh is the surprise the switch in concepts causes. Recognizing that one or the other usually predominates as a laugh provoker is important to you as a joke maker. If it is incongruity, you will do everything you can to create the impression that the elements in a situation do not fit together very well. If it is surprise, you will concentrate on leading your audience into thinking a train of events is following one path only to reveal suddenly that it is going down quite another one.

Incongruity

Let us begin with a first principle. In using incongruity to make audiences laugh, you must never make it explicit by referring to it in a direct way. It is the task of your listeners to infer from the material you present in your expressed idea the existence of incompatible elements. Pointing out the incongruity denies the audience the pleasure of arriving at a perception of incongruity on its own. In saying this, of course, I am merely reiterating the point made in Chapter 4 that in constructing all jokes, listeners must be left free to draw conclusions and make inferences by themselves.

Sometimes the incongruity developed by a joke can be so obvious that everyone will notice it, and sometimes it can be so delicate that only the most discerning listeners will grasp it. In a few cases it may amount to nothing more than mere contrast. One of the factors that made the Laurel and Hardy comedies so amusing was Laurel's thinness and Hardy's fatness.

The Incongruity of Language with Character and Situation. One way of creating incongruity is to use words that do not fit the character who speaks them. The writer of *The Cosby Show* showed how to do this in a scene in which Bill Cosby, playing Dr. Huxtable, sat down with his granddaughter, Olivia, to have a serious talk. The tiny girl opened the conversation by saying, "May I be frank?" The studio audience burst into laughter.

The practice of having children respond to situations with adult-sounding expressions is common in the writing of situation comedies. Their wisecracks often excel in sophistication the gags that come from adult characters. Child characters in comic strips, such as *Peanuts*, frequently exhibit a precocious grasp of language.

Joke makers sometimes jar us by putting profane or near-profane words into the mouths of children. One of the most celebrated cartoons ever published in *The New Yorker* employed this device. Drawn by Carl Rose, it showed a mother trying to persuade her young son to eat broccoli. "It's broccoli, dear," she said enticingly.

"I say it's spinach," the child replied, "And I say to hell with it."

Incongruity can also be achieved by having such words come from people at the other end of the age spectrum. When a little old lady with blued hair and dressed in lavender and lace, whose language to a certain point has been conspicuously correct, suddenly bursts into profanity, audiences are almost certain to laugh. *The New Yorker* cartoonists through the years have been masters at creating laughter with language that fails to fit the character who speaks it. Two other examples, both drawn by Edward Koren, illustrate this type of contrast. In one, a mother is admonishing her child for being naughty and in so doing used a very unmotherlike word: "You have been a very, very bad sibling." The other cartoon, inspired by the scene in Shakespeare's *Macbeth* in which the three weird sisters recite the recipe for a wizard's brew, shows a witch stirring a vile looking concoction in a large kettle and asking a fellow sorcerer, "Would you be a dear and fetch me a toad." That one word "dear" throws the whole scene into incongruous disarray.

Portraying animals acting and talking like humans is another form of incongruity which humorists have used down through the years. It was the main device employed by Don Marquis in his stories about archie, the cockroach, and mehitabel, the cat (Archie, who ostensibly wrote the stories, couldn't reach the shift key to type capital letters). Much of the fun in the comic-page cartoons *Marmaduke* and *Garfield* comes from their assumption of human characteristics. Half the drawings in a collection of cat cartoons first published in *The New Yorker* elicit laughter by showing a cat or some other animal behaving like a human. A *New Yorker* cartoon, drawn by J. B. Handelman, achieved a double-effect incongruity first by having a bird talk and second by putting words into its mouth that clashed with what we might expect a bird of that type to say. The cartoon showed two birds sitting on a branch. One of them, apparently reacting to a complaint from the other, says, "Of course, I love you—I'm programmed to love you. I'm a goddam love bird."

Another way to create incongruity is to mismatch words with the activity to which you connect them. The newspaper humorist Kin Hubbard, who wrote under the nom de plume of Abe Martin, provided an example when he switched a word usually associated with one aspect of a druggist's work to another. "Druggist Len Small severed an artery while filling a prescription for a pork sandwich."

Professional humorists are not the only ones who create incongruity by using language that seems out of place. The Duke of Wellington, Napoleon's conqueror at Waterloo, disrupted our usual concept of the majesty and impact of that crucial battle when he said of the cavalry, "They added tone to what otherwise would have been an ugly brawl."

140

The Incongruity of Understatement. One thing that makes words sound ill-fitting is their failure to provide the force, energy, and descriptive power that a certain situation would seem to deserve. The English writer Charles Lamb, for example, titled one of this essays, "The Inconvenience Resulting from Being Hanged." Inconvenience is scarcely the word most of us would use to describe that climactic event. The same kind of delicate understatement marked a description of a similar happening by the early American humorist, Artemus Ward:

> Mr. Coe unintentionally dislocated his neck a few years since by falling from a scaffold in Illinois, a rope being twined about his neck at the time. There was a large crowd present, including the sheriff of the county.

Mark Twain was masterly in his use of the technique of understatement. A celebrated example was his cable to the Associated Press from London after some English newspapers had announced his demise: "The reports of my death are greatly exaggerated." In another instance he described a ferocious fight as "a misunderstanding conducted with crowbars."

As a boy Mark Twain had an experience that left an indelible imprint on him. He had run away from school, and to avoid going home to receive an almost certain thrashing, he crawled through the window of his father's office late at night and tried to get to sleep on the couch. But as his eyes grew accustomed to the darkness, he became aware that a "long dusky, shapeless thing lay stretched out on the floor." Moments later the moon drifting across the sky sent light through the window, revealing that the object was a corpse with its eyes "still fixed and glassy in death." On its chest he saw a ghastly wound.

To this point the language Twain used to describe his experience matched perfectly the horror of the scene. But then his tone subtly changed. In depicting what happened next—presumably a panic-stricken, headlong flight from that hideous figure on the floor—the strength of his words suddenly diminished. They became almost prosaic, coming nowhere near to reflecting the terror that was undoubtedly coursing through him.

> "I went away from there. I do not say I went away in any sort of hurry, but I simply went—that is sufficient. I went out at the window, and I carried the sash with me. I did not need the sash, but it was handier to take it than to leave it, and so I took it."

A cartoon published in *The New Yorker* many years ago used the same technique of understatement to evoke laughter. It showed a trapeze artist who had just missed catching his partner. At the bottom of the picture, you could see the victim of his clumsiness plunging to the floor. The reaction of the man who had fumbled the catch was to say, "Oops—sorry," words that might be adequate to reflect concern at dropping a dish belonging to a friend, but which did not quite measure up to the compunction one should presumably feel at sending a colleague tumbling to his death.

Euphemisms, words we substitute for the more obvious ones to soften the impact of an unpleasant truth, sometimes sound funny because they result in understatement. It is said, for example, that the makers of Rolls Royces never admit their cars break down. Their way of describing the problem is to say "The vehicle failed to proceed." The money lost by a bank because of a robbery was listed in its financial report as an "unauthorized withdrawal." A company that experienced a loss during one of its quarterly periods reported it had incurred a "negative investment increment."

<u>The Incongruity of Reactions</u>. Sometimes it is not just the use of inadequate words that creates incongruity but also the way people react to a situation. When the response is less than one would expect, it has the same laugh-producing effect as understatement. The "Oops—sorry," in *The New Yorker* cartoon just referred to was not the only incongruity. Another was the look on the face of the trapeze artist whose partner's carelessness sent him plunging to his death. Instead of reflecting outrage and fear, his expression conveys a feeling of mere annoyance.

A master at the art of under reaction was the silent-film actor, Buster Keaton. No matter what was happening to him—a devastating calamity or a blissful resolution—his face remained utterly expressionless. Underreaction was also a prime weapon in the comedy armory of Laurel and Hardy. One of their early two-reelers demonstrated the use of the technique at its best. Caught in a long line of traffic, their automobile inadvertently nudged the one in front of them. The aggrieved driver walked slowing back and stood for a moment as he gave their car an appraising look. Then suddenly bursting into maniacal action, he proceeded to rip off one of its fenders. Laurel and Hardy made no attempt to stop him; they watched with what almost appeared to be an expression of disinterest. The participants then reversed roles. Laurel and Hardy dismembered the other car in a similar fashion as its driver looked on with the same apparent complacency they had shown. This sequence was repeated over and over again until both cars were reduced to piles of rubble.

Two other great comedians of the silent-film era also made use of the technique of underreaction. Harold Lloyd in *Safety Last* kept audiences in terrified suspense as he floundered, slipped, and stumbled high above the street. His audiences gasped, but they also laughed uproariously at the incredible composure he showed as he encountered one perilous situation after another.

Charlie Chaplin in the movie many consider to be his masterpiece, *Modern Times*, also demonstrated how funny underreaction can be. Roaming about after hours with his girlfriend in the department store where he served as the night watchman, he decided to show her how well he could roller skate even while blindfolded. Unknown to him, the area he chose for his demonstration was being repaired, and the guard rail that would have kept him from plunging to the floor below had been removed. Unaware of the danger, Chaplin glided blithely around the floor. Each time he sailed with carefree insouciance to within an inch or two of the yawning abyss, the audience held its breath. And when he avoided disaster at the last moment with a dainty pirouette, it howled with laughter.

Chaplin produced rib-tickling incongruity of another sort when his girlfriend took off his blindfold. The fun arose then from the contrast between what his behavior had been and what it now became. As the realization of his danger flooded in on him, his limbs, so supple a moment before, suddenly became as rigid as sticks. Gyrating clumsily on the edge of disaster, he finally managed to crawl in stiff-legged terror away from the brink.

Sometimes reactions create incongruity not only because they fail to measure up to the gravity of what is happening but also because they are so clearly out of place. Classic examples of this type of absurdity occur in one of Woody Allen's early films, *Take the Money and Run*. Woody, playing a man embarked on a career of crime, enters a bank and presents a note to the teller demanding money and warning that he has a gun. Instead of complying, the teller explains that a withdrawal of the type he is requesting must be approved by a vice president. That gentleman, whose arrival Woody patiently awaits, then points out that Woody has misspelled a number of words in his robbery note.

The Incongruity of Exaggeration. Giving a situation less than it deserves creates an imbalance which makes it funny. Giving it more also creates incongruity by producing a different kind of imbalance. We call this effect exaggeration. It occurs when you take an idea, a characteristic, or a situation further than your audience might reasonably expect it to go. Caricaturists do this when they expand their subjects' ears, noses, and chins into grotesque magnifications of the real thing. Some editorial cartoonists, for example, make the ears of the second President George Bush so large that were he to run down the street, one can almost see him taking off in flight.

Words can also build images that exceed ordinary expectation. Mark

Twain, a master of the art of understatement, was equally proficient at making readers laugh by using the technique of exaggeration. In his short story "The Jumping Frog of Calaveras County" he told about a man who won a frog-jumping contest by pouring buckshot down the throat of his rival's frog. The story's publication made Mark Twain famous overnight. It is still commemorated today in a yearly frog-jumping contest held in the county in California where the story was set.

The radio and television comedian Jack Benny used exaggeration to make clear to his audience how incredibly stingy he was. He had a pay telephone installed in his home for the use of his guests. He had a vault built far below his home in which he kept his money. At intervals he made a journey into the depths to make sure that his fortune was still intact. In the radio version of his program, this piece of exaggeration was particularly effective because sound effects stimulated the audience into recognizing the extreme steps Benny had taken to safeguard his money. As the clanging of metal on metal and the rattling of chains echoed in the tunnel leading to his vault, listeners could visualize the opening and closing of immense steel doors and the removal and replacement of the chains used to reinforce them. The climactic exaggeration came when Benny reached his guard, Ed, who spent his life in the abyss below guarding Benny's money. Ed's plaintive question, "How are things on the outside?" was guaranteed to send the audience into paroxysms of laughter.

A similar flight of fancy characterized a remark the comedian Henny Youngman made about a man who had a vasectomy performed at a Sears department store. "Now every time he makes love the garage door opens." In the same imaginative league was the stand-up comedian Jack Douglas's story about the sad end his girlfriend met in the Radio City Music Hall. On her way to the ladies room, she made a wrong turn and ended up on the stage where the Rockettes kicked her to death.

You do not have to use exaggerations as elaborate as these, however, to make audiences laugh. Going just a little bit beyond normal expectation can also be highly amusing. An Irish attorney once used subtle overstatement to fend off a judge who liked to humiliate lawyers with insulting questions. Interrupting the attorney while he was arguing a point, the judge asked sarcastically whether the attorney's clients were aware of the doctrine of *de minimas non cural lex*? "I assure your lordship," the attorney responded in a silky voice, "that in the remote village where my clients live that doctrine is a constant topic of conversation." A response less subtle might well have earned him a contempt citation. The Latin phrase means, incidentally, that "the matter is so small the law has no cure for it."

Two cartoons in *The New Yorker* illustrate how funny modest exaggeration can be. The inspiration for one, drawn by Dean Vietor, came from the habit some overly solicitous waiters have of returning to a table over and over again to ask, "Is everything all right?" The cartoon showed a woman who has just answered the telephone at home turning to her husband and saying, "It's the waiter at the restaurant where we ate tonight. He wants to know if everything is still all right."

The other *New Yorker* cartoonist, Michael Crawford, went about the same distance beyond normal expectation when he showed a man in an office with his feet on the desk. Apparently he was one of those bosses who expects his secretary to serve him coffee and perform other menial tasks. Punching the intercom, he said, "Sandy, could you step in here and put my feet back down on the floor, please?"

A framework for jokes employing exaggeration was often used by Johnny Carson on the *Tonight* show. He would make a statement such as, "I have a very fat girlfriend" and then look meaningfully at the audience. It had learned from watching previous shows to shout back, "How fat was she?" and he would respond with something like "She was so fat she had to let out the shower curtain." Sometimes Carson responded with more than one exaggeration. When he mentioned that he had stayed at the swankiest hotel in the country, the audience naturally shouted, "How swank was it?" He replied, "It was so swank the outside was air conditioned. It was large too. You had to make a long-distance call to reach room service. And when you ordered a sandwich, it came by carrier pigeon."

Words are not always needed to create an exaggeration. Actions alone can do it. In one of the routines presented by the pianist and raconteur Victor Borge, a soprano standing next to him emitted a note so high and piercing that the startled Borge fell of the bench. Scrambling to his feet, he opened the cover of the bench and took out a seat belt.

The television comedian Sid Caesar often took a simple act far beyond its usual bounds with a visual exaggeration. Playing a doctor, he would not only put the stethoscope on the patient's chest, but on his shoulder, his arm, his hand, and on the floor as well. In this case words capped the effect as he said, "I'm afraid you have termites."

The Incongruity of Sound-Alike Words. In an earlier chapter I mentioned Mrs. Malaprop, one of the most famous characters in all literature. She helped make Richard Sheridan's play, *The Rivals*, a comic masterpiece by using words that seemed to fit a situation, but which actually only resembled in sound the words she should have used. She said, for example, that "Few gentlemen nowadays know how to value the ineffectual

WILLIS - How to be Funny on Purpose

qualities in a woman." She advised her niece regarding a certain young man to "illiterate him, I say, quite from your memory," and in another instance she said, "Lead the way, and we'll precede."

Sheridan was not the first dramatist to make us laugh by using that technique. Shakespeare in *Much Ado About Nothing* created the character Dogberry, a political official, whose slightly off-center words is the main comic element in a number of scenes. After making an arrest he says, "I have comprehended two aspicious persons." In another scene he denounces a rascal with these words: "O, villain! Thou wilt be condemned into everlasting redemption for this." General practice, however, has conferred on Sheridan rather than on Shakespeare the honor of naming such errors, for they are now known as malapropisms, not dogberrys.

Words that are simply misused even though they do not resemble a correct word can also be funny. In *Roughing It* Mark Twain remarked that "the horses are bituminous from long deprivation." And in one of O. Henry's short stories, a woman whose choice of words reminds one of Mrs. Malprop, complains that a certain man "has made proposals to me sufficiently obnoxious to ruffle the ignominy of any lady."

The Incongruity of Conflicting Connotations. Ill-chosen words (or well-chosen in the case of a humorist) can make us laugh by creating a conflict that disrupts our perception of a generally accepted concept. A famous *New Yorker* cartoon showed two Greek gods sipping a drink as one of them commented, "This is good ambrosia but it's not great ambrosia." The line generates conflict by qualifying a substance that by its very nature as a drink fit for the gods can never be qualified.

An even more direct conflict between perception and statement was created by James Hilton in his novel *Lost Horizon* when a character named Chang, explaining the philosophy of life prevailing in Shangri-La, the strange land into which some visitors had wandered, said this:

> Our private belief is in moderation. We inculcate the virtue of avoiding excess of all kinds—even including, if you will pardon the paradox, excess of virtue itself. I think I can claim that our people are moderately sober, moderately chaste, and moderately honest.

A manifestly ill-suited verb clashed with the dialogue line it followed in a passage in one of Ring Lardner's short stories. A father out for a walk with his son became confused about where they were. "Are you lost, Daddy?" the son asked. "Shut up," the father explained.

Laughable conflicts often arise because the impression a person is trying to make nullifies what the person actually says. That was true of the man who remarked, "Of my traits, the one that pleases me most is my humbleness," and of another who said, "I don't believe all this astrology nonsense. We Scorpios aren't gullible enough for that."

Conflict in thought is readily apparent in the complaint a woman made to a restaurant owner, "Your food is rotten and the portions are too small." Conflict between intent and words leaps out in the counsel a woman gave a friend: "You simply *must* stop taking advice from other people." And the last word in the following classified ad creates a conflict that turns the whole sequence of ideas upside down. "Lost—brown and white dog, blind in one eye, left ear bitten off, can't hear, recently castrated. Answers to the name of *Lucky*."

The Incongruity of Irrelevance. Another way of creating incongruity is to drop an irrelevancy into an otherwise logical statement. In one of his movies, Groucho Marx said, "I'd horsewhip you if I had a horse." It takes a moment to realize that a horse has nothing to do with his contemplated action. The same kind of inspired irrelevancy appears in a comment Marx made in another movie after feeling the pulse of a man he found lying unconscious in the street. "Either this man is dead or my watch has stopped."

It was a frequent practice of the Canadian humorist, Stephen Leacock, to introduce irrelevancies at unlikely moments. His parody of romantic fiction, "Gertrude the Governess," began with two of them, one in two lines that followed the title, and the other in the opening paragraph.

Synopsis of Previous Chapters:
There are no Previous Chapters.

It was a wild and stormy night on the West Coast of Scotland. This, however, is immaterial to the present story, as the scene is not laid in the west of Scotland. For the matter of that the weather was just as bad on the East Coast of Ireland.

The Incongruity of Ambiguity. Sometimes ideas in a joke swirl about in such a confusing way that our reaction becomes equally confused. Ambiguity can be funny at times because it creates incongruity. In the musical comedy, *Anything Goes*, the actor, Victor Moore, spoke this line: "As to capital punishment: If it was good enough for my father, it's good enough for me." Two people asked to interpret the line's meaning are likely to reach different conclusions. The point of a statement made by Jay Leno is equally difficult to pin down. He said that when he came from his native Massachusetts to California, the first thing he noticed was that the beaches all faced the wrong way.

In one of his books, the novelist Peter De Vries commented that "Someone who goes to a psychiatrist ought to have his head examined."

The writer Goodman Ace, fighting a sinus infection, said, "I need a sinus like I need a hole in the head." And a doctor told by his receptionist that there was a man in the waiting room who claimed to be invisible, responded, "Tell him I can't see him." Reacting to the first joke, the puzzled audience is likely to think, "But that's what psychiatrists do—examine heads"; to the second, "But a sinus is a hole in the head"; to the third, "Of course, he can't see him—he says he's invisible"—all examples of meaning receding into the kind of ambiguity that causes laughter.

<u>The Incongruity of Nonsense.</u> When ambiguity is carried far enough, all meaning vanishes and the result is nonsense. In an earlier chapter I quoted Yogi Berra's statement: "Nobody goes to that restaurant anymore; it's too crowded." Because he seems momentarily to be making sense, we may even nod our head in understanding. Then we realize that the two ideas in his statement completely nullify each other. The collapse of meaning creates an incongruity which makes us laugh.

Conveying an aura of plausibility for an instant or two is an important factor in making nonsense funny. A statement that is patently absurd from the moment you hear it is not likely to make you laugh. The line "I went to a garden to find a pumpkin to make an apple pie" may amuse children but not their parents. Mere gibberish is also deficient in laugh-producing power. President Gerald Ford once said, "Things are more like they are now than they have ever been." Listeners would have difficulty drawing out of this sentence any line of thought at all.

This suggests another characteristic of the best nonsense. Even though its elements when rigidly analyzed add up to nothing, it is still possible to draw from it some nugget of meaning. Yogi Berra's comment about the restaurant no one goes to is obviously absurd on the surface, but we can nevertheless see the point he was trying to make. A statement Groucho Marx made about the actress Doris Day—"I knew her before she was a virgin"—causes us to reflect on the movies in which she managed to remain pristine despite the efforts of heavy-breathing males to seduce her. A little boy's plaintive question to a baggage handler in an airport—"Have you seen a woman around here without a kid that looks like me?"—at least makes clear the kind of predicament in which he finds himself. And the statement "If you put a baby into water and it gets pink, you know the water's too hot for your elbow" gives an audience the chance to rearrange the words into a familiar admonition about child care.

Having said all this, I must admit that nonsense without any redeeming air of plausibility or suggestion of meaning can still be funny if it is done well enough. Most of us laugh at the utter absurdities in Lewis Carroll's

Alice in Wonderland. In Gilbert and Sullivan's *The Mikado*, the hero Nanki-Poo disguises himself as a second trombone. The idea of doing so is absurdity at its purest without any taint of reason and yet it still convulses audiences with laughter. In one of his stand-up routines, the comedian Steven Wright reported that "A fellow had been caught counterfeiting pennies because he got the heads and the tails on the wrong side." This is also sheer, unadulterated nonsense lacking any semblance of plausibility or hint of logic, yet it is funny nevertheless.

Nonsense often seems to spring to the lips of those who are best at it in a seeming flash which reveals no hint of technique or prior design. If you want to help inspiration along, however, the examples cited suggests certain useful approaches. One way to create nonsense is to put words into a sentence that do not merely conflict with each other but which totally nullify the other's meaning. Tallulah Bankhead is reputed to have said, for example, "We spent last night reminiscing about the future." In his novel, *The Tunnel of Love*, Peter De Vries accomplished the feat of constructing a sentence made up entirely of two mutually incompatible words. It came when an adulterous man, panting to begin the culminating act, mumbled to his partner, "Foreplay later."

A second way of creating nonsense is to begin with a plausible statement and then negate it with an absurdity. To the examples of this technique already given, one can add Rodney Dangerfield's confession. "To stop drinking I joined Alcoholics Anonymous. I still drink, but now I do it under an assumed name."

A third way of creating nonsense is to make characters exhibit what one might call illogical unreasonableness. This technique is illustrated in a story the columnist Sidney Harris said was the only mother-in-law joke he found amusing. It told of a woman who gave her son-in-law two neckties for his birthday. When he appeared the next day wearing one of the ties, she challenged him with this question: "What's the matter? Didn't you like the other one?"

This next story also reflects unreasonableness, but it is meant to be helpful rather than antagonistic:

A father went for a walk one day with his son. They happened to go by a store selling TV sets, and the son asked his father to explain how television pictures travel through space. "I'm afraid I can't tell you that," the father replied. "I never studied electronics."

Continuing their walk, they came to a man who had raised the hood of his car and was looking down intently at the motor. "Can you tell me how a gasoline engine works?" the boy asked.

"You're out of my area again," the father explained.

A little while later it began to rain. The youngster looked up at the sky, "Say, Dad," the boy began, and then said, "Well, never mind."

"Go ahead," said the father. "Ask the question. How else are you ever going to learn anything?"

Surprise

We turn now to the type of joke in which an unexpected twist or sudden shift in concept is the prime factor in triggering audience laughter. Just as we saw that certain types of patterns can create a perception of incongruity so we can discern a group of patterns that produce the phenomenon we call surprise. The major ingredient in all of them is deception. You lead your audience into believing you are following one line of thought and then abruptly switch to another.

<u>Multiple-Meaning Words</u>. The major instrument for creating surprise is a word that has more than one meaning. Fortunately for comedians, a great many words have that characteristic. When you produce surprise by using the same word to mean two different things, we call the result a pun. You can also create puns by using words that sound the same but have different meanings, such as "scent" and "cent" and "bear" and "bare," and even by using words that sound almost the same, such as "closed" and "clothed."

Puns are an element in a great many different kinds of jokes. Their use is so prevalent that they have been called the foundation stone of humor. This does not mean that everyone likes them. They have been condemned as superficial instruments of humor which trick audiences into laughter, and have even been denounced as scourges upon humanity. Despite all this condemnation, puns, like death and taxes, have always been with us and probably always will be. We can be pretty sure our cave-dwelling ancestors began creating them as soon as their primitive grunts evolved into language many thousands of years ago. Puns appeared in the writings of the Greeks and Romans, and they have been a significant element in most of the cultures that followed.

Puns can do more for the comedian than merely create surprise. They can contribute materially to developing the kind of humor we call wordplay. I discuss wordplay later in this book, and I also take up the vexing question of whether puns deserve the bad reputation they seem to have earned. For now, however, we concentrate on the use of puns to create surprise. Here is an example:

Two old maids went for a tramp in the woods. The tramp got away.

The surprise in this joke comes from a switch in the meaning of two different expressions—"tramp" and "went for." Note how deceptively the joke maker deludes the audience into thinking they refer to a type of exercise before suddenly revealing that "tramp" refers to a person, not an activity, and that the term "went for" twists around to connote something quite different from the bland meaning first suggested.

The comic versifier Richard Emmons engaged in a similar type of deception in the following quatrain:

Our bathroom has besides the ones
Connected to the water,
A fixture others may not boast,
A fifteen-year-old daughter.

The Hallmark Company used a different kind of pun to communicate the same kind of thought in designing a card meant to be sent to a daughter about to be married:

We have been trying to decide
What to do with the room in
Which you spent so many years.
We have decided to keep it
A bathroom.

Sometimes you can assign the task of misdirecting an audience to a character you create, rather than doing it yourself. In the following story, it is clear that one of the participants lures his companion down the wrong track by deliberately applying a commonly used expression in a way no one would anticipate:

After a college student had returned to his dormitory after a date, his roommate asked him how the evening with his new girlfriend had gone. "Not too well," the roommate answered. "She used too many four-letter words for my taste."

"Really? I didn't think she was that kind of girl."

"Well, she is. All she kept saying was 'stop,' 'don't,' and 'quit that.'"

In some instances you can reveal a difference in meaning simply by arranging to have one person in your story view a word or phrase in one light while a second person sees it in another. The result is that their thoughts go careening down different tracks. In the following story, for example, one character uses a word as an adjective, the second thinks of it as a disparaging nickname.

151

A woman went to a marriage counselor hoping to track down the cause of the marital discord she was experiencing. At one point in the interview, the counselor asked, "Did you wake up grumpy this morning?"

"No," the wife responded. "I let him sleep."

In this next story, the same word is meant by one character to refer to a type of activity, but is snatched at eagerly by the second as a reference to a person.

A husband was telling his wife what he would do if he won the state lottery. "I'll buy a new car, fix up the house, and make some investments. And you, honey, can have any cruise you want."

Without a moment's hesitation, the wife replied, "I'll take Tom."

A similar type of preoccupation led the young women in the next two stories to place meanings on terms never intended—in one case by the designer of a questionnaire, and in the other by a convention visitor.

A girl who had just graduated from high school was filling out a college application form. In the space that called for her to list her graduation date, she wrote "Bill Foster."

A young woman had volunteered to serve at the information desk for a convention of business people. One of the delegates came up to her and asked, "Do I register with you?"

"Not particularly," she replied, "but what did you have in mind?"

Having one character use a term in a conventional manner while the second takes an unconventional track is another way of surprising an audience, as the following story illustrates:

A young reporter was interviewing a woman on her hundredth birthday. The old lady's eyes danced with excitement as she talked about a life which had spanned the period of the covered wagon to that of the airplane. The conversation then moved to matters of health. "Have you ever been bedridden?" the reporter asked.

"Hundreds of time," the old lady replied, "And twice in a haystack."

Having a character take an expression that is meant figuratively and apply it literally can also be a fruitful source of surprise.

In an opening statement to a PTA group, the president emphasized it would be better for everyone if schools and parents could get closer together. A father rose to his feet and said, "I certainly agree because then I wouldn't have so far to walk to the PTA meetings."

Sometimes you can give your joke a double-barreled effect by having different characters interpret two expressions in two different ways. The following joke illustrates the technique:

A French visitor to England was being given a tour of a college for women. "Notice that lady in front of us," the guide said. "She is the mistress of Ridsley Hall."

"And who," asked the visitor, "is Ridsley Hall?"

Puns are powerful instruments for achieving surprise as the preceding illustrations show, but you can also use them on occasion to accomplish other purposes. Sometimes they can serve to stimulate a thought or reflection which can materially enrich the effect of a joke. In the following story, for example, a classical pianist employed a play on words to suggest in a subtle way his disdain for a certain type of contemporary music. When he was asked to name his favorite rock group, he replied, "The one on Mount Rushmore."

The wry switch in the meaning of a phrase in the following statement from a friendly to hostile interpretation not only surprises, but it may also evoke thoughts about the nature of humankind.

It's a sure sign someone has been thinking of you when you find a tack on your chair.

John Ralston used a play on words to convey a refreshing admission of a certain type of failure when he explained why he had quit as the coach of the Denver Broncos. "I resigned because of illness and fatigue. The fans were sick and tired of me."

By assigning different meanings to the same expression you can also show how age groups differ in their outlook on life. The following story, for example, suggests that young people may be mistaken about the thoughts that occupy their elders:

A young person talking with his grandfather said, "I suppose as you get older, you tend to think more about the hereafter than you used to."

"You're certainly right about that, son," the old man responded. "I keep opening closets and refrigerators, and then I have to stop and think, 'What am I here after?'"

Switching the Perception of a Situation. Suddenly substituting one interpretation of a word or phrase with another is unquestionably an effective way of surprising an audience, but it is by no means the only one. You can accomplish the same result by suddenly revealing that the impression of a situation you have led the audience into accepting is the wrong one. Again, deception is involved. An episode from a Jack Benny radio show illustrates the technique:

153

Jack: It's a little embarrassing to say this, but your bathing suit is a bit snug and skimpy.

Mary: If you don't like it, go in and take it off.

This may be a good time to point out that the medium in which you work exerts some control over the way in which you should present your material. Radio was a perfect vehicle for the sequence just cited, but Jack Benny obviously couldn't transfer the gag to his television program without making some modifications. To avoid spoiling the surprise, he would have to tell the story in retrospect, with Mary, perhaps, as the narrator. "Jack told me my bathing suit was a bit snug and skimpy so I told him that if he didn't like it, he could go in and take it off." That surprises communicated in this way can still be funny was demonstrated by Groucho Marx in one of his films. The joke, one of his best remembered ones, also involved the question of who was wearing a particular garment. "I shot an elephant in my pajamas. What he was doing in my pajamas I'll never know."

It would be difficult to tell some jokes on either radio or television without giving the point away. The only way to conceal the surprise in the following joke until the end is to present it orally or in print:

A husband became worried that his wife was losing her hearing. He decided to test it by speaking to her from different distances. Standing 30 feet away he called out, "Can you hear me?" Hearing no response, he moved to within 20 feet of her and repeated his question. Still hearing no answer, he moved 10 feet closer and called out, "Now can you hear me?"

This time he did hear her response.

"Yes, dear, for the third time, yes."

You can dramatize some jokes of this type, however, by keeping the element that would telegraph the surprise out of the picture. The following story provides an example:

A young couple had planned to elope during the early morning hours. When the appointed time came, the prospective groom began tapping on the upper story window of his loved one. She opened the window to find her future husband standing on a ladder. "Are you all packed?" he asked.

"Yes," the woman answered, "But don't talk so loud. You'll wake my father."

"Wake him?" the groom responded. "Who do you think is holding the ladder?"

For most of you the critical question regarding the medium in which you present a joke is to decide whether the funniness of something seen in print will carry over when you deliver it orally. Consider the following, for example:

An Annapolis midshipman taking a course in English wrote that Sancho Panza "always rode a burrow." His professor wrote in the margin, "*Burro* is an ass. *Burrow* is a hole in the ground. As a future naval officer, you are expected to know the difference."

The problem in simply telling this joke is that the distinction between the words "burro" and "burrow" disappears because they sound the same. Recognizing that distinction is crucial, of course, to getting the point. You might spell out the words, but the clumsiness of doing so would probably snuff out most of the humor.

Another example of the same problem is a notice posted on a campus bulletin board: HOTEL WORKERS WANTED. ONLY THE INN-EXPERIENCED NEED APPLY. There is no good way of using this item in an oral presentation without losing the ingenious pun. An audience hearing it would simply be confused about what the point is. The same problem would arise if you tried to insert the following joke into a conversation: "Do you know what 'ecumenism' means? It means getting to know the opposite sects." The clever play on words, which would be obvious to a reader, would be lost on listeners, and they would be baffled as well.

It is clear that when considering whether to tell a joke you have seen in a magazine, newspaper, or on the Internet, you must make sure your audience will understand the point when they hear rather than see the words. Does the same kind of admonition apply when you convert a joke you have heard into print? To begin with, this situation arises much less often than the previous one. It can also be said that a printed version of a spoken joke is almost certain to communicate the point. However, there are some jokes that may work a little better in oral rather than in printed form. One reason is that a skilled comedian can sometimes make even a bad joke sound good. There also are some jokes, it seems, whose points can be grasped more readily by listeners rather than readers. I saw the following in a newspaper, for example:

The golfer, Chi Chi Rodriquez wonders whether he speaks English well enough. He asked his caddie for a sand wedge and he brought him a ham on rye.

I think the pun would have leaped out a little more quickly if we could have heard Chi Chi say those words rather than seeing them in print. The same applies to the following somewhat artificial build up to a forced pun:

A bartender was startled to hear a voice coming from one of the bottles behind him. It appeared to be issuing orders to the other bottles on the shelf. "Straighten up," it ordered. "Get your labels around to the front and shake off that dust."

Turning around, the bartender said, "It's fine to hear you talk. But why are you giving orders?"

"I just can't help it," the bottle replied, "I guess I'm just a born liter."

For my part, and I may be a little obtuse, I found I didn't really grasp the pun until I had read the last sentence aloud.

Coming back now to the various ways to achieve surprise, let us turn from jokes that mislead an audience about the nature of a situation to those that surprise by having a character respond in a totally unexpected way. The Pepsi-Cola Company made skillful use of this technique in one of its commercials. It showed the star basketball player Shaquille O'Neal walking off a court after a grueling practice session. It is a hot day and the perspiration is streaming down his face. On the sidelines he sees a tiny boy holding a cold bottle of Pepsi-Cola in his hand. Next to him is an ice bucket, but Shaq sees immediately that all the bottles are gone. Looking back at the boy, he smiles ingratiatingly and tentatively reaches out his hand. Instead of handing over the bottle to this celebrated player, as one would think he would, the tiny tyke's features tighten into a threatening grimace, and between clenched teeth he pipes a warning, "Don't even think about it."

It is interesting to compare that commercial with one produced several years ago by Pepsi's chief rival, the Coca Cola company. The ingredients were the same—a star athlete—in Coca Cola's case, Mean Joe Greene, a player for the Pittsburgh Steelers—leaving a stadium after an exhausting game and a little boy standing at the exit with a cold bottle of Coca Cola in his hands. In the Coca Cola commercial, however, the normal expectations of the audience were realized. The boy impulsively hands over his drink to the athlete he obviously idolizes. In return, the football player rips off his jersey and tosses it to the big-eyed boy. Both commercials were impressive examples of the advertiser's art. The effect of the Coca Cola commercial was to warm viewers' hearts. The effect of the Pepsi-Cola commercial was to make them laugh.

The humorist Will Rogers once used the technique of defying normal expectation to win a wager with his friend Harvey Firestone, founder of the tire company. Both had been invited to a reception at the White House, which was occupied at that time by President Calvin Coolidge. Coolidge was noted for the grim, unsmiling face he usually presented to photographers. People might well wonder whether his stern visage ever loosened into a smile, much less a laugh. This public impression was reflected in a remark made by Dorothy Parker, a well-known wit of the period. When told that Coolidge had died, she responded, "How can they tell?" Firestone bet Rogers $100 that he couldn't make Coolidge laugh and Rogers accepted the wager. Arriving at the White House, he joined the reception line and finally made his way to where the president stood. The usual introductions took place. Rogers then leaned forward to the president and said, "I'm sorry I didn't get the name." He won the bet.

Sometimes reactions are unexpected because they fail to conform with the image the audience has of the person from whom they come. Most of us, for example, have a general perception of how psychiatrists would respond in certain situations. The reaction of the psychiatrist in the following story violates that perception:

> A man became worried about the strange behavior of his brother so he decided to visit a psychiatrist. "My brother goes into a bar," he explained, "orders wine in a goblet, and after he's swallowed the wine, he eats all of the goblet except the stem. I've seen him do that several times in one sitting."
>
> "You mean he keeps eating goblets and leaving the stems?"
>
> "That's right. Don't you think that's odd?"
>
> "I certainly do," the psychiatrist replied. The stems are the best part."

The same kind of unexpectedness characterizes a comment made by a man who was operating a business with a partner. He had been invited by a professor at a local college to talk to a class about business ethics. During the course of this lecture he presented this hypothetical problem:

> "Suppose a customer buys a product costing five dollars and hands you a twenty-dollar bill to pay for it? When you get to the cash register, you realize there's another twenty-dollar bill stuck to it. Now you have an ethical decision to make. Are you going to tell your partner?"

Double-Track Surprises. As noted earlier in this chapter, you can achieve surprise by having characters interpret the same word in two different ways. You can achieve the same kind of surprise by having characters focus on two different aspects of a situation. The surprise comes when you reveal the existence of this dual focus. In the following joke, for example, it suddenly becomes clear that the thoughts of the wife and the husband are on different tracks:

> A young wife came up to her baby's crib to find her husband staring down at it with an intent expression on his face. She looked

at the little form the crib held and turned eyes glowing with love on her husband. "Isn't this wonderful?" she breathed happily.

"It certainly is," he replied. "I just can't figure out how you ever managed to find a crib like this for just $69.75."

The switch in that joke is from an emotional to a practical concern. In the following joke it is clear that one of the participants is thinking about the characters in a play, the other about the actors who performed them:

One of John Barrymore's most notable portrayals was of the title character in Shakespeare's *Hamlet*. At the end of one of his performances, a reporter asked him whether he thought Hamlet really had an affair with Ophelia.

Barrymore replied, "Only in the Chicago Company."

Sometimes the elements in a situation are both human and animal, and a double-track joke results when one participant is obviously concentrating on the human, the other on the animal, as the following jokes illustrate:

A circus owner instructed a friend of his to watch a woman animal trainer, noted for her beauty, working in a cage filled with lions. One of her tricks was to put a lump of sugar between her lips and command the lion to take it from her. "Would you like to try that?" the owner asked facetiously.

"I certainly would," the visitor replied. "But first you've got to get rid of those vicious looking lions."

A young farmer who was on the lookout for a wife met an attractive prospect at a church ice-cream social. After they had become acquainted, he asked whether she would like to come out sometime and see his farm. The date was arranged and as they were walking though a pasture, they saw a cow and calf tenderly nuzzling each other. Seizing the opportunity to make an overture, the farmer said, "You know, seeing that makes me want to do the same thing."

"Be my guest," the young woman responded. "It's your cow."

The next story utilizes precisely the same framework, the only difference being that the switch in the story is from one human to another human:

A man and wife saw a young couple sitting on a bench kissing passionately. "Why don't you do that sometime?" the wife asked.

"But I don't even know her," the husband protested.

Children often surprise us simply because their minds fasten on an aspect of a situation we had thought of as only incidental. The following joke illustrates such a shift, one that involves a change in focus from the human to the heavenly:

After bringing his wife and their new baby home, a father went to tell his five-year-old daughter the good news. "An angel has just brought you a little baby brother," he told her. "Would you like to see him?"

The little girl's response came without hesitation: "First, I'd like to see the angel."

Sometimes double-track jokes require an audience to keep in mind through most of the telling, elements on which the two tracks focus. This means that as a joke maker, you must be particularly clear about what those two tracks are. The following story exemplifies this type of joke:

A sociology professor was asked by a PTA group to talk on sex. Afraid that his wife would deluge him with wisecracks if he told her what the actual topic was, he said he had been asked to speak on sailing. The next morning the president of the PTA saw his wife in the supermarket and told her what a marvelous talk her husband had given the night before.

"I was really surprised he was willing to talk about it at all," the wife responded. "As far as I can remember, he's only done it twice. The first time his hat blew off, and the second time he got sick to his stomach."

The Matter of Length. It is axiomatic that a joke should be just long enough to make its point effectively. Some jokes can establish an expectation and reverse it in just a few seconds. The stand-up comedian, Henny Youngman, was a master at getting to the punchline in the minimum amount of time. Here are two examples of the crispness for which he is noted:

A girl kept me awake all night knocking on my door. Finally, I had to get up and let her out.

The doctor says, "You'll live to be 70.
"But I am 70."
"See, what did I tell you?"

Two cartoons deliver surprises with almost equal concision. One shows a man lying in a bed with his leg in a sling. Sitting beside him are a doctor and the patient's wife. The caption reads, "He appears to have broken his leg in two places: Charley's Lounge and Buster's Bar and Grill." The second cartoon is one in *The Lockhorns* series. In just two succinct lines it demonstrates that the thoughts of the two characters are traveling on different tracks. "How much money do we have in the bank?" Mr. Lockhorn asks. His wife replies, "I don't know. I haven't shaken it lately."

Such brevity is not always possible, however. Sometimes the delivery of a surprise requires a long and elaborate build up, as the following story illustrates:

A man was dismayed when his Rottweiler appeared at his back door with the dead body of his next-door neighbor's white rabbit in his mouth. Looking over at his neighbor's house, he saw that the door of the rabbit cage in the backyard was open. He assumed immediately that his dog had gotten into the cage and killed the rabbit. Appalled at what this would do to what had been a friendly relationship, he picked up the dead animal, cleaned it, and fluffed up its coat with a blow drier. He then sneaked over to the neighbor's yard, shoved the rabbit into the cage, and shut the door. He had been in his house only a few minutes when he heard a horrendous scream. Rushing out he saw his neighbor looking at the cage with terror in her eyes. "What's wrong?" he shouted as he ran toward her.

"Our rabbit died yesterday," she said in a shaking voice, "and we buried him. Look," she said, gesturing at the cage with trembling hand, "He's come back!"

The type of double-track joke in which the shift is from the main development of a story to what would seem to be an infinitesimal detail also requires a long development. As the man in the next story tells about his experience, you will undoubtedly think he is going on for quite awhile. I believe you will agree, however, that including all the details is necessary to stress with sufficient emphasis the difference between the main thrust of the story and the one detail on which his listener focuses:

One day a man, breathless and shaking with excitement, came dashing into his office where his secretary immediately noticed his agitated state. "My goodness, Mr. Baxter," she said, "What happened?"

"You'll never believe what I've been through," he gasped. "I had just come out of the restaurant where I have chili and an egg every morning and suddenly I found myself in the middle of a gunfight between the police and two masked men. The siren on the police car was shrieking and the police were behind their car shooting at the men who were dodging behind cars parked on the street. I ducked behind a telephone pole to get out of the way. Bullets whizzed past my head and ricocheted off the building behind me. Glass was flying everywhere. Cars coming up the street went up on the sidewalk to get out of the line of fire. Some of them crashed into garbage cans and sent them rolling everywhere. I ran back into the restaurant. I was lucky to get out of there with my life."

His secretary looked at him with amazement in her eyes. "I can't believe this, Mr. Baxter, do you mean to say that you have chili and an egg *every* morning?"

Multiple Triggers

At the beginning of this chapter I pointed out that distinguishing incongruity and surprise as independent triggers of laughter is difficult because the presence of one usually involves the presence of the other. They are not the only triggers that appear together. A given joke may include all of the triggers I have mentioned.

All jokes, of course, contain the trigger of self satisfaction, for to qualify as a joke, it must confront audiences with a puzzle or an idea which they must solve or connect with another idea. As we have already noted, completing this task successfully gives rise to a feeling of self satisfaction that triggers laughter. In a few jokes it is the only trigger there is.

The playwright George S. Kaufman commenting on the problem of keeping the various factions in the Middle East apart, said "One man's Mede is another man's Persian." The task for listeners, of course, is to recognize that his remark is a play on the familiar aphorism, "One man's meat is another man's poison." Those who make the connection are likely to feel some pleasure at their perceptiveness. But that seems to be the only trigger in the joke.

Compare Kaufman's joke to one attributed to the actress Tallulah Bankhead. She is reported to have called up a male friend one day and said, "I'll be over at five o'clock to make love. If I'm late, start without me."

To begin with, this joke has an expressed idea that invites the audience to infer an intriguing conclusion, and one, moreover, that approaches the realm of the forbidden. Thus it contains two elements that produce self satisfaction. It also suggests an incongruity, and the remark is surprising as well.

Another story with the same multiple triggers is the one cited earlier about the old woman who when asked whether she had ever been bedridden, answered, "Hundreds of times, and twice in a haystack." First, there is a play on words for listeners to figure out. Second, that play involves the thinking of taboo thoughts. Third, the old lady's response is not one we would expect from such a person. Thus, it generates both the triggers of surprise and incongruity.

Talullah Bankhead's remark and the old lady's reply involve all the

161

triggers of laughter there are except one—the self satisfaction that comes from a put-down. The story about the stuttering golfers, cited in the previous chapter, makes use of that trigger as well as all the others. You recall that the two stutterers, a man and a woman, were invited to introduce themselves. The man responded by saying, "M-my n–name is P-P-Peter, but I'm n–not a s-saint." The woman came back with, "M-my n–name is M-M-Mary, but I'm not a v-v-very good player."

This joke presents an opportunity for generating self satisfaction in three ways: by suggesting an implied word the audience must supply; by making that word one which some might consider taboo, and by making fun of a disability—a put-down. It also includes the trigger of surprise, and the ludicrousness of the exchange adds the element of incongruity.

In my lecture on humor I have used both Kaufman's remark about the Medes and Persians and the story about the stuttering golfers. If the first elicited any response at all, it was no more than a slight smile of appreciation. The second generally evoked gales of laughter. The difference in the number of triggers each joke involved explains this difference in reactions. As stated earlier, the Kaufman comment produces only one—the self satisfaction one might feel at making the connection between the remark and the aphorism. There isn't any detectable surprise or incongruity or any of the other components that might enhance the trigger of self satisfaction. Indeed, the main reaction to Kaufman's comment might well be envy of the wit that could produce such a dazzling double pun. It is exquisitely clever, but it is not particularly funny. The other joke, in contrast, as we have just seen, gives rise to all the triggers there are. The lesson from all of this seems clear. The more triggers you put into your jokes, the more likely you are to make your audience laugh.

Chapter 7
Finding Your Way to a Joke

Comedy is simply a funny way of being serious.
Peter Ustinov

Thus far we have seen that the delivery and reception of a joke involves three major elements. First, a joke maker conceives an idea or a group of ideas and presents it to an audience. We refer to this part of the joke, you may recall, as the expressed idea. Second, the audience is prompted by what the joke maker has said, written, or pictured to arrive at an idea of its own—the inferred idea. Third, the combination of the expressed idea and the inferred idea produces one or more of three laugh-inducing effects: a feeling of self satisfaction, the recognition of an incongruity, or a surprise.

The crucial element in this series of events is the formulation of the expressed idea. If it is well-constructed, all the other events will follow almost automatically. If the task is fumbled, on the other hand, nothing will be forthcoming except an embarrassing silence.

In Chapter 4, I pointed out that the task of composing an expressed idea may be carried out from two different perspectives. In the one case you have decided on an inferred idea, and you must now devise an expressed idea that will lead the audience to it. In the other case you have come across an item you think has some potential for playing a role in an expressed idea. You must now develop it to the point that it will cause an audience to respond to it with some kind of connecting idea of its own. In the first instance you begin with an inferred idea, in the second with all or part of an expressed idea.

In Chapter 4, I used several examples to show how a joke progresses from either of these starting points to its final form. In Chapters 5 and 6, I added to this information by discussing the kinds of ideas and devices that make audiences laugh. This may be a good time to draw all of this together by doing again what I did in Chapter 4—namely, tracing the development of another sample joke. You will see what gave it its initial impetus and what was done along the way to fashion the finished product. This description of the various stages in the joke-creation process will provide you with a step-by-step model to follow when you come to producing your own jokes.

Formulating an Expressed Idea

<u>Finding a Starting Point</u>. The development of a joke must begin with something and in the case of our sample it was a news item reporting that a book written by the comedian Al Franken had reached the best-seller list. The main part of its title was eye catching: *Rush Limbaugh is a Big Fat Idiot*. The author's eschewing of all subtlety and finesse in making his point might cause some people to smile, excepting, of course, Rush and his

devoted admirers. Still, it was not quite a joke, for it required no inference from the audience to complete the thought. The meaning was all there in blunt, unequivocal language. It did seem to possess a potential for becoming the foundation for what could be a joke, however.

Determine the Initial Idea's Role. Having found a springboard for our joke, we now have the task of deciding whether it will become the inferred idea or all or part of the expressed idea. Let's think about it first as a possible inferred idea. If we are to give it that role, members of the audience must be familiar with it. How many are likely to know the title of Franken's book? Few, I presume, even though it was a bestseller. Concocting an expressed idea that will cause people to recall an item they've never heard of is obviously impossible. It was clear that making the book's title the inferred idea was not a practical option. It might serve, however, as all or part of the expressed idea. In that role the audience wouldn't have to recall the book's title. The expressed idea would give it to them.

At times the initial idea all by itself can constitute the expressed idea. That was not true of the item that inspired our sample joke, nor is it true of most initial ideas. They may become elements in expressed ideas, but other material must be provided if the audience is to be led into inferring a connecting idea of its own. As we noted in Chapter 4, we call this added component the bridge of the joke.

Develop a Bridge to the Inferred Idea. This is the step that will test your creative ability to the utmost. How can you produce the additional ideas you need? You should focus on the initial idea, spinning off from it as many connecting ideas as you can. They may be variations, elaborations, extensions, or examples that distill its essence. These ideas in turn may give rise to other related ideas. Concentrate on the main line of thought, but within that focus let your mind operate in a free-wheeling mode. Some of you will recognize this as a process called brainstorming. Don't take time at this point to decide which ideas are good and which are bad. That can come later. Simply let them flow in.

Select and Arrange the Ideas. Presumably your brainstorming has produced several ideas from which you select one or two to put into the expressed idea. You must then arrange the initial idea and the ones you have just thought up into an appropriate order. There is no pattern to guide you in carrying out these tasks. The construction of each expressed idea involves its own unique considerations. In the case of our sample joke, its initial idea obviously contained two key words: "fat" and "idiot." Of the two it was clear that "idiot" should get most of the attention. Franken's main emphasis was on Limbaugh's low mental capacity, not on his corpulence. The brainstorming phase produced an idea for extending and exemplifying the meaning of the word "idiot" in a way that seemed promising:

> If Rush Limbaugh traded his brain for a sparrow's, he'd get the better of the deal.

It was immediately apparent that this statement by itself could serve as the expressed idea, for it was enough to lead an audience into making the desired inference. The title of Franken's book wasn't needed after all. But discarding it would deprive the joke of a context. It would seem to spring out of nowhere without any motivating rationale. Retaining the title also opened up another possibility. Franken could be given the line the brainstorming phase had produced. That he probably had never said it, unless two minds were traveling exactly parallel courses, wasn't an issue. Joke makers constantly put lines they have invented into other people's mouths. Further, it was a natural step to have Franken extend the insult he had made the title of his book. It was also in tune with the reputation for irreverency he had earned as a performer on *Saturday Night Live*. The expressed idea finally concocted for our sample joke goes like this:

> The comedian Al Franken has written a book entitled: *Rush Limbaugh is a Big Fat Idiot*. In a radio interview, Franken was asked whether he really thinks Limbaugh is stupid. "I'm not sure I'd go that far," Franken replied, "but if he traded his brain for a hummingbird's, he'd get the better of the deal.

<u>Evaluate the Result</u>. The process of evaluation should begin as soon as you start putting your expressed idea into words. Keep looking for ways to make improvements. The steps you take may include moving sentences around, substituting one word for another, pruning away verbiage, or adding something that will enhance the effect. Those of you who have been paying attention will immediately notice that one bird has been switched for another in the sample joke. A hummingbird is smaller than a sparrow. That makes the insult somewhat sharper and the joke funnier.

When you are satisfied you have written as tightly composed and highly focused an expressed idea as you can, you should step back, and try to measure its overall effect. Determine first whether you have actually produced a joke. Does it have a point, and is it subtle enough to make those who get it feel a glow of pleasure at their perceptiveness? If you can answer affirmatively, you have struck one of the triggers of laughter—self-satisfaction. But that alone may not provide all the merriment you would like. It may be necessary to reinforce the self-satisfaction trigger or add others.

An analysis of our sample joke reveals that it does have a point. It is not particularly elusive, but it is subtle enough to make those who get it feel some self satisfaction. That effect is intensified by the feeling of superiority most people experience when someone, particularly a celebrity, is ridiculed. Self satisfaction, then, is the main trigger the sample joke uses.

In a minor way it also employs the two other triggers. The idea of exchanging brains with a bird introduces an incongruity. The idea even delivers a tiny surprise. As Franken begins his response to the interviewer, he seems about to modify the derisiveness of his book's title. Then suddenly he reverses course and blisters Limbaugh with another zinger.

My detailing of the steps involved in creating a joke may make the process seem more laborious and prolonged than it usually is. As you gain experience, you will find that telescoping takes place as the line between the steps begins to disappear. In some instances you may carry out several of them simultaneously. There may even be times when you proceed from a beginning idea to a polished expressed idea in one instantaneous flash. In such cases your task has no hint of drudgery. Instead it is glorious fun.

On the other hand—and I'm sorry there is another hand—you may sometimes find that your creative machinery has come to a dead stop. Beginning ideas stay tantalizingly out of reach no matter how hard you try for them. To help you in such a situation, the rest of this chapter reviews some of the approaches and devices that may get the wheels of invention moving again.

Taking Advantage of Different Word or Phrase References

Many jokes turn on the fact that a word or phrase can be interpreted in more than one way. An abrupt switch from one reference to another produces a surprise which generates laughter. That suggests one route you can take to finding your way to a joke. Look for a word or phrase that may apply to two different contexts. Then try to invent a situation in which you can make a sudden shift from one context to the other. *Airplane* (1980) and *Airplane II: The Sequel* (1982), which burlesqued aviation disaster movies like *Airport*, used this device in a special kind of way. One of the scenes in the original *Airplane* movie shows a young man taking a seat on an airplane next to a nice, old lady. We know that he has a good reason for feeling upset and nervous, and his agitation is clearly evident. The nice, old lady immediately takes a motherly interest in him and tries to calm him down by engaging him in conversation:

Woman: Nervous?
Man: Yes.
Woman: First time?
Man: No, I've been nervous lots of times.

Exactly the same device is used in other scenes. In one a woman becomes ill, and a doctor who happens to be among the passengers describes the situation to a flight attendant:

Doctor: Tell the captain we have to land immediately. We have
to get this woman to a hospital.
Attendant: What is it?
Doctor: It's a big building with patients, but that's not important
right now.

Jokes of this type must be constructed with care if a laugh is to be realized. If the nice, old lady has asked, "Is this your first time on an airplane?" there would have been no joke, of course.

Here are two more jokes that show how you can create a laugh by having two characters see different meanings in the same words:

The cashier at a supermarket checkout counter rang up the cost
of a bag of pears and then realized he had made a mistake.
"Whoops, I've charged you for plums instead of pears," he told the
customer.
"What's the difference?" the customer asked.
"Well, plums are smaller and rounder."

"Can I try the trousers on in the window?" a customer in a men's
shop asked.
"You can if you insist," the salesman replied, "But we do have
dressing rooms for that purpose."

Jeff Daniels, known to most people as movie actor, is also building a reputation as a writer of stage comedies. A number of his plays have been produced in a theater he founded in Chelsea, Michigan. He, too, takes frequent advantage of the double-track technique to produce a laugh. One of his plays deals with the experiences of a man who is thinking about having a vasectomy. Entitled *The Vast Difference* (an ingenious pun), Daniels increases the potential for fun by making the urologist a woman. At one point the man says:

"The procedure, I take it, is performed with no pants on."
"No, I'm fully clothed at all times," the doctor replies.

Children often startle us by seeing a meaning we never intended. That happened to a father who was driving with his young son past a race track. When the boy asked what it was, the father answered, "It's place where people go to race horses."

"I bet the horses win," the boy responded.

You will note that the switch in many of these jokes arises because one party to the conversation interprets the meaning of a word or phrase in a more direct and literal way than the other party. That is true of the following jokes:

"How did you happen to become a nudist?" asked a first-time visitor to a nudist camp.

"I was born that way," the nudist replied.

A man passing a country estate saw a sign reading "Please ring bell for caretaker." The man rang the bell and shortly the caretaker appeared.

"What is it you want?" he asked.

"I'd just like to know why you can't ring the bell yourself," the man said.

A man making out an employment application, listed his street number and city in the proper place, but when he saw the word "zip" he appeared to be puzzled. Finally, he wrote down, "Normal for my age."

George Carlin was taking a literal approach when he said in one of his monologues:

"I read the other day that a motorist had been arrested for being legally drunk. If he was legally drunk, why was he arrested?"

Literal meanings lurking behind seemingly positive statements in advertisements may turn the message in an unfortunate direction. For a number of years the Arbor Drug Company of Michigan ended its radio and TV commercials proclaiming the benefits of using its medicinal products with the glowing declaration, "You can't get any better!" Perhaps the copywriters should have taken another look at their work. And some picky critics have pointed out that the slogan used by the maker of Maxwell House coffee—"Good to the Last Drop"—suggests there may be something wrong with that last drop.

The double meaning in most jokes is usually instantly apparent, but for some, filtering out the second meaning may require a moment or two. A far-fetched pun can wrinkle brows for a bit. And a few ticks may go off the clock before you figure out what precisely was going on in the mind of the character portrayed in this next joke:

A woman on a subway escalator was trying to control a struggling dog she was carrying in her arms. Reaching her destination, she put the dog down, and in a state of high irritation, marched over to a transit guard. "I'll have you know it took me an hour to find this dog," she said angrily. "I think that's ridiculous."

"But madam," the guard said soothingly, "Why would you try to find a dog?"

"That's why," the woman said, pointing to a sign at the top of the escalator. It read:

DOGS MUST BE CARRIED ON ESCALATOR

I have no way of knowing how the originators of the jokes I have quoted began the process of creating them. At one point, obviously, the joke makers had to hit on a word or phrase that could be taken in two different ways. When you realize you are bereft of comic ideas, that can be a first step toward finding your way to a joke. The invention of circumstances that utilize the double meaning you have found must then follow.

The detection of double meanings, in fact, can be a means of producing spontaneous humor. Secondary meanings lurk everywhere. By unexpectedly pulling them to the surface, you can surprise your friends and associates with your spur-of-the-moment wit. One comedian who made a specialty of turning what people said into instant jokes was Steve Allen. He listened carefully to the words used by ordinary folks—contestants on quiz shows, people he intercepted on the street, or audience members who shouted questions at him—and took their remarks in a totally unexpected direction. The following examples show his technique in action:

Allen:	What business are you in?
Contestant:	Tool and die.
Allen:	Oh, that's too bad. But then we all have to go sometime.
Allen:	What is your name sir?
Contestant:	Tom Francis, Central Steel Works, Pittsburg, Pennsylvania.
Allen:	That's a rather long name, Mr. Pennsylvania.
Audience member:	Is that your own hair?
Allen:	In another two payments it will be.

Most of you can't hope to match the lightning wit Steve Allen displayed. But even though creating instant jokes may be beyond your reach, the detection of a double meaning can lead to the finding of a joke if you are given enough time to think about it. A questionnaire sent to a government agency requested it to list the names of all its employees broken down by sex. The double-meaning phrase is glaringly obvious. Now see what you can do with it.

Beginning with a Standard Framework

Many jokes are built around specific frameworks or patterns. Thinking about the direction a standard framework can take you may provide the impetus you need to get your joke-making faculties working. What do I mean by a framework? One that has been around for more than fifty years begins, "Knock-knock....Who's there?" Some may feel it has worn out its welcome, but it still has its adherents and is a particular favorite of children. One admirer of knock-knocks is said to have collected 147,000 of them, and that was before the Internet existed. The Internet produced almost 134,000 web sites when "Knock-knock jokes" was entered into the Google search engine.

A particular advantage of using the knock-knock-joke framework is that it permits you to commit an atrocious pun without usually inviting assault and battery. Here is an example of such a pun:

> Knock-knock.
> Who's there?
> Don Ameche.
> Don Ameche who?
> I'll be Don Ameche in a taxi, honey.

People's names, both real and fictional, have been a constant source of material for knock-knocks. Plays have been made on the names Will Durant (Will Durant be paid this month?) and Tarzan (Tarzan stripes forever). A little thought should produce some puns with equal potentialities for making your listeners cringe. Or, perhaps, you will think of a way of varying the formula with a clever twist, as the creator of the following knock-knock did:

> Knock-knock.
> Who's there?
> Opportunity.
> Can't be.
> Why not?
> Opportunity only knocks once.

A formula of more recent vintage is the good news-bad news approach. A story told by the Israeli scholar and statesman Abba Eben illustrates the format:

> The first time Moses came down Mount Sinai, he said, "I have twenty commandments." The Israelites responded, *"Twenty* commandments? Don't do this, don't do that. Impossible! Go back

and get them reduced."

So Moses went back up the mountain and after forty days and forty nights, came back down again. This time he said, "I've got good news and bad news. The good news is that the commandments are now down to ten. The bad news is that the one about adultery is still in."

It is possible to reverse the formula and make it a bad news-good news sequence, as Mark Russell did during one of his PBS half hours. He was commenting on a proposal by President Bill Clinton to make certain tax raises retroactive:

"The bad news is that even if you die after January 1, you still have to pay those taxes. The good news is that you can still vote in Chicago.

In the opening decades of the twentieth century a writer (or writers) turned out a long succession of books about an ingenious lad named Tom Swift, who invented startling new machines that foreshadowed major scientific developments of the future. Two characteristics marked the writer's style. First, the characters rarely just said something. They declaimed, or argued, or expostulated, or shouted. Second, an adverb almost always added a further modification of the thought. Joke makers picked up these two peculiarities to create a form of humor called a Tom Swifty, in which the adverb, and sometimes the verb constitute a pun. Here are some examples:

"I've decided to become a nudist," she declared starkly.

"The days are getting shorter," she groused darkly.

"I'm going to play Puck in *Midsummer Night's Dream*," the actor bragged impishly.

"Sure, I can climb cliffs," he bluffed haughtily.

(An etymologist would see two puns in this example.)

"I've had a great many children," Mother Hubbard boasted overbearingly.

"Can't you see I'm studying for an exam," she barked testily.

If you go to the Internet you can find hundreds more. Google produced over 26,900 web sites for Tom Swifties.

Creating a Tom Swifty is fairly simple. The first step is to pick out an adverb and see where it takes you. If that gets you nowhere, discard it, and try another one. If you persist long enough, you are almost certain to end up with a joke.

There are other punning frameworks which, like the Tom Swifty, can set you on the road to creating your own humor. One matches real place names to the type of business or enterprise the name suggests. Thus, Sioux City, Iowa, would be an ideal location for a law firm. And what better town to set up a sex clinic than Climax, Michigan?

A similar type of framework requires the joke maker to link descriptive words with various kinds of occupations. Suppose you ask the question, "How was your day?" Now you must find a word that constitutes an appropriate response by workers in various fields. A veterinarian, for instance, might reply "beastly," the lawyer, "trying," the judge, "fine," and the wrecker, "smashing."

A somewhat more exotic framework executes a play on words in which the aim is to find an English meaning in a foreign phrase. The following guesses at what some French names and phrases mean provide examples. *Pas de deux*—father of twins; *Jeanne d'Arc*—there's no light in the bathroom, *Coup de grace*—lawnmower.

These punning frameworks, incidentally, can be the basis for party games that can test the ingenuity of your guests. Some may discover they have a capacity for inventing jokes they never knew they possessed.

A formula familiar to many because of its use by Johnny Carson on the *Tonight* show was the three-step answer to a question. Johnny would say something like: "The girl I went out with last night is really fat." The well-trained audience would shout back, "How fat is she?" Johnny would then expand on his statement with three specific examples of her fatness:

She's so fat that her bathtub has stretch marks.

She's so fat that every time she gets on an elevator, it goes down.

She's so fat that when she does the dance of the seven veils, she has to use fifty.

Sometimes he tried a fourth answer but usually regretted it. When the laugh fell off, he would ask himself, "When will I ever learn that three is enough?"

Johnny Carson is by no means the only comedian who employs the three-step formula. Phyllis Diller made use of it on occasion. Well before their time, Fred Allen, one of the most notable of the radio comedians, built laughs by delivering successive comments on the same topic. After visiting California, he made these three observations, all inspired by his visit:

California is a wonderful place to live—if you're an orange.

Hollywood is a place where people from Iowa mistake each other for movie stars.

An associate producer is the only guy in Hollywood who will associate with a producer.

In a feature on his program called "Allen's Alley" he created what amounted to a variation of the three-step formula by getting the reaction of various inhabitants of the alley to the same question. One of them, Senator Claghorn, rarely appeared without emphasizing his extreme southern proclivities and usually his comments came in threes.

I never go to a baseball game unless a south-paw is pitching.

I always drink water out of a dixie cup.

I never drive through the Lincoln tunnel.

The obvious first step in carrying out the three-step formula is to think up a statement which you can expand with funny comments. Let's suppose you say, "I met a really dumb guy last night." To the question, "How dumb was he?," you might reply:

"He's so dumb he had his Olympic gold medal bronzed."

Can you devise two other statements that carry out the "dumb" motif?

A formula created by that ever fruitful fount of comedic ideas, Steve Allen, is worth mentioning. It is quite simple and yet it can generate a great deal of amusement. He picked a word some people were likely to misunderstand and put it into a question he asked passersby.

A good example: "If an admitted heterosexual were running for president, would you vote for him?" Note that the use of the pejorative word "admitted" helps mislead those who might otherwise know the meaning of the word. The confused answers and misguided floundering of the respondents were often hilarious. Allen enhanced the effect by keeping a straight face throughout, no matter how ridiculous the reply.

A formula widely used by burlesque comedians of the past generated laughs by presenting two people simultaneously following two different lines of thought. In a discussion between the comedian and his straight man, a topic would come up with potentialities for double entendre. The laughs would come when the comedian went in one direction, the straight man in another. I saw an example of this technique on an episode of the British comedy series *Are You Being Served*, broadcast in the United States by PBS stations. In this episode, the employees of a department store were being given physical examinations, the results of which would determine the amount of pension they received. At one point a group of anxious employees gathered outside the closed door of the owner's office where they presumed the results of their physicals were being reported. In actual fact, the one person whose voice they overheard was discussing the condition of the furniture in the owner's office. At one point one of the employees was led to believe that his legs were suffering from dry rot. There were other examples of misinterpretation, most of them involving a double entendre, a common ingredient in this series.

The frameworks I have mentioned are only a sampling of the many currently being used. I once heard Gene Shalit, the movie critic for the *Today* show, make use of another standard pattern. It consists of taking a proverb or popular saying and reversing the order of its key words. The one to which Shalit gave that treatment was the saying, "I wouldn't put a dog out on a night like this." He conveyed his low opinion of the movie *First Knight* by closing his review with the comment: "I wouldn't put a knight into a dog like this." Another reversal of a familiar saying provides the cap to a story about a moth that unwisely flew over a two-year old's birthday cake. He burned his end at both candles.

Topics of Humor

A great many lists have been drawn up that classify the general subjects around which jokes have been created. Scanning such a list may start you on the path toward developing your own joke, based on one of these topics. They might include subjects like the following:

Fatness	The wedding night
Old maids	Boarding houses
Seasickness	Stinginess
Vice presidents	Drunkenness
Sex	First-time fathers
Precocious children	Misadventures by politicians
Mothers-in-law	Marital spats
Farmers' daughters	Traveling salesmen

The list, of course, could go on and on. One of the things you will note is that some of the topics in the list are outdated. Changes in our culture, society, economy, and mores have deprived jokes based on certain topics of their ability to make us laugh. Max Eastman, one of the most perceptive analysts of matters humorous, learned during his career as a lecturer that some subjects can go out of style. In the 1920s he could call forth gales of laughter by reading excerpts from one of Stephen Leacock's most celebrated essays, "My Financial Career," which tells about a hapless depositor so befuddled by the intricacies of banking that he immediately withdrew money he had just deposited. As the twenties edged into the thirties, Eastman found that the response to the story was declining. Deciding it had lost its power to amuse, he finally dropped it from his repertoire. Perhaps the bank failures of the 1930s were responsible for changing audience reactions to Leacock's humor. People may have had difficulty laughing about an institution that had just cost them their life savings.

In the nineteenth century living in a boarding house was an experience many people shared. Stephen Leacock wrote funny pieces about them also. Few nowadays would understand what he was talking about. Other changes have outdated once sure-fire topics. The transition from family farms to large agricultural enterprises have made jokes about traveling salesmen and farmers' daughters sound old fashioned. Put-downs about old maids are likely to call forth frowns of disapproval in this age of feminism, rather than laughs. The development of a greater sensitivity about race and the desire to be politically correct has consigned a vast array of jokes to the dumpster.

On the other hand, some topics have demonstrated impressive staying power. Fatness still makes us laugh, and some of us still find amusement in the miseries suffered by the victims of seasickness. We can also put vice presidents on the list of humorous topics that have endured. From the beginning of our republic, jokesters have made fun of them. In 1900 Mark Twain twitted vice presidents in a speech he made to the Lotus Club. In the 1930s the plot of a popular musical, *Of Thee I Sing*, revolved around the desperate effort of a Vice President Throttlebottom to find out what it was he was supposed to do. More recently, Vice President Dan Quayle was the butt of more jokes than anyone who had ever served in that office. Much of the damage was self-inflicted, of course. Comedians could get a laugh simply by drawing attention to the school-boy howlers he sometimes committed. The assault diminished when Al Gore succeeded him, but it did not disappear. Most of the jokes focused on Gore's habitual stiffness of speech and demeanor. In his appearance with David Letterman, he even made fun of it himself.

The ridicule didn't stop when Dick Cheney became vice president. Oddly, much of it was aimed at the serious heart trouble from which Cheney suffered. One might have thought that the condition would have drawn the sympathy of the late-night comedians, but instead they were unremitting in their mockery of it. An example is this comment by David Letterman: "Dick Cheney has laryngitis....That's from yelling all day: 'Quick, my heart-attack pills, quick!'" A more legitimate target for the comedians' taunts, perhaps, is Cheney's passion for keeping governmental activities secret. That was the focus of this item in one of Jay Leno's monologues:

Dick Cheney finally responded today to demands that he reveal the details of the Enron meetings. This is what he said: "He met with unnamed people, from unspecified companies, for an indeterminate time, at an undisclosed location." Thank God he cleared that up.

Another topic that has always stimulated laughter and probably always will is sex. In his book *Enjoyment of Laughter*, Max Eastman included a story that is hoary with age, and yet its capacity to make audiences laugh is as strong as ever. It demonstrates how effective a joke with sexual connotations can be:

> To refute a certain vicious slander, a preacher asked all the women in his congregation who were virgins to stand up. A deathlike silence followed.
>
> Once more the preacher urged all women who could claim virginity to stand up. Still no one moved. As he glared down at the congregation, a young woman with a baby in her arms struggled to her feet.
>
> "But my good woman," the preacher remonstrated, "Surely you misunderstand my meaning. You have a child in your arms."
>
> "Of course," the young woman responded, "You wouldn't expect this little baby to stand up by herself, would you?"

I can testify from personal experience that referring to a list of humorous topics can sometimes help one find the way to a joke. The name of the captain of a cruise ship on which I once traveled was Victor Hugo. There seemed to be a joke lurking there somewhere, but none came immediately to mind. In an effort to start something germinating, I tried to recall the titles of the books his French namesake had written, still without any result. Finally, in desperation, I turned to the topics I listed at the beginning of this section. One of them caught my eye—"seasickness." The next instant a connection leaped out at me. I hadn't been seasick on my trip, but why not exaggerate a little? This was the joke as it finally crystallized:

> The captain of a cruise ship I once sailed on was named Victor Hugo. It was an appropriate name. The first day at sea, I felt *tres misérable*.

Turning Old Jokes Into New Ones

One step many humorists have taken when they find their creative machinery idling is to take a look at material other people have written. When they find a joke that appeals to them, they make some changes in it and present it as their own. This practice is called *switching*.

I sense that some of your eyebrows are rising at this point. Am I suggesting it is proper to appropriate other people's material? Let me say to begin with that when you switch a joke, you do not take it over just as it is. You put it into new surroundings, supply new characters, or add an original twist of your own. A further point is that some of our best and most esteemed humorists have regularly engaged in switching.

During his long and fruitful career as a comic novelist, Peter De Vries originated many jokes and witty comments of his own. But when his well of inspiration ran dry, he did not hesitate to switch jokes he had found elsewhere and incorporate them into his novels. In *Slouching Towards Kalamazoo*, I came across this passage:

> My old eighth-grade teacher, Miss Maggie Doubloon, said she "was half Spanish, half French, and half Irish," a plethora of halves not entirely unnoticed by the brighter students.

That, of course, is a switch on a line Stephen Leacock had written many years before in one of his humorous essays: "The legendary Bulbeks were a fabulous race—half man, half horse, half bird." In De Vries's novel *I Hear America Swinging*, a wife delivers this admonition to her husband: "I wish you wouldn't eat in your undershirt. It's too common. Nobody does that." Compare that remark with Yogi Berra's oft-quoted comment, "No one goes to that restaurant anymore. It's too crowded." It's obvious that both are using the same comic device.

James Thurber, whom some critics rank even above Mark Twain as a humorist, was, like his close friend Peter De Vries, a fount of inimitable, funny ideas. But he, too, sometimes resorted to switching. An example occurred in one of his fables in which a male crow falls in love with a female oriole. He pleads his cause to her, or as Thurber, an inveterate punster put it, "Caws his please." The lady oriole rejected his suit with the comment, "I don't see how that could interest anybody but another crow." Harrison Kinney, in his biography *James Thurber: His Life and Times*, points out that was a switch on a joke current at the time Thurber wrote his piece. It told about a lady visiting the Central Park Zoo who asked the attendant about the sex of the caged hippopotamus she saw there. The attendant replied, "I don't see how that could interest anyone but another hippopotamus."

Will Rogers, who like De Vries and Thurber, could stand with anyone as a wit, also switched other people's comments into jokes of his own on occasion. When a Republican orator at the 1924 convention defended his long windedness by saying he was speaking for posterity, Rogers observed: "If he don't get done pretty soon, they'll be here." You may recall my earlier citing of a similar comment made many years before by Henry Clay in the House of Representatives about an equally verbose congressman who also claimed he was speaking for posterity. Clay said: "Apparently you are determined to speak until the arrival of your audience." The relationship between Clay's remark and Roger's slight variation of it is clear.

A similar relationship exists between a comment King George II of England is supposed to have made in the mid 1700s and one credited to Abraham Lincoln one hundred years later. They both involved generals. In King George's case the general was James Wolfe, who commanded British forces in Canada in the war against the French. When told that Wolfe had gone mad, King George is reputed to have said, "I wish you could persuade him to bite some of my other generals." In Lincoln's case, the general was Ulysses S. Grant, and the issue was his alleged drunkenness. As you will recall from an earlier chapter, when informed of it, Lincoln is said to have responded, "I wonder if you could get me a few barrels of that same whiskey, and I'll give it to my other generals."

When I quoted this remark earlier, I mentioned that Lincoln denied ever saying it. It probably came from some anonymous wit. I suspect the King George comment was also created by an unknown joke maker. But whoever originated those remarks, their close relationship suggests that one is a switch on the other.

When humorists make switches, they usually begin with material from an outside source. At times, however, they recycle their own witticisms. A good example is a Jay Leno joke I quoted earlier: "Some people in Washington, D.C., have tried to put together a Christmas crèche but have been unable to find either three wise men or a virgin." A year later he presented a revised version which went something like this. "In trying to construct a crèche for a Washington Christmas celebration, the Republicans and Democrats found they had to cooperate. The Republicans couldn't come up with three wise men and the Democrats couldn't come up with a virgin."

In the comic strip *Frank and Ernest*, its creator, Bob Thaves, rang a couple of variations on the theme of upside-down cakes. In one cartoon he showed his characters looking at two signs in a bakery window. One read CAKES—$6.66, the other, UPSIDE-DOWN CAKES—$9.99. In the second cartoon, which followed three months later, one character said to the other, "I bought an upside-down cake from China. It's right side up."

One of the more startling examples of what one might almost call self-plagiarism occurred in *The New Yorker*. In 1994 the magazine published a drawing showing an Oriental father trying to persuade his son to eat what was on his plate. The response of the son was "I say it's seaweed, and I say the hell with it." That, as many of you will recall, was almost identical to the caption of one of *The New Yorker's* most famous earlier drawings. It showed a mother trying to persuade her son to eat what she claimed was broccoli. In that case the son replied, "I say it's spinach, and I say to hell with it."

Most humorists who switch jokes would probably prefer you didn't remember the original. I'm sure that wasn't true of *The New Yorker* editors. Even though the first version was published more than sixty years ago, they would expect their more mature readers to recall it. I suspect they even invited that recollection, for the feat of connecting the two versions provides a special kind of pleasure. For those who weren't familiar with the original, the second would stand on its own.

A switch similar to *The New Yorker* one appeared in a 1995 episode of the *Born Loser* comic strip. A man sitting at a luncheon counter looks at the man next to him who is enjoying a hamburger, and says, "I will gladly pay you Tuesday for a hamburger today." Again, for mature readers that would spark recollections of a comic-strip character of many years ago named Wimpy who regularly made that identical appeal to his fellow comic-strip inhabitants. The clue that the joke came from someone other than the *Born Loser* cartoonist appears in the response the man eating the hamburger makes to his strange friend, "I think I'm in the wrong comic strip."

Some switches not only invite recollections of the original, but would scarcely qualify as jokes unless they did. That is true of the following:

> Why did the germ cross the microscope?
> To get to the other slide.

> Why did the lion cross the jungle?
> To get to the other pride.

> Why did the polygamist cross the aisle?
> To get to the other bride.

Those lines acquire real meaning only if you remember the answer to the question, "Why did the chicken cross the road?" The following lines amount to no more than gobbledegook unless you recall the story about the man who when asked "Who was that lady I saw you with last night?" replied, "That was no lady that was my wife." There is the musician's version, "Was that an oboe I saw you playing last night? That was no oboe that was my fife." The kitchen version, "Who was that ladle I saw you with last night?" "That was no ladle, that was my knife." The magician's version, "Who was that lady I saw you saw last night?" "That was no lady, that was my half-sister." And the truncated version, "Who was that lady I saw you outwit last night?"

There are many routes to making switches. One is to find a word or phrase other joke makers have converted into puns. You can then make up new puns using that same word or phrase. A word a number of joke makers have had fun with is "Czech." In a *Frank and Ernest* comic strip, for example, the manager of a talent agency tells someone on the phone, "We don't have any Russian ballet dancers available right now....Will you take a Czech?" Exactly the same pun appears in a sign posted in a cafè in Crete, Nebraska, home of many people of Czech ancestry: "We accept out-of-town Czechs." Another play on the same word appeared in an episode in the *Winthrop* comic strip. It showed one little boy telling another what had happened to his father while he was visiting Czechoslovakia. "He got arrested for walking past a hobo in Prague. They charged him with passing a bum Czech." The story is told that when the tennis player Martina Navratilova defected from then communist Czechoslovakia, she wrote a letter to the U.S. State Department which combined the "Czech" pun with another clever play on words. Her double-pun question was, "Would you be willing to cache a Czech?"

The fact that the word "see" pertains both to vision and to the area under the jurisdiction of a bishop has opened the door to several puns. One came from the hand of a headline writer: BLIND BISHOP APPOINTED TO SEE. Jean Kerr introduced a familiar saying into the mix when she made this comment about a bishop who had been defrocked: "Long time no see." She claimed it was the only pun she had ever committed and added that she was not proud of it. Bob Thaves gave the same phrase a slightly different twist in a *Frank and Ernest* episode. It showed the explorer Balboa explaining to a couple of natives that he had been traveling for several days trying to find the ocean. The response of the natives was "Long time no sea."

Another way to make a switch is to identify the idea behind someone else's pun and then invent a new pun to express it. Comments made by two English literary figures, the playwright Richard Sheridan and the poet Lord Byron, contain different puns inspired by the same thought. Asked to describe the difference between men and women, Sheridan replied, "Madame, I cannot conceive." Byron once likened one of his acquaintances to an old woman. When challenged to explain why, Byron responded, "Because she's past all bearing."

One of the simplest ways of carrying out a switch is to give a framework you have found in someone else's joke a new setting and new characters. That's what Peter De Vries did with Stephen Leacock's "half man, half horse, half bird" description of the Bulbeks. There is an old joke about a visitor to New York who stopped a man on the street and asked how he could get to Carnegie Hall. The man's answer was "practice, practice, practice." Bob Hope picked up the framework of that joke but moved the setting to Nashville, Tennessee, and changed the place the visitor had in mind to the Grand Old Opry. In Hope's version the answer to the question about how to get there became, "Sing through your nose." The other day I ran across still another switch on this pattern. A new student who had become lost in Boston went up to a passerby and asked, "How do I get to Harvard University?" The answer was: "First get a good SAT score."

During his run for the presidency in 1976, Morris Udall sometimes asked his Midwestern audiences if they knew the difference between a pigeon and an Iowa farmer. The answer was, "The pigeon can still make a deposit on a tractor." Some years after that I ran across a switch on the joke that changed the farmer to a yuppie stock broker and the tractor to a BMW. The propensity of pigeons for making deposits still remained the key to the joke.

In Chapter 5 and 6 we looked at the basic triggers of laughter—self satisfaction, incongruity, and surprise. In switching an old joke into a new one, an obvious first step is to determine what triggered the laughter in the old joke. In an earlier chapter I quoted a joke about a physician who told a patient he needn't apologize for calling him out on a cold night because "I have to call on someone near you, and I'll just kill two birds with one stone." One trigger of laughter in that joke is the self satisfaction created by putting down a professional person most of us view as an authority figure. To switch it into a new joke, however, you must determine the precise nature of the put-down that generated a feeling of self satisfaction. That's fairly easy as far as this joke is concerned. The joke maker casts doubts on the physician's healing powers. To switch it you must now find another way to create the same type of doubt. The next joke does just that:

A patient who was leaving the hospital offered to give a plant he had just received to the doctor who had treated him. "I'd better not take it," the doctor responded. "Everything I touch seems to die."

One of the delightful features in the now defunct *Saturday Review* was a column written by Goodman Ace. In one of them he made this comment:

I was so upset by the articles the *Reader's Digest* was running on the dangers of smoking that I decided to do something about it. I gave up reading the *Reader's Digest*.

The trigger of laughter in this comment is clearly surprise. Describing it more specifically, we can say it is the kind of surprise produced when the joke maker leads us to believe he is adopting one solution to a problem and then abruptly switches to another. Henny Youngman used precisely the same kind of surprise to trigger laughter in the following joke:

My wife finally did something about her weight. She stopped getting on the scales.

Many other switches involving the substitution of an unexpected solution for an expected one are possible. Another joke using the smoking motif presents a different situation and a different solution, but the trigger of laughter is identical to the one in the Goodman Ace comment:

My wife keeps telling me to give up smoking so I've decided to do something about it. I'm buying myself some earplugs.

Let's look now at another type of surprise, illustrated by the following joke:

A woman went to a psychiatrist complaining that her husband had come to the conclusion he was a horse. When she asked the psychiatrist whether he thought he could help him, the doctor said he thought he could, but warned her the treatment would cost a lot of money.

"Money's no problem," the woman replied. "He's just won the Kentucky Derby."

The surprise in this joke comes when a condition represented as a delusion is suddenly seen as a reality. A great many jokes have used that particular twist. Sometimes the approach is a very simple one, as it is in the story about a woman who came to a psychiatrist complaining that her husband seemed to think he was a chicken. When the psychiatrist offered to cure him, she protested, "But what would we do for eggs?" This joke can be switched to one about a husband who thinks he's an airplane. When the psychiatrist tells his wife to bring him in on Thursday at two, she counters, "He can't make it that day. He has to appear in court for flying too low over Flatbush." Four other jokes feature even more complicated switches on the delusion theme:

A couple went to see a psychiatrist. "My wife has a problem," the husband explained. "For the last six months she's been thinking she's a lawnmower."

"That's serious," the psychiatrist said, "Why didn't you bring her in sooner?"

"I've been waiting for the neighbor who borrowed her to bring her back."

A woman complained to a psychiatrist that her husband had a strange delusion. "He thinks he's a television set," she explained.

183

"Have him come in," the psychiatrist said, "I think I can cure him."

"Oh, no doctor. Don't cure him. We enjoy the entertainment he gives us. We just want you to adjust his horizontal linearity."

Another joke almost identical to the previous one changes the instrument from a television set to a computer. When the therapist invites her to bring him in so that he can cure him, the woman says: "Oh, no doctor. Don't cure him. I enjoy all the entertainment he gives us. I just want you to give him more RAM!"

A woman told a psychiatrist that her husband had been acting oddly for a long time. "He seems to think he's the Lone Ranger."

"Bring him in and I'll see what I can do to help him."

"Yes I suppose I should," the woman conceded. "But Tonto is so good with the children."

In one of the *Born Loser* comic strips this episode took place:

A man slipped on a banana peel and injured his ankle. A dog observing the incident commented that he'd probably broken it. The astonished man scrambled to his feet and asked a disreputable looking character nearby, "D-d-did you hear what that dog just said?"

"Y'mean that stray that hangs around here?" the character responded. "Don't pay him no nevermind. He don't know beans about orthopedics."

You recall that in Chapter 6 I pointed out that surprise and incongruity are often found in the same joke. We decide what the main trigger is by determining which of those elements actually sets off the laugh. The above joke certainly contains surprises, but I think the element that makes us laugh is an incongruity. To be more specific, it is the incongruity of accepting as normal and natural a dog's ability to talk. That incongruity is given a further amusing extension when it is implied that the dog might be able to discourse intelligently about some aspects of medicine, but not about orthopedics. The same type of incongruity is the trigger of laughter in the next two jokes. Only the animals and the field of knowledge under scrutiny are different:

A car running down a country road suddenly sputtered and came to a complete stop. The puzzled driver got out and was about to raise the hood when a cow standing in a nearby field offered him some advice. "I think it's your radiator," the cow said.

The startled driver looked at the cow in astonishment and then ran up to the farmhouse and knocked on the door. When the farmer appeared, the driver said, "I can't believe it. One of your cows just told me what is wrong with my stalled car."

"Was the cow white with big black spots?" the farmer asked.

"That's right."

"Well, that's Sarah. Don't pay any attention to her. She doesn't know a thing about cars."

A clerk selling two-dollar tickets at a race track window reacted with open-mouthed amazement when a horse stepped up and placed a bet on himself.

"What's the matter," snorted the horse. "Are you surprised I can talk?"

"Not at all," the clerk replied. "I'm just astonished that you think you can win."

In the normal course of life, we expect people to react in a certain way to the development of certain kinds of situations. When their behavior does not meet our expectations, an incongruity arises. People bereaved by the loss of loved ones, for instance, usually show signs of grief and interrupt their everyday activities. A violation of that pattern produces a specific type of incongruity around which a number of jokes have turned. Stephen Leacock included one of the best in his book on *Humor*:

A Scotsman's wife was dying. Calling her husband to the bedside, she said, "John, I know you didn't like Aunt Janet, but you'll let her ride with you in the carriage to the funeral?"

The husband, much moved, answered, "I'll do it for you, Maggie, but it'll spoil my day."

The circumstances and characters in this next joke are different, but the wife's remark produces an incongruous effect identical in nature to the one created by the Scotsman's comment:

A widow had been busy for several days working out the disposition of her late husband's estate with the family attorney. "I'm sorry this is taking so long," the attorney said apologetically, "but settling an estate is a complicated process."

"It certainly is," replied the widow with a sigh. "You know, sometimes I just wish John hadn't died."

Those of you interested in switching this type of incongruity into jokes of your own should note that a further qualifying characteristic of these statements is their impulsiveness. It is quite likely that the Scotsman and the wife regretted making them as soon as the import of what they had said dawned on them. These next two jokes illustrate the same kind of impulsive—and markedly incongruous—outbursts. The circumstances and characters differ, but the similarity in the patterns of development make it easy to believe that one is a switch on the other. You will note, further, that the concluding words are identical:

The wife of a Maine farmer was subject to fits from which she quickly recovered. Not knowing her history, his neighbors would call him from his work in the field whenever they saw her behaving oddly. When he arrived at the house, he would find that she was perfectly normal again. As this interruption of his work went on, he grew more and more irritated by it. One day a neighbor called out to him, "You'd better see to your wife, John. I think she's in a bad way." Reluctantly he left his plowing and went up to the house. This time he found his wife lying dead on the floor. "Well," he said, looking down at her. "That's more like it."

Zeb, a pioneer farmer, settled down with his wife, Martha, on land where settlers were sometimes subject to attacks by Indians. Zeb hung a big bell on a tree and told his wife she should ring it if she saw anything suspicious. "But don't call me in from the field unless you think it's a real emergency," he emphasized.

Apparently his wife wasn't listening because the first time she called him in it was to ask whether he'd like a cup of coffee. "Tarnation!" Zeb expostulated. "I told you to ring the bell only in an emergency."

He returned to the field, and a little while later heard the bell ring again. This time she told him the washtub was leaking. "That's not a blasted emergency!" he shouted at her as he went back to his plowing.

Two hours later the bell rang again. He hesitated a moment and then decided he'd better find out what was up. As he approached the house he saw flames shooting from it and near the bell, he found his wife with an arrow through her heart. "Well, Martha," Zeb exclaimed. "That's more like it."

These next two jokes feature reactions to the loss of loved ones that are out of keeping with normal expectations. They differ from the previous jokes in that the aberrant behavior is not impulsive in any way. What the characters say and do is obviously planned and deliberate.

A member of a golfing foursome came up to another foursome on a tee and requested permission to play through. "Why should we let you do that?" one of the other foursome asked. "It's like this," the first speaker explained. "My wife's funeral is scheduled for two o'clock and my friends and I don't want to be late for the service."

A woman at a matinee noticed that an empty seat separated her from another woman. During the intermission, she expressed her surprise that the seat was unoccupied, considering how many people had been clamoring for tickets. The second woman explained that the seat had been reserved for her husband, but he had passed away suddenly. "I'm sorry to hear that," the first woman answered, "but couldn't a member of your family have come with you?"

"Oh, no," the second woman replied. "They're all at the funeral."

To help you understand and carry out the process of switching an old joke into a new one, I have quoted a number of closely related jokes. Some of them came into existence, I'm sure, because one author saw the work of another, picked up its basic concept, and clothed it with new circumstances and characters. There is good reason to believe, for example, that Peter De Vries was familiar with Stephen Leacock's "half, half, and half" description of the Bulbeks and converted it to his own use. The Jay Leno joke and *The New Yorker* cartoon I cited are unquestionably switches, but in both instances they switched their own material. Another example of an obvious switch not mentioned thus far is a remark made by a movie critic about Audrey Hepburn: "I can describe her in two words: dee-lectable." That comments brings instantly to mind what Samuel Goldwyn is supposed to have said when asked whether a certain project could be carried out: "I can answer that in two words: Im-possible." I'm certain the movie critic was familiar with Goldwyn's remark and made his own adaptation of it.

Other examples that look like switched jokes may not be switches at all. Peter De Vries's joke about the woman who chided her husband for eating in his undershirt with the words, "It's so common. Nobody does that," and Yogi Berra's comment about the restaurant nobody goes to anymore "because it's too crowded," are obviously closely related. One may not be a switch on the other, however. It's quite possible that De Vries and Berra thought them up quite independently. Other jokes I have quoted, which appear to be switches, may also be independent creations. Even if the De Vries and Berra comments do represent switches, we can't know who did the switching because we don't know which came first. That is true of some of the other switches I quoted. The order in which I have put them, in most instances is purely arbitrary.

All of this material, the actual switches and the apparent ones, can guide you as you attempt the task of switching an old joke into a new one. The first step you must take is to determine the fundamental comic ingredient in the joke you want to switch. My analyses of closely related jokes can give you an idea of what a particular ingredient might be. There are many others, of course, which you must discover for yourself. The true test of your creativity will come as you attempt to devise a new context of circumstances and characters in which to place the ingredient you have found.

Let's look again at Stephen Leacock's joke: "The legendary Bulbeks were a fabulous race—half man, half horse, half bird." We have already seen how Peter De Vries switched that bit of nonsense. Another switch concerned a woman who asked her husband when the football game he was watching on TV would be over. "It's in the middle of the second half," he told her.

"How many halves are there?" she asked.

Your assignment is to think up still another switch on the "half-half-half" idea.

Using Other People's Material

Producing a joke from scratch requires the greatest inventive effort. Switching someone else's joke into one of your own is less demanding, but it still calls for the exercise of some ingenuity. Taking over a joke created by another person, just as it is, requires no inventive effort at all. Before you raise your hands in dismay at what I'm suggesting, let me remind you that the funniness most of us transmit comes from telling jokes other people have invented. Being able to remember a joke and tell it well, in fact, is a talent we respect. Our admiration increases when a person can store up a number of jokes and then select one that precisely fits a particular situation or incident.

Senator Tom Harkin showed he had that talent during his 1992 run for the presidency. On one occasion he found he was the final speaker on a very long list. When the time for his speech finally arrived, he opened it by saying: "I see I'm the last speaker for today. I feel like Elizabeth Taylor's seventh husband on his wedding night. I know what I'm supposed to do. I'm just not sure I can make it interesting."

Harkin didn't invent that joke. Many years before Milton Berle had said the same thing about the husband of another multiple bride, Zsa Zsa Gabor. Berle probably didn't invent the remark either. The point is that it fit Harkin's need perfectly. It had a direct application to the situation in which he found himself and possessed just the tinge of naughtiness that might wake up an audience whose attention was flagging.

A further point is that Harkin didn't suggest in any way that the joke was his. Because it is a common practice for speakers to tell other people's jokes, his audience would assume he had picked it up somewhere and was simply applying it to the circumstances in which he found himself. When most of us tell jokes, we don't suggest that we invented them. Our listeners conclude correctly that we are simply passing along a joke we have heard or read. That is also what happens when a joke is sent from one person to another by means of the Internet. Generally, there is no credit line. That does not cause the recipient to assume that the joke originated with the sender.

Do we have any obligation to the authors of the jokes we tell? If we do know who they are, it would be a graceful note to mention their names, especially when we make their work part of a formal presentation, such as a speech. In most cases, of course, we have no idea who originated the material.

Even when a person and a joke are connected, we can't always be sure the attribution is correct. In a number of instances, two or more people have been given credit for originating the same joke. One of the more scintillating puns to come out of the 1920s was "You can lead a horticulture but you can't make her think." Both George Kaufman and Dorothy Parker had the wit to concoct that dazzling bit of word play, but which one did? Both have been named as its author.

Dorothy Parker has also had to share the credit for another oft-quoted comment. As mentioned earlier in this book, when someone told her that former President Calvin Coolidge, the "Silent Cal" of the 1920s, had died, she is supposed to have asked, "How can they tell?" In a profile written for *The New Yorker* Alva Johnson attributed that remark to a show business figure named Wilson Mizner.

A politician famed for his expertise in the art of repartee was Nicholas Longworth, who served as the Speaker of the House of Representatives from 1925 to 1931. One day one of his House colleagues ran his hand over Longworth's bald pate as he remarked: "You know your head feels just like my wife's behind." Rubbing his own head, Longworth presumably responded: "Why so it does." Was he really the one who made that unsettling response, or did it come from the playwright Marc Connelly, a contemporary of Longworth's who sported a dome equally as bald? Both have been credited with it.

Suppose you had a young niece who was addicted to biting her fingernails. Suppose further that you were visiting the Louvre in Paris and found a postcard in a gift shop with a picture of one of the museum's most noted exhibits, the armless Venus de Milo. Wouldn't it be clever of you to send that postcard to your niece after writing on it, "This is what will happen to you if you don't stop biting your fingernails." Two world famous wits are said to have done just that—the playwright Noel Coward and the comedian Will Rogers.

At times we may feel absolutely sure a certain famous person is responsible for some witty remark, and we may be absolutely wrong. Most people believe that W. C. Fields said, "Any man who hates dogs and babies can't be all bad." Why shouldn't we think he said it? It sounds just like the kind of remark his acerbic wit would produce. In actual fact, however, the comment wasn't made *by* Fields, it was said *about* him. It came from a speaker who was introducing Fields at a Masquers' Club dinner held to honor him. The source of that revelation is Leo Rosten, who included it in an article he wrote for the March 11, 1972, issue of the *Saturday Review*. Rosten says he knows he's right about this, because he attended the dinner. Unfortunately, the originator remains anonymous because Rosten didn't identify him.

Further complicating the problem of giving due credit is that we often don't know when a certain joke came into being. Earlier I referred to one of the nastier put-downs of the 1988 presidential campaign—"beware of Greeks wearing lifts"—which belittled the Greek ancestry and short stature of Michael Dukakis, the Democratic candidate. I had always thought that this ingenious revision of a well-known saying was the work of some witty Republican. The other day, I was watching a TV rerun of the movie *Pete and Tillie*, which was released in 1972, and there was that same wisecrack.

In Chapter 1, I mentioned a joke I heard some years ago from my pastor, Bob Wallace. It concerned a little girl who found her grandmother's driver's license and came to the conclusion that she had received an F in sex. Several years later Paul Harvey told that same story at the end of one of his newscasts. It was obvious that he had just heard it and was passing it along as a new joke.

The joke we tell today, in fact, may be hundreds, even thousands, of years old. You may have heard someone say of a new bridegroom, "The only way he can get any rest is to get out of bed." That joke appeared in the first edition of *Joe Miller's Jests*, published about 200 years ago.

One humorist who learned that some jokes have a long lineage was Johnny Carson. During one of his monologues on the *Tonight* show, he told this joke: "The life insurance company I do business with pays a claim only if death isn't permanent." One of his guests that evening, Tony Randall, who had a reputation for being ostentatiously erudite, pointed out that William Shakespeare had used that same joke in his play *Antony and*

Cleopatra, written some 400 years ago. It occurs in the scene in which Cleopatra is preparing to commit suicide. Under her orders, the court clown has brought her a poisonous snake concealed in a basket. As he approaches her, this exchange takes place:

<u>Cleopatra</u>: Has thou the pretty worm of Nilus there, that kills and pains not?

<u>Clown</u>: Truly, I have him: but I would not be the party what should desire you to touch him, for his biting is immortal; those that do die of it, do seldom or never recover.

Some of the things we say today may actually have been said for the first time in ancient Greece. You probably have heard someone remark of a certain city: "It's a nice place to visit, but I wouldn't want to live there." You may have said it yourself. The Greek rhetorician Isocrates made that remark around 400 B.C. The place he had in mind was the city of Athens. And even he may have heard it from someone else.

Around 1865 Mark Twain wrote one of his best known stories, "The Notorious Jumping Frog of Calaveras County." As he himself said, it was the first piece of writing that "brought me into public notice." It told of a gambler who won a contest between two jumping frogs by surreptitiously pouring quail shot down the throat of his opponent's frog. After Twain's story was published, a Professor Van Dyke of Princeton called his attention to the fact that a story virtually identical to his had been told in Greece some 2000 years ago. The only difference was that pebbles had been used to weigh down the Greek frog, rather than quail shot.

The anonymity of many joke makers and the ancient vintage of some of the stories they tell have tended to make us look on humorous material as public property. We say, "It's a dirty job, but someone has to do it," with an almost proprietary feeling that the remark is our own. In making it, of course, we are in the company of hundreds, perhaps thousands of others. Another smart saying that receives multiple renderings is "When I get the urge to exercise, I lie down until it goes away."

In discussing the propriety of repeating a joke originated by someone else, I have been thinking mainly about those for whom the transmission of humor is an avocation not a profession. Since humor can liven up a social situation or a workplace or add sparkle to one's speaking and writing, I see nothing wrong with using it as long as it is appropriate to the occasion.

Should the same standard apply to the professional humorist? In answering that question we must take into account a significant difference between the two groups. As I noted earlier, listeners to the jokes most of us tell don't assume that we invented them. The assumption with professionals is exactly the opposite. We take for granted that they have made up the jokes they use in their routines.

Do professionals take over other people's material without signaling that it came from another source? Sometimes they do. One of the places we are most likely to see the recycling of old material is in comic strips. One can scarcely blame the cartoonists for resorting at times to the use of other people's ideas. They must produce a strip every day of the week. They do not even get a respite from their daunting task on weekends. And acknowledging the source of the material would probably disturb the rhythm of the joke.

I once came across a surprising instance of the simultaneous use by two comic-strip artists of the identical pun, which I presume some third party had originated. At least one artist couldn't have picked it up from the other because their strips appeared in the *Ann Arbor News* on the same day, August 25, 1980. One of the strips, *Frank and Ernest*, showed two men in a laboratory setting. One of them had turned to the other to say, "Do me a favor, Ernie, stop referring to our cloning project as 'Designer Genes'." The other strip, *Priscilla's Pop*, showed two little girls engaged in the following conversation:

First Girl: You have a real talent for design, Priscilla.
Second Girl: Thanks.
First Girl: It must run in the family.
Second Girl: My grandma is a good designer.
First Girl: Well, you probably inherited her genes.
Second Girl: Hey, I've heard of those.
First Girl: What?
Second Girl: Designer jeans!

I may be wrong, of course, in thinking that this pun came from an outside source. It's possible that the two cartoonists thought it up independently. After all, identical ideas do come to different people simultaneously at times.

An equally astonishing duplication occurred in April 2004 when two editorial cartoonists drew cartoons based on exactly the same idea. One signed by Peters appeared in the *Dayton Daily News*, the other signed by Morin appeared in *The Miami Herald*. Both cartoons sprang from the often repeated speculation that the presidential decisions in the administration of the second George Bush are actually made by his vice president, Dick Cheney. The event pictured in the two cartoons was the joint appearance by Bush and Cheney before the commission investigating the 9/11 disaster. The treatment of the situation by both cartoonists is virtually identical.

192

George W. Bush appears as a puppet being manipulated by Dick Cheney, and Cheney is shown using the old ventriloquist's trick of drinking a glass of water while the puppet talks. Was this another case of two agile minds coming up simultaneously with the same idea?

Comic strip artists are not the only humorists who use other people's material. In watching a TV rerun of the movie *Chitty, Chitty, Bang Bang* the other day, I heard a line indelibly associated with Groucho Marx: "I saw an elephant in my pajamas. What he was doing in my pajamas I'll never know." No mention was made of Groucho nor of the movie in which he delivered the line.

Earlier I mentioned the comment made by either Dorothy Parker or Wilson Mizner when they heard that Calvin Coolidge had died: "How can they tell?" That line, slightly switched, turned up in the movie *Quiz Show*. When one character said to another, "There's a rumor Eisenhower died," the other responded "How can they tell?" No nods were made in either the direction of Parker or Mizner.

Earlier I mentioned some switching the comic novelist Peter De Vries had done to provide jokes for his novels. I also discovered that he sometimes appropriated material more directly. Some years ago I ran across the following gags in one of his novels:

> Anybody who goes to a psychiatrist ought to have his head examined.

> Top soil in Connecticut is dirt cheap.

I was working on a textbook at the time and realized that those jokes would make fine illustrations for a point I was making in the chapter on comedy writing. I wrote to De Vries requesting permission to use them, and much to my surprise, he wrote back to say they weren't his jokes. He had seen or heard them somewhere and had no idea where they had come from. (Since then, incidentally, I have seen the psychiatrist joke attributed to Samuel Goldwyn.)

De Vries, like comic-strip artists, had to maintain a constant flow of jokes and witticisms to fill up the pages of the comic novels he kept writing. Most of them, I'm sure, were the product of his own inimitable wit. When he ran across a bon mot that fit a particular need, one can understand why he would use it. But because we expect professionals to be the inventors rather than the mere purveyors of the material they present, it might have been appropriate to let his readers know that the jokes weren't his. Making such an acknowledgment might have disturbed the tone and flow of the passage, of course. If that was the case, we can understand why he didn't do it.

Using anonymous material without acknowledgment is one thing; doing so with material whose source is known is quite another. A publication for senior citizens I once received contained a signed column called "Observations," made up of pithy comments, jokes, and philosophical musings. Because of the way it was set up, one was led to believe that the various items were the work of the person whose name appeared under the title. The column contained this entry: "Did you know that man is the only creature that blushes, but then he's probably the only one who needs to." Mark Twain expressed that same idea more than one hundred years ago, and he did it somewhat more crisply: "Man is the only animal that blushes—or needs to." It seems to me that some recognition of Twain's contribution was in order, or if the column writer couldn't remember or didn't know who had said it, he might have added, "As someone once remarked," to indicate that that particular "observation" wasn't his.

It's possible, of course, that he believed he had thought it up. Have you ever given birth to a bright remark you felt you had invented only to discover later you had merely remembered it? Most of us have had that experience. Helen Keller, whose life was marked by great achievement despite her blindness and deafness, once submitted a poem to a magazine which turned out to be an almost word-for-word copy of a poem published many years earlier. Horribly embarrassed, she realized she must have memorized it as a child, forgotten its origin, and then when the words came into her mind again, thought they were hers. If the author of "Observations" was tricked by memory in the same way, he is to be excused.

Among comedians, having other people appropriate one's jokes is a touchy business. It can take bread and butter out of their mouths. During his prime, Milton Berle was routinely accused of stealing other comedians' material. He didn't deny it, and, in fact, made a joke about it by calling himself "The Thief of Bad-Gags"—a pretty good joke itself. In an article he wrote for *TV Guide*, which dealt with the ruthless way vaudeville performers used to treat their rivals, he said, "The success of another performer was a pebble in your shoe on your march to the headliner's spot. Selfishness didn't lead to damnation. Nor was pilfering a sin. If you 'borrowed' a line, the theft was for the greater glory of mankind—your act!"

Most performers reject that point of view. At times the loss of even a single gag to another comedian can be exceedingly damaging. An incident involving Robin Williams and a local Los Angeles comedian named John Witherspoon shows how it can hurt. Witherspoon had turned a common greeting heard among Black people, "What's happening, blood?" into "What's happening, plasma?" and had given it a key place in his comedy routine. One night he tuned into *Mork and Mindy*, the situation comedy that

194

made Robin Williams a national celebrity, and to his dismay heard Williams use his line. When Witherspoon included it in his routine the following night, the laughter it had always evoked before did not materialize. Instead his listeners looked up at him, silent and stony faced. Ironically, they thought he had stolen the joke from Robin Williams. When Witherspoon asked Williams why he had used it, Williams explained that he often ad libbed, and the line had just slipped out. He offered to pay for it. That was small recompense for Witherspoon. Robin William's borrowing meant he could never again use the line he had invented.

Stealing a specific line from another comedian and presenting it as one's own seems indefensible. Does that same prohibition apply to switching? In his book *Make 'Em Laugh*, Steve Allen appeared to be firmly opposed even to that practice. He took Johnny Carson to task for making use of frameworks other people had devised. The fact that he made slight changes in the format didn't excuse the theft in Allen's view.

One framework Allen mentioned was the gimmick of beginning the items in a quiz routine with answers rather than questions. Calling it "The Question Man," Allen made it a regular feature of the Sunday-evening comedy series he did on NBC. Carson took over the idea and retitled it "Carnac the Magnificent." Allen thought that he had originated the gimmick until he heard from a Los Angeles radio comic named Bob Arbagast, who claimed he had been the first one to use it. Thereafter Allen paid Arbagast a fee every time "The Question Man" appeared. Arbagast also wrote to Carson, but Allen said that he never received a response.

Allen also claimed that Carson's portrayal of the late-night pitchman Art Fern was a copy of a character he had originated and that Carson appropriated his idea of making members of the audience characters in a soap opera. Allen added that he was not the only comedian to whom Johnny Carson turned for ideas. According to Allen, Carson's Aunt Blabby was based on a character created by Jonathan Winters, and the squeaky voice Carson used for certain characters was inspired by the vocal pattern Jackie Gleason gave to his character Reginald Van Gleason. Allen remarked further that he was not the only one who had noted Carson's predilection for taking over other people's ideas. He mentioned that Dick Cavett in his autobiography drew attention to the close resemblance between The Mighty Carson Art Players and the Allen's Alley troupe Fred Allen had introduced on his radio program many years before. Cavett also commented that Carson's habit of gazing directly into the camera when something untoward happened was copied from Oliver Hardy of "Laurel and Hardy" fame.

In another passage in *Make 'Em Laugh*, Steve Allen pointed out that as the initial host of the *Tonight* show, he was the first comedian to engage audience members in conversation or to go out into the street to interview passersby. The implication seemed to be that he thus acquired proprietary right to those gimmicks. In making the comments, he seemed to be taking aim at others in the late-show field, among them Jay Leno and David Letterman. In the years after he wrote *Make ''Em Laugh*, it was clear that the fact he had originated a number of the routines currently being used was still on his mind. In an interview published by *TV Guide* in early 1996, Allen again reminded readers of the debt other comedians owed him, but he did it somewhat more gently than he had in his book. He said "David Letterman gives me credit when he does all my old routines." His feelings about Johnny Carson also seemed to have softened. He advised other comedians that "I think it would profit each of them well to watch old Johnny Carson tapes."

An ironic note in this controversy is that Steve Allen, who played the role of an accuser, also found himself among the accused. Jack Paar in his memoir *I Kid You Not*, mentioned that other comedians stole some of the material he delivered on an afternoon comedy show broadcast in the 1950s on CBS. The only filcher Paar identified was Steve Allen. He noted that some of the jokes Allen presented on a nighttime show bore a striking resemblance to ones he had originated. When he complained to Allen, he said the only response he received was a "long, ponderous letter giving me a tedious lecture on comedy."

What are we to make of all this? It is clear that both Steve Allen and Jack Paar at one time or another felt bitter about what they looked on as the appropriation of their ideas. But are their accusations justified? Allen did not accuse Carson of stealing any specific gags. The questions matched to the answers Carnac was given all came from Carson and his writers. And Carson added new wrinkles, the Carnac character and costume, and his inevitable stumble as he made his entrance. Moreover, the idea of beginning a quiz with answers instead of questions is not limited to comedy shows. That particular gimmick is a distinguishing feature of the game show *Jeopardy*. Jack Paar's charge is somewhat more pointed. He mentioned a specific routine he claimed Allen took over.

Back in the early days of broadcasting someone began making audiences laugh by spoofing commercials. Since then Allen, Carson, and a host of other comedians have done the same thing. Was it improper for them to make use of that framework? How unique and different must an idea be to qualify as the sole property of the person who originated it? The Steve Allen complaint, an unusual one for a person of his normally sunny disposition, suggests that a comedian is well advised to think carefully before even switching a fellow comedian's material.

I recognize that in discussing this issue, I have probably raised more questions than I have answered. On one point, I think, most people would agree: a comedian who uses specific lines or gags invented by another professional without acknowledging the debt is clearly stepping out of bounds. Whether it is equally reprehensible to switch someone else's joke or employ a framework another person developed, as Steve Allen implies, is debatable, however. In making a decision about what to do in a particular instance, you are pretty much on your own. In this difficult terrain, there are few markers to guide you.

Chapter 8
Helping a Joke Along

Time spent laughing is time spent with the gods.
Japanese proverb

L et us assume that the suggestions about creating jokes presented in the previous chapters have inspired you to invent at least one joke of your own. Let us assume, further, that you feel your joke meets the basic comic criteria and is therefore likely to make an audience laugh. Should you be satisfied? Unless you think your little bit of whimsey has exhausted all of its inherent laugh-producing possibilities, you should not be satisfied. "Is there anything I can do to make the laugh bigger?" is a question you should ask. A number of devices exist that might help you increase the laugh potential of your joke. Indeed, at times most of them can evoke laughter entirely on their own. In this chapter we take a look at what some of these devices are.

Using Funny Words and Sounds

Your first step is a simple one. Examine the specific words you have used in your joke with this question in mind: Are they the ones best calculated to amuse? Some words, for reasons that are hard to pin down, are just naturally funny in and of themselves. It is obvious that you can help your joke along if you use words possessing that built-in power. The comedian Don Rickles, for example, could make audiences chuckle simply by calling someone a "hockey puck." He wouldn't get the same result with the word "baseball." It isn't a funny word.

Another word that seems to have an innate power to provoke laughs is "peanut." For some reason people found it amusing that Jimmy Carter had been a peanut farmer before he was elected president. Would they have had the same reaction if he had raised cotton?

No one has ever been able to explain why certain words are funny and others are not, but there have been some theories. Thomas Middleton, in an article he wrote for the *Saturday Review* speculated about why "peanuts" is a funny word. One reason, he thought, is that peanuts look funny. Another is that they are the cheapest nut around. From this may come the expression, "He's working for peanuts." They are certainly cheaper than walnuts, which, incidentally, isn't a funny word. Charles Schulz obviously recognized the comic potential in the word when he called Charlie Brown, Snoopy, Linus, Lucy, and the other inhabitants of his comic strip *Peanuts*.

In his play *The Sunshine Boys*, Neil Simon has the character Willie Clark discourse for awhile about funny sounds and words. He explains to his nephew that words with a *k* in them are funny. That may be why Don Rickle's "hockey puck" made audiences laugh. It has two *k*'s. Comedians in the New York area often get laughs by weaving references to Brooklyn and Hoboken into their monologues. In my area the funny sounding place name is Hamtramck, a suburb of Detroit.

The problem with this theory is that putting a place name with a *k* into a joke doesn't necessarily make it funnier. Pike's Peak has no special power to make people laugh, and yet it has two *k*'s. And no one giggles at the mere mention of New York. By locating a joke in Flatbush, on the other hand, you can enhance its laugh-producing power, and the name doesn't even have a *k* in it.

What this all adds up to is that you are pretty much on your own in deciding what words are funny and what aren't. A reference to herring or chopped liver, for example, is likely to make an audience titter. Mentioning salmon or roast beef in and of itself won't do anything for a joke. Somehow you have to be aware of this. Walt Kelly, the creator of the comic strip *Pogo*, obviously had that kind of sensitivity. He might have made his characters inhabitants of the Everglades. Instead he wisely chose to have them live in the Okeefenokee swamp. Just saying it makes us laugh.

Let's see how replacing an unfunny word with a funny one can help a joke along. This is the first version:

A lawyer and his wife were giving a dinner party for a group of friends. After they had assembled, he asked his wife, "Is dinner ready yet?"

"Yes, counselor," she answered. "You may approach the table."

Does that joke make you laugh? Not very loudly, I'm sure. Now let's change just one word and see what happens:

A lawyer and his wife were giving a dinner party for a group of friends. After they had assembled, he asked his wife, "Is dinner ready yet?"

"Yes counselor," she answered. "You may approach the beans."

The basic comic peg on which both these jokes turn is an incongruity— the transferring of language used in a courtroom to a social situation. I think you will agree, however, that changing just one word makes the second version funnier.

Let's look at another example. In the "Periscope" section of the February 12, 1996, issue of *Newsweek*, there was a feature on the pets owned by a number of the candidates who were vying for the 1996 Republican presidential nomination. Most of the candidates the magazine contacted willingly provided information about their pets and pictures of them. The exception was Steve Forbes. According to the story, he "stonewalled" all requests for names, breeds, or photographs. The feature concluded with these questions: "Just what is Steve Forbes hiding? Could there be an unlicensed Chihuahua lurking behind the wall of his New Jersey estate?"

This is another illustration of the difference one word can make to the funniness of a joke. Making the breed of the undercover dog a Chihuahua was an inspired choice. Had the writer speculated it was a collie, the story would not have been nearly so amusing.

Once in awhile we come across a phrase already stocked with funny sounding words. The line from the familiar nursery rhyme "Eenie, meenie, miney, moe" is an example. One joke maker used this phrase as the starting point for a well-crafted joke. "We call our children Eenie, Meenie, Miney, and we don't expect no Moe."

Funny place names can be a rich source of humor. In his radio programs Jack Benny could make his studio audiences laugh uproariously simply by having a train announcer reel off a list of destinations ending with "Anaheim, Azuza, and Cucomonga." He didn't have to make those names up. They are the names of actual places in California. There are lots of names like them waiting to be discovered by alert joke makers. This headline appeared in an Illinois newspaper, for example, NORMAL MAN WEDS OBLONG WOMAN. Normal and Oblong, of course, were the names of the towns from which they came. The United States is dotted with a great many places blessed with funny sounding names. Walla Walla, Washington, and Oshkosh, Wisconsin come immediately to mind. In my own state of Michigan, we have Kalamazoo, Bad Axe, and Hell.

As a child in Canada, I was always amused when my father mentioned the names of two nearby towns: Moosejaw and Medicine Hat. England is a particularly rich source of funny sounding place names. In the Cotswold area, I remember seeing signs pointing the way to North Piddle. The possibilities for having fun with that name seem endless. In Washington there's a town called Peculiar, and in Indiana there is one called Nonesuch.

The humor in the following story mainly arises from the odd-sounding names of places in the United States and Canada:

A woman on the road in New Mexico wanted to get in touch with her folks who lived in Canada. She stopped at a gas station to use the phone and asked for the long-distance operator. "This is Babe Clatterbuck in Tucumcari, New Mexico, and I want to speak with Pa Quackenbush in Saskatoon, Saskatchewan."

The operator hesitated for a moment, then said, "Would you mind spelling any one of those?"

This story combines the use of funny sounding place names with funny sounding people's names. The place names are real, the people's names

202

were probably made up. Some real people have been given amusing names, of course. The Texas couple named "Hogg" who inexplicably named one of their daughters "Ima" comes to mind. The potential for using it to provoke laughs seems obvious. But professional humorists who go too far in that direction might find themselves in legal trouble.

There is no restraint on making up funny names, however, and many humorists have enriched their material by doing so. In this regard one is likely to think of Charles Dickens. He peopled his stories with characters whose names alone have the capacity to make us laugh—Mrs. Gummidge, Joseph Sniggers, Mr. Pecksniff, and a host of others. People attending a production of William Wycherley's restoration comedy *The Country Wife* are likely to start laughing even before the play begins when they see in the playbill that they are about to be introduced to such characters as Sir Jaspar Fidget and Old Lady Squeamish. Humorists of more recent vintage, S. J. Perelman and Jonathan Winters, have often evoked appreciative chuckles by inventing funny names. Two that came from Perelman were Ernest Void and Motley Throng, and Winters gave birth to Granny Frickert and Elwood P. Suggins. The British writer H. H. Munro, who used the pen name Saki, was not only adept at coining curious names for people—Crispina Umberleigh and Arlington Stringham among them—but he once applied this talent to devising a name for a breakfast cereal. He called it Filboid Studge, and featured it in one of his short stories.

Some comedians have helped their careers by giving themselves funny sounding names. Jacob Cohen used the stage name Jack Ray when he began to work as a comedian. When he failed to attract any particular notice, he changed it to Rodney Dangerfield, and his career took off. One of the most inspired of name changes was carried out by three brothers name Marx. They retained their last name but changed their first names to Groucho, Chico, and Harpo. Would they have been as successful had they decided to use the names their parents gave them—Julius, Leonard, and Adolph? (Adolph maybe.)

Thus far we've been thinking about how words with funniness built into them can raise the laughter quotient of a joke. Can words that aren't intrinsically funny do the same thing? They can if they are used in the right combination. Consider the following joke:

> It was a young physician's custom to drop into a neighborhood bar after working hours and order a daiquiri cocktail sprinkled with nutmeg. One evening the bartender found that he was out of nutmeg so he ground up a hickory nut and used the grains as a substitute. After tasting it, the doctor asked, "What's this?"

"A hickory, daiquiri, doc," the bartender replied.

Heard in isolation, none of these words is particularly funny. But put together they can make us laugh. How perfectly ordinary words can evoke laughter if one strings their sounds together in a certain order is also illustrated by the following joke:

A kindly woman had provided lunch for a hobo who had knocked on her back door. After he had finished eating, she gestured toward a saw sitting next to a pile of uncut wood. The hobo took one look and said before taking off, "You saw me see it, but you ain't gonna see me saw it."

These two previous jokes both have points. One reminds us of a well-known nursery rhyme, the other causes us to reflect about the work attitudes of the class of people we call hobos. Sometimes the deft manipulation of words with similar sounds can make an audience laugh even when the combination ends up making no point at all, as the following demonstrates:

In one Catholic parish, the Mother House of the Sisters of St. Francis was situated across the street from a Franciscan monastery. One day a nun at the switchboard heard this message: "Sister, this is Brother. Father wants to talk to Mother."

One of the most notable sketches on the *Jack Benny Show* was also the sort of material that garners big laughs without making any point. It was funny simply because of the kind of sounds the audience heard. Those sounds came from that master of dialects Mel Blanc:

Travel Agent: You're going to Mexico?
Blanc: Si.
Agent: Flight 341?
Blanc: Si.
Agent: You will be staying at Hotel Amigo?
Blanc: Si.
Agent: What's your name?
Blanc: Cy.
Agent: Your wife is traveling with you?
Blanc: Si.
Agent: What's her name?
Blanc: Sue.

A good way to get the most out of a funny sound is to repeat it. One such sound is the *oi* we hear when "bird" and "third" come out as "boid" and "t'oid." See how the following verse builds the laugh by constantly repeating this sound.

Toity poiple boids,

Sittin' on de coib,
A choipin and a boipin,
And eat'n doity woims.

Even sounds that aren't funny in and of themselves can become funny at times if they are repeated. A sketch featuring the British comedy performer Beatrice Lillie provides an example. It showed her entering Harrods, the London department store, and telling a saleslady she wanted to purchase "Two dozen double-damask dinner napkins." When the saleslady asked her to repeat her request it came out "Two dazzle dimask dibble dinner naples." There were several other variations employing initial *d* sounds before the sketch came to its hilarious conclusion.

A notable example of material whose funniness was produced entirely by a recurring sound came from Johnny Carson. It satirized the *Dragnet* TV series and featured Carson as a witness and Jack Webb as Sergeant Friday, the role that made him famous. The sketch began with Carson reporting the theft of some copper clappers from a closet. The loss, it turned out, had been discovered by Clara Clifford, the cleaning woman, and the clean copper clappers had apparently been copped by Claude Cooper, a kleptomaniac. The sketch ended with Carson warning that if he caught Claude Cooper, the kleptomaniac, he'd clobber him. Carson included this sketch in the set of videotapes he produced after his retirement as host of the *Tonight* show.

Occasionally a sound that is funny in and of itself can be used to elicit laughter even when it is not repeated. The best example is a sketch originated by Victor Borge. His device was essentially simple. He converted the punctuation marks we see on printed pages—periods, commas, exclamation marks—into individual sounds. They were all different, all unique. Then while he was reading a piece of straight material with no humorous content at all, he interjected his vocal representations of the punctuation marks as they might occur on the printed page. Those sounds alone were enough to make his audiences rock with laughter. The sketch was so successful that it made Victor Borge famous overnight.

Sometimes humorists magnify the effect of repeating sounds and words by setting them into a rhythmic, rhyming pattern. A good example appeared in Louis Untermeyer's collection of funny material, *A Treasury of Laughter*:

A tutor who tooted the flute
Tried to tutor two tooters to toot.
Said the two to the tutor,
"Is it harder to toot or
To tutor two tooters to toot?"

Many of you will recognize this example as a form of verse that, for reasons unknown, is called a limerick. Their creators, many of them anonymous, use a number of comic devices besides that of repeating sounds. Puns abound. Louis Untermeyer pointed to another characteristic when he said, "It is a lamentable fact that the best limericks are the unprintable ones." Most of us, told that we are about to hear a limerick, expect it to be bawdy. Morris Bishop, a writer of light verse put that thought into limerick form:

The limerick's furtive and mean;
You must keep her in close quarantine,
    Or she sneaks to the slums,
    And promptly becomes
Disorderly, drunk, and obscene.

W. S. Gilbert, the composer of the lyrics for the Gilbert and Sullivan operas, showed how to use the limerick form to create surprise by tampering with its conventional rhyming scheme. His limerick reads as follows:

There was an old man of St. Bees
Who was stung in the arm by a wasp.
    When asked, "Does it hurt?"
    He replied, "No it doesn't—
I'm so glad it wasn't a hornet."

The limerick is not the only verse form that uses catchy rhymes and rhythms to produce a humorous effect. Some of them are so catchy that they are difficult to get out of one's mind. Mark Twain wrote a piece entitled "Punch, Brothers, Punch" which described the travail he suffered after reading the following verse:

Conductor, when you receive a fare,
Punch in the presence of the passenjare!
A blue trip slip for an eight-cent fare,
A buff trip slip for a six-cent fare,
A pink trip slip for a three-cent fare,
Punch in the presence of the passenjare!
            Chorus
Punch, bothers, punch, punch with care!
Punch in the presence of the passenjare!

Mark Twain claimed that those words "took instant and entire possession of me. All through breakfast they went waltzing through my mind." As he kept repeating them relentlessly, his feet even kept time to them. The verse maintained its hold on him until he thought of reciting it to someone else. As his victim went away mumbling the verse, Twain found that a miracle had taken place. The pernicious rhymes were no longer resounding in his mind. I have a confession to make. I read Twain's piece when I was a teenager and the verse made the same indelible imprint on me as it did on him. Perhaps I too am free of it at last. For you, my dear readers, I can only close with the warning Mark Twain used to conclude his essay—and it may be a little tardy. "Avoid these rhymes as you would a pestilence."

Giving the Impression of Spontaneity

In a conversation involving a number of people, Stephen Leacock mentioned a college student who earned tuition money by winning prizes in golf tournaments. Someone in the group remarked, "I gather he's putting himself through college." This comment drew an uproarious laugh from the rest of the group. Did it deserve that kind of reaction? On the face of it, the pun is pretty weak. As part of a prepared monologue, it even might have drawn groans rather than laughs. What gave it exceptional comic power was the fact that it had been created on the spur of the moment. The aura of spontaneity can make any joke seem funnier than it really is.

There is a lesson in this for joke makers. You can help a joke along by giving your audience the impression that it has just popped into your mind. A joke that actually is a product of the moment is the one most likely to give an impression of spontaneity, of course. There have been some memorable examples of witticisms that were clearly the result of sudden inspiration.

The opera singer Leo Slezak, father of the film actor Walter Slezak, while performing in *Lohengrin* was supposed at one point to step into a boat shaped like a swan. Just as he was about to enter it, the stage hands mistakenly pulled it away. As he stood looking forlornly at the departing vessel, he made a remark that has been cherished down through the years: "When does the next swan leave?"

Beatrice Lillie showed she could react spontaneously to unexpected events when a pigeon suddenly flew into her apartment while she was entertaining some guests. It alighted on the arm of her chair, fluffed its wings, and looked up inquiringly at her. Her instant response was, "Any messages?"

One of the gifts that help explain Johnny Carson's thirty-year tenure as host of the *Tonight* show was his ability to turn unexpected happenings or statements by guests into jokes. There was the time, for example, when he asked a guest who raised pigs why he had taken up that particular vocation. The guest replied, "My old father had a farm," Carson promptly responded, "EI-EIO."

Perhaps Carson's most notable ad lib came during the celebrated episode referred to earlier in this book, in which his guest Ed Ames was demonstrating how to throw a tomahawk. You will recall that it landed in the crotch area of a cardboard cut-out of a cowboy in a totally unexpected and highly suggestive position. After the audience laughter died down, Carson sent it to new heights by commenting, "I didn't even know you were Jewish."

A political figure noted for his ready wit was the former presidential candidate Adlai Stevenson. An example of his spontaneous humor was his response to some words yelled at him after he had concluded a speech. A woman called out, "Mr. Stevenson, you have won the vote of every thinking American."

"Yes," Stevenson responded somewhat sadly. "But I need a majority!"

People who are not celebrities often hit the mark with a spontaneous comment. An authority on human behavior, whose name has not been recorded, once responded with biting wit to inconsiderate treatment accorded him by an organization he was scheduled to address. Unfortunately, his talk was preceded by a long business meeting, and when it finally wound down, the chairman said, "I see that the time is getting very late. We're going to hear from our speaker now, and I hope he will be as brief as possible. As you know, he is going to talk on sex."

"It gives me great pleasure," the speaker said, and promptly sat down.

An equally anonymous history professor was just as quick witted in responding to a trick some of his students played on him. They took advantage of the fact that he gave his lectures in a college theater from a section of its stage that could be raised or lowered. Some practical jokers in his class attached a timing device to the lowering mechanism and set it to operate half way through the class period. As he began a slow descent in the middle of his lecture, the professor calmly remarked, "This may be the first time a professor has gone down in history."

Even a written comment can retain an air of spontaneity at times. As we read the following examples we can see sudden smiles flash across the faces of those who wrote them, and we smile too, as we enjoy their spur-of-the-moment wit:

An advertisement on the back of a bench in Phoenix, Arizona, read: "CROSSTOWN BUSSES RUN ALL DAY." A whimsical passerby had written beneath it in large letters, "DOO-DAH, DOO-DAH."

"Why am I so mizzerable?" read the message scrawled on a poster in London. Underneath it someone wrote: "You're just going through a bad spell."

The inspired response of a stagehand who was caught on stage during the performance of a ballet demonstrates that spontaneous wit does not necessarily have to be communicated in words. Suddenly seeing the audience staring up at him, he raised his arms above his head in a graceful arc, stood up on his toes, and pirouetted off stage. The burst of applause he received was as great as any accorded the dancers in the ballet.

Being able to react to an unexpected situation with instant humor is a gift few comedians possess. One willing to gamble on the inspiration of the moment was Steve Allen. He sometimes went on the air without preparing a script ahead of time. In Jonathan Winters' appearances on the *Tonight* show, he sometimes invited the audience to suggest topics, which he used as springboards to routines he invented on the spot. Another comedian who has made a specialty of spontaneous humor is Robin Williams.

Most comedians, in contrast to these ad-lib specialists, prepare their material well before they deliver it. In fact, they may have honed and polished it through a period of years. Can an impression of spontaneity still be conveyed in such circumstances? Much depends on the manner of delivery. It is deadly simply to *recite* what one has prepared. The most successful comedians give the impression that their jokes and witticisms are taking form in their minds as they go along. Jerry Seinfeld is a good example of that skill. As he talks about the foibles of everyday life, one idea seems to give birth to another while he's standing there. The naturalness of his delivery and his own seemingly impulsive reactions to the comments he makes further enhance the aura of spontaneity he develops.

Another comedian who was eminently successful in giving the impression that he had just thought up the jokes he spouted was Groucho Marx. The vehicle that gave him the reputation of being a spontaneous wit was a television quiz show called *You Bet Your Life*. The stream of hilarious comments he made about the contestants he interviewed seemed, as the saying goes, to come right off the top of his head. Some of them may have, for Groucho was an expert at creating instant humor. In an article Dick Cavett wrote about him, he tells of the time he heard Groucho pick up a hotel phone and ask for room 4-8-2. Then quick as a flash he turned to

Cavett and said, "Sounds like a cannibal story." But even a wit as resourceful as he was might have had trouble producing a succession of jokes on an ad-lib basis for a full half hour. Most of the wisecracks he made on *You Bet Your Life* came from a corps of comedy writers, who interviewed the contestants ahead of time and prepared funny comments, which were then flashed on a screen located offstage where only Groucho could see it. Thus, when he asked a tree surgeon whether he had ever fallen out of a patient the audience thought it was his own spontaneous reaction to the man's profession when, in fact, one of his comedy writers had originated it.

Johnny Carson, whose skill as an ad libber I have already noted, also depended on comedy writers to create some of his spontaneous humor. On the quiz show *Who Do You Trust,* on which Carson served as MC before he became host of *Tonight,* almost all of the jokes, both those that had obviously been prepared ahead of time and those that seemed to be spur-of-the-moment remarks, were originated by Carson's head writer, Ray Kannerman. So skilled was Carson at delivering those "ad libs" that most people, including members of his crew who weren't in on the secret, were led to believe he had just thought them up. Many of the spontaneous comments he delivered on the *Tonight* show were legitimately spontaneous, as I have already pointed out, but some of them were also the product of his comedy writers.

The actor and comedian Billy Crystal has made several appearances as host of the Academy Awards program. His ability to pick up on happenings that occurred on the show unexpectedly made him one of the most successful of the many comedians who have performed the hosting duties. There is no question that Crystal is quick witted enough to invent on the spur of the moment some of the gags that made his audience of movie celebrities roar with laughter. He has acknowledged, however, that he had help. The producers of the program employ comedy writers who stand in the wings and write jokes for the host. Some of Crystal's spontaneous gags come from that source.

A good way of making a remark sound spontaneous is to anticipate something that may happen and have a joke ready in case it does. During the Academy Awards show of 1974, the actor David Niven was in the process of introducing Elizabeth Taylor when a nude man suddenly darted out of the wings and streaked across the stage. Niven paused for a moment and then remarked, "Isn't it fascinating to think that probably the only laugh that man will ever get is by stripping off his clothes and showing his shortcomings." Niven's apparently spontaneous wit drew a tremendous burst of applause from the people in the theater. Only later was it learned that the show's producers, anticipating that a streaker might make an appearance, had prepared the gag ahead of time. During rehearsal they made it available to the various presenters, including Niven, and instructed them to use it if the streaker showed up while they were on stage.

A similar type of preparation brought a Detroit minister one of the biggest laughs he had ever drawn. He was painfully aware that the area's professional football team, the Detroit Lions, would be playing their biggest game of the season close to the time the Sunday service was scheduled. It was likely that many of his parishioners would choose to go to the game rather than attend church. When he stepped up to the pulpit on Sunday morning, he saw that his worst fears had been realized. The attendance was sparse indeed. But he was ready with a joke he had worked out the night before. Surveying the empty seats, he said, "Well it looks like the lions are beating the Christians again." The congregation responded with a loud laugh and tumultuous applause. The seeming spontaneity of his comment was the main reason for their boisterous reaction.

Sometimes you can give an impression of spontaneity even when the joke is not yours. My friend Joe Moffatt did that when he announced during a faculty lunch hour that he was going to tell a Polish joke. One of our number, a young female faculty member, fixed him with a gimlet eye and said, "I'll have you know I'm Polish." The retort of the story teller came instantaneously: "That's all right. I'll tell it very slowly."

The group dissolved in laughter. Even the young woman laughed and then applauded him. Largely responsible for our appreciative response, of course, was the belief that his riposte was the product of his own wit. Sometime after that, I happened to run across a joke in a magazine which concluded with the same put down, though the target was different—White House workers instead of Polish people. I wondered whether he had seen it, too, and had stored it in his memory bank ready for use in case a similar opportunity presented itself. Whether or not he did, the point is that you can give an impression of spontaneity by applying jokes or witticisms you have remembered to situations or comments that suddenly develop around you.

The way a joke is written is an important factor in determining whether it will appear to be spontaneous. Above all, it must sound conversational. Skilled writers can make it seem that characters in a sketch are responding with instantaneous wit to what is happening. A story told by Redd Fox about an incident that occurred during the Watts race riot provides a good example:

I was in Watts when the riots started. Maybe you saw my cousin on TV with a couch on his head. "Are you a looter?" a cop asked him.

"Absolutely not," my cousin responded. "I'm a psychiatrist making a house call."

Taking Advantage of Visualization

We noted in a previous chapter that in order to be called a joke, humorous material must cause an audience to do something, such as connecting one idea with another, recalling a well-known story, arriving at a conclusion, or reflecting on a philosophical point. One of the most powerful producers of laughter is a funny or ludicrous picture created in the audience's mind by material the joke maker presents. Sometimes this visualization acts on its own to evoke laughter. In other instances it contributes to stimulating the maximum laugh response.

In the following joke, visualization is the main inciter of laughter:

A friend of mine was run over by a steamroller yesterday. He's in the hospital now in rooms 16, 17, and 18.

A joke utilizing the same technique, which may make mothers in the audience cringe a little, goes as follows:

A question came into a newspaper asking it for the birthdate of the longest baby ever born. The answer was duly printed the next day, July 12, 13, and 14.

In the following joke visualization is the final cap to a story that also generates amusement as it goes along:

A 130-pound man came to a lumber camp to seek a job as a lumberjack. The foreman was about to reject him out-of-hand because of his puny size, but the little man begged for a chance to demonstrate his skill. "All right," the foreman said pointing to a tree that was five feet thick. "Cut that tree down." The tiny man picked up an axe and in a moment its blade became an arc of silver as the axe sliced with blinding speed into the huge tree. In almost no time it came crashing down. The foreman stared at it in open-mouthed astonishment. "Where did you ever learn to swing an axe like that?" he asked.

"Cutting down trees in the Sahara," the little man replied proudly.

"But the Sahara's a desert."

"Sure, now it is."

That joke requires an audience to venture into the past to visualize a still verdant Sahara. Other jokes lead audiences into seeing a scene that is about to take form, as the following one does:

A married woman, engaged in a tryst with another man, hears a car drive up. Realizing that her husband has come home unexpectedly, she hisses into her paramour's ear, "Quick, get out of here. My husband's coming."

"Where's your back door," the man gasps.

"There's no back door."

"Where would you like one?"

Jokes depending on visualization by the audience to make or accent their points differ in the kinds of challenges they present. Some pictures are relatively easy to call up. The images the joke teller wants listeners to visualize in the following two jokes should leap immediately into their minds:

A plumber who was called to repair a pipe that was gushing water into a basement arrived several hours after he had been summoned. "I'm sorry I'm late," he apologized. "Have you been getting along all right?"

"I've been making good use of my time," the woman of the house replied stiffly. "While I've been waiting for you, I've taught the children how to swim."

The old-time comedian Bobby Clark was eating in a restaurant when the waiter came by to check on how everything was going. "How was the soup, sir?" he asked solicitously.

"To tell the truth," came the answer, "I'm kinda sorry I stirred it."

Some jokes, on the other hand, require considerable mental assembling before the picture takes form. The following two items need an audience that is intellectually agile:

A story in the *Denver Post* reported that a park safety plan directs pedestrians and joggers to stay to the left and travel in a clockwise direction. It further directs bicyclists to stay to the right and ride counter clockwise around the park.

The New Yorker magazine followed the reprinting of this item in its pages with the comment, "Good luck, everybody!"

The manager of a boat-rental concession, noting that one of his customers had been out the allotted time, went to the water's edge and shouted through a megaphone, "Number 99, come in, please, your time is up."

When several minutes went by without any response, he called again, "Boat 99, come in, please. If you don't return immediately, I'll have to charge you overtime."

At that point the manager's assistant broke in with, "I don't think we have a 99, Boss. All we have are seventy-five boats."

The manager pondered this a moment and then raised his megaphone again. "Boat 66, are you having trouble?"

Visualization is a particularly effective way of delivering a funny put-down. Through the ages obesity has been a common topic of humor. In the next two jokes adroitly conceived suggestion stimulates pictures that cause audiences to see the sometimes ludicrous result of over-abundant flesh:

When the fashion cycle brought short dresses back into favor, a woman went rummaging through her closet and found a mini-skirt she had worn as a young woman. She pulled it on then stopped with a puzzled expression on her face. Her problem was that she couldn't figure out what to do with her other leg.

A sobbing woman called a weight-reducing salon to say her husband had just given her a lovely present and she couldn't get into it. The salon manager replied soothingly, "We'll make an appointment for you, madam, and don't worry, we'll have you wearing that dress in no time."

"Dress?" the woman sobbed. "It's a Porsche."

Visualization can enhance the effect of one of the most commonly used humorous techniques—exaggeration. Cliff Arquette, known professionally as Charlie Weaver, was adept at calling up pictures of exaggerated action. A joke he told during one of his appearances on the *Tonight* show demonstrates the technique in action:

I was about to leave a hotel to catch a train when I found out the elevator was broken. I was on the twelfth floor, but I had no choice but to run down the twelve flights of a circular staircase. By the time I reached the bottom, I was going around in circles so fast, I screwed myself into the floor.

Visualization can help reveal an unexpected element in a situation, which, as surprises usually do, causes the audience to laugh. The following joke illustrates:

A woman who had had a phone installed in her bathroom heard it ring while she was taking a shower. She stepped halfway out, picked up the receiver, and then turned and handed it back through the shower curtains with the comment, "It's for you."

One of the greatest triumphs of visualization occurred in the stage play

214

Arsenic and Old Lace. Oddly enough it appeared in the curtain call rather than in the play itself. The main story line concerned two kindly but slightly dotty sisters who concluded that the elderly gentlemen who visited them had really little to live for. Deciding they could perform no greater service than to ease them gently from this world into the next, where presumably a better fate awaited them, they served elderberry wine spiked with arsenic to a succession of gentlemen callers, then buried them one after the other in the basement of their house.

The curtain call began in the usual way with the appearance of the actors. As they finished taking their bows, men began emerging from the door in the set leading to the basement, and continued doing so in a steady stream until they had formed a long row across the stage. For a moment the members of the audience stared at them in puzzlement, wondering who they were. Then suddenly the image of all those bodies buried in the basement flashed into their minds. As they realized they were witnessing the resurrection of the old gentlemen the kindly sisters had dispatched to their eternal rest, the theatre reverberated with the loudest laugh of the entire performance. Incidentally, it was a costly one. The backstage workers recruited to take part in that curtain call had to be paid an acting fee.

We all know that a great deal of humor revolves around topics some think of as taboo. The adroit use of visualization can materially heighten the effect of one of the most common types of such humor, the joke with sexual connotations. Sometimes the pictures it arouses merely skirt the edge of the forbidden, as this one does: "Whenever I go to a wedding where the bride is pregnant, I always throw puffed rice." A comment made by Barry Goldwater during a *Tonight* show appearance called up a picture equally innocuous. Speaking of the then Vice President Hubert Humphrey, Goldwater said, "He talks so fast listening to him is like trying to read *Playboy* with your wife turning the pages." This next joke evokes a somewhat more graphic picture:

Members of a women's-lib group paraded nude in front of City Hall. When asked why they had taken that step, one of them responded: "We wanted to get our differences out in the open."

Whether this next joke should be told in polite society depends on how polite the society is:

A dejected mother, who had been going through a continuous succession of pregnancies, came to her doctor seeking advice. "I've tried to help," he told her, "but you keep getting pregnant. I can think of only one more thing to do. I want you to put a ten-gallon crock in your bed, and before you go to sleep, put both your feet into

215

it, and keep them there until you get up."

Six weeks later the woman came back. She was pregnant again. "Didn't you put your feet into a crock the way I told you?" the exasperated doctor demanded.

"Well, sort of," the woman replied. "The trouble was we didn't have a ten-gallon crock, so I put my feet into two five-gallon ones."

Bathrooms and bathroom functions are also frequently referred to in the kind of humor that challenges taboos. The early creators of comic strips often provoked snickers by inserting drawings of outhouses into their cartoons. The development of modern plumbing outmoded this type of humor. There was a recent resurrection of it, however, in the contemporary comic strip *Born Loser*. It did not picture an actual outhouse, but led the readers into visualizing one. The strip showed a man telling his wife that his cousin was named Arson because he once set fire to the bathroom. To the wife's question, "Was anyone hurt?" the man replied, "It never reached the house."

Until fairly recent times, the makers of Hollywood films were not permitted to show toilets in bathroom scenes. The only permissible clue to the nature of the location was the presence of a washbasin or bathtub. The makers of a 1940s film, however, led the audience into "seeing" a toilet through the clever use of visualization. The scene showed the actress Mary Martin standing next to a washbasin as she tossed a wadded-up piece of paper off screen. It was pretty clear what its destination was. Not until the 1960s were audiences actually permitted to see toilets. The first film to show a toilet flushing was Alfred Hitchcock's *Psycho*.

In its early days television was equally pristine. The most essential item in a bathroom was never shown. *All in the Family*, the situation comedy that broke many taboos, broke another when it let its audience hear a toilet flushing. In the years since, of course, most prohibitions have vanished and, to some people's regret, there are now almost no restrictions on what can be said or shown in the movies and very few in television.

Thus far we have been thinking about visualization that takes place in audience's minds. Before leaving this subject, we should note that there are laughs to be found in actual visualization. It is obviously the main source of humor in cartoons. I recall a panel in the *Heathcliff* comic-strip series which showed the title character during a visit to a veterinarian. To escape the doctor's ministrations, he had taken refuge between the legs of a shaggy dog. All you could see of him was a pair of anxious cat eyes peering out from the dog's fleecy coat. There was a caption—"You're next, Heathcliff'—but all that was necessary to make a reader laugh was the picture.

Another artist who often generates laughs solely by visualization is *The New Yorker* cartoonist George Booth. His specialty is drawing frazzled cats and scrawny dogs. I remember one of his drawings, made up of four panels, which showed a dozing dog gradually losing its balance and finally toppling over. The last panel showed the dog sitting bolt upright once again his big puzzled eyes obviously asking the question, "What on earth happened?"

One of the funniest bits of actual visualization was the work of a practical joker, who happened to be the ticket-seller for a New York opera house. Through the years he had become acquainted with the personal characteristics of its patrons. For one performance he used this knowledge to play a prank. He parceled out the tickets in such a way that the bald heads of the male opera goers occupying the seats on the lower floor formed an identifiable pattern. Its victims were quite unaware of what had been done to them, but to those in the balcony it was clearly visible. As they took their places, they broke out into unrestrained laughter. Spelled out by the shining hairless pates of the baldheaded patrons below was the word SHIT.

Using Familiar Names

A simple way to beef up the laugh potential of a joke is to make its characters people the audience knows or recognizes. That is why celebrities often pick up newspapers to find they are being credited with witticisms they never uttered and funny exploits they never performed. When a humorist thinks up a line marked by the addled drollness associated with the remarks Yogi Berra is supposed to have made, why not pretend that Yogi is responsible for this one, too. Doing so probably will give it added circulation. I presume that Yogi did say some of the things attributed to him. Was "It's *deja vu* all over again" one of them? We can't be sure. Producing Yogi Berra *non sequiturs* seems to be a thriving cottage industry.

The technique of using familiar names becomes even more effective when the person in question is a local celebrity. Putting the name into your joke isn't being dishonest. It's just a way of having fun. Take the following joke, for instance:

After a coach's team blew a close game that lost the conference championship, he was asked how he had slept that night.

"I slept like a baby," he replied. "I'd sleep for an hour and then I'd wake up and cry for an hour."

That's not a bad joke as it stands, but you can substantially increase its voltage by giving a familiar name to the coach. I frequently spoke to

University of Michigan alumni clubs during the time Bo Schembechler was serving as the football coach. He was remarkably successful in winning Big Ten championships, but for some reason his special touch did not carry over into bowl games. If one of his bowl losses occurred near the time of my speech, Bo Schembechler became the coach in the story. That role can be easily transferred to other coaches who have just suffered bitter losses. Usually there are plenty of them around. In 1995 the Michigan basketball team was eliminated in the first round of the NCAA tournament after having been a Final Four team three times in recent years. Steve Fisher, the team's coach, became the person who "slept like a baby."

This "name" technique works equally well with people who are not necessarily celebrities, but who are acquaintances or friends of those in your audience. You are even more likely to get a laugh if the person you make your target is actually present while you are giving your speech. In my talk on humor, I find out the names of lawyers, doctors, teachers, and any others whose profession I may be referring to. They then become characters in the stories. Let's suppose that a Dr. Edwards is one of your listeners. You can enhance the effect of the following joke by making him the leading character:

> Dr. Edwards is highly regarded in his community. One reason is his ability to decide on treatments for various ailments with great speed and authority. One patient complained that when he pressed on a certain part of his arm, it caused pain. Dr. Edwards's advice came instantaneously: "Don't press on that part of your arm anymore." Another patient said that his leg hurt. Dr. Edwards's prescription for treatment was equally quick and terse, "Limp." (Incidentally, those jokes originated with Henny Youngman.) In a similar case, when a patient complained of pain, Dr. Edwards's asked, "Have you ever had this sort of pain before?" "Yes," the patient replied, and Dr. Edwards, always fast on the draw, said, "Well, you've got it again."

No one seems to resent being given this kind of treatment. I have never heard a single objection. In fact, the butt of the joke is often the person who laughs the loudest.

Suppose you want to tell a joke about someone who doesn't fit any of the special material you have on hand—your introducer, perhaps. In that situation you need an all-purpose joke that can exploit some kind of general quality, either one the person actually possesses or one you make up. I used such an all-purpose joke in responding to an introduction made by Bill Colburn, then an officer of the University of Michigan Alumni Association.

After he had finished detailing my many sterling qualities to a group of Michigan alumni, I made this comment:

Thank you very much for those kind words, Bill, most of which are true. Of course, I can be equally charitable in return. Bill has a number of personal qualities I could mention. One that has especially impressed me is his quick wit. Like all of us he occasionally puts his foot in his mouth. But I have never seen anyone faster at extracting it before too much damage has been done. There was the occasion, for example, when he was talking with a person he didn't know very well, and the subject of Columbus, Ohio, came up. At one point Bill remarked, somewhat intemperately perhaps, that the only thing Columbus is noted for are ladies of easy virtue and football players."

His companion's face flushed red, and he blurted angrily, "I'll have you know my wife was born in Columbus."

Quick as a flash, Bill responded, "What position did she play?"

That story exploited the intense football rivalry existing between Ohio State University, which is situated in Columbus, and the University of Michigan. In preparing your version of the story, you would naturally look for the name of a city capable of evoking a similar hostile reaction in the group you were scheduled to address. Such a city should be easy to find. Arch rivalries of the kind mentioned exist everywhere.

Testing Your Jokes

One of the best ways of finding out what to do to help a joke along is to try it out on other people. In some instances it may reveal you don't have a joke at all. In others it may indicate you have something going, but a puzzled look or a laugh that dies still-born may indicate that some repairs are necessary. Drama producers, particularly those specializing in comedy, often test the effectiveness of their material by performing their plays in Boston or Philadelphia before bringing them to their most important venue, New York. During this process substantial changes in scripts are often made. After Jerry Seinfeld decided to end the production of his highly successful TV program, he was scheduled to perform a comedy routine as an HBO special. To prepare for it, he took his comedy act on the road, and as audiences reacted to it, he made changes. When the time came to shoot the HBO program, he had honed every emphasis, every pause, every punchline to polished perfection.

Revising the scripts of films, of course, is more difficult, but the reactions of sneak-preview audiences sometimes result in the re-shooting of certain scenes. One of the problems faced by TV comedians is that they have no time to test their jokes before delivering them to a national audience. Johnny Carson often made this fact clear after one of his jokes had fallen flat. The producers of situation comedies have the same problem.

One way comedians make up for the lack of a try-out opportunity is to assemble a corps of writers. Its members then become audiences for one another's jokes. The main reason for having more than one writer, of course, is that the burden of producing humorous material five nights a week, or even once a week, is usually too much for a one person to handle. There have been exceptions. A writer name Harry Conn is reputed to have invented the character portrayed by Jack Benny on his radio show and to have written all or most of the scripts during its first four years on the air. He was succeeded by two writers and they, in turn, were succeeded by four. Another prolific producer of comedy material was Fred Allen. He is credited with creating three-quarters of the jokes he broadcast. Jack Benny was not an originator of comedy material, but he was a remarkably astute judge of what would work and what wouldn't. His writers could not have had a better try-out audience.

During his long career on NBC, Bob Hope had the regular assistance of about a dozen writers. The staffs of the contemporary talk-show hosts, Jay Leno and David Letterman, number about the same. That they serve as audiences for one another's jokes is obvious from the remarks Leno and Letterman make on occasion. When a joke fails to come off, Leno will sometimes turn to the head writer, who is watching his performance from off-stage, and remind him that he had expressed doubts about the joke's effectiveness. Letterman in one instance had a similar reaction. Before the broadcast, he had apparently been so sure one of the jokes would expire pitifully that he bet $100 to back up his opinion. When the joke surprised him by drawing a big laugh, he turned to the writer who had produced it and expressed his mock dismay at its success. He particularly mourned his lost $100.

Another big advantage of the group production of humor is that writers, working together, stimulate one another's funny bones. George Kaufman was one of the keenest wits who ever wrote comedy material, and yet he was almost never willing to work alone. He depended on his collaborators to bring out the best in him.

Most of the assignments in my writing classes were completed by students working alone. The exception was my comedy-writing assignment. I always gave it to teams of three. I knew for one thing that some students asked to write a comedy script themselves would be so paralyzed with fear that they would produce nothing. I also knew that by assigning three writers I was providing them with a preview audience for their jokes and that this combined with the social facilitation developed from working together would produce the best results. For you, as a beginning comedy writer, two steps would seem to be in order. Try to find someone with similar interests to work with you. At the very least, take advantage of your friends by trying out your jokes on them before presenting them to an audience.

Developing an Individual Style

For professional comedians it is difficult to think of anything more important in helping their jokes along than the development of an individual style. Knowing something of what to expect, audiences come to a performance with an attitude of anticipation. Because they are poised to laugh, the laughs come more readily. Even more important, a unique style gives comedians an identity that helps them emerge from the crowd of their competitors.

You may wonder how uniqueness can be achieved, considering that comedians all strike the same few triggers of humor—self satisfaction, incongruity, and surprise. We can compare their situation to that of composers of music. They have a limited number of notes available to them, yet the great composers combine and treat them in such a distinctive way that a work bearing their own individual stamp emerges. A musicologist listening to a few bars from an opera can instantly recognize the style of a Puccini or a Verdi. In the same way, the ability to manipulate the triggers of laughter in a distinctive, personal way is an important element in winning widespread recognition for a humorist. Take the following remarks, for instance:

> That woman drove me to drink. I just remembered I never wrote to thank her.

> I always carry whiskey with me in case I get bitten by a snake. And just to be sure, I always carry a snake.

Who said those words? People familiar with the great comedians of the last fifty years would probably focus immediately on W. C. Fields as the prime suspect. And they would be on the right track. The best clue to the identity of the author is the nature of the subject matter. Fields's comments often expressed his preference for a certain type of liquid refreshment. In other instances he was equally forthright in making clear his disdain for humankind's most commonly consumed potable. His comment—"I never drink water. Fish make love in it"—is a good example.

These items suggest that one of the best ways comedians can establish a unique identity is by concentrating on a particular kind of material. Gary Larson earned a special niche for himself by drawing cartoons that explored the world of the fantastic and the freakish. The series title he chose, *The Far Side*, indicated the nature of his material. Ernie Kovacs, a television comedian, whose career was cut tragically short by an automobile accident, was noted for the whimsical eccentricity of his subject matter. In one program he picked up a book entitled *Camille*. When he opened it, the book coughed. In another program he was a champion chess player about to play twelve other players simultaneously while blindfolded. His projected exploit came to an ignominious end when he stumbled into the row of tables at which his opponents were sitting and sent tables, chess boards, and chess pieces flying in every direction. He suffered the same kind of humiliation when he portrayed an Indianapolis race-car driver who couldn't get his car started.

Steven Wright is another comedian who specializes in the sort of humor many would call weird. He said, for example, "I'm not frightened by heights, but widths scare the hell out of me." On another occasion he remarked that he was once arrested for walking in someone else's sleep. And he told an audience mournfully, "I spilled spot remover on my dog's head, and now he's gone. Poor Spot." Wright's delivery matches his material. As I noted earlier, he maintains an expressionless face and speaks in a doleful monotone. Often his comments come spilling out with no connection to what he has just said or what he is about to say. His whole presentation shimmers with the rib-tickling aura of absurdity.

A number of comedians draw most of their laughs by making fun of themselves. In this regard we are likely to think first of Rodney Dangerfield's oft-repeated complaint, "I don't get no respect." Even as a child he apparently failed to inspire admiration among his playmates. "When I played hide and seek," he told an audience, "No one would look for me." His situation didn't improve as he grew older. Apparently even his wife found him unattractive. "She never makes love to me except for a reason," he once said. "One night she used me to time an egg."

Self denigration underlies much of Joan Rivers's humor. She describes herself as a person whose chances of winning a husband were almost nil. Her mother in her desperate struggle to get her married even went so far as to write her name and telephone number in men's restrooms. And one night that same mother put a sign in front of their house reading: <u>LAST GIRL BEFORE FREEWAY</u>.

Jokes that make fun of personal inadequacies are also a major element in the humor of Woody Allen. In his films he constantly portrays himself as a weak, fearful, wimpish bungler who has difficulty coping with life's simplest crises. He worries about his sexual attractiveness, he fears death, and he wonders what to believe. "If God would only speak to me," he once pleaded. "If he would only cough."

Woody Allen is by no means a one-note humorist, however. In his written material—short stories and essays—he has shown great skill in activating the trigger of incongruity. He often drops in a word or phrase so out of keeping with other items in the material that it jars readers into laughter. An excerpt from his private journal, published in *The New Yorker*, illustrates how an extended lament about the major miseries of his life is capped with a reference to an exquisitely minor irritation:

> I believe my consumption has grown worse, also my asthma. The wheezing comes and goes, and I get dizzy more and more frequently. I have taken to violent choking and fainting. My room is damp, and I have perpetual chills and palpitations of the heart. I noticed, too, that I am out of napkins. Will it never stop?

Still another technique we associate with Allen is the use of psychiatric or philosophical jargon. He frequently inserts it unexpectedly into a film, scene, or essay. In his movie *Manhattan*, for example, the characters played by Allen and Diane Keaton engage in a conversation marked by a long list of pseudo psychoanalytic terms. Allen's predilection in this area is illustrated by his comment, "I was thrown out of school for cheating on my metaphysical final. I looked within the soul of the boy next to me."

Some humorists find their special kind of subject matter in the world outside themselves. A particular target for a number of them are political happenings and characters. In the 1920s Will Rogers became famous for the barbs he tossed at politicians. In the 1950s a stand-up comedian named Mort Sahl moved into the limelight with monologues primarily directed at political figures and events. He became so prominent, in fact, that his face appeared on the cover of *Time,* and his life and work were covered in a *New Yorker* profile. Other aspects of his performance also drew attention. He discarded the tuxedo favored by other comedians of his period for a sweater and rumpled slacks. He was a forerunner of Woody Allen in his use of psychoanalytic terms. He told a story about a bank teller, for example, who was handed a note by a robber reading, "Give me all your money and act normal." The teller responded, "First, you must define your terms. What do you mean by normal?"

Many other humorists make fun of politicians and political events. They are the almost exclusive targets of Mark Russell's witticisms purveyed on PBS and CNN. Political satire is a major ingredient in Gary Trudeau's comic strip *Doonesbury*. The humor of Johnny Carson ranged widely through many different topics, but his slicing up of politicians often drew the greatest public notice. During the Watergate scandals he made Richard Nixon a laughing stock and thus helped grease the rails for his inglorious exit. He was equally merciless when the Iran-Contra crisis enveloped Ronald Reagan. In one instance he combined the two scandals by converting the question Howard Baker asked about Nixon during the Senate Watergate hearings, "What did the president know and when did he know it?" into a question that applied to Reagan, "What did the president know and when did he decide he didn't know it?" Political satire is also an important element in the monologues of Jay Leno, David Letterman, and Jon Stewart.

Focusing on a certain type of material has given identity to a number of other comedians. Bill Cosby rose to prominence by talking about such childhood characters as Fat Albert. He carried this focus on the ups and downs of childhood into *The Bill Cosby Show*, one of the most successful situation comedies ever broadcast. A major source for Louie Anderson's monologues are the idiosyncrasies of his family members and relatives. Jerry Seinfeld concentrates on the petty irritations and minor crises of urban life. Don Rickles's specialty was delivering insults aimed both at celebrities and people in his audiences. George Carlin is best known for railing at meaningless cant and clichés. In one routine he itemized a list of words he had banned from his vocabulary: "I will not *share* anything with you," he said, "I will not *relate* to you and you will not *identify* with me. I will give no *input* and I will expect no *feedback* in return." As I noted earlier, some comedians like Jonathan Winters have carved a special niche for themselves by permitting audiences to dictate the subjects for their humor.

The way material is worded can also be a significant factor in giving a comedian special identity. Henny Youngman is noted for the crispness and conciseness of his jokes. He has the ability to condense a humorous idea to its essence. His most famous joke referred to earlier in the book, "Take my wife...please" is a prime example of his skill in the art of compression. Somewhat longer, but still a model of succinctness, is his remark, "A man told me he hadn't had a bite in three days so I bit him." Sudden journeys like that from the beginning of a joke to its end caused him to be called "The King of the One Liners."

Another way to draw public notice is to invent a catchy phrase, slogan, or routine, and then impress it on the public mind by constantly repeating it.

Comedians know they have been successful when they hear other people reciting it. While Jackie Gleason was on the air, phrases he invented—"And away we go" and "How sweet it is"—could be heard everywhere. The "Top Ten List" which David Letterman introduced on his NBC *Late Night Show* and then carried over into his CBS program, was of immense help in winning him special recognition. Others began using the same framework to express their ideas, among them Vice President Al Gore, who listed ten advantages of being vice president when he appeared as a guest on David Letterman's program. *Newsweek* began a major article on late-night comedians with a take-off on the "Top Ten List" routine.

The use of a catch phrase has played a significant role in advancing the career of one of the most successful comedians of all time. Jeff Foxworthy has become the largest selling comedy artist in history. He appears regularly on Comedy Central, has starred in HBO and Showtime specials, has sold millions of DVDs, and attracts sold-out audiences to his Blue Collar Comedy Tour. A regular and always anticipated segment of his presentation is a series of jokes which begin with the catch phrase: "You might be a redneck if...." It can be said that these words launched a career.

We should note that although a catchy phrase or a distinctive routine can be a valuable element in a comedian's battery of material, they alone can't sustain a career. You must offer your audiences much more than that. In the 1930s a radio comedian named Joe Penner suddenly grabbed the spotlight with some inimitable sayings. He would begin a conversation by asking, "Wanna buy a duck?" or end one by shouting, "Oh, you nasty man!" For awhile those sayings, and others like them, became part of the national dialogue. But as the weeks went by and they continued to be about the only solid meat in his routines, their hold on the public loosened. Before his untimely death from a heart attack, Joe Penner had all but vanished from the airwaves.

Catch phrases and unique gimmicks can also be overdone. They can attract attention in the beginning by giving a presentation a distinctive flavor, but too much repetition may dull their appeal. One of the comedians who helped usher in the modern age of radio comedy in the early 1930s was Eddie Cantor, who had gained his first fame as a stage performer. At the beginning of his career he often provoked laughter by quacking like a duck. One day he made a personal appearance in a New York movie theater. As he stepped out on the stage a thunderous wave of quacking from the audience greeted him. Completely taken aback, Cantor resolved at that moment never to quack again.

A similar type of decision was made by the producers of radio's *Fibber McGee and Molly Show*. One of its funniest routines was the accidental opening of a door to a closet which Fibber had packed to overflowing with all kinds of miscellaneous objects. As they cascaded out onto the floor, a cacophony of well-orchestrated sound effects pictured what was happening. The sequence never failed to evoke a constant succession of laughs. And then after it seemed all the bumps, crashes, and thumps had ended, the sound of a tiny, tinkling bell was heard. It always drew a final, uproarious guffaw. The sequence was so funny it seemed repetition proof, yet the producers decided it could be overdone. They didn't eliminate it, but they severely rationed its use. By the time it made one of its rare appearances, the audience was hungry to hear it all over again.

We have noted already that David Letterman's "Top Ten List" helped give his program distinction. but one may wonder at times whether he is overdoing it. Sometimes I detect a little sigh from him as he begins the routine, suggesting that he may wish he didn't have to do it that particular night. He may feel caught by the pattern he has created. His audience expects to hear a "Top Ten List" on every program, and he feels obligated to fulfill that expectation. The result is that on nights when the fires of inspiration are burning low, the sequence creaks with artifice. Some rationing may be in order.

Thus far we have noted a number of ways in which a comedian may establish a special identity. I have not focused yet on the most important one of all—the development of a unique, individual persona. Some have used props or a special kind of dress to give their presentations distinction. Will Rogers wore a cowboy costume and twirled a lasso. George Burns and Groucho Marx smoked cigars. In fact, it is possible to do a recognizable impersonation of Groucho simply by pretending to tap a cigar in the inimitable way he did. Henny Youngman came out carrying a violin which he always seemed about to play but seldom did.

Props and costumes have their place in creating a personal trademark. If nothing else, a prop can solve the perplexing problem of what to do with one's hands. But alone they cannot produce a distinctive persona. To achieve that result comedians must establish themselves as unique personalities. The kind of attitude they convey is an element in it as well as their individual mannerisms, their gestures, and even their way of walking. Most important of all are the particular characteristics marking the delivery of their material.

In calling Bob Hope "The All-American Wisecracker," *Time* found a term that summed up the overall impression he made. The fast pace of his delivery was a major factor in creating the image of the quintessential wise guy. The gags that peppered his radio and television shows and his movies kept exploding like firecrackers. Someone once measured him zipping along at 120 jokes an hour.

A quite different image was created by Bob Hope's contemporary Jack Benny. One difference was that Benny did not specialize in gags at all. His comedy grew out of character and situation. His pace was also much slower than Hope's. In fact, some of the funniest moments in Benny's routines came when he was doing nothing at all except standing there. That was true of his most famous joke which we referred to earlier in the book, the one in which he answered a robber's challenge—"Your money or your life" with a long pause. Pressed into responding, he finally said, "I'm thinking it over....I'm thinking it over." Nothing could more eloquently convey his overriding concern for his money than that long pause.

I was privileged to see Jack Benny make personal appearances in movie theaters on two different occasions. What impressed me the most was his ability to use long, silent moments to make audiences laugh. I recall that he came out from the wings with that idiosyncratic stroll of his and took a position at the front of the stage. For more than a minute, it seemed, he did nothing more than stare quizzically out at the audience. A rumble of laughter began and kept rising until it was a roar. No words were necessary to incite that reaction. Better than anything else I have ever seen, his performance illustrated the kind of crucial contribution a well-established persona can make toward helping a comedian along toward a laugh.

Johnny Carson was a performer with a many-faceted talent. He was adept at delivering his monologues. One critic said that "He taught American how to tell a joke." Often funnier than his gags, however, was the way he responded when a joke went sour. He would distance himself from the wreckage with an attitude of philosophical resignation. His reaction was often so funny that one might wish more of his jokes would fall flat.

His image as the consummate responder was further burnished by the way he reacted to other happenings. Sometimes he underreacted. That was true the time a marmoset crawled slowly up his arm and shoulder and came to rest on the top of his head. During the marmoset's leisurely journey, Carson's face remained almost expressionless. He spoke only after it had made itself comfortable, and then it was to say, "Do you realize that I'm probably the only person on the face of the earth who at this moment has a marmoset on top of his head." Sometimes he overreacted. On one occasion he came too close to an unfriendly cheetah. The animal's snarl sent him jumping panic-stricken into the protective arms of Ed McMahon. More than anything else, I remember Johnny Carson as the masterly responder.

The late-night battle for audiences between David Letterman and Jay Leno has drawn a great deal of public and press attention. Of the two, Letterman was the first to win national prominence when he presided over the late-late show that followed Johnny Carson's *Tonight* program. Ironically, he was instrumental in propelling Leno into the national spotlight by inviting him more than thirty times to be a guest on his program. As I noted earlier, NBC's decision to make Leno the host of the *Tonight* show when Johnny Carson retired surprised almost everyone and was apparently a numbing shock to Letterman. He recovered quickly, however, with his appointment as host of CBS's *Late Night* show. In the early years of their head-to-head competition, Letterman drew the larger audience, but Leno eventually caught and passed him. Letterman, however, garnered more Emmy nominations and awards.

In my view, Letterman projects a sharper, better defined persona than Leno. For young people particularly, he became the embodiment of hip sophistication. Contributing to this image is his gap-toothed grin, his frowzy hair, his cackling laugh, his fidgety unbuttoning and buttoning of his coat, and his disdainful grimaces. His program tends to be more centered on stunts than it is on jokes. On one program he dropped watermelons from a roof top, for example, and he often leaves the studio to engage in other far-fetched ventures. Binding all this together is the almost continual sound of music in the contemporary mode, which provides riffs for the pay-off lines of his jokes and accompanies the entrances and exits of guests. He also interrupts his presentations to engage in banter with his orchestra leader, Paul Shaffer.

Leno's persona is fuzzier and more resistant to description than Letterman's. He is more conservative and less inclined to take risks, and in the tradition of most stand-up comedians, he puts most of his emphasis on jokes rather than on the physical action that characterizes the Letterman show. His monologues are a much more important element in his programs than they are in Letterman's, and they contain two to three times as many jokes. Leno never developed a special routine that caught the public ear the way Letterman's "Top Ten List" did, though many viewers look forward with anticipation to his weekly "Headlines" segment, which presents a group of wayward and wacky headlines and advertisements. Leno is particularly skilled in the construction of jokes. It is my impression that his quips, especially the ones dealing with political personalities and events, are more often quoted in the news media than those of any other comedian.

During the period that Leno trailed Letterman in audience ratings, he clearly worked hard to sharpen his image. He became more relaxed and more flexible in his reactions to unexpected happenings on the program. He took to leaving the studio at times to participate in pre-taped segments. He also made his orchestra a more significant element than it had been in his earlier years. His first orchestra, under Branford Marsalis's direction, performed almost as a separate entity and Marsalis rarely took part in any other part of the program. When Leno replaced that orchestra with one directed by Kevin Eubanks, music became a constantly pulsing presence, growling and burbling throughout the monologue and providing the riffs to punch up Leno's pay-off lines. Eubanks also engages in interchanges with Leno during the monologues and sometimes takes part in pre-taped comedy sequences. Some cynics might say that many of the changes Leno made in his show were inspired by his close observation of what Letterman was doing.

The image Leno now projects is of a regular fellow enjoying himself. He sometimes laughs along with the audience, but his reactions do not seem to be stimulated by his own wit, as is the case with some comedians. He just happens to be a purveyor of the humor and is enjoying it along with everyone else. Some of what he says is as biting and sarcastic as anything heard anywhere, but his happy demeanor works to dull its edge. Taking full advantage of the loosening of network standards for the late-night hours, Leno gives his material a somewhat racier touch than Letterman. His jokes are honed and polished with loving care, and yet in delivering them, he produces an ad-lib effect that enhances the image of a nice guy having fun with ideas that sometimes just pop into his mind.

Recently Leno and Letterman have been joined in the late-night race for viewers by Jon Stewart, whose *Daily Show* is broadcast four nights a week by the Comedy Central cable network and is rebroadcast the following day in an earlier time slot. Stewart is getting more and more public notice. The special gimmick that distinguishes him from his late-night competitors is his extreme bodily reactions to statements made by people in the news. He sets up each sequence by playing a tape of the comment on a screen located behind him. He then reacts to it with what can only be described as a series of facial gymnastics which convey feelings ranging from horror, disgust, and utter amazement to expressions of resignation or mere bemusement. He buttresses his presentation of what is supposed to be a news program with interviews and commentary by a corps of skilled associates. The half-hour program concludes with an interview of a person in the news. Stewart carefully managed to lure such luminaries as John McCain into helping him maintain the air of satirical fun that pervades the show. He differentiates himself from his late-night rivals by performing his routines from a sitting position. For that reason, it would be inaccurate to refer to him as a stand-up comedian.

There are a number of women comedians who have had or are finding successful careers as stand-up performers in comedy clubs and in other venues. For a time Joan Rivers served as host of a late-night show for the Fox network, but her tenure in that role was brief. As of this writing, no woman is serving in that capacity. However, Ellen De Generes has been attracting much favorable attention with a syndicated show that follows the pattern of the late-night shows hosted by David Letterman and Jay Leno. It is broadcast during daytime hours by TV stations around the country.

The quality that distinguishes Ellen De Generes is her refreshing air of sunny good nature. It pervades the entire program—the monologue, the special features, and the interviews with guests. She smiles and laughs a lot, but her good humor never seems forced. She is simply having fun. She employs physical stunts to some degree: the introduction to the program shows her falling down, and she dances and struts at times in response to what is happening on the show. Like Letterman and Leno, she exchanges quips with Tony, her music director. The monologues I've heard spring from her personal experiences. One, for example, dealt with the measures she has taken to keep spiders out of her bedroom. I have not heard her make a political personality or event the focus of a joke. The format she has adopted plows no new ground, but she has managed to place on it the stamp of a unique personality.

For all comedians, the development of a distinctive, recognizable persona is obviously a matter of great importance. In this section you have seen the approaches various humorists have taken to accomplish it. They cannot be a model, of course, for copying someone else's persona will never set you apart. They may stimulate your thinking, however. But finding the specifics that will give you a unique identity is a task you must carry out for yourself. Meeting that challenge will be the ultimate test of your capacity to be original.

Chapter 9
Distinguishing Good Jokes
From Bad Ones

*Against the assault of laughter nothing can stand,
not even the most colossal humbug.*
Mark Twain

231

You have noticed, I'm sure, that at times the reactions of different people to the same joke can vary widely. What may draw an uproarious laugh from one individual, another may greet with a supercilious look that clearly says—"How silly can you get?"—and still another may turn red-faced with anger. Ogden Nash referred to this phenomenon when he said, "In this foolish world there is nothing more numerous than different people's sense of the humorous." Divergent views on what is funny can even damage relationships as the novelist George Eliot noted in her comment, "A difference of taste in jokes is a great strain on the affections." Many factors have a bearing on a person's response to a joke, among them age, nationality, educational background, occupation, religion, living experience, mood, the situation, and the sex of the responder. A joke that makes a man laugh, may make a woman grit her teeth.

Even people who are experts in the field of humor may differ about the quality of a joke. An investigator named Rebecca Kaplan submitted a list of forty puns to a panel of such experts and asked them to rate them in order of merit. In some instances a pun one expert ranked the best another said was the worst. Goodman Ace, who was both a writer and a performer of comedy material, described an experience he had which demonstrates how difficult it is to determine the effectiveness of a joke. While he was serving as the chief writer of the *Perry Como Show*, Bob Hope was one of the guests. In preparing for the broadcast, Ace asked Hope to think of something funny to say after Perry Como had completed one of his songs. Hope came up with the line, "His voice sounds like the mating call of a mashed potato." Ace was not impressed. In consulting with the program's producer, he said, "No one will understand it. Let's not use it."

"Hope didn't object to any of the jokes you wrote for him," the producer pointed out. "I think you should leave it in."

"Okay," Ace responded, "But I'll bet it will be a loser."

You can guess the end to the story. Much to Ace's surprise, the "mashed potato" joke got the biggest laugh of the entire show.

Even people working on the same writing team may disagree about whether a particular piece of material will work. From the side comments Jay Leno and David Letterman make about the jokes that succeed or fail, it is clear they have argued with their writers about whether to include them in the program.

In the light of all this, setting out to define the good and the bad in joke making seems extraordinarily presumptuous. Let me hasten to say that because the appreciation of humor is so personal a matter, I do not in any way intend to foist my tastes on you. I fully expect that in some instances you will disagree with my evaluations, perhaps violently. I take this questionable step because it is important for creators of humor to develop criteria for measuring the effectiveness of their own product. They are also needed by performers who have material written for them. Jack Benny rarely produced jokes of his own, but he was a skilled evaluator of the jokes his writers created. His ability to distinguish the good from the bad and to improve the jokes he decided to use was one of his greatest assets as a comedian.

My hope is that my listing of jokes I liked and jokes I found wanting, and particularly my detailing of the reasons for those judgments, will lead you into setting up standards of your own. Armed with a set of personal criteria, you should become a better judge of what will work and what will not. That doesn't mean you will avoid unpleasant surprises. I will never forget the look of amazement that sometimes crossed Johnny Carson's face when one of his jokes emerged inert. And he, like Jack Benny, was an expert at evaluating humor. A set of standards will not eliminate occasional misfirings, but it should cut down on their number.

In establishing criteria for evaluating jokes, I followed a two-step process. I first determined whether a particular joke made me laugh and, if so, how much. Second, I tried to figure out why different jokes produce different results. Why did some jokes fail, I asked myself, and why did others succeed?

I quickly discovered that the reason for the funniness of some humor is difficult to explain. In a newspaper article Goodman Ace once wrote, "The more I think about it, the more I realize that what's funny, per se, escapes me." Other writers on humor have expressed the same frustration. In my case, for example, I find the humor of one scene in Charlie Chaplin's movie *Modern Times* difficult to analyze. I laugh every time I see it, and yet I've never been quite sure why. The scene depicts an incident that occurred during Charlie's first day of employment at a shipyard. His boss shows him a piece of wood and tells him to find one just like it. After a long search, Charlie finally spots such a piece wedged beneath a ship that is under construction. Failing to pull it out with his hands, he picks up a sledgehammer and knocks it loose. Immediately he hears a grinding noise behind him and looks around to see the half-built ship sliding majestically into the sea. No obvious explanation for the irresistible funniness of that scene leaps out at me. Fortunately, the explanations for the funniness or unfunniness of the jokes I am about to analyze are much more evident.

<u>Why Jokes Fail</u>

<u>They Have No Point</u>. If a joke is to work, it must present an idea that will stimulate a listener into thinking of another related idea. Sometimes what seems to be a joke isn't a joke at all because it doesn't lead to such a connection. Among the ideas a joke may arouse are the recollection of a well-known story of a common human experience, a philosophical reflection, the recognition that words have more than one meaning, or anything else that links meaningfully with what the joke maker has said. If nothing like that happens, the joke has no point and therefore fails.

For a number of years the Sunday newspaper supplement *Parade* ran a feature that focused on the favorite jokes of a variety of comedians. Among the gems was the occasional dud. This one contributed by Ed Bluestone:

This incredible thing happens in our apartment building. Say you're watching a movie on TV and someone else in the building turns on the same movie—some of your actors will leave and go to the other apartment.

I've gone through this presumed joke a number of times trying to think of an idea I can connect to it. Nothing occurs to me. Perhaps you will see something I've missed. To me, however, it is a prime example of a non-joke. Another in the same category was contributed to the *Parade* series by Jack Eagle:

I was sitting in a restaurant the other day. A guy was watching me. I ordered a steak smothered with lamb chops. He came over to me and said, "Listen, a lot of people dig their graves with their teeth." I told him, "You're right, you got to take care of your teeth."

I would think an audience hearing this joke would be baffled. Perhaps there is a tiny flicker of something funny in the idea of smothering a steak with lamb chops. Is there anything else?

The next two items were also identified as jokes by the publications in which they appeared. They succeeded only in wrinkling my brow rather than nudging my funny bone:

<u>Question</u>: What's a sitcom family?

<u>Answer</u>: Single income, two children, and an outrageous mortgage.

A friend of mine explained that the point to this joke is that the word "sitcom" is formed from the initial letters of the three items in the <u>Answer</u> portion. Not much of a point I'd say, and besides the connection doesn't exactly leap into one's mind. In the joke that follows, I discern no point at all:

A patient in the doctor's office was listing his complaints to the nurse. "I've got a bad case of arthritis," he enumerated. "There's a buzzing I in my ear, my ankle is sprained, I see spots in front of my eyes, and I've thrown my thumb out of joint."

"You must be awfully healthy," replied the nurse, "to stand all the pain."

As I noted earlier, Johnny Carson sometimes told jokes that left his studio audience silent and wondering. In many instances the point was simply too subtle for his listeners to grasp. There were times, however, when even Carson gave birth to a non-joke. In one of his monologues he tried to create a joke out of the fact that the first Black Miss America, Vanessa Williams, and the first Black astronaut, Lloyd Buford, were chosen at about the same time. Johnny's comment was, "They both obviously had the right stuff." There was no laughter from the studio audience. Some might have been reminded that Tom Wolfe had written a book about astronauts entitled *The Right Stuff*, but that didn't connect with Miss America. Puzzlement rather than amusement was the result, and unfortunately puzzlement doesn't provoke laughter.

Jay Leno fared no better with one of his attempts at joke making. He said in one of his monologues that a teacher of wrestling graded his students by locking them in a cage and letting them fight it out. The utter silence of the studio audience made him realize he had a non-joke on his hands. Leno responded, as he often does when a joke misfires, by saying "I didn't tell you that because I thought it was humorous; I just thought it was an interesting fact." That did get him a laugh.

<u>They Feature a Feeble Pun</u>. As far as I know, no one has ever tried to find out what percentage of jokes depend for their comic effect on a pun. From looking at jokes in general, one can conclude that the percentage is very high. It follows that the success of a great many jokes depends on the quality of the puns they employ. It they are weak or ineffective, the joke is almost bound to fail.

Before exploring this point further, it may be well to make some general observations about puns. In Chapter 6 I described the raw material from which puns are created—a word or phrase that has two or more meanings, two words that are spelled differently but sound the same, and words that are closely related in sound. Other types of word play have also been called puns, such as combining elements of two different words to make a new word, and creating a clever rhyme.

235

Humans have been creating puns ever since they began to speak. Aristotle, in the Fourth Century, B.C., analyzed their various characteristics, and the Greek playwrights of his time put puns into their dramas. The Roman orator Cicero maintained that one way to make a speech great is to include some plays on words. A pun that had a crucial impact on the development of the Roman Catholic hierarchy occurs in the Bible. Matthew 16:18 records a message addressed to Peter which contains two words that in the original Greek had a similar sound: "And I say also unto thee, that thou art Peter (Petras in Greek) and upon this rock (Petrai in Greek) I will build my church." In the eyes of Roman Catholics, Jesus with that statement made Peter the first pope.

Puns abound in the plays of William Shakespeare. In 1887 F. A. Bather counted them and came up with an exact number—1,062. Contemporary scholars would probably find more, for our knowledge of Shakespearean language has increased since Bather's time. Other notable English punsters were Samuel Johnson and Jonathan Swift, who published a book in 1719 on *The Art of Punning*. It set down seventy-nine rules for creating an acceptable pun.

A pun is enshrined in the history of the American Revolution. Benjamin Franklin crystallized the choice faced by those who were determined to throw off the British yoke in these memorable words: "We must all hang together or assuredly we shall all hang separately."

There is a great ambivalence about puns. Some people abhor them. Others seem to spend most of their waking hours trying to think them up. A notable pun hater was Joseph Addison, who in 1711 expressed concern that "our Posterity will degenerate into a Race of Punsters." The American writer Oliver Wendell Holmes shared his distaste. He felt that a pun was a prima facie insult to the person at whom it was directed. He called it "total depravity" and went so far as to suggest that if someone retaliated with a blow that caused death, the jury might well "return a verdict of justifiable homicide." On the opposite side of the controversy was the English writer Charles Lamb. "A pun is a noble thing per se," he told his fellow writer Samuel Taylor Coleridge. "It fills the mind; it is as perfect as a sonnet."

Pun lovers sometimes use puns to turn back the criticism of those who scorn them. One called such criticism "sour japes." Echoing the same thought, Doug Larson said, "A pun is the lowest form of humor unless you thought of it yourself."

The novelist Victor Hugo took the middle ground. He said, "Far be it from me to insult the pun. I honor it in proportion to its merits—no more." As far as I know he didn't explain how merit should be judged. Max

Eastman did take that bold step in his book, *Enjoyment of Laughter*. He identified three categories of puns: the atrocious, the witty, and the poetic, and provided examples of each type. I have followed this example. I call my categories the bad, the middling, and the good. My criterion for putting a pun in one or another of these groups is the kind of challenge it presents to listeners. If it makes a simple, one line demand, it falls into the lowest group. If it asks listeners to make more than one connection, it rises higher. Another way of stating this criterion is to say that the quality of a pun is directly proportional to the richness of the associations it stimulates.

One of Charles Lamb's favorite puns was this:

A passerby asked a man who was carrying a hare through the street, "Prithee friend, is that thy own hare or a wig?"

If this was one of Lamb's favorite puns, one must conclude he had a taste for the abominable. All it asks listeners to do is connect the word "hare" with "hair" and "wig," not a very demanding challenge. It provides enough double meaning to create a joke, but it's a feeble one.

Further illustrating the point that one person's favorite is another person's groaner is a selection made by the comedian and musician Max Morath for the *Parade* feature "My Favorite Jokes." In my view, it scarcely qualifies as a joke. True, it presents a play on words, but one so slight that it is not likely to provoke a smile, much less a laugh. Here is Morath's selection:

A man went to visit a friend in a mental hospital. Later he ran into the patient's brother.

"I've just seen your brother," he said.

"What did he have to say?"

"He's crazy to see you."

Some other puns that provide little exercise for the listener's mind are the following. They feature an extremely simple, one-line play on words.

Said one Turk to another: "I didn't know his name, but his fez was familiar."

Surgeon to his assistant after beginning an operation: "How is that for openers?"

"Do you shoot quail?"

"I quail at the thought."

The second President George Bush appeared on CBS's *Late Show* shortly after its host, David Letterman, had returned after heart bypass surgery. Bush began by saying "It's about time you had the heart to invite me." The studio audience greeted his remark with boos. Whether this hostile reaction was prompted by the weakness of the pun or the feeling that it was in poor taste, no one can know.

Of the thousand or more puns Shakespeare perpetrated, some would fall in the atrocious group, some were middling, and some deserved outstanding ratings. A comparison of two of his puns—one bad, the other good—should help to clarify the basis on which I rate the quality of puns. Shakespeare's *Merry Wives of Windsor* tells how the attempts of Sir John Falstaff to seduce a pair of virtuous wives were thwarted by a series of clever tricks. Three times the wives feigned interest in his propositions and then deftly turned the tables on him. On the third occasion, they persuaded him to don the antlers of a deer and then humiliated him before a group of merry makers. The episode concluded with one of the wives saying to Falstaff, "I will never take you for my love again; but I will always count you my deer." When I include this example in a lecture, my audience usually greets it with a groan, and rightly so. It is a contrived and simplistic play on words.

Perhaps Shakespeare's best known pun occurs in *Romeo and Juliet*. It is uttered by Mercutio after he has been fatally stabbed in a duel with Tybalt. Romeo tries to comfort him by saying, "Courage, man; the hurt cannot be too much," and Mercutio responds:

"No, 'tis not so deep as a well, nor so wide as a church door; but 'tis enough, 'twil serve; ask for me tomorrow and you shall find me a grave man."

This pun is not so much funny as it is foreboding. I rate it as far better than the shallow pun from *The Merry Wives of Windsor* because it foreshadows events that will bring the play to its tragic climax. It widens the vision of the audience by asking them to reflect on the consequences of careless bravado.

Two puns with an Egyptian motif further illustrate differences in the quality of puns. This one I would place in the lowest group:

An ancient Egyptian surveying a newly built pyramid says: "Personally I wouldn't be caught dead in it."

This is too obvious to be really funny. This next pun moves a step up to the middling class because the play on words is somewhat more sophisticated, and it challenges the listener to visualize something:

One mummy looking critically at another says: "I see you got a bum wrap."

In their *Book of Lists* Irving Wallace and his collaborators classified items in a great many different categories. One of them is a list of the "worst" puns. It included the following:

"It's raining cats and dogs," one man remarked.

"Don't I know it, " said another. "I just stepped into a poodle."

I must admit I found that pun rather amusing. In any event, I would scarcely put it into a list of the "worst puns," as Wallace did. It features a funny sounding word, and I found its touch of absurdity amusing. I would call it middling.

Charles Dickens was not noted for his puns, but at least one has come down to us. It, too, belongs in the middling category:

> It is said that in the middle of the nineteenth century London was terrorized by the arrival in the Thames of a tremendous sea monster. The townspeople finally killed it, but they then faced the problem of disposing of the remains. A butcher found a solution by making sausage of it. Charles Dickens commenting on the story said, "It was the beast of Thames, it was the wurst of Thames."

I rate this joke better than bad because it cleverly combines three puns, beast, wurst, and Thames. Further, it challenges the reader to recall the memorable lines with which Dickens opened his novel *A Tale of Two Cities*. Perhaps it should be placed in the "good" category.

Here are several more puns I would place in the middling category and my reasons for doing so. The first, like the Dicken's example, requires something of the audience, namely, a recollection of a historical figure's last name:

> The writer of a column on cooking hints responded to a reader's comment in this way: "We prepare a dish similar to your 'Chinese Chicken' except that we call ours 'Chicken Napoleon' because we use only the bony parts."

A second pun which makes me laugh every time I see it, also requires the recall of a name we find in the history books:

> Remember the famous words of Eli Whitney—"Keep your cotton-pickin' hands off my gin."

Though I know little about Whitney, I have always visualized him as a dedicated and somewhat solemn inventor. It is not just the pun that makes me laugh, but the incongruity between my image of him and the words he utters.

The third pun ranks in the middling group because the connection it requires listeners to make is somewhat more complicated than those demanded by puns in the lowest group:

> Spongecake: "Dessert made by ingredients borrowed from the neighbors."

A fourth pun deserves a place in the middling group because of its play on words:

239

WILLIS - How to be Funny on Purpose

Remember the little Dutch boy who saved his country by standing for long hours with his finger plugging up a hole in the dike? When a repair was finally made, the townspeople greeted him with hurrahs and begged him to make a speech.

"Not now," he responded. "I've had a tough day at the orifice."

You may be wondering whether there are any puns I would place in the "good" category. One does come along once in awhile. A number achieve this ranking because of the funny visualization they call forth. These next two are examples:

A circus owner said to his human cannonball who had submitted his resignation, "You can't quit. Where would I find another man of your caliber?"

A man whose home was washed away in a California flood told a friend that the experience revealed he had an unsuspected musical talent. "You see," he explained, "My wife floated down the canyon hanging on to a bed."

"How does that prove you have musical talent?" the friend asked.

"I accompanied her on the piano."

We have seen examples of puns that call for literary and historical knowledge. To get the point to this next one, you need some acquaintance with biology. Reinforcing the pleasure that comes from making that connection is the subtle reference to a situation familiar to most men and women. The combination of those two factors puts this pun in the top rank:

Amoeba: Not tonight, dear, I have a splitting headache.

One way that puns achieve the merit Victor Hugo looked for is by making full use of the main triggers of laughter. Puns are good when they surprise us, when they intrigue us with an incongruity, or when they put someone or something down. This next pun benefits from that last trigger. It uses a clever play on words to twit an authority figure:

While a university marching band was practicing, a thunderstorm came up unexpectedly. Seeing lightning crackling overhead, one of the brass players mentioned the danger of electrocution.

"Don't worry about it," said the director from a stand high above the group. "If anyone is in danger of being struck by lightning, I am."

"No, you're not," the brass player responded. "You're not that good a conductor."

If I had been asked by *Parade* magazine to submit my favorite jokes, the following pun by Fred Allen would have been in the group. On one of his radio programs, he broadcast this announcement:

240

Next Sunday the Reverend Dr. Jones will preach on "Skiing on the Sabbath," or "Are our Young Women Backsliding on Their Week-ends?"

This item, though relatively brief, succeeds in actuating the three triggers of laughter and thus provides a rich experience for the listener. A surprise comes with the recognition of the two puns' double meanings. There is a touch of incongruity in the clash between the ministerial status of the preacher and the title of his sermon. Self satisfaction is achieved in three ways. First, listeners can take pleasure in making the connections the joke requires. Second, the ludicrous picture the joke evokes amounts to a delicate put-down. Third, listeners can experience the triumph that comes from defying a taboo. Admittedly, that joke would scarcely qualify as spicy in today's world, but in the period Allen was broadcasting, even the indirect reference to the part of the anatomy alluded to in the sermon's title took considerable daring.

The Point is Too Subtle. Jokes sometimes fail because making the required connection is beyond the reach of most people in the audience. If the point is so elusive that listeners cannot see it, obviously they are not going to laugh. Determining whether the point to a joke is likely to be understood, is one of the most crucial decisions you must make. The line you tread is a narrow one. If you are too consistently simple, your listeners will be denied the self satisfaction that comes from responding successfully to a difficult challenge. On the other hand, if you keep shooting over their heads, they will experience nothing except frustration.

Let's look at some jokes whose points might elude some audiences.

An English professor was in a motel room engaged with a female student in some extra-curricular activity.

"I feel good," the student said, and turning to the professor she said, "And you feel well."

The professor smiled happily. It was clear that his teaching had not fallen on fallow ground.

To get the point to that joke you must be acquainted with one of the more subtle distinctions grammarians make. A group of English majors might laugh at it. An audience of business people would probably be baffled. There is another reason why the use of this material is questionable. The explicit picture it calls up might offend some of those who do succeed in making the connection.

Subtlety of another type occurs when a joke focuses on circumstances affecting a particular occupation or profession. A group of university professors would probably laugh heartily at the following joke. University students might too, for most of them are familiar with the requirement to which it refers. Still, it is an "inside" joke that is likely to get a far greater response from the group it deals with than from the public at large. It also requires knowledge of the way the ideas of the people referred to came down to us.

The stone facade of Butler Library on the Columbia University campus is etched with the names of ancient Greeks and Romans whose contributions have enriched our cultural heritage: Homer, Herodotus, Sophocles, Plato, Aristotle, Demosthenes, Cicero, Virgil. Looking up at it one day, a professor said to a colleague, "I wonder why Socrates's name isn't up there."

"Simple," replied his fellow professor. "He never published."

Sometimes audiences may not get the point to a joke, not because it is particularly subtle, but because the joke teller uses the wrong means of communication. Consider this example:

Two strings went to a restaurant to get a bite to eat. The maitre d' refused to seat them saying, "We don't serve strings in here."

One string gave up and went home, but the other disguised himself by putting a fringe around his head and feet. His disguise didn't work. The maitre d' immediately recognized him. "Aren't you one of those strings I refused to serve a few minutes ago?"

"No," replied the string haughtily, "I'm a frayed not."

To a reader the pun is immediately obvious, but only the most perceptive listener would be able to identify it. This joke illustrates the fact that some jokes are likely to make sense only if the words are seen in print. That would also be true of the "You've had a bum wrap" joke I included earlier. If you are presenting material orally, make sure that it will be clear to those who only hear it. Another pun whose point would be obvious to readers but which might elude listeners came from columnist James Kilpatrick. He was commenting on his fellow columnist, William F. Buckley, Jr.:

Both actor and satirist—a kind of ham on wry.

Some jokes fall on the borderline. Listeners with agile minds might be able to make the connections they call for. The safe policy would be to use them only in a print medium. If you do decide to tell them, make sure you pronounce the key words very clearly.

Question: Why did they ban Ivanhoe?
Answer: Too much Saxon violence.

And then there was the stock broker who was led astray by false prophets.

Another type of joke that may get no reaction when orally presented is one that requires a period of contemplation before the point becomes clear. Two jokes dealing with the reading dysfunction dyslexia provide examples:

My mother belongs to an organization known as D A M— Mothers against Dyslexia.

Hear about the dyslexic theologians? They got into an argument about the existence of dog.

To get the point to these jokes, listeners, to begin with, must know that people suffering from dyslexia reverse the order of letters in words. Then they must recognize that the words "DAM" and "dog" represent such a reversal. Seeing the joke in print, one has time to make the required connections.

Some jokes may elude understanding simply because the facts one must know to make the connection are too distant in time. In 1995, Robert McNamara, Secretary of Defense in the cabinets of John Kennedy and Lyndon Johnson, wrote a book in which he admitted he had been wrong to urge our participation in the Vietnam War. Mark Russell, in an appearance he made on CNN, referred to McNamara's book in this way:

I see that Robert McNamara is now admitting that the Vietnam War was a mistake. I wonder if he's going to write another book in which he'll concede the Edsel was a lemon.

That's a very good joke but only to those with long memories. To get its point you must remember that before Robert McNamara went into government, he was an executive of the Ford Motor Company. You must further remember that during his time there, Ford produced one of the great disasters of automobile history—the Edsel. The response of Russell's audience to this joke was noticeably muted. Many of his listeners weren't even born at the time the Edsel made its debut.

Another very good joke, which requires acquaintance with the life of an actor who has dropped from the public eye if one is to get the point, was contained in a comment a critic made in reviewing a biography of the film actress Ava Gardner. "In a short time she had an experience common to many young women: she married Mickey Rooney." That is a delightfully indirect way of reminding audiences that Gardner was just one of some eight women Rooney married. But how many of today's readers will remember that fact?

The passage of time can blunt the effect of almost any joke, but it is particularly damaging to those which were subtle to begin with as this one is:

It seems that Wade Boggs, Steve Garvey, and Pete Rose were together in a bar when a very attractive woman walked by. Wade

243

Boggs said, "Wow, she's certainly beautiful. I think I'll ask her for a date." Steve Garvey then interjected, "Don't waste your time. She's carrying my baby." To which Pete Rose responded, "Wanna bet?"

The Pete Rose line is likely to get a laugh from almost everyone, for most people will remember the gambling indiscretions that denied him entrance to baseball's Hall of Fame. The peccadilloes that inspired the Boggs and Garvey quotes received much less publicity. Even at the time they happened, some might not have heard about them, and those who did might soon forget the relevant details. Yet to appreciate all of the implications this very clever joke provides, one must know and remember those details.

Sometimes a joke focuses on a minor detail. Heard at the time of the event, it will be understood, but listeners hearing it years later may be baffled because minor details fade quickly from the collective memory even though the main outlines of a story remain vivid. People are likely to remember for a long time that O. J. Simpson was accused of murdering his wife, for example, but they may forget that for a period of many months the news media made some reference to the case in almost every issue or broadcast. At the height of the frenzy, *The New Republic* published an issue which did not mention O. J. Simpson. To signify that fact, it printed a message on its cover reading "O. J. Free." At the time of the trial that was meaningful and funny to most readers. I've wondered, however, what readers seeing that message on a library copy of *The New Republic* twenty years from now would make of it.

There is another point to be made about the influence of time on the effectiveness of a joke. Even though the details of an event remain clear in listeners' minds indefinitely, they usually laugh louder at a joke about it immediately after its occurrence than they do later. Take the Lorena Bobbitt story as an example. Some people may remember that in retaliation for her husbands' infidelity, she cut off his penis. I recall two jokes that came out at the time of her trial. One was an editorial cartoon drawn by Mike Luckovich entitled "Thanksgiving at the Bobbitt's." It showed a woman wielding a carving knife while under the table the male members of the household were cowering. The second was a remark Jay Leno made about Lorena and John Bobbitt: "Both would have trouble getting dates." Each joke qualified as an exceedingly amusing reference to the case. I suspect, however, that encountered years later the passage of time would dull the funniness of both of them.

<u>They Contain Logical and Factual Errors</u>. It may seem ridiculous on the face of it to argue that a joke may fail because it contains an absurdity.

Aren't some jokes funny precisely because they make no sense? We laugh, for example, when Yogi Berra says, "If people don't want to come to the ball park, nobody's going to stop them," because his words are so utterly illogical. The kind of joke I have in mind is one that incites laughter for reasons other than the perception of an absurdity. The response to such a joke can be dampened if it contains something illogical. The problem, however, is that you often can't eliminate the illogicality without eliminating the joke. That is true of this next item:

> The skipper and engineer of a ship got into an argument about which was easier—steering the ship or running its engines. They decided to settle the matter by changing places.
>
> Ten minutes later the captain was ready to concede defeat. Calling up to the engineer who was on the bridge, he said, "I can't get these darn engines to start."
>
> "Don't bother," the engineer called back dejectedly, "We've run aground."

Some in your audience may wonder how the engineer managed to run the ship aground before the skipper could get the engines started. That question may not kill the joke, but the jokester should be aware that it can affect the response. But I see no way of getting rid of the logical inconsistency and still preserve the joke.

The *Mary Tyler Moore* show had a similar problem. As you laughed at the nerdish, bumbling antics of the newscaster Ted Baxter, didn't you sometimes wonder, as I did, how such an obvious incompetent could hold a job in a news operation that was otherwise staffed by cool, rational professionals like Lou Grant and Mary? But turning Baxter into the same kind of competent professional would have eliminated the fun his inane shenanigans and childish insecurities generated. The *Mary Tyler Moore* show managed to survive its logical inconsistency to become one of the most successful programs in broadcasting history.

Some logical inconsistencies, however, damage a joke so seriously that it's not worth telling. I submit the following as an example:

> A woman had made several trips to a dentist to have her false teeth fitted. After the fifth visit, the dentist said, "There, I've done all I can. There's no reason why these shouldn't fit your mouth easily."
>
> "Who said anything about my mouth?" the woman answered. "They don't fit in the glass."

The problem with this joke is that the last line makes no reasonable connection with anything that has gone before. It all adds up to nonsense, but it's not funny nonsense.

Summing up, we can see that three kinds of nonsense play a role in humor. First, there is the kind that is truly and delightfully funny. Second, there is nonsense that is not funny in and of itself which may inflict some damage. In many instances, however, it must be retained because it makes the humor possible. Finally, there is contrived nonsense that creates no funniness at all.

Just as a logical inconsistency may diminish the effect of a joke, so may an error in fact. A joke from one of Johnny Carson's monologues illustrates the point:

When the Pope went to Venice, he was arrested for jaywalking.

The factual inaccuracy in this joke, of course, is attributing the gift of walking on water to popes. It connects instead with an episode in the life of Jesus. The problem is that the erroneous implication, like the logical inconsistencies I have just cited, makes the joke possible. I think it's worth telling just as it is, but the jokester should be aware that its inaccuracy may bother some people.

A joke of more recent vintage also exhibits this problem. It stemmed from the fact that in the spring and summer of 2004, the price of a gallon of gasoline rose to its highest point in history:

If gas prices keep rising, President George W. Bush and Vice
President Dick Cheney will have to carpool to work.

The problem with this joke is that, as Jon Stewart pointed out on his *Daily Show*, President Bush both lives and works in the White House. I'll leave it to you to decide whether the joke can survive its logical inconsistency.

They Reek of Contrivance. Jokes may fail because they sound too planned. They fall short of projecting the impression of spontaneity, which, as I have already noted, is a factor of crucial importance in joke making. The best jokes are those that seem to erupt suddenly in a natural, unpremeditated way. Some jokes represent the exact antithesis of that quality. They sound so manufactured, you can almost hear the clank of the machinery that produced them. Here is an example:

A funeral procession is plodding along. All at once the door at
the back of the hearse suddenly opens, and the casket goes sliding
down a hill and into a drugstore. The lid springs open and the corpse
sticks his head out and says, "Maybe you've got something to stop
my coffin."

It's obvious that the circumstances of this joke were put together simply to make the pun possible. And it's a "groaner" type of pun at that. We can see the same artificial building of a situation to justify a pun in this next joke:

> Joe was visiting his friend Bill when all of a sudden a huge gray dog rushed out of the kitchen and bit him on the leg. Joe left, vowing never to visit his friend again until he got rid of the dog.
>
> Several years later Bill called to tell Joe that the dog had died and invited him over. Reassured, Joe went for a visit, but as soon as he arrived, a huge gray dog rushed out of the kitchen and bit him on the leg. "What's going on?" Joe howled. "I thought you told me your dog had died."
>
> "He did," Bill assured him. "This is the heir of the dog that bit you."

A joke that almost always sounds contrived is the type that uses the reversal of a well-known saying or aphorism as its tag, as this next example illustrates:

> Before leaving on a canoeing trip with his friend Frank, John reached down for his paddle and found he couldn't straighten up. Frank pulled and tugged at him, but his back still wouldn't come unstuck. Finally Frank grabbed the paddle and handed it to John. "Stand it up on the ground," he instructed him, and gradually work your hands to the top."
>
> Frank's advice worked. Before long John was up the paddle without a crick.

I do not find this joke funny. At the same time I recognize that some people take particular delight both in formulating such material and in hearing it from others. There is no question that it qualifies as a joke, for it requires the audience to make a connection by recalling the saying in its original form. And conceiving circumstances that will lead to its reversal demands considerable ingenuity. Its obvious contrivance, however, puts me off.

Another problem with jokes of this type is that they often take an awfully long time to get to the snapper. I find them somewhat more bearable if the lead-in is short and crisp. This next one, at least, has the virtue of being admirably succinct:

> Said an orthopedic specialist to a girl with an arthritic knee,
> "What's a rough joint doing in a nice girl like you?"

Some jokes of this type also earn my begrudging respect by providing a challenge to the listener that is sterner than most such jokes manage to present. This next one falls in that category:

> Did you hear about the unfortunate woman who forgot to take

the pill? She got into trouble by practicing license without a medicine.

And despite their general air of contrivance, some such jokes still manage to convey an impression of spontaneity. The reversal at the end of this next joke emerges in an almost natural way:

> A music major at a midwestern university was advised by her father to take some business courses. In music her grades were excellent, but the ones she earned in business were mediocre to poor. Asked by her father to explain, she replied, "There's no taste for accounting."

Jokes that sound labored often suffer from other defects. This is an example:

> "Have you heard about the boy and girl vampires who couldn't get married?"
>
> "No, what happened?"
>
> "They loved in vein."

Let's count the problems. Number one, you can sense the joke maker's struggle to create a pun from the words "vain" and "vein." Number two, there would be no joke at all for those who only heard it. Number three, the circumstances add up to sheer nonsense, but it's not funny nonsense.

This next joke exhibits two of those problems—obvious contrivance and puzzlement for those who only hear it—but it crispness redeems it somewhat:

> The king had to leave his country because tigers and elephants had overrun it. In other words, he had to call the reign because of the game.

The Joke is too Clever. It may seem heretical to suggest that a joke can be too clever for its own good. That doesn't mean that a joke maker shouldn't be clever. Creating effective humor requires cleverness of the highest order. But a joke that is merely clever doesn't necessarily produce laughs, and that is what the humorist is after. The reversal jokes we have just been considering are examples. That is also true of other types of jokes. An example is one Max Eastman included in his *Enjoyment of Laughter*. He noted that it was the only triple pun he had ever encountered:

> A father who operated a ranch in company with his three sons named it Focus. It's where the sons raise meat (suns rays meet).

In the first place, you can't tell this joke to an audience and expect it to get the pun. It must see the words to have any chance at all of making the proper connections. During my lectures, I've printed them on a chalkboard and even then the pun is difficult to comprehend. But those who do get it aren't likely to laugh. They may emit a grunt of understanding, but that's about all. The pun is too clever for its own good.

A triple pun apparently overlooked by Max Eastman is sometimes used as the name for a motel or bed-and-breakfast house—Dew Drop Inn. You've probably seen it at one time or another. You may have smiled, but I doubt you have ever laughed.

Earlier I referred to the comment George Kaufman made about problems in the Middle East: "One man's Mede is another man's Persian." I've included that comment in a number of lectures, and so far it has failed to elicit a single laugh. Apparently most people don't connect it with the aphorism, "One man's meat is another man's poison." Those who do may be overwhelmed by admiration for Kaufman's ingenuity, but it doesn't seem to tickle their funny bones. A similar play on the familiar saying, "Big oaks from little acorns grow," executed by James Thurber, falls into the same category. In discussing the idiosyncrasies of Soviet officialdom, he said, "Big oafs from little icons grow." I've never tried out this remark on an audience, but I suspect it would get the same result as Kaufman's comment. Thurber's twist on the words of the saying is breathtakingly clever without question, but it would probably stir admiration rather than laughter.

Admiration is also the main response audiences have to the verses of Ogden Nash. A good example is the following quatrain:

I am a conscientious man, when I throw rocks at seabirds I leave
no tern unstoned.

I am a meticulous man, and when I portray baboons I leave no
stern untoned.

Audiences clearly enjoy hearing this clever verse. It is therefore worth reciting. But don't expect a big response. You may see some smiles and hear some chuckles, but it's not likely to draw a belly laugh.

They Suffer from Faulty Wording. It is obvious that a joke will fail if its wording is ineffective. That generalization, however, needs to be made specific if it is to be truly meaningful. What are some of the faults that can drain the fun out of a joke? Perhaps the most common one is to use too many words. Nothing is more likely to dampen the response to a joke than language that is soggy with verbosity. A good joke is marked by succinctness and crispness; it marches briskly to its conclusion. As Polonius said in Shakespeare's *Hamlet*, "Brevity is the soul of wit," and immediately showed how true that was by becoming long and wordy.

One reason that unnecessary words creep in is that joke makers clutter their material with irrelevant details. Consider the following example:

Three cross-eyed prisoners with different colored eyes stood before a cross-eyed judge. The judge glared at the first prisoner who had brown eyes and then asked, "What's your name?"

"Jim Bowers," answered the second prisoner, a blue-eyed man.

"I wasn't talking to you," the judge growled.

"I didn't say anything," the third prisoner with hazel eyes replied.

I'm sure you immediately spotted the unnecessary details. The color of the prisoners' eyes has nothing to do with the point to the joke. Besides making it longer than it needs to be, mentioning the prisoners' eye color creates two other problems. It takes attention away from the fact on which the audience should focus—the cross-eyedness of the judge and prisoners—and referring to it suggests that it has significance, thus creating confusion.

Wordiness can also creep in when joke makers try to be too clear. Concerned that their listeners may miss the point, they explain it as part of what they say, thus denying audiences the pleasure of arriving at it on their own. As an example, I quote a comment Willard Scott made about one of the jobs he had held before becoming the weatherman on the *Today* show:

I began my professional career as a clown in Washington, D. C. It was difficult to be a clown there because there was so much competition from the House and Senate.

That leaves something for listeners to do. They must draw out the inference that members of Congress are clowns. But did Scott go too far in suggesting that idea? A sharper, crisper version might go like this:

I was once a clown in Washington, D. C., but I gave it up. Too much competition.

This version requires the audience to make two connections: recall that Washington, D. C. is the home of the House and Senate and associate clowning with their members. Is that asking the audience to do too much? If you think it is, then Scott's version is preferable.

Let's look at another example. It comes from one of Jay Leno's *Tonight* show monologues and concerned the first President Bush who made news at one time by granting what some thought were ill-considered pardons:

This was on the news tonight. Two students skipped school to go and hear President George Bush speak at West Point, and to avoid getting the kids into trouble, the President personally gave the kids an excuse to give their teacher. Boy, this guy will pardon anyone.

In preparing the routines that first brought him national attention, Jay Leno had time to hone and polish his material. As host of the *Tonight* show, he doesn't have that luxury, considering that he has to produce fifteen to twenty new jokes a night, five nights a week. Cutting unnecessary words takes time. George Bernard Shaw implied just that when he wrote to someone, "I'm sorry this letter is so long; I didn't have time to write a short one." In my view Leno's joke needs pruning. It tends to waddle rather than march to its conclusion and the snapper isn't brisk enough. Here is a shorter version that calls forth the same ideas:

> Did you hear that two kids skipped school to hear President George Bush speak at West Point? When he heard what they had done, he solved their problem. They went back to school with pardons in hand.

Is it possible to use too few words? That can happen if cutting words makes the point too elusive for most audiences to get. It can also happen if you fail to use enough words to exploit fully all of the comic potential inherent in your idea. I use another Jay Leno joke to illustrate the point. In one of his monologues he mentioned that currently orbiting astronauts were having trouble with their $30 million toilet. He then said, "Imagine getting a plumber up there to fix it." It occurs to me that he might have given his joke a further dollop of humor by adding, "And you figure he'd have to go back at least once for tools."

Avoiding faulty wording isn't merely a matter of cutting unnecessary words, of course; you must also find words that best develop the humorous idea you are trying to convey. "The difference between the nearly right word and the right word is the difference between lightning and the lightning bug," Mark Twain said. Let's see how this dictum applies to humor.

During a stay in a hospital, TV personality Hugh Downs's greeted an intern wearing a white coat with the comment, "You look like the Good Humor man." I suppose that qualifies as a joke, but it's a pretty feeble one. Can it be made funnier? Let's turn for help to an expert in the field of humor, Joey Bishop, a stand-up comedian and former talk-show host. When he heard Downs comment, he remarked, "That's not what I would have said. I would have said, 'I'll take two chocolates and a vanilla.'" Why do Bishop's different words make a better joke? The reason is that they require the audience to work a little harder to make the connection than the Downs's version does. Downs plants the "Good Humor" idea in their minds in an obvious way. Bishop merely suggests it.

My second example comes from Ronnie Corbett, the British comedian, whose programs were sometimes broadcast in Canada:

> Harold Johnson, who swallowed a boomerang, was discharged from the hospital twenty-seven times.

That's pretty good joke just as it stands. It suggests the boomerang's unique characteristic: two-way movement. But does it focus on it strongly enough? In my view, and I concede that I'm nitpicking, the emphasis is mainly on one direction—movement out of the hospital. Another version using different words equalizes the attention given to the movement out and the movement back. Is it funnier? That's for you to decide.

> Harold Johnson, who swallowed a boomerang, was discharged from the hospital at 10:00 A.M. and was back in at 10:01 A.M.

Let's conclude this section with a little problem in joke construction. An instrument that shares with the boomerang the capability of moving in opposite directions is the yo-yo. Can you find a joke in that fact? To help you out, let's assume that a ship carrying a cargo of yo-yo's hits an iceberg, which inflicts damage serious enough to make it sink. Now connect the idea of that sinking ship with the yo-yo's ups and downs. Can you find the words you need to develop those ideas into an effective joke?

The Sequence is Faulty. Sometimes jokes fail because the ideas they contain come in the wrong order. A common mistake is to follow the pay-off line with further words. In almost all instances the snapper to the joke should be the last thing the audience hears of that particular joke. To illustrate the point, I return to a sequence from one of Jack Benny's radio programs, which I quoted in an earlier chapter. Jack and Mary were sitting on the edge of a swimming pool when this exchange took place:

> Jack: It's a little embarrassing to say the least, but your bathing suit is a bit snug and skimpy.
> Mary: If you don't like it, go in and take it off.

You will note that the topper to the joke comes just where it should—at the very end of the last line. Mary's last six words, "go in and take it off," suddenly reveal what the true situation is. Reversing the order of words in that last line would have given us the following:

> Mary: Go in and take it off, if you don't like it.

That version might still get a laugh, but it would be muffled and tentative. The point of the joke is muddled by the words that follow it.

For a second example, I turn again to Jack Benny, who this time is talking with George Burns. In his chat with Mary, the ideas come in the right sequence. In my view that is not true of this interchange with Burns:

> Benny: You said friends of yours had eight sets of twins.
> Burns: Yes, they made book ends for a living. It affected their whole lives.

Your first step in determining the order in which you should present your ideas is to decide what the joke's basic comedy idea is. You should then arrange a sequence in which that idea gets the greatest emphasis. The best way of doing that is to put it last.

In the Benny-Burns exchange, I think the basic comedy idea is the connection between twins and book-ends, not the fact that having twins and making book ends affects their whole lives. For that reason, I would place the reference to book ends last, preceding it with the line about their lives being affected, as in this version:

Benny: You said friends of yours had eight sets of twins.

Burns: Yes, it affected their whole lives. They made book ends for a living.

You may feel that my tampering has succeeded only in downgrading the quality of the joke. (My wife thought so and now that I've reviewed it again, I'm inclined to agree with her.) There is no question that deciding the order in which to present ideas is a delicate and challenging task, for which there are few absolute guidelines. Consider these two arrangements of the same joke, for example. Which one is better?

I'd call you a barefaced liar, if it weren't for your mustache.

If it weren't for your mustache, I'd call you a barefaced liar.

I think I'd vote for the second arrangement, though with no strong conviction that it is superior. I feel the same ambivalence about two versions of a Rodney Dangerfield joke, although again I lean toward the second arrangement:

I wouldn't have any sex life at all if it weren't for pickpockets.

If it weren't for pickpockets, I wouldn't have any sex life at all.

In repeating a story they have heard, people sometimes reverse the order of ideas inadvertently. Usually a mistake like that has a disastrous effect. But there is at least one instance in which the goofed-up version seems as funny or even funnier than the original version. The story begins with an interchange between two men:

First man: Did you hear the story about the dirty window?

Second man: No.

First man: Aw, never mind. You couldn't see through it anyway.

When the second man came home, he decided he'd tell his wife the story. This is how it came out:

Man: Hey, Bertha, did you hear the story about the window you couldn't see through?

Wife: No.

Man: Never mind. It's too dirty to tell.

Which is the better version? The best advice probably is to present the two versions as a package.

<u>The Telling is Botched</u>. Even the best of jokes needs to be told well if it is to succeed. One problem with many people is that they feel inadequate as joke tellers. It is natural for them to begin by saying, "I don't tell jokes very well, but there's a story I thought you might like to hear." That admission alone throws a pall over the situation. Forget the apologies, and tell the joke as straightforwardly and as well as you can. If you don't mention your supposed ineptness, perhaps no one will notice it. And it just may be that you are not as inadequate as you think.

A first rule, of course, is make sure you have a firm grasp on what you are about to say before you begin your story. Your joke is likely to collapse if you flounder around or get mixed up. Nothing can be more damaging than having to stop just as you are approaching your punchline to say something like, "Oh, I forgot to tell you. There was an owl in the window." Even stumbling on a single word can be damaging. Jay Leno tends to slap his face in frustration when his articulatory mechanism breaks down.

If you do mangle a joke, don't try too hard to fix it. When a joke fails to get a laugh, the teller sometimes repeats it. Rarely does that accomplish anything. And you aren't likely to get a laugh by explaining the point either. The best thing you can do in most instances is recognize you have a lost cause and abandon it.

In telling a joke there are a number of factors to keep in mind. You should give words the proper emphasis, vary your pitch, and pause in the right places. Stating those instructions is easy, following them is difficult. The top comedians seem to have an instinctive grasp of the right technique. Many of them develop a characteristic rhythm in telling a joke. Bob Hope is a good example. He once participated in an experiment which demonstrated that he could evoke laughter with rhythm alone. The material was not funny in any way, yet audiences laughed at it because it sounded like a joke.

President Ronald Reagan can also be cited as a consummate master of the art of telling jokes. The day after his death on May 6, 2004, CBS devoted most of its *60 Minutes* program to commemorating his life and achievements. One of the segments, narrated by Dan Rather, showed Reagan telling jokes at various stages of his career. As I watched I was impressed again by how well he did it. His native talent for speaking well was undoubtedly sharpened by his years of experience as a radio announcer and actor. The elements of good speech—articulation, patterns of emphasis, and phrasing—were all performed impeccably. In addition, he met the special challenges that joke telling requires with signal effectiveness. For one thing, I never heard him botch the delivery of a joke. For another, his timing was superb. He would pause as he reached the climax for that infinitesimal part of a second that arouses audience anticipation and adds power to the punchline. Perhaps more important than anything else, he showed how much he was enjoying telling the joke. The crinkling of his eyes and the smile enveloping his face played as big a role in triggering laughter as the joke itself.

To learn how to tell a joke well, a good first step is to watch expert comedians in action. You will see, for example, how important timing is by looking at tapes of Jack Benny as he performed in his TV shows. He could make audiences laugh with timing alone.

Comedians can teach you some other valuable lessons if you pay close attention to their delivery techniques. You will learn that when you are telling more than one joke, you should not step on a laugh by starting the next joke too soon. On the other hand, you will see that you should not wait too long to move on. Silence between jokes can give your audience the impression that you are trying to milk your material for laughs. The best procedure is to begin your next joke just as the laughter incited by the previous one is dying out. Also, you should let the joke carry itself. Don't overdo the emphasis. Some joke tellers tend to do this when they reach the snapper. If it's a good one, it will stand on its own. You don't have to tell your audience—this is the point to the joke—by pounding on it. On the other hand, you shouldn't drop your voice just as you reach the concluding line, as some do. Doing so has two damaging effects. It gives your listeners the impression that you aren't certain your joke is funny enough to tell. Even more serious, they may not be able to catch what you have said, and the joke collapses. You must be sure that everything you say is delivered loudly and forcefully enough to be easily heard and understood. That is particularly true of the climactic, final line.

What you must do is strike the correct point between pushing too hard and being alert and animated enough to hold attention. Watching comedians, you will note how energetic they are. When Jay Leno comes out to do his monologues, he seems completely vital and alive. More important than anything else, perhaps, he conveys the impression that he is having a good time. Does that mean you should laugh at your own jokes? Red Skelton did and often cued the audience into laughing along with him. I see nothing wrong with letting listeners know that you have a keen appreciation for your own material. On the other hand, some comedians like Jerry Seinfeld deliberately hold down their reactions, yet they still manage to make us feel they are enjoying themselves. That is what is important.

To sum up, hone your material to its sharpest edge, be sure you have command of it, show that you have confidence in your joke, and be brisk and energetic in the telling.

Why Jokes Succeed

In discussing why jokes succeed, I might simply turn around many of the points I have made about why jokes fail, converting a series of "don'ts" into a series of "do's." I could also repeat the information I provided in previous chapters about the anatomy of a joke and the triggers of laughter. I will do neither of those things, of course. My purpose in this section is to draw attention to some special techniques that help to assure a joke's success. Some I have mentioned before, some will be new.

For most of us, there are stories we found especially amusing at the time we heard them and which we recall with particular relish. What is it that makes those jokes stand out in our memories? Why did they succeed so well? In answering these questions, we can complement what we have already learned about joke construction with a knowledge of some further techniques. By applying them we may be able to create material on occasion that will also reverberate in our audiences' minds with distinctive and lasting force. Let us look now at a few of the reasons some jokes evoke special appreciation.

They Call Up Funny Pictures. In Chapter 7 I discussed how effective visualization by the audience can be in enhancing the laugh potential of a joke. Indeed, an amusing visualization may be all that is needed to get a laugh. It follows that a joke that causes the audience to see a funny picture is almost certain to be successful. Just such a picture takes form in the listener's mind on hearing the following joke, and the picture is created by a simple two-letter word:

Two moving men were struggling with a big crate in a doorway. They pushed and tugged until they were out of breath without moving it. Finally the man on the outside said, "We'll have to give up. We'll never get this crate in."

In breathless astonishment, the inside man gasped. "In?"

Quite a different picture, but one equally funny, is created by a joke told by Ronald Reagan while he was president:

Two men were out on a hike when they saw a large bear coming over a hill directly toward them. Immediately one of the men sat down, dropped his knapsack, pulled out a pair of tennis shoes, and began putting them on. The other man, seeing what he was doing, said, "I hope you don't think that putting on those tennis shoes is going to help you outrun that bear."

"I don't have to outrun the bear," the other man replied, "I only have to outrun you."

<u>The Point Sneaks Up</u>. Some jokes gain impact, oddly enough, because the point is not immediately obvious. In fact, for a moment the listener may think there is no joke there. Then suddenly two meanings connect with a click and a laugh explodes. The delay, for some reason, makes the laugh louder than it might otherwise have been. Jokes of this type usually involve puns, as is the case with this first example:

A man made the worrisome discovery that he was shrinking. Realizing that every day he had been getting smaller and smaller, he made a hasty visit to the doctor and demanded that he see him immediately.

"He's very busy," the nurse said soothingly, "Just take a seat and be a little patient."

The question the policeman asks in this next joke sounds so natural and ordinary, it is difficult to believe it will lead to a funny answer. For that reason the injured man's reply may puzzle listeners for a moment before they realize he has gone off in an unexpected direction:

A policeman came up to a man lying injured in the middle of the street. "Are you comfortable?" the policeman asked.

"I make a nice living," the man replied.

Reaction to this next joke may be delayed because listeners must do two things—identify a pun and make a literary connection:

A group of men were fishing off a dock when they made the delightful discovery that a school of fish had arrived and were swimming around right where they had dropped their lines. They began pulling fish in one after the other when the line of one of the men suddenly broke. "Give me a line," he yelled frantically. "Somebody give me a line."

"How's this one?" one of the others answered. "All the world's a stage and all the men and women merely players."

A comment that can still amuse decades after it was first uttered has been attributed to Robert Benchley:

Coming into a party out of a driving rain, Benchley is reputed to have said, "I've got to get out of these wet clothes and into a dry martini."

At first glance this joke seems to have no point. Then two things happen. The listener sees that a pun has been committed and recognizes the existence of an absurdity. You don't get into a dry martini, it gets into you—and the laugh comes.

Absurdity is at the core of this next joke, and again it is one that is not likely to be grasped instantly:

Thomas Edison spent many years trying to find a substance that would glow when subjected to electricity. He succeeded one day and the electric light was born. He ran out of his laboratory, into the house, and up the stairs to his bedroom. "I've done it!" he said to his dozing wife. "At last I've done it!"

She rolled over and said, "Thomas, will you please turn off that light and come to bed."

The Suggestion is Especially Subtle. All jokes employ suggestion to stimulate listeners into making some kind of connection with the ideas the joke maker presents. The more subtle the suggestion, the greater the self satisfaction listeners are likely to feel when they get the point. One method of achieving subtlety is to use the technique of indirection. We can see this technique in action in a joke Mark Russell told during one of his PBS presentations:

You recall that Hillary Rodham Clinton recently had an audience with the pope. During the session she explained to him the doctrine of infallibility.

This joke uses indirection in a particularly adroit way to accomplish two objectives. First, it leads the audience into recognizing that explaining the doctrine of infallibility to the pope, the world's leading authority on the subject, is highly presumptuous. Second, it lampoons Hillary Rodham Clinton by picturing her as a person who fancies herself an expert on everything.

This next joke portrays a woman who is obviously easily influenced. No description is needed. The idea is conveyed by the most subtle indirection:

A woman was telling her neighbor about her husband's occupation. "Harold writes children's stories. His stories are good. Children like Harold's stories. Sometimes I help Harold. I like to help Harold."

They Provide Richness of Experience. In reacting to a joke, listeners are looking for two things. One I have just mentioned. They want the point to be sufficiently elusive to make grasping it a satisfying accomplishment. They also want it to stimulate thoughts they can savor and enjoy. When a joke achieves those two objectives, it succeeds.

The challenge must not be so great, of course, that listeners cannot handle it. When a point remains beyond their grasp, they gain no satisfaction. Moreover, they are deprived of any kind of experience at all except one of disappointment.

Making an intelligent assessment of the kind of challenge a joke presents and the experience it evokes is of crucial importance to joke makers. This next series of jokes provides a test of your evaluative powers. I have arranged them in what I consider to be an ascending order of effectiveness. In studying them, focus your attention on the factors that determined my decision—challenge, and the evocation of experience. You may not agree with my rankings, but in formulating your reasons for agreeing or disagreeing, you should sharpen your ability to make sound evaluations of the material you produce.

I place this first joke at the low end of the spectrum because its challenge is slight, and the picture it evokes is vague and diffused. It probably would invite a groan from most audiences.

<u>Man</u>: I just got the job in the tube works up in the Bronx.

<u>Friend</u>: Oh, yeah, I've heard of the bronchial tubes.

The next joke represents a step upward both in the sternness of the test and the quality of the experience. The ingenious pun is a little more difficult to decode than the previous one, and the image produced in the listener's mind is more concrete.

I went to the store to buy myself a feather duster. And you know what? Inflation is so bad even the down is up.

I rank this next joke a touch higher than the preceding one because the test for the listener is somewhat more challenging. To unravel the pun, listeners must catch a clue that comes in the middle of the joke.

"Doc," said the cannibal to the witch doctor, "I have a terrible case of heartburn."

"What have you been eating?"

"The last thing was a missionary who wore a hooded robe and had a bald head."

"How did you cook him?" the witch doctor asked.

"I boiled him in my big iron pot."

"That's your problem," the witch doctor replied. "He isn't a boiler, he's a friar."

The challenge of getting the point to these next two jokes is about equal to that of the one above, but they move up a notch on the quality scale because they provide a somewhat richer, more enjoyable experience.

If your college daughter complains about having the Egyptian flu, you'd better start worrying. That's the latest college term for being pregnant, and it comes from the idea that those who suffer from it turn into mummies.

The bounty hunter came into the sheriff's office to ask if there were any outlaws around with prices on their heads.

"There sure is," said the sheriff. "We've got a weird one out there who'll be real easy to identify. He wears a brown paper shirt, brown paper pants, and a brown paper hat."

"What's he wanted for?" the puzzled bounty hunter asked.

"Rustling," said the sheriff.

Some of you might rate this next joke about equal in quality to the two I have just cited. I place it a step higher because getting its point requires the listener to visualize an object not commonly seen and to make a quick inventory of its attributes. The richness of experience the joke provides is about equal to that of the two previous ones.

An English professor was lecturing about the necessity of being precise in defining words. "How would you describe a mammal?" he asked one student.

"Well, let's see," the student responded nervously. "It has a hard skeleton...it's hairy...and it...uh...provides milk."

The professor gave him a cold look and then snapped, "So far, young man, you haven't eliminated the coconut."

Jokes that require listeners to connect what the joke maker says to such things as a literary work, a familiar saying, a famous quotation, or an historical event usually stand high on the quality list for two reasons. First, achieving the desired linkage produces marked self satisfaction. Second, the act of recollecting something from the past is likely to induce a pleasant contemplation that enriches the present. A *New Yorker* cartoon drawn by Mike Twohy illustrates both those virtues. It requires readers to recall a story most people heard as children, "Goldilocks and the Three Bears." They will remember the empty porridge bowl and the bed slept in by an interloper. The cartoonist has enhanced the incongruity of associating porridge and beds with bears by introducing an item even more out of keeping with their usual activity. The cartoon shows Papa Bear, Mama Bear, and Baby Bear looking down at three bicycles equipped with odometers. Baby Bear is saying, "Somebody's been putting additional mileage on my bike too."

Of all the jokes I have been analyzing the one I rank highest is also a *New Yorker* cartoon. Drawn by Charles Barzotti, it shows a corkscrew walking abruptly away from what is obviously a female cork as she says plaintively, "Will you call me?" It requires readers to make several connections, involving the incongruity of inanimate objects indulging in what might be thought of as very human behavior. Added to the mix is an enticing touch of naughtiness.

<u>The Language is Felicitous</u>. It goes without saying that to succeed, joke makers must find words that fit the ideas they want to express. The term "felicitous," however, implies more than mere appropriateness. To earn that approbation, joke makers must do more than find words that fit the thought. One must feel that the words they have chosen carry out the joke's purpose better than any others one can think of. When that goal is reached, the joke is bound to succeed.

One of the missions a clever choice of words can perform is to create an impression of suddenness. Many students of humor have emphasized its importance. Max Eastman listed it as one of the qualities that distinguishes the best jokes. Note how often Thomas Hobbes, who advanced a theory of humor in the 1600s, used the word in his oft-quoted statement about the cause of laughter: "*Sudden* glory is the passion which maketh those grimaces called laughter; and is caused either by some *sudden* act of their own that pleaseth them, or by apprehension of some deformed thing in another, by comparison whereof they *suddenly* applaud themselves." The word appears in Immanuel Kant's equally famous statement: "Laughter is an affectation rising from a *sudden* transformation of strained expectation into nothing."

Notice in the following joke how adroitly and swiftly the word "hardened" establishes the pun and concludes the joke:

NEWSFLASH: A cement truck collided with a police van carrying a group of prisoners. Be on the lookout for twelve hardened criminals.

This next joke is also marked by a choice of words that makes its point with admirable succinctness. They were added to a notice inscribed on a bulletin board standing outside a church. The notice read:

If you are weary of sin, come inside.

A whimsical passerby completely demolished its effect with just six pithy words:

If you're not, ring Bayswater 6-3000.

Earlier I referred to the type of joke that seeks its laugh by reversing the order of words or sounds in a familiar saying or by turning them into a pun. Most such jokes subject listeners to a build-up so long and laborious that by the time the pay-off line is reached, much of the humor has drained away. The best jokes of this variety are those whose words have some degree of terseness and snap. Here are two distinguished by the suddenness with which they make their points:

Jacques Plante, the one-time National Hockey League goal tender, took the TV personality Foster Hewitt and his son out to dinner. Seated around the table were the father, the son, and the goalie host.

While playing a short hole, a golfer hit his drive into the rough where it sent a quail flying into the air. He realized it was the first time he'd seen a partridge on a par three.

Let us turn now to some jokes that are marked not only by crispness in the telling, but also by a fine sensitivity to the subtle nuances which certain words can transmit. The words need not be grand or imposing to be effective. Often the best word is the simplest one you can find. The challenge is to find the word that fits the idea better than any other. The author of this next joke, the comedian Woody Woodbury, was highly successful in that endeavor. Note that his "right" words are all simple and short:

I love those slow-talking Southern girls. I was out with a Southern girl last night who took so long to tell me she wasn't that kind of girl, she was.

The movie *Some Like it Hot*, written by Billy Wilder, shows how simple words, chosen well, can be hilarious. The movie's closing line has been called the best tag to a movie ever created. The story tells how two men, played by Jack Lemmon and Tony Curtis, dress up as women to escape gangsters who are trying to kill them. A rich man, played by Joe E. Brown, falls in love with Jack Lemmon, thinking he's a woman. When Lemmon's masquerade is finally revealed, his ardor is in no way diminished. He expresses his intention to keep pursuing Lemmon in just two simple words: "Nobody's perfect."

Another tag equally hilarious came at the end of an episode in the *Maude* television series, a spin off of *All in the Family*. It was an expression most of us use at one time or another. Employed in ordinary circumstances, it is not funny at all. In this instance, it was adroitly slipped in at just the right moment.

The story concerned a neighbor of Maude's, a character played by Rue Clanahan. Rue thought her husband had gone away for the weekend, but when a man who looked just like him showed up on Saturday night, she concluded he had changed his plans. Actually he was her husband's twin brother, a person she didn't know existed. The brother played his role well, even to the extent of going to bed with her that night. The next day her husband returned to find that his long-lost brother had come to visit them. They had an affectionate reunion and when it was time for the brother to go, he said goodbye to Rue with the conventional, "I'm happy to have met you." She responded with the equally conventional, "It was my pleasure." Her words in that context rang with a double-layered meaning that provided a perfect ending to the show.

Well-chosen words are not necessarily simple, of course. Sometimes language has to be somewhat elaborate to convey the intended meaning. An anecdote concerning George Bernard Shaw shows him using language that is a little more sophisticated than the examples cited thus far. Nevertheless, I think you will agree that they deftly and economically made the point Shaw had in mind:

Seated next to a beautiful woman at a dinner party, George Bernard Shaw, demonstrating his penchant for being adventurous, asked her if she would be willing to sleep with him for £10,000. She indicated she might be willing to consider it.

"Would you be willing to do it for sixpence?" Shaw then asked.

"What kind of woman do you think I am?" the woman responded indignantly.

"We've established what kind of a woman you are," Shaw replied. "Now we're merely haggling over the price."

One of the most felicitous choosers of words was *The New Yorker* humorist James Thurber. One gets the feeling in reading his stories, essays, and cartoon captions that of all the words available to him, he has found exactly the right ones to express his ideas. These choices did not occur to him instantly. He kept revising his work until he was satisfied that every word was the right one. An example of his skill is a caption he wrote for one of his most memorable cartoons. Like the Shaw example, the words have an air of sophistication. The cartoon shows a group of people gathered around a dinner table. The host introduces the wine with the comment:

It's a naive domestic Burgundy without any breeding, but I think you'll be amused by its presumption.

It is difficult to articulate the point this joke makes, and yet it is still funny. The humor, I think, derives almost entirely from the precision with which Thurber chose the words. Each one of them is to be savored and enjoyed.

Sometimes felicity in language consists of drawing humor out of words that aren't inherently funny by inserting them into a situation in such a way that it makes them comic. This next joke shows how two unquestionably serious expressions, devised by creators of a religious doctrine, can become the focus of a joke when they are combined in an artful way:

Two boys who were studying religion in two different classes their church had set up were heard discussing the progress they were making. One boy announced proudly, "We're up to original sin."

"That's nothing," the other boy scoffed. "We're past redemption."

They Build to a Climax. All jokes, especially the longer ones, should maintain a steady movement forward to the final climactic line. A good way to attain this quality is to develop anticipation. Audiences will listen closely when they wonder where all this is leading. This next joke illustrates the technique. Note how meaningfully and directly it moves from one idea to another until the punchline is reached:

Two women who had known each other in high school met for the first time after graduating. "Have you managed to live a well-planned life?" one woman asked of the other.

"Oh, yes," her friend replied. First I married a millionaire, then an actor, then a preacher, and now I'm married to an undertaker."

"Why does that add up to a well-planned life?"

"One for the money, two for the show, three to get ready, and four to go."

Jokes, particularly those that go on at considerable length, are essentially stories with a funny ending. A major ingredient in the story teller's art is the ability to build events until they reach a climax. Listeners to these next two jokes are pulled along by the realization that something amusing is going to happen, and the jokes proceed step by step until that expectation is rewarded. An intriguing point is that both last lines include the same surprising word, one that also takes full advantage of the laugh-producing power of incongruity:

Michelangelo was painting the ceiling of the Sistine Chapel when he lost his grip on his brush and it clattered to the floor. Looking down, he emitted a hearty, "I'll be damned."

A nun walking by heard his expletive and, as he came down to retrieve his brush, reproved him with, "Michelangelo, you shouldn't swear like that. When something bad happens, just say 'Heaven saves.'"

Michelangelo nodded and climbed back to the ceiling. A few minutes later, he leaned too far out and his ladder began to topple backwards. He was about to utter another "damn" when he remembered the nun's admonition and muttered, "Heaven saves."

Miraculously the ladder steadied and then moved back to its proper position. The nun seeing all this from the floor below gasped, "Well, I'll be damned."

A minister and one of his parishioners went out to play golf together. The parishioner had a bad day. He missed an easy putt on the first hole and couldn't keep from saying, "Damn." On the third green, another putt trickled by the hole and he muttered, "Damn, missed again." The same thing happened on the sixth hole and another "Damn, missed again" followed. The minister looked reproachfully at him after each profane utterance but said nothing.

The parishioner's game didn't improve on the back nine. After another "Damn, missed again," the minister could take it no longer. "This can't go on," he burst out. "If you say 'damn' one more time, I'll call on the Lord to strike you."

The parishioner bit his lip and tried to restrain himself. He was successful until the last green when a putt that would have given him a birdie stopped at the edge of the hole. "Damn! damn! damn!" he exploded, "missed again!"

A huge black cloud suddenly formed in the sky. Then a lightning bolt flashed by the parishioner and vaporized the minister. Immediately a thundering voice filled the heavens with a frustrated, "Damn, missed again!"

This next joke also demonstrates how humor so often takes the form of a story. One can sense a vigorous movement toward a climactic conclusion, in which irony is the main provoker of mirth:

Mr. and Mrs. Brown were ecstatic when a child they had long hoped for finally arrived. They rejected all ordinary names in favor of one that described the wonderful thing that had happened to them. They called their son Fantastic Brown.

As soon as the child was old enough to understand his name, he hated it. When he went to school, his classmates made fun of it, and he hated it even more. He continued to hate it as he grew up, married, had children, and enjoyed a successful professional life. When the final reckoning came, he begged his wife as he lay on his deathbed not to put Fantastic on his tombstone. "Just put Brown," he ordered her. "Leave off the Fantastic."

She followed his instructions, but she felt uncomfortable about just using his last name. To make up for the omission, she added a line that defined what a fine, faithful husband he had been. It read: "During his marriage, he never looked at another woman."

And now everyone who goes by murmurs, "That's fantastic."

A joke is most easily recognized as a type of story when it is relatively long. But shorter forms also qualify and with them, as with the longer types, the joke maker must take care to create a pattern that moves inevitably to the pay-off line. The following joke, which you will recognize as a close relative of the previous one, is made up of just a few words, and yet it manages to develop sustained movement toward its amusing conclusion:

> A man named Homer Strange lived such an unsatisfactory life that he wanted to be forgotten after he died. He therefore ordered that his tombstone be left completely blank. People going by stop and stare at it and then mutter, "That's strange."

A joke does not even have to be told in conventional narrative form to become a story. The item below is an example. Note that it does what all good stories should do—provides insight into a character. Note also how it builds step by step to the surprise that provides the funny climax:

> The pilot pulled out the checklist he always consulted after a trip overseas. It read as follows:
> 1. Engine analyzer—OFF
> 2. Lights—OFF
> 3. Inverter—OFF
> 4. APP—OFF
> 5. Batteries—OFF
> 6. Wedding band—ON

They Shoot More than One Barrel. A characteristic of a number of jokes we recall with particular relish is that they make us laugh more than once. Sometimes the two or more parts making them up can stand on their own as separate jokes. In others, the first part, though it may provoke a chuckle or a grin, is designed primarily to provide a launching pad for the major laugh-producing punchline. Let's look first at examples of this latter type. Here is one that Jerome Beatty Jr. included in a "Trade Winds" column in the *Saturday Review*:

A lady tells me she was at a party in Houston where they were talking about odd yet authentic names of people, such as Gizella Werberzerk-Piffel and Rinetta Davydink. A man recalled a girl in Waxahachie, Texas, named Naughtybird Curtsey.

My friend says she was reluctant to believe this, until a young woman spoke up and said to the man, "I know a Naughtybird Curtsey in Waxahachie. I wonder if it could be the same one?"

The element in the first part of this story that may draw a chuckle from listeners is, of course, the succession of funny names. It would not stand on its own as a joke, but it does provide a perfect foundation for the funny bit of nonsense with which the story concludes.

A more elaborate build up to a punchline is illustrated by a story the singer Andy Williams told during one of his appearances on the *Tonight* show. The reiterated line "Did I say" becomes steadily funnier as the story proceeds, but the material does not become a full-fledged joke until the last line is heard. Those preliminary steps, besides being amusing on their own, build an expectation that is almost certain to make the final laugh bigger than it might otherwise be:

The following dialogue took place between an elderly man and his doctor.

"For a man of 60 you're in remarkable shape."

"Did I say I was 60? I'm 84."

"How old was your father when he died?"

"Did I say he was dead?"

"You mean he's still alive? How old is he?"

"102."

"How old was your grandfather when he died?"

"Did I say he was dead?"

"He's alive, too? How old is he?"

"123—and he's getting married."

"Why would a man that old want to get married?"

"Did I say he *wanted* to get married?"

This next joke represents a transition between the type in which only the last item really qualifies as a joke and the type in which the two or more items it includes can stand independently as jokes:

A monastery needed more money so the monks opened a fish and chips restaurant. One day a fellow who really enjoyed the repasts it provided went up to one of the cooks and said, "Are you the fish frier?"

"No, that's my brother over there," the cook replied, "I'm the chip monk."

The first part does not quite qualify as a joke in its present form, but it could easily be turned into one with a little touching up. As it stands, however, it is meant to prepare the audience for the funnier pun that follows.

Let us turn now to an example that truly qualifies as a double-barreled joke. Its two puns should both draw laughs (modest ones perhaps), and if one is removed the other still survives as a fully rounded joke. The item was reported in the *San Francisco Chronicle* by Herb Caen:

> There was a break-in at Heidi's Lingerie Shop. Taken were seven bras, size 36D and 38D. The police are keeping abreast of the case and are looking for a bust.

Here is another double-barreled joke:

> While Margaret Thatcher was serving as prime minister of Great Britain, she told the first President Bush that when she was considering someone for her cabinet, she always asked the candidate a certain riddle to make sure the person was smart enough to do the job. Before he succeeded her as prime minister, John Major was one of those candidates, and this is what she asked him: "If it's your father's son and it's not your brother, who is it?"
>
> "It's me," John Major said, and she made him a cabinet member.
>
> Bush decided to test his vice president, Dan Quayle with the riddle. After hearing it, Quayle said, nervously, "I'll get back to you." He then rushed to his office and called Henry Kissinger.
>
> "The answer's 'me,'" Kissinger said promptly after hearing the riddle.
>
> Quayle returned to Bush and reported triumphantly, "It's Henry Kissinger."
>
> "You are a numbskull," Bush responded. "It's not Kissinger. It's John Major."

If you ended this story with Dan Quayle's statement—"It's Henry Kissinger," you would have a full-fledged joke. You could also make George Bush's comment an independent joke, by having Quayle reply, "It's me." Bush's reaction, "It's John Major," would then become an independent joke of its own. No one would want to do that, of course, because the first part makes the second part, in which the dunce cap moves from Quayle's head to Bush's, much funnier than it would be standing alone.

Other jokes that shoot with more than one barrel show how a succession of jokes enhances the laugh-producing impact of all the funny lines that follow from the first one. This triple-barreled example illustrates the point as the two concluding items bring different variations on the motif introduced by the first item:

A friend visited an old lady in a nursing home and asked, "Do you know who I am?"

"I don't," the old lady said, "but if you ask at the desk, perhaps they can tell you."

"Well, do you know who you are?" her friend asked.

"How soon do you need to know?" the old lady replied. Then she added, "If I'm going to find out, I'd better knock on wood," whereupon she rapped the table next to her. Immediately she stood up and said, "I think someone is at the door."

In creating jokes that shoot with more than one barrel, a quality to strive for is to make each successive joke funnier than its predecessor. This put-down of lawyers illustrates the principle. You will note that as the joke goes along, the barbs get sharper:

Have you heard that some testing laboratories have begun to use lawyers in their experiments instead of white rats for three reasons: There are now more lawyers than there are white rats. Sometimes scientists get attached to white rats. And there are still some things white rats won't do.

The next joke, one that has been around for a long time, but which keeps popping up as a new item, is another example of a triple-barreled joke in which the humor of the punchline grows as the joke proceeds. In telling it, incidentally, it helps a great deal to fake a French accent:

Three Frenchmen were discussing the meaning of the term savoir-faire. "I can tell you what it means," said the first Frenchman. "If I came home to find my wife making love to another man, and back out quietly saying, 'Excusez-moi,' that is *savoir-faire*."

"I think we can be more precise," said the second Frenchman. "If when you leave you say, 'Excusez-moi. Please continuez.,' that is *savoir-faire*."

"You are thinking about the wrong person," said the third Frenchman. "If after you say to your wife's visitor, 'Excusez-moi. Please continuez' and he *can* continuez, that is *savoir-faire*."

Can a joke shoot with more than three barrels? One that often does is the type favored by now-vanished burlesque comedians, in which the humor arose from a contrast between two trains of thought inspired by the same stimulus, one completely innocent, the other highly suggestive. The multiple-barreled example that follows has an interesting history. Jack Paar told it while he was host of the *Tonight* show on February 10, 1960. The squeamish NBC censor clipped it from the tape. When NBC refused to honor Paar's request to play it the next night, Paar, outraged at what he viewed as petty censorship, walked off the set, leaving a startled Hugh Downs to carry on in his absence. I found the item in Paar's memoir, *I Kid You Not*. Incidentally, I'll be referring to it again when I discuss good taste in humor in the next chapter. For now, however, it provides a further illustration of how jokes on the same theme, heard one after the other, become funnier and funnier as the jokes proceed:

An English lady who was planning to spend a year in Switzerland made a preliminary visit to find an apartment. After deciding on one, she returned to England to make final preparations for her move. The thought suddenly struck her that she had not seen a water closet in the apartment, so she wrote to the schoolmaster who had rented it to her. Being a person of delicate sensibilities, she refrained from using the term itself, but referred to it by the abbreviation W. C." The schoolmaster, who knew very little English, had no idea what she meant so he asked the parish priest for help. He was puzzled too, but finally decided that "W. C." must stand for Wayside Chapel. He then helped the schoolmaster write the following reassuring letter:

Dear Madam:

I take great pleasure in informing you the "W. C." is situated nine miles from the apartment you will occupy, in the center of a beautiful grove of pine trees surrounded by lovely grounds.

It is capable of holding 229 people and is open on Sunday and Thursday only. As a great number of people are expected during the summer months, I would suggest that you come early; although there is plenty of standing room as a rule.

You will no doubt be glad to hear that a good number of people bring their lunch and make a day of it. Others who can afford to go by car arrive just in time.

I would especially recommend that Your Ladyship go on Thursday when there is musical accompaniment.

It may interest you to know that my daughter was married in the "W. C.," and it was there that she met her husband. I can remember the rush there was for seats. There were ten people to a seat usually occupied by one. It was wonderful to see the expressions on their faces.

The newest attraction is a bell donated by a wealthy resident of the district. It rings every time a person enters. A bazaar is to be held to provide plush seats for all the people, since they feel it is a long-felt need. My wife is rather delicate, so she can't attend regularly.

I shall be delighted to reserve the best seat for you if you wish, where you will be seen by all.

For the children, there is a special time and place so they will not disturb their elders. Hoping to have been of some service, I remain

Sincerely,
The Schoolmaster

Wisdom Jokes

Before concluding this discussion on the characteristics that distinguish good jokes from bad ones, I should like to refer briefly to a type of joke that falls into a category of its own. The measure of its effectiveness is not the strength of the laugh it calls forth but rather the kind of thinking it provokes. If a function of humor is to reveal the truth, as so many commentators have said, then a joke that accomplishes that objective in a striking and original way can be said to be a success, even though the laugh it incites is minimal. William Davis once said: "The kind of humor I like is the thing that makes me laugh for five seconds and think for ten minutes." The jokes I am about to quote are of that variety.

Some may question whether this first example should be called a joke at all. Attributed to Louis E. Boone, and published originally in *Quotable Business*, it was picked up by the *Reader's Digest*. Instead of putting it in one of its humor columns, however, the *Digest* included it in a feature called "Points to Ponder":

> It is often argued that the people who will be affected by a major decision should be involved in it. Paul Kruger, president of the Transvaal in southern Africa, once resolved a dispute between two brothers about a land inheritance they were to share. Kruger's decision: Let one brother divide the land, and let the other brother have first choice.

The tone of this item is essentially serious and thought provoking, yet it concludes with the evocation of a picture that will make readers smile. Most of them will visualize the two brothers struggling to adapt to President Kruger's ingenious solution in a way that will benefit them the most. It is a

271

prime example of what I call a wisdom joke. Incidentally, my wife tells me the idea isn't new to her. As a child, when her mother told her to divide up a piece of cake with one of her sisters, she would use the expression, "You cut, I'll choose."

In a column called "Observations," which Al Failka wrote for a newspaper aimed at senior citizens, there was another example of a wisdom joke. It manages to bring a serious subject into focus in an intriguing and amusing way:

I found a St. Christopher medal that had a note attached, "Good only up to 55 mph."

Here are some further examples. Most would agree they are thought provoking. Whether they qualify as jokes may be debatable. I find them amusing enough to be placed in the wisdom-joke category:

The Rev. Robert Ard, president of the Black Leadership Council, explained the difference between involvement and commitment in this way: "When you look at a plate of ham and eggs, you know the chicken was involved. But the hog was committed."

The difference between a conviction and a prejudice is that you can explain a conviction without getting angry.

If the human brain were so simple that we could understand it, we would be so simple that we couldn't.
Emerson M. Pugh

Defeat is an orphan, but victory has a thousand fathers.
President John Kennedy after being
assailed for the Bay of Pig's disaster.

It should be the function of medicine to have people die young as late as possible.
Ernst L. Wynder, M. D.

My last example clearly qualifies as a joke, but one might wonder whether its subject matter is serious enough to place it in the wisdom category. It was part of a monologue delivered by Conan O'Brien on NBC's *Late Show*. The joke was prompted by a series of newspaper reports about the childish reactions of some major-league baseball players to umpires' decisions. It happened that the Little League World Series was going on at the time the program was to be broadcast. O'Brien seized on this fact to express his disdain for the childish behavior of the major-league players with this comment:

I've been watching Little Leaguers play baseball in their World Series. It's just like the Major League World Series, except the players are smaller and more mature.

Chapter 10
Should I Tell This Joke?

A good laugh and a long sleep are the two best cures..

Irish proverb

Though being funny can produce undeniable benefits, humor can also snap back and hurt you if your audience concludes it is inappropriate or in poor taste. Some topics have a built-in potential for giving offense. There are also occasions when simply telling a joke can work against you even if your material kindles no complaints. If you use humor at all, you are bound to be faced at times with the problem of deciding whether to tell a particular joke. Making the right decision is often difficult. In this chapter we look at some of the criteria you should keep in mind as you ponder what to do.

The Hazards of Being Funny

A general problem humorists face is that their art has sometimes been held in low esteem. A passage in the Bible, for example, stands on the side of seriousness. In Ecclesiastes 7:3 we read: "Sorrow is better than laughter." Plato thought that laughter was unseemly for dignified men. Aristotle placed comedy on a lower plane than tragedy, suggesting that there was something base and ignoble about it. The eighteenth century British statesman, Lord Chesterfield, echoed that thought by condemning comedy for providing "mirth for the mob, who are only pleased with silly things." The English poet Percy Bysshe Shelley went so far as to say, "There can be no entire regeneration of mankind until laughter is put down." Even when humorists do achieve recognition, their product often does not win the high regard accorded the work of serious writers. Many of them might say along with Rodney Dangerfield, "I don't get no respect."

Most of us view Abraham Lincoln's ability to find a funny story to fit almost every occasion as one of his most attractive characteristics. In his own times, however, his constant use of humor probably hurt him more than it helped. Many of his contemporaries looked on him as a mere buffoon. We can find parallels to that judgment about politicians in our own day. One who comes to mind is Adlai Stevenson, who won the Democratic nomination for president in 1952 and 1956, but lost both times to the Republican nominee, Dwight Eisenhower. Like Lincoln, Stevenson was constantly making jokes. His humor charmed some, but it made others think he was superficial. As one commentator put it, he violated the Republican law of gravity. Morris Udall, who lost the Democratic nomination for president to Jimmy Carter in 1986, recognized that his jokes might have contributed to his defeat. He wrote a book about his failed quest entitled *Too Funny to be President*.

One authority on the presidency even thought that Ronald Reagan told too many jokes. There was at least one occasion in which his attempt to be funny did go awry. During a voice check preceding the delivery of a radio speech, he said, "My fellow Americans, I am pleased to tell you I have just signed legislation that outlaws Russia forever. The bombing starts in five minutes," never realizing that his words were being broadcast. As one might expect, those words caused a disapproving stir in foreign circles.

A hazard all joke makers face is that they may be taken seriously when they are simply trying to be funny. Jimmy Carter ran into that problem while he was president. In a talk to government employees, he made what he meant to be a jocular reference to employees who lived together without benefit of marriage. Betty Ford, the wife of the man he defeated for president, thought he was trying to impose his moral values on government workers and publicly chastised him for it.

Is it possible for a person who makes a living by being funny to tell too many jokes? According to Roger Angell, a writer and editor for *The New Yorker*, Woody Allen may sometimes be guilty of that fault. In reviewing a humorous essay Allen had submitted, Angell noticed that some sentences contained as many as three jokes. In Angell's view, that was too many, and he told Allen.

"Do you mean you want me to write fewer jokes?" Allen responded unbelievingly.

Angell answered with a nod and a pleading, "Yes—yes, please."

The great Canadian humorist Stephen Leacock once wrote a funny piece entitled, "A, B, and C," which many consider to be a classic example of the humorous essay. His fellow Canadian, Robertson Davies, who put together an anthology of Leacock's best work, hailed it as "perfection in its kind." In it Leacock puts human faces on the characters who inhabit arithmetic problems, those that begin, "A, B, and C do a certain piece of work. A can do as much work in one hour as B in two, and C in three." Leacock turned these symbols into real people with specific personality characteristics who experienced triumphs and failures. As it goes along the essay gets funnier and funnier. It is indeed a gem, but in my view it contains one defect. The flaw occurs when Leacock inserts one joke too many. It comes when Leacock is telling how C, who always ends up last, comes to this melancholy end:

It seems that A and B had been rowing on the river for a wager, and C had been running on the bank and then sat in a draught. Of course, the bank had refused the draught and C was taken ill. A and B came home and found C lying helpless in bed. A shook him roughly and said, "Get up C, we're going to pile wood.

The flaw, as I see it, is the inclusion of the pun about the "draught." It sticks out awkwardly, sounds forced, and is out of keeping with the tone of the rest of the piece. Even masters sometimes stumble.

In his book *How to be Funny* Steve Allen concedes that at times he is too intent on being funny, especially around the house. On occasion his wife, Jayne Meadows, asked him plaintively to stop making jokes for awhile to give her mind a rest. You may feel that way at times about some of your funny friends, who never seem able to resist the urge to wisecrack.

One built-in hazard humorists face is that a great many jokes get laughs by making fun of people, institutions, and ideas. Most people are willing to accept a certain amount of joshing, but if it cuts too deeply, the teller may suffer. As Will Rogers said, "We all enjoy a joke as long as it's aimed at someone else."

Former Senator Bob Dole can make most people laugh most of the time, but sometimes, his wit took on a very sharp edge. Some think it became so sharp in 1976, when he ran as the vice-presidential candidate with Gerald Ford, that he hurt the Republican ticket. His cut-and-thrust attack on his Democratic opponents, in the opinion of some, may have alienated just enough voters to account for Ford's razor-thin loss to Jimmy Carter.

That verdict cannot be proved, but the impact of offensive humor on the downfall of two other Republicans is beyond dispute. Earl Butz, Secretary of Agriculture in the Ford administration, while on an airplane trip told a distasteful story about the sexual preferences of Blacks. Word of his story leaked out, and before Butz quite knew what was happening to him, he was out of a job. A similar fate befell James Watt, Secretary of the Interior in the Reagan administration. In a clumsy attempt at using humor to persuade his listeners he was non-discriminatory in his choice of personnel, he announced he had appointed a committee "made up of a Black, a woman, two Jews, and a cripple." His blunt language lost him his job also.

In telling his story, Earl Butz was being deliberately offensive. He just didn't expect the public at large to learn about it. James Watt probably didn't intend to offend anyone. He was just trying to be funny.

A similar type of incident occurred on a local level. In 1995 the Ann Arbor City Council was interviewing three finalists for the position of city manager. One of them had surged to the top with an impressive performance, and it seemed he was about to win the appointment. Near the end of the interview, however, he was asked how he would deal with the inevitable reversals and disappointments he was bound to experience. In an apparent attempt to be funny, he responded: "I'll take out my frustrations by going home and beating my wife." The council members recoiled in shock.

In their eyes spousal abuse was not an appropriate subject for humor. Still, most of them were inclined to overlook the remark, realizing that he wasn't serious. One member made an issue of it, however, and the candidate was dropped from the list of prospects.

The columnist and TV news commentator Jeff Greenfield once wrote: "Humor is the nitroglycerin of politics. Used skillfully it is a powerful weapon; used carelessly, it can blow up in your face and cause big trouble." The three incidents I have described show how harmful the clumsy use of humor can be. But sometimes comments much less crass than those I have just cited can damage political figures. During the 1992 presidential campaign, Hillary Rodham Clinton inadvertently offended a legion of homemakers when she made what she no doubt meant to be a jocular response to a question about why she had decided on being a career woman. "I didn't want to spend my time making cookies," she said. Unfortunately her reply created a supercilious image which she has never succeeded in completely erasing.

A common joke among people who experience intestinal distress while on a trip to Mexico is that they are suffering from Montezuma's revenge. Most people can make that remark with impunity. That is not true, however, when you are the President of the United States and have made your trip as a guest of the Mexican government. The president in question was Jimmy Carter. His use of the Montezuma comment to explain his temporary indisposition naturally affronted his hosts.

Misplaced or ill-chosen humor may not have quite the disastrous consequences which some of the examples I have cited illustrate, but it can nevertheless be damaging. The most common result is that the reputation of the joke teller suffers. What worried Jack Paar most about NBC's cutting of this "W. C." routine was that the public would assume he had told a smutty story. It is not just off-color material that can affect what people think of you, of course. If you make fun of people's afflictions or direct barbs at ethnic groups, your listeners may conclude you are callow and insensitive, or even worse, a racist.

One way to avoid difficulty, it would seem, is not to tell any jokes at all. Ohio Senator Thomas Corwin, one of President Garfield's counselors, gave him precisely that advice. "Never make people laugh," he told him. "If you would succeed in life, you must be solemn as an ass. All great monuments are built over solemn asses." If you adopt that solution, of course, you casually toss away all of the benefits that the use of humor can bring.

A less dramatic approach would be to tell some jokes, but to make sure that none of them will offend anyone. That solution eliminates from your repertoire a whole host of subjects about which to be funny. As I noted in a previous chapter, seventy percent of all jokes get laughs by making fun of somebody or something. They may well make those who are their targets unhappy. Another type of material that may offend listeners with delicate sensibilities are jokes involving sexual references. I've never seen an estimate of how much humor falls into that category, but it must be substantial. On the Internet the word Jokes brought up 12,600,000 web sites on Google and the words Jokes about Sex brought up 2,560,000 which reveals a very rough estimate of 20.3%. Of course, that percentage would increase dramatically if those jokes that are faintly risqué were included. Deleting all put-downs, jokes about sex, and anything that is even faintly risqué will leave you with very little else to be funny about.

A second problem is that by excluding everything that might possibly offend the few, you may deprive the many of material they would find enjoyable and satisfying. Let's face it, a lot of people like to hear spicy jokes. Put-downs of people, particularly of those in high places, bolster a lot of egos.

A third problem is that no matter how careful you are, you can't be sure you have eliminated everything that might offend. I discovered that early in my career when I was writing radio programs for the Detroit Board of Education which were designed for use in classrooms. In one program dealing with the history of dentistry, I had an ancient Egyptian dentist begin a session with a patient by saying, "This isn't going to hurt you a bit." What I thought of as an innocent little line provoked the president of the local dental association into writing a letter to the Superintendent of Schools denouncing me for making youngsters afraid to go to the dentist. The incident had a satisfying ending for me, however. The superintendent, Frank Cody, simply handed the letter to me with a smile and didn't even admonish me to be more careful in the future.

I think we can conclude from all of this that telling jokes involves some risks. But playing it absolutely safe isn't the answer. Professional comedians are well aware that their humor may offend a few listeners. Sometimes Jay Leno tries to ward off protesting letters and emails by saying somewhat wistfully, "Please don't write to me about this. I'm only joking." The knowledge that those objecting letters will come in doesn't keep him from telling the jokes, however. Much to my amazement, he sometimes goes so far as to make fun of products advertised on his program. The wry comment, "Well, there goes another sponsor," often follows. Even more amazing is that the network lets him do it.

I do not imply that complete license is desirable, of course. The damage you can incur is too great to make such a course advisable. In considering whether to use a particular piece of material, you need to make a careful assessment of the risk you face. In deciding whether it is worth taking, you should consider a number of factors.

The Nature of the Audience

Your first step should be to think about the kind of people who will hear or read your material. Jokes that are suitable for one audience may be inappropriate for another. For a number of years I have been giving a lecture entitled "The Anatomy of Humor." The groups who hear it vary widely in their characteristics. The basic principles I discuss are the same for all of them, but the jokes I use to illustrate the principles may differ to some extent as I move from one group to another. Before giving the version I had used for a Rotary Club to a church women's society, for example, I would do a little winnowing and substituting.

In deciding what jokes to use, most people think first about whether certain material is a little too racy for the prospective audience. A joke that Rotary Club members would find entirely acceptable might draw disapproving clucks from the church women. It is certainly necessary to think about how your listeners will react to material some may look on as risqué, but you also need to consider how they will respond to other types of material. In making that assessment, some of the characteristics you might mull over are your listeners' occupations, political views, religious affiliations, educational background, and prevailing age. One item that has nothing to do with giving offense is their level of sophistication. A joke whose point would be easily grasped by one audience could shoot over the heads of another. You want to entertain your listeners, not baffle them.

A good guide to making the right decisions is to think about your audience's expectations. People flipping through *Playboy* would anticipate seeing material quite different from the kind they look for in the *Reader's Digest*. The same sharp contrast would characterize the expectations of a comedy club patron and those of a person attending a scholarly lecture.

Should the fact that your audience is exclusively male or female, or includes both, influence the type of jokes you tell? Conventional wisdom would say it should. Research carried out at the University of Connecticut by John Parrish Sprowl indicated that men and women have somewhat different tastes in humor. Men almost always find sexual jokes funny. Women are more inclined than men to enjoy humor that comes out of everyday events, but most of them also like to hear material that has sexual

281

references if they are not too crude and explicit. That last conclusion is supported by an experience Goodman Ace wrote about in the September 17, 1977, issue of the *Saturday Review*. In the early 1970s he became affiliated with a lecture bureau, and before he went out into the field, the crusty, elderly gentleman who managed the bureau gave him this instruction: "Since almost all your audiences will be mixed company, we have one strict rule for all our speakers. Never say anything or tell any story that is off color." After giving a number of lectures, Ace began to wonder about the mixed company, off-color admonition. He decided to test it by dipping his toe, as he put it, "into the polluted off-color waters." At his next lecture he told this joke:

> The Italians are going to put a clock in the Leaning Tower of Pisa. Why are they putting a clock in the Leaning Tower of Pisa? Because the Italians feel, "What's the use of having the inclination if you don't have the time?"

As far as he could see, there was no hostile reaction to his little venture into the risqué. Both his male and female listeners laughed at his joke. Encouraged, he tried other jokes of the same type. One dealing with the world's first humans, went like this:

> When Adam came into the world, he was lonely. So the Creator made Eve out of one of his ribs. After completing His task He said to Adam, "See that girl over there. Why don't you go over and give her a hug?"
>
> "What's a hug?" Adam asked.
>
> The Creator explained, and the deed was done.
>
> The Creator then said, "Now give her a kiss." Again He had to explain. When the kiss had been successfully delivered, the Creator then told Adam to go over and make love to Eve.
>
> "What's make love?" Adam asked.
>
> The Creator explained the intricacies of the maneuver, and Adam said, "I'll try." A few seconds later he was back. "What happened?" asked the Creator.
>
> "What's a headache?" Adam responded.

Though this joke seems somewhat racier than the first one and includes elements some might think of as sacrilegious, it still drew loud laughter and no visible forms of disapproval. Ace reported that the women actually laughed more boisterously than the men. Apparently it was their kind of sex joke.

It is not enough to think only about the general characteristics of your audience. It is possible that it may contain people who will react with peculiar sensitivity to something you say. Suppose, for example, that you are considering telling a joke about elderly forgetfulness. You would obviously avoid doing so if you knew that the life of one of your listeners was being ravaged by the burden of caring for someone with Alzheimer's disease. There is no way of knowing all about the individual backgrounds of your listeners, of course. But you need to think long and hard about using material that might evoke painful recollections from someone in your audience.

The Nature of the Occasion

In pondering whether to tell a particular joke, there is more than the audience to consider. You also need to think about the objective you are trying to achieve with your article or speech. Why has an audience assembled to hear you? What are the people who will read your words looking for? If your purpose is simply to entertain, your humor is justified if it does no more than make your audience laugh. If your principal aim is to enlighten or persuade, however, the prime purpose of your humor should be to support and reinforce the information or arguments you present.

There are other aspects of a situation you need to consider. As I noted in Chapter 1, humor at a funeral service is not necessarily out of place, but you must exercise special care in choosing it. Most of us would agree that snappy wisecracks are not suitable for such an occasion. On the other hand, a funny story that illuminates an attractive personality characteristic of the person whose life is being celebrated can add a welcome lightening touch to the service.

Should preachers use jokes in their Sunday sermons? In Chapter 1, I answered "yes" to that question and cited some of the benefits that humor can bring. Some would disagree with that position. One, oddly enough, was the writer we know as Lewis Carroll, whose masterly use of humor in his *Alice in Wonderland* books has made millions of people laugh. After the Bible and Shakespeare's works, they are the most widely quoted and translated books in the Western world. But when it came to religious services, Carroll's attitude was starchy and restrictive. He once wrote to a bishop to rebuke him for allowing a touch of humor to creep into one of his sermons.

I see no reason for such an attitude. People attending church like to laugh as much as anyone. If nothing else humor can make a sermon easier to listen to. It is important, however, that preachers make sure it is relevant to their central message. Because the sound of laughter is sweet music to a speaker's ears, preachers are sometimes lured into telling jokes for their own sake. Too many of them can damage the spiritual atmosphere religious services aim to create. A discordant note may also be introduced if the humor does not fit the situation, whether it is a funeral, a church service, or some other type of occasion. An experience Mark Twain had illustrates how unfortunate the consequences can be when humor is used inappropriately. In 1877 he was invited to speak at a dinner commemorating the seventieth birthday of John Greenleaf Whittier. Instead of spouting the shopworn clichés usually marking such events, Twain decided he would do something different and unexpected. That intent was wholly admirable, but he made the mistake of going too far.

Oddly enough, he completely ignored the guest of honor and concentrated instead on making fun of three other American literary giants he knew were going to be in the audience—Oliver Wendell Holmes, Ralph Waldo Emerson, and Henry Wadsworth Longfellow. Twain pretended that during a trip to the Sierras, he had knocked on the door of an isolated log cabin and introduced himself to the miner who occupied it. The miner responded by saying, "You're the fourth literary man that has been here in twenty-four hours—I'm going to move." The other three, it turned out were Emerson, Holmes, and Longfellow. The miner described Mr. Emerson as "a seedy little bit of a chap, red headed. Mr. Holmes was fat as a balloon; he weighed as much as three hundred, and had double chins all the way down to his stomach....Mr. Longfellow was built like a prizefighter. His head was cropped and bristly, like as if he had a wig made of hairbrushes." The miner added that the three had obviously been drinking. Their conversation was mainly made up of quotations from their own literary works. After inspecting the cabin, Mr. Holmes said, for example:

Through the deep caves of thought I hear a voice that sings,
"Build thee more stately mansions, O my soul."

Mr. Emerson, feeling hungry, took the miner by the buttonhole and said:

Give me agates for my meat;
Give me cantharids to eat;
From air and ocean bring me foods,
From all zones and altitudes.

When Longfellow was about to leave, the miner noticed he was wearing his boots. "Hold on there, Evangeline," he protested. "What are you going to do with *them*?" Longfellow replied, "Going to make tracks with them because—"

Lives of great men all remind us

284

We can make our lives sublime;
And, departing, leave behind us
Footprints on the sands of time.

At the end of his speech Twain revealed that the three visitors wer
imposters, but by then it was too late; his audience had been stunned int
silence. Albert Bigelow Paine, a biographer of Twain, said that the speech
exploded like a bombshell "of planetary proportions....The thought o
associating, ever so remotely, those three old bummers...with the venerabl
and venerated Emerson, Longfellow, and Holmes...seems ghastly." Willian
Dean Howells, the chairman of the occasion, and Twain's close friend
noted that the audience's excited expectancy about what the distinguishe
humorist was going to say soon turned into a black frost. In a few moment
Twain had become a solitary and lonely figure standing before his appalle
listeners with his presumed joke dead in his hands.

Twain realized almost immediately that he had made a hideous mistake
but unable to stop, he staggered on to his speech's conclusion. Later as h
writhed under the recognition of his own stupidity, he thought for awhile
about abandoning his career as a lecturer and writer. The incident haunte
him for the rest of his life. Thirty years later he still thought about it
Sometimes he became defensive, describing his speech as "smart" an
"saturated with humor." Clever it undeniably was—and funny, too. As w
read it today, Twain's ingenious coupling of developments marking th
three bleary outcasts' visit to the cabin with quotations from the three poets
works is likely to make us laugh. But just as undeniably his coarse ridicul
of Emerson, Holmes, and Longfellow was totally out of keeping with th
occasion.

One of the shocking aspects of the Mark Twain presentation was that h
ridiculed famous literary figures in their presence. That same kind o
behavior provoked a similar controversy more than 100 years later. In 199C
a New York broadcaster named Don Imus, known as a "shock" talk show
host because of the raunchiness of his material and the derisive tone of the
comments he makes on his morning radio program, was invited to speak a
the annual dinner of the Radio and Television Correspondents Association
He remained true to form. With two notable guests sitting just a few fee
from him, President Bill Clinton and his wife, Hillary, he proceeded to taun
them with jokes about Clinton's presumed womanizing and Hillary'
alleged Whitewater shenanigans. They were not the only victims of hi
abuse. He also dissected publicly and explicitly the embarrassing misstep
and personal idiosyncrasies of a wide range of broadcasters and politicians
most of whom were also present at the dinner.

WILLIS - How to be Funny on Purpose

The nature of his material drew some critical comments. A few jokes were unquestionably clever and funny, but much of what he said descended to the level of direct personal insult, unredeemed by the saving grace of humor. An aura of nastiness pervaded his whole presentation. What drew most attention, however, was the fact that he had mocked the president and first lady while they sat there looking at him. Bill Maher, a comedian who had hosted a TV program entitled *Politically Incorrect*, which often included humor some would describe as outrageous, concedes that he has told jokes about Clinton and Hillary similar to those Imus told—and so have other comedians. He said, however, that he would never tell such jokes in the first couple's presence. In doing that, Maher argued, Imus crossed the line into the unacceptable. Others expressed similar views, using such adjectives as crass, sleazy, and insensitive to characterize the performance.

Unlike Mark Twain, Imus was unrepentant. Interviewed on *60 Minutes* by Mike Wallace, he refused to admit that he had done anything wrong, saying that "They knew what they were buying when they asked me to speak."

This incident demonstrates how subtle the circumstances are that must be considered in deciding whether to tell a certain joke. Other celebrities were ridiculed to their faces, among them Newt Gingrich, Dan Rather, and Sam Donaldson, but that didn't seem to bother most people. It was the fact that he made fun of the President of the United States and his wife in an extremely personal way, while they were present in the audience. It should be noted that Imus's misstep, if that's what it was, has not damaged his broadcasting career. His radio program still reaches a national audience, and it is simulcast on cable television by MSNBC.

The Nature of the Times

Those among you old enough to recall the kind of world we lived in a few decades ago recognize that a tremendous change has taken place in the language used by writers for all the various media and in the sort of situations they portray. People tuning in the radio soap operas of the 1930s became accustomed to a dramatic form in which the heroines were not even permitted to smoke for fear it would sully their pristine purity. Suppose listeners to such entertainment had fallen suddenly into a deep Rip Van Winkle type of sleep and had awakened years later to be abruptly exposed to one of the steamy sex scenes so prevalent in today's TV soap operas. How, one wonders, would they react? In the nineteenth century women in Victorian England found this bit of advice in *Godey's Lady's Book*:

286

The perfect hostess will see to it that the works of male and female authors are strictly separated. Their proximity on the shelves—unless they happen to be married—should not be tolerated.

We may laugh at the kind of mind that produced such an absurdity, and yet some of the prohibitions observed in the twentieth century were not far removed from it. In the 1930s NBC would not permit the word "diaper" to be used in any of its programs. CBS stayed even in the primness sweepstakes by banning the use of the word "pregnant." Some wag remarked that you couldn't even use the word to describe a pause.

Driving networks down this prudish path were expressions of outrage received from listeners when programs violated what they considered to be standards of good taste. A notable protest occurred in 1937 when Mae West, an actress best known for the sexually oriented roles she played on stage and screen, appeared in an NBC program portraying Eve in a sketch set in the Garden of Eden. The part of Adam was performed by Charlie McCarthy, the ventriloquist's dummy whose voice was provided by Edgar Bergen. The NBC censor saw nothing untoward in the script, but when Mae West read the lines with the suggestive intonations that were her trademark, they acquired a meaning no one had anticipated. The FCC responded to a deluge of complaining letters and phone calls by warning NBC that such material would not be tolerated. It delivered a warning equally stern when the producers of a radio adaptation of Eugene O'Neill's play *Beyond the Horizon* failed to cut out the "damns" and "hells." From then on networks became extremely skittish about what they would permit in their programs. In one instance the expression "Holy Cow" was excised. In another, the line "Out damned spot" was cut from a broadcast adaptation of Shakespeare's play *Macbeth*.

The same kind of attitude influenced what could be advertised on radio in those early days. At one time toothpaste was considered too intimate a product to be mentioned in commercials. That proscription was soon dropped, but other products about which listeners might be sensitive remained on the forbidden list. Broadcasters once had a "Code of Good Practice" which banned advertising for hemorrhoid remedies. That kind of restriction is now a distant memory, and so are most other such restraints. In the interests of public health, Congress has prohibited the advertising of cigarettes and some other tobacco products, and most stations refuse to carry commercials for hard liquor for fear of arousing the prohibition crowd, but beyond that there are virtually no restrictions on the products and services broadcasters advertise.

Movies now have almost unlimited freedom in the words they can use and the situations they can portray, and so do TV cable systems. Producers of broadcast radio and TV programs are still more circumscribed than movie and cable producers, but they, too, have taken long steps toward complete permissiveness. Part of this may be a result of the unbridled freedom revealed on the World Wide Web. The censors who carefully cut out the "damns" a few years ago would be astonished to hear the words now commonly heard on television and radio programs, not just from the so-called "shock" disc jockeys, but from characters in situation comedies and dramas as well. The producers of *Seinfeld* delivered one of the most startling challenges to commonly accepted taboos when they made a contest among the program's leading characters about who could avoid masturbating the longest the focal point of an episode.

Certain current events opened doors that had previously been closed. The development of the AIDS crisis, with its emphasis on the importance of safe sex, meant that "condom," a previously taboo word, could now be used. During the period that Lorena Bobbitt's commission of very personal mayhem on her husband was in the news, broadcasters of the event could not avoid using the word "penis." It now occurs in other contexts. In a 1995 *20/20* interview conducted by Barbara Walters with the shock disc jockey Howard Stern, the word was bandied about with complete abandon.

The elimination of most restrictions in the entertainment industries has influenced what goes on in other situations. Lecturers use words and discuss subjects many people would have scarcely dared even to think about a few years ago. The same change has taken place in the content of private conversations.

In deciding whether to tell a certain joke you should naturally take the changes I have described into account. That does not mean that anything goes, of course. Even in these permissive times, restrictions still exist. The fact that the bars are lower than they used to be does not mean you can ignore them, however. In the early 1960s when Jack Paar told his "W. C." joke on NBC, the prudish taboos of broadcasting's earlier years were disappearing. Perhaps that is why he thought this once questionable material would be acceptable. What he overlooked was that "bathroom" humor was still on the forbidden list. He could argue, as he did later, that the routine must be totally innocent because he had obtained it from his thirteen-year-old niece, who had received it in turn from her seventh-grade teacher, but none of that made any difference. The material was still a bathroom joke.

Today, of course, the "W. C." routine would cause no ripples of any kind. Some might even consider it too mild for the *Tonight* show. When the words "bathroom humor" were entered into the Google search window 886,000 web sites were generated, and the words "bathroom jokes" produced 689,000; obviously, there is a different set of standards operating today than in the past, and the Internet has played no small part in lowering the bar.

Indicative, too, of the astonishing changes that have taken place in what censors will accept was a conversation Jay Leno had with Jack Paar when he made a return visit to the *Tonight* show as a guest in 1994. The two were discussing why Madonna and Michael Jackson had the habit of grabbing their crotches during performances. Paar speculated that "Madonna is trying to find her talent and Michael Jackson is trying to find anything." Despite the bawdiness of his comment, the NBC censors, as far as I know, remained completely quiescent.

No matter what the standards are at a given time, people will disagree about what is seemly, as Jack Paar and the NBC censor did in 1960. In the 1930s, CBS refused to accept commercials for Sal Hepatica, a treatment for constipation, or for deodorants. NBC accepted commercials for both types of products. In this area of greater permissiveness, people still disagree about what is appropriate even though the issues are vastly different. That means it is just as difficult as it ever was to decide whether to use a certain joke.

Today's TV producers of situation comedies disagree, for example, about how free their woman characters should be as far as sexual activity is concerned. Brett Butler, star of the situation comedy *Grace Under Fire*, recalls that the production group agonized about whether her character, a single woman, should have sex with the man she was dating. No such compunctions seem to have troubled the producers of *Seinfeld*. In that series, Elaine, the leading female character, seemed to be allowed as much bed time as the three male leads—Jerry, George, and Kramer.

Indicating how complex the task of deciding what is appropriate no matter what the standards, are the sometimes quirky decisions made by network censors. The criteria they use are often difficult to discern. For example, they cut this line from a proposed network script: "She sits among the cabbages and peas." One can see why. But why did they accept "She sits among the cabbages and leeks" as a suitable substitute?

A decision equally baffling cropped up during a censor's review of a sketch scheduled for production on the comedy hour program on which Carol Burnett appeared. In it Carol played the part of a woman who was a member of a nudist colony. Clad only in a barrel from which her bare shoulders protruded, she answered questions about the group's activities. At one point the interviewer asked what they did on Saturday night. "We have dances," she replied. "How do nudists dance?" was the next question. Her answer as originally written was "Very carefully." The network censor refused to pass it. After some thought the writers came back with a substitute line, "Cheek to cheek." It was approved. Both lines evoked a visualization that was undeniably explicit. What differences did the censors see that made one line acceptable and the other not?

One truth we can draw from all this is that performers can never be sure what is permissible and what is not. The standards are constantly changing. Some events occurring in 2004 suggest that the pendulum may be swinging back to a situation requiring a little more restraint. During a dance routine performed on television during halftime at the 2004 Super Bowl by Janet Jackson and Justin Timberlake, one of her breasts was exposed. That incident aroused a storm of protest. In trying to quiet the furor, the producers of the sequence claimed that the exposure was accidental. There is evidence, however, that the gesture responsible for bringing it about was actually rehearsed. Howard Stern, noted for the raunchy material he uses on his radio and television program, has recently run into trouble. Six stations carrying his program, which are owned by "The Clear Channel Company," abruptly canceled it.. The FCC is threatening to impose heavy fines on all broadcasters who violate standards of good taste. Stern has decided to take his radio show to satellite radio, where presumably he can do or say anything he wants to, without fear of retaliation.

Troublesome Topics

In telling jokes, certain types of subject matter are likely to evoke disapproval or even outrage. The danger flags should start flying if a joke you are thinking of using deals with one of those potentially troublesome topics. Certain ones come immediately to mind. Any joke with sexual overtones or one that refers to intimate physiological functions may be offensive. Crude language or bawdy behavior can be equally objectionable. The tremendous flap aroused by the sketch in which Charlie McCarthy and Mae West portrayed Adam and Eve illustrates what can happen when humorists violate current standards of propriety. One result was that Mae West was never again invited to take part in a radio broadcast. Some thirty years ago the career of a promising young comedian named Jackie Mason went into a similar tailspin because Ed Sullivan thought he had used an obscene gesture during an appearance on his Sunday night variety show. Mason remained in the shadows for three decades. Only recently has he emerged to gain the limelight once more as a monologist on the New York stage.

Though performers today enjoy much greater freedom than they used to in their treatment of sex and their use of language and gesture, they can still go too far. After Joan Rivers's appearance as the host of the thirty-fifth Emmy Awards show, a flood of protesting phone calls deluged the stations that carried the program. Among her taboo-breaking comments were the following: To something that the actor and comedian Eddie Murphy whispered in her ear, she shot back, "I wouldn't go near her. She gave a friend of mine herpes." She flouted another canon by using profanity, saying, "I've been waiting to get on the Emmys for many years, but they always wanted me to sit in the goddamned audience." Some viewers denounced her for wearing costumes that were too revealing. One newspaper headline employed a pun to sum up what many thought of her performance: HOSTING EMMYS MUDDIES RIVERS.

An irony of the incident was that Joan Rivers had used sexual humor and inelegant language many times before as a guest of Johnny Carson on the *Tonight* show without arousing hostile reactions. This difference underlines how important it is to take the nature of the audience into account in deciding what kind of humor to use. The expectations of people who watch a late-night show are markedly different from those who tune in a general-audience show broadcast during prime time.

Another type of joke that can seriously damage a career or a reputation is one that suggests its teller is a bigot or a racist. If the joke that lost Earl Butz his job as Secretary of Agriculture had been merely salacious, he might have survived. What did him in was that it also ridiculed African-Americans.

An unfavorable light that racist humor can throw on a person was demonstrated by an incident involving Ted Danson, the actor who portrayed the libidinous bartender on *Cheers*. In 1993 at the Friar's Club he appeared in a skit designed to make fun of his then girlfriend, Whoopi Goldberg. Appearing in black face and with his lips painted white in the style made famous many years before by Al Jolson, he proceeded to use scurrilous ethnic terms, ate watermelon, and told lewd jokes. Many in his audience laughed uproariously, but some were outraged. One of the latter was Montel Williams, the talk-show host, who walked out on the presentation and then resigned from the Friars, claiming he didn't know he had been invited to "a rally for the Klan or Aryan nation." Danson went into seclusion after the incident and refused to talk to reporters. More voluble was Whoopi Goldberg, the target of the sketch. In an ironic note, she revealed she had written most of the material and had found the make-up artist who created Danson's black-face character. The incident did not end Danson's career. Later he resurfaced to appear as the star of another situation comedy, *Becker*, which had a modest run on CBS.

Ethnic humor got Ronald Reagan into trouble during his first campaign as the Republican nominee for president. A joke told privately to some fellow politicians while he was in New Hampshire was picked up by the press and reported to the country at large. In it he managed to arouse the ire of both Polish- and Italian-Americans. The joke went like this:

How do you tell who the Polish fellow is at a cock fight?

He's the one with the duck.

How do you tell who the Italian is at a cock fight?

He's the one who bets on the duck.

How do you know the mafia was there?

The duck wins.

A Manhattan GOP leader name Victor Albano said Reagan should apologize "because no nationality should be subjected to ridicule," adding that Reagan's quip "was not funny to anyone." Reagan made no response, but his wife, Nancy, did apologize for him.

The comedian Billy Crystal found himself in similar trouble when he also made fun of the mafia during one of his appearances as M. C. of an Academy Awards presentation. Noting that an Italian group had purchased MGM, Crystal commented that the lion would no longer roar but would take the Fifth Amendment. Italian-American organizations and some members of Congress registered protests. When Crystal failed to respond, the Commission for Social Justice of the Order of the Sons of Italy in America took out a full-page ad in *Variety* calling on him to make a public apology. As far as I know, he never did.

Any joke that targets a particular segment of the population may cause trouble. Humor that makes fun of a specific occupational group, for example, is almost certain to draw protests. President Ronald Reagan found himself in a censorious spotlight once again when the columnist Tom Wicker severely chastised him for directing one of his humorous barbs at farmers. Commenting on the shipment of American grain overseas, Reagan had said, "I think we should keep the grain and export the farmers." The remark drew this response from Wicker: "With so many farmers losing their land—often through no fault of their own—and suffering from outmoded government policies, a declining farm economy, and crippling trade restrictions, Reagan's graceless quip at their expense suggests that he just doesn't care."

Johnny Carson discovered, as I did, that dentists are peculiarly sensitive to pain, especially when someone suggests they are responsible for it in others. In April, 1986, Carson made the following remark during one of his *Tonight* show monologues:

> According to a recent business report, dentists are going out of business due to improvements in dental techniques and in the use of fluoride. Imagine dentists going out of business. I haven't been so happy about a group disbanding since the Gestapo.

A dentist named Michael Mendelson sued Carson for five million dollars, claiming he had defamed the profession by trying to amuse his audience with "an anachronistic and damaging myth of a dental appointment as a sadomasochistic vaudeville act. To compare this same group of doctors to a gang of sadistic and bigoted thugs is ludicrous." The dentist demanded a "smirk-free apology."

An unrepentant Johnny Carson refused to back down. He read the dentist's letter on the air and then said, "Lighten up Michael Mendelson, DDS." He proceeded to point out that dentistry has an honorable tradition dating back to the Spanish Inquisition, adding that dentists take off only three days a year—"Christmas, Thanksgiving, and the Marquis de Sade's birthday."

Plaintiffs like Mendelson rarely win such suits. A case in point occurred in the 1980s when *Hustler* magazine published a parody of a Campari advertisement in which the television evangelist Jerry Falwell was portrayed as admitting that he had lost his virginity to his mother in an outhouse. Falwell was naturally outraged, and he sued the magazine for spreading lies which caused him great emotional distress. Most people would probably conclude that the law was on Falwell's side, and indeed a lower court awarded him two million dollars for the damage he had suffered. The Supreme Court, however, unanimously reversed that ruling. Chief Justice William Rehnquist, who wrote the decision, said that although the accusation was undeniably false and was "doubtless gross and repugnant in the eyes of most," it was clearly satire that did not pretend to be factual and therefore contained no statements with a reckless disregard for the truth. For that reason, it was protected by the First Amendment.

Even before that the Supreme Court had made it difficult for public figures to win suits for defamation. In the *Sullivan* decision, promulgated in 1964, it ruled that public figures could not collect damages for defamatory falsehoods unless the statements were made with "actual malice." The actions of the Supreme Court provide humorists who want to make fun of people in the news with a great deal of protection. Still, suits for damages are not only irritating, but they can also be costly to defend even though the plaintiff's claim is eventually denied.

Another topic that may invite trouble, is the treatment of religious principles and beliefs in a satirical way. The novelist Salmon Rushdie was put under a sentence of death by the late Iranian leader, the Ayotollah Khomeini, for including what the Ayotollah considered to be sacrilegious passages in Rushdie's novel *Satanic Verses*. The death sentence has been withdrawn, but it is possible that his life may still be in jeopardy.

I suspect that two entries in the *Frank and Ernest* comic strip may have raised some hackles. Both stemmed from the same comic idea, the attempt by the Creator to escape some onerous responsibilities. The first cartoon depicted Him saying to two representatives of the Creation Production Control Department, "I'm tired of making decisions. Let's just go with natural selection." The other again showed the Creator and two underlings engaged in a colloquy. One of the underlings, apparently responding to something the Creator had just said, remarked "Free will?—Isn't that sort of passing the buck?" The mere depiction of the Deity, especially in this farcical way, would be offensive to some. There are also other reasons why certain readers might find these cartoons sacrilegious. If there have been objections, they have not deterred the artist who draws the strip from regularly making the Lordly figure of the Deity one of his characters.

Drawing lines with respect to humor dealing with religion is extremely difficult. Even people with similar religious backgrounds may differ on what they consider to be fitting. In Chapter 1 I referred to a sign a minister of the First Baptist Church of Ann Arbor had put up in the church's parking lot in an attempt to discourage interlopers. It read "We forgive those who trespass against us—but we also tow them." When his successor in the pulpit saw the sign, he clearly felt uncomfortable with the play on a passage from the Bible. Before too long he had it replaced with a conventional warning to unauthorized parkers.

Another topic humorists should approach with care is anything to do with physical ailments and disease. While Ronald Reagan was president, comedians had fun with his tendency to be forgetful. It was simply an intriguing little quirk which at the time seemed to have no serious implications. That attitude changed abruptly when Reagan revealed after his retirement that he had Alzheimer's disease. The result was that for most humorists forgetfulness connected with Ronald Reagan was no longer a proper subject for humor. A few could not resist the temptation to make jokes about it, however. One was the cable channel Comedy Central. In announcing that it was going to rebroadcast some of its programs, it aimed one of its promotional messages about the reruns directly at the former president, saying, "They'd be great for someone in your condition." The "Cheers 'N' Jeers" section of *TV Guide* pummeled the channel "for pushing the boundaries of taste too far," adding that "there's just nothing droll about a debilitating and deadly disease." *Newsweek* made a similar misstep in the opinion of one reader when the editors of its "Conventional Wisdom Watch" in mentioning Reagan's letter announcing he had Alzheimer's disease added the comment, "But CW forgets what's in it." In the February 13, 1995, "Letters to the Editors" column, Betsy Bloom asked, "Where are your collective hearts? By your comment you treat this insidious disease as something to joke about. Shame on you."

Comedians generally show no mercy in making fun of people whose actions are strange or bizarre. Some draw back, however, when they discover that the erratic behavior is caused by illness. Jay Leno displayed such sensitivity in dealing with the case of a woman who was planning to donate a kidney to her diabetic husband. At first Leno had fun with the idea of such a transfer, but when the husband's condition took a life-threatening turn, he stopped making jokes about it. After the transfer had been successfully completed, however, his jokes resumed. He clearly feels that when a situation becomes too serious, humor about it is no longer appropriate.

The misadventures of the singer Michael Jackson have been heralded in headlines for many years. Before he was accused of sexually misbehaving with a child, a charge that resulted in a criminal indictment and a trial, an incident with no hint of fault on his part, generated a headline. Jackson collapsed while rehearsing for a TV show and was rushed to a hospital. Jay Leno, who had made him a regular focus of his barbs, also made a joke about that unfortunate event. In one instance he said the hospital had "upgraded Jackson's condition from bizarre to strange." Before making his comment, however, and others like it, he called the hospital to find out how Jackson was getting along. Assured he was making satisfactory progress, Leno felt free to tell his joke. After he had delivered it, he let his audience know he had called the hospital and had been told Jackson was improving. Had the situation been serious, he assured his audience, he would have cut it from his monologue. He has shown Jackson no mercy, however, in deriding him for the alleged sexual misbehavior that brought him into court.

In addition to his concern about hurting the feelings of people who are ill, Leno has avoided exploiting other types of situations for the sake of a joke, particularly when the target of the humor was an innocent victim of circumstances. The children of presidents certainly fall into that category.

They draw a laser beam of public scrutiny simply because they are who they are. When Bill and Hillary Clinton moved into the White House, they resolved to do as much as they could to keep their daughter Chelsea out of the limelight. Leno respected their wish. He pointed out in an interview that poking fun at Chelsea simply because she was the president's daughter wouldn't be fair. Though he shot many arrows in Bill and Hillary Clinton's direction, as far as I know, he never mentioned Chelsea. I never heard him say anything about the second President Bush's twin daughters either.

Should Leno have shown similar restraint in dealing with the O. J. Simpson murder case? It involved events that were undeniably tragic. The two victims died terrible and agonizing deaths and Simpson, though acquitted of the crime, saw his reputation as one of the nation's most admired athletes crumble. Yet Leno, night after night, was unremitting in his caricaturing of the principal participants. An example was his creation of the Dancing Itos, a chorus line of men in judicial robes made up to look like the presiding judge, Lance Ito.

Leno's late-night rival, David Letterman, sniffed haughtily that such humor was out of place, and he wouldn't indulge in it. He was quite willing, however, to squeeze a joke out of the practice of terrorism, which causes human carnage on far wider scale than that dealt with in the Simpson trial. In one of his programs he made this comment: "In Lebanon switching to daylight saving time is a problem because they have to turn all the time bombs back an hour."

These inconsistencies and differences of opinion illustrate how difficult it is to make judgments about the propriety of a particular piece of material. President George W. Bush, apparently, stumbled badly when he made a joking reference to the failed search for weapons of mass destruction in Iraq. It came in a speech he delivered to the annual banquet of the Radio and Television Correspondents' Association. The joke revolved around a series of photographs showing Bush in the White House peering under a table, looking behind draperies, and moving furniture back and forth in the Oval Office. The pictures were accompanied by captions saying such things as: "Those weapons of mass destruction have got to be somewhere." "Nope, no weapons over there." "Maybe under here." The problem was that this unsuccessful search for weapons of mass destruction nullified the Bush administration's main reason for going to war in Iraq, a war that snuffed out the lives of hundreds of young people and left thousands more crippled for life. The Democrats immediately denounced the joke as tasteless and insensitive. When CNN ran a tape of the sequence on its *Morning Show*, it was deluged with emails from outraged viewers, one of whom called the joke "stomach turning."

A comment by John Kerry about the Vietnam War, in which he served as a naval officer, caused a minor backlash. During Kerry's campaign for the presidency in 2004, in a ponderous attempt to be funny, he remarked that one of his opponents, John Edwards, was in diapers at the time Kerry volunteered for service. The problem was that by then Edwards was sixteen years old, as I believe Edwards himself pointed out.

Earlier I mentioned that Hillary Clinton had raised eyebrows during her husband's first run for the presidency with her "staying at home to make cookies" comment. After being elected to the Senate by New York voters, she went slightly astray again by saying jokingly that Mahatma Ghandi once ran a gas station in St. Louis. Later she apologized for what she called "a lame attempt at humor."

I have by no means mentioned all the topics that can invite vigorous disapproval. Anyone who makes a joke touching the abortion issue, for example, is taking a dangerous step. Bill Hicks, a comedian from Texas, found that out when he made fun of pro-lifers in a sketch he taped for David Letterman's *Late Show*. The producers cut the episode from the program and never invited him back. Any comedian who tries to extract humor from illicit drug use is likely to meet the same kind of fate. Homosexuality is another touchy subject. The producers of the *Seinfeld* series have managed to make it the theme of a program without arousing any passionate protests, however, by including a phrase that has since become something of a byword, "Not that there's anything wrong with that."

To indicate how irreverent, politically incorrect, and, perhaps, disrespectful the Internet is, a quick search of each of the taboo subjects above netted a substantial amount of humorous material. Abortion jokes, entered into the Google search window brought forth 500,000 web pages. Pro-life jokes produced 75,800 pages. Illicit-drug jokes garnered 6,420 hits. Homosexual jokes received 242,000, but the largest number of web pages, 697,000, was supplied when lesbian jokes was entered into the search window. Once again, this reveals the potential influence of the Internet in lowering the bar regarding what is acceptable and unacceptable in the marketplace of jokes.

Sick Humor

Sometimes jokes are made about subjects so macabre or loathsome that one wonders about the mental health of the person who creates or tells them. As with other types of humor, people differ about how far a person can go in that direction before being viewed as sick or perverted. Some years ago I was sharing a brown-bag lunch with some of my university colleagues when a member of the group told a joke involving a series of rapes. At the end of the joke, the faces of two of the women became fiery red. The reasons for their reaction were different, however. One doubled up with laughter. The other rose to her feet and in a voice filled with fury said, "You should never joke about rape—never, never, never!" and with that she stalked from the room. The clear implication of her action was that anyone who enjoyed such humor must be a little depraved.

In trying to draw a line between what is normal and abnormal, we must confront the fact that many of the situations with which humor deals would in another context be seen as disagreeable at best and, in some instances, as downright repulsive. The idea of cannibalism, for example, is likely to send a shiver of disgust through most people. Is it a proper subject for humor? Gary Larson, the creator of *The Far Side* cartoon series obviously thought so for one of his cartoons evoked recollections of the tragedy that befell the Donner Party in 1846 when it attempted to get through the Sierra Nevada mountain range in the middle of winter. When some of its members perished in a brutal snowstorm, survivors kept alive by eating the bodies of their dead companions. Larson's cartoon showed one of the group lunching on a sandwich from which a human foot protruded. One reader found this satirical portrayal of human tragedy so revolting that he condemned its publication with these words:

> The mind that conceived it must be terribly sick, and the mind
> that permitted this to be printed is even sicker.

One might argue that people who followed *The Far Side* series should have become accustomed to humor on the outer limits of acceptability. Even its title warned potential readers of what was in store for them. But the *Reader's Digest*, which its audience expects to publish a more conventional type of humor, has on more than one occasion passed along a joke involving cannibalism, as in this example:

> Two cannibal chiefs were talking after dinner. "Your wife
> makes a wonderful pot roast," one chief remarked.
>
> "Yes," the other chief replied, "And I'm certainly going to miss her."

Another lugubrious subject about which humorists have joked is cremation, and reputable publications have printed the results of their efforts. In its issue of July 24, 1976, *The New Republic* published an essay by Woody Allen entitled, "Remembering Needleman at the Cremation." It opened with the following paragraph:

It has been four weeks and it is still hard for me to believe Sandar Needleman is dead. I was present at the cremation and at his son's request brought the marshmallows, but few of us could think of anything but our pain.

Newspapers around the country printed a strip in the *Born Loser* series which also employed a cremation motif. It showed two women engaged in the following conversation:

First Woman: Is that Blanche over there?
Second Woman: Where? Why yes...yes, it is.
First Woman: Poor dear....Just cremated her third husband.
Second Woman: Ironic, isn't it?
First Woman: Ironic?
Second Woman: All I've got is Brutus, and she's got husbands to burn.

Jay Leno made an oblique reference to cremation in a joke primarily designed to stimulate his *Tonight* show viewers into recalling that the wife of the former Philippine's dictator, Ferdinand Marcos, was an inveterate collector of shoes—thousands of them.

When Imelda Marcos was told she could return her husband Ferdinand's ashes to the Philippines, she wondered what she could carry them in.

Surely she must have an old shoebox around somewhere.

Another type of joke associated with death and bereavement is the funny epitaphs we sometimes see engraved on tombstones. Whether the following are all legitimate tombstone epitaphs or the creation of some clever joke maker, I don't know:

Stranger, tread this ground with gravity,
Dentist Brown is filling his last cavity.

Here lies Jim the Brewer,
Who in life was both ale and stout.
Death brought him to his bitter bier,
And now in heaven he hops about.

Here lies the body of
Detlaf Swenson, waiter,

God finally caught his eye.

Here lies an atheist
All dressed up
And no place to go.

Here lies Lester Moore
Four shots from a .44
No Les—no more.

The raconteur Robert Benchley also indulged in graveyard humor when he suggested that the following line would be an appropriate epitaph for a promiscuous actress:

She sleeps alone at last.

In the early nineteen hundreds an Englishman named Harry Graham wrote a series of quatrains which evoked images of death in its grimmest and most repellant forms. This is one of them:

In the drinking well
    Which the plumber built her,
Aunt Eliza fell.
    We must buy a filter.

Louis Untermeyer included this verse and others like it in his collection of humorous pieces, *A Treasury of Laughter*. He went on to say that Graham's work inspired others to follow his example and soon American newspapers were printing quatrains sent in by readers, each of whom according to Untermeyer, "tried to invent a catastrophe more gory in event and more nonchalant in effect than its predecessor." Because the person mentioned in most of these verses was named Willie, they came to be called "Little Willies." Here is an example:

Willie fell down the elevator—
Wasn't found until six days later.
Then the neighbors sniffed, "Gee Whizz!
What a spoiled child Willie is."

The printing by reputable publications of the jokes I have just cited suggests that most people view them as legitimate examples of humor. This makes one wonder whether any jokes at all deserve to be called sick. Alan Dundes, a professor of anthropology and folklore at the University of California, Berkeley, would answer that indeed there are. In his book *Cracking Jokes: Studies of Sick Humor Cycles and Stereotypes*, he quotes one of them:

How many Jews will fit in a Volkswagen?
506. Six in the seats and 500 in the ashtrays.

What differentiates this example from the others I have mentioned? I think it is clear that those previous examples, although dealing with unsavory subjects, were created in a spirit of fun. Moreover, they have no reprehensible intent. The last one, in contrast, has no such saving graces. It is not just that its referent is a tragedy so overwhelming and so immense that its true dimensions are almost impossible to comprehend. It is that its undiluted nastiness reflects an attitude of chilling contempt. Thus it becomes a vehicle for expressing a rabid anti-Semitism rather than an instrument for making people laugh. There is not a scintilla of anything good humored in it.

Another joke similarly racist in its aim was cited by Nicholas von Hoffman in "Shuttle Humor," an article he wrote for the March 24, 1986, issue of *The New Republic*. It came from a radio disc jockey while he was commenting on the festivities surrounding the celebration of the martyred Martin Luther King, Jr's. birthday. "If somebody would shoot four more, the country could have a whole week off."

Some people have even made jokes about the *Challenger* disaster, which took the lives of six astronauts and a teacher who had won a contest to accompany them into space. It is difficult to think of anything that saddened the nation more, yet von Hoffman has counted at least a score of jokes about it. One lost a Los Angeles radio announcer his job. He remarked that the *Challenger* blew up because the crew was free-basing on Tang. The station manager immediately fired him. Von Hoffman wondered whether screwing up one's face and saying "Tasteless" after telling such a joke is enough to take the curse off it.

The Internet makes a substantial contribution when it comes to strange, sick, twisted, or tasteless jokes. Entered into the Google search engine, sick jokes produced 1,190,000 web sites, and twisted jokes garnered 837,000. Tasteless jokes brought forth 172,40200 hits. Challenger Jokes yielded 112,000 web sites, World Trade Center jokes supplied 1,640,000, terrorist jokes generated 574,000, Iraq jokes 1,110,000, Osama Bin Laden jokes had 611,000 hits, and 9/11 jokes supplied 611,000 web sites. If one were doing a study of this kind of humor, obviously the Internet would be a significant resource.

The tragedy of the 9/11 attack on the World Trade Center in New York was so overwhelming that almost no one—the Internet notwithstanding—has dared make jokes about it. The search for the author of the disaster, Osama Bin Laden, has generated some jokes. However, most of them can be told without fear of arousing disgust or loathing. This is one of them:

    The government of the United States sent this threatening

message to the leaders of the Taliban in Afghanistan: "Give us Osama Bin Laden, or we will capture your women and send them to college."

That joke aside, most of us would probably hesitate before telling most of the jokes I have quoted unless the purpose is to explain what we mean by a sick joke, as is the case here. But illustrating how difficult it is to draw a line that divides the admissible from the inadmissible is a joke cited by Professor Dundes, which he puts into the sick category. After reading it I'm wondering whether you would do the same. True, its last line is likely to make most readers gulp a little, but does it go beyond the "Little Willie" quatrains and the jokes about cannibalism and cremation that reputable publications have seen fit to print? The jokes goes as follows:

A man who was in an automobile accident woke up and asked what had happened to him. "Well, I have bad news and good news," the doctor said.

"What's the bad news?"

"The bad news is we had to amputate both your legs."

"What's the good news?"

"The man in the next bed wants to buy your shoes."

Let's look at another example. I bring it up not because it deals with tragedy but rather with behavior that some would find extremely distasteful. I found it in one of the *Reader's Digest's* humor columns:

The novice ice fisherman wasn't having any luck, but another man was pulling up fish after fish through the ice. "What's your secret?" the newcomer asked.

"Mmnpximdafgltmn," mumbled the other man.

"I'm sorry, I couldn't understand you," said the novice.

"Mmnpximdafgltmn," the fisherman mumbled again.

The neophyte shook his head and began to turn away. Then the other man held up his hand. Spitting twice into his coffee cup, he said, "You've got to keep the worms warm."

As my wife typed the last line of this joke, I heard her utter a long, drawn-out "Ugh," which I'm sure was accompanied by a grimace and a shiver of disgust. How do you react? Does this joke deserve to be called sick?

Other Circumstances Affecting Acceptability

Thus far I have described the main conditions that can determine whether the joke you tell will cause your audience to laugh or gasp. There are a few more conditions you should think about in deciding whether to tell a certain joke. One of them relates to one of the circumstances I have already discussed—the nature of the occasion. Will the joke you are thinking of telling be delivered to an audience gathered for the express purpose of hearing you speak or will it be merely an item in an informal conversation with one or two friends? Does this difference in circumstances have a bearing on a particular joke's propriety? Two thousand years ago the philosopher Plato said something that suggests an answer to that question. In Book X of *The Republic* we find this observation:

> There are jests which you would be ashamed to make yourself, and yet on the comic stage...when you'd hear them, you are greatly amused by them, and are not at all disgusted at their unseemliness.

The way audiences react to the sexual and scatological material sometimes dispensed by comedians in comedy clubs confirms the truth of Plato's observation. Both men and women laugh at jokes and four-letter words which many of them would never consider repeating themselves. Can we infer from this that speakers can get away with more in a large audience situation that they can in a conversational setting? I think that is sometimes true. We may safely tell some jokes to an audience we would hesitate to include in a conversation with one of its individual members. But it is also true that we may pass along a story to an intimate friend we would never dream of telling an audience—or anyone else for that matter.

Another circumstance affecting an audience's response to questionable material is its source. Earlier in this chapter I mentioned that audiences tend to differ in their reactions to libidinous characters in situation comedies depending on whether they are men or women. The same difference applies to the telling of jokes. Jean Lipman-Blumen, a professor of public policy and organizational behavior at the Claremont Graduate School, points out that "men can tell off-color jokes, and they're seen as kind of good guys if they do. If women tell the same kind of joke, there's a gasp. Joan Rivers' type of humor is totally off limits for most women in the workplace." We may decry this double standard, but there is no doubt it exists. The fact that Joan Rivers is a woman undoubtedly magnified the reaction to her Emmy Awards performance. She has argued that women have as much right to be bawdy as men. She says, "Shocking people is my business....If I'm vulgar the whole country's vulgar." But vulgarity coming from a woman is still more shocking than it is coming from a man.

A practical joke someone played in a hospital laboratory illustrates the point. A male technician surreptitiously poured apple juice into a urine specimen container, and then held it up for all to see. One of the other technicians commented, "It looks rather cloudy to me."

"Perhaps it needs another pass through the system," the prankster said and promptly swallowed the container's contents. The others in the group gasped and then laughed. As Professor Lipman-Bluman suggests, they probably looked on him as a funny guy. But what if the impish technician had been a woman? Isn't it likely that some in the group would wonder what kind of person she was?

There is another way in which the nature of the source can influence the reaction to a joke. An experience of the humorist Burgess Johnson provides an illustration. He was giving a lecture to an audience of women about the surprising statements children sometimes made. As an example he quoted the remark of a little boy, "Ma, they is a kind of dog what has two rows of shoebuttons along his stommick." The audience reacted with a chilly silence. Realizing he had misstepped, Johnson quickly added, "I just read that in the latest issue of *The Ladies Home Journal*." Immediately, the chill evaporated and the audience laughed. The name of the magazine provided an imprimatur that made the joke acceptable.

Most people think of the *Reader's Digest* as a wholesome family magazine, yet it occasionally prints surprisingly spicy material. When I use such an item, I often take a cue from the experience of Burges Johnson by telling the audience ahead of time that I found the joke in the *Reader's Digest*. That is usually enough to sanitize it.

Making other types of associations can also confer respectability on questionable material. An incident connected with one of Jack Benny's radio programs illustrates the point. On one occasion the NBC censor directed him to cut one of his sketches because it might offend the tender sensibilities of the audience. The sketch showed Benny and his singer Dennis Day making a call on Eddie Cantor. Coming into the living room, Benny noticed the photos of a number of celebrities hanging on the walls, but his was not included. The snapper came when Dennis Day emerged from the bathroom to announce he had found Jack Benny's picture hanging there.

The censor's reaction to the sketch was prompted by the rigidly proper standards broadcasters observed in the 1940s. For them bathrooms didn't exist, and any reference to them was almost always blue-pencilled. Benny persuaded the censor to reverse himself, however, by pointing out that the sketch clearly indicated that Dennis Day had gone into the bathroom to return a toothbrush he had borrowed rather than for the usual reason. Establishing that connection made all the difference.

In Woody Allen's film *Crimes and Misdemeanors*, this line appears: "Comedy is tragedy plus time." It underlines the point that an important factor in determining the acceptability of humor based on a tragic event is the year it took place. We are usually safer in making jokes about calamities that happened a long time ago than we are about those of recent origin. The passage of years softens the shock. Thus, we laugh when a reporter asks Mrs. Abraham Lincoln, "Other than that, Mrs. Lincoln, how did you like the play?" A comparable joke about President Kennedy's assassination or the 9/11 tragedy would still be out of place. Not enough time has gone by to produce the healing effect of distance.

A further mitigating influence on jokes dealing with past events is that the people they refer to are either unknown or are familiar only through the reading of history. We can laugh at the graveyard humor we see on seventeenth- and eighteenth-century tombstones because their subjects are persons without faces.

Two other factors are of immense importance in determining whether a joke about a questionable topic will be acceptable. One is the nature of the joke itself. Is it truly funny or is it merely salacious? Is it designed to make people laugh or is its primary purpose to exploit a prejudice?

The second crucial factor is the attitude of the joke tellers. They can take the sting out of disagreeable or potentially objectionable material by communicating it in a playful manner. Some University of Illinois researchers who studied the effect of demeanor on the reception of humor defined the result you should seek as "mirthful shock." By developing a manner that invites your listeners to have fun, you can make them feel comfortable with what you say even when it challenges taboos.

Some Test Cases

Let me conclude this chapter by presenting some jokes for your evaluation. They all deal with topics or circumstances that might raise some people's eyebrows. Your task is to decide whether you would pass them along, and if so to what kinds of audiences and under what circumstances. Your first step should be to determine whether they are funny enough to tell. If they meet that criterion, your next step should be to decide whether their subject matter disqualifies them despite their funniness or whether they bear telling under certain conditions.

The source of the first joke is Woody Allen:

I've just heard my ex-wife claims that she has been violated. I'm sure it wasn't a moving violation.

This is the type of joke that is likely to draw a snicker rather than a belly laugh. Is its humor quotient sufficiently strong to justify taking the chance of upsetting someone? Its put-down of women is somewhat snide and the sexual image it conjures may be too explicit for some tastes. Would the audience you are thinking about find it acceptable?

The ethnic group which this next joke satirizes has been the target of a continuous series of barbs in recent years. In its framework and in the kind of ridicule it conveys, it is representative of its type:

How many Poles does it take to screw in a light bulb?

The answer is five—one to hold the bulb, and four to turn the chair he's standing on.

One possible conclusion with respect to this joke is that humor which makes fun of an ethnic group is unacceptable under any circumstances. In taking such a stand you cast into oblivion a multitude of jokes which have made audiences laugh down through the centuries. That doesn't necessarily mean that more of them should be told, of course.

Can anything be said in its defense? Some might argue that the absurd picture it evokes is so extreme that a connection with any kind of reality fades away. Thus it conveys no actual insult. Further alleviating its sting is the familiar ritualized form it takes. At the same time we must recognize that any denigration of an ethnic group, however slight, may be offensive. Proof of this is the firestorm of criticism that enveloped the advice columnist Ann Landers when in a *New Yorker* interview she referred to Pope John Paul II as a Polack. When ethnic sensibilities are pricked, passions sometimes explode.

My third test case appeared in the comic strip series entitled *Non Sequitur*, which was published by newspapers on November 12, 1995. Produced by the Washington Post Writers Group and drawn by an artist identified as Wiley, it shows a woman attired in colonial garb tied to a post. A group of men similarly dressed are raking up leaves around her. At the left top of the cartoon this notice appears: "How Air Quality Regulations Steered American History: 1692, Salem, Massachusetts." At the left bottom of the cartoon a character holding a clip board and with the letters E. P. A. on his uniform makes this statement: "Hey, I love the scent of burning leaves in the Fall as much as anybody, but if you can't find another way to burn witches, then I'm afraid you'll have to stop altogether."

Let's think for a moment about the incident that inspired this cartoon. The Salem witch trials constitute one of the most shameful and tragic episodes in American history. For a period of time irrational passion triumphed over reason and before the affair had run its course, twenty completely innocent people had lost their lives. One might point out that more than 300 years have now gone by since the martyrdom of those pitiful victims. Does that amount of time provide enough distance to make a jocular approach to such a terrible event proper and acceptable? The manager of the syndicate that distributed the cartoon and the editors of the newspapers that published it obviously thought so. They might also point out that those who turn to the *Non Sequitur* comic strip on a regular basis should expect to see material of this type. Do you agree with those editors? Would you have printed this cartoon?

Down through the ages people who suffer disease and disfigurement have been the constant targets of humor. Modern day examples are jokes dealing with Alzheimer's disease. As my final test case, here is one of them:

> There are three advantages to having Alzheimer's.
> One, you can make new friends every day.
> Two, you can hide your own Easter eggs.
> Three—I forget.

We have learned in recent years that Alzheimer's is one of the most appalling disasters that can strike a family. The chief sufferers are usually not its immediate victims, but the care givers who must stand helplessly by while loved ones change from kind and considerate people into people dominated by hate and paranoia. Even worse perhaps is to watch a once beloved personality gradually vanish into nothingness. Nancy Reagan referred to such a development in poignant terms when she described former President Reagan's condition as *The Long Goodbye*. Is the mocking of such awful human tragedy ever appropriate?

I don't know how you would respond to that question or to the other test cases I have presented. It is possible in some instances for two people to take entirely opposite stands and still be correct. As we have already seen, one person telling a certain joke may offend whereas another may not because of the differences in their personality, sex, and demeanor. Differing circumstances and conditions call for different answers.

As a final note, I come back to a point I made earlier—namely, that adopting the simple solution of avoiding anything that could possibly offend anyone is not the answer. Our catalogue of humor would be drained of a great many wonderful jokes if everyone followed that practice. Reflecting on the career of the late James Reston, *The New York Times* editor and columnist, Jonathon Alter, writing in *Newsweek*, recalled a sly little dig Reston had taken at Thomas Dewey, who in 1948 was expected by almost everyone to defeat Harry Truman for the presidency. On one occasion Dewey complained rudely that his campaign train was starting and stopping too suddenly. Reston ended his report of the incident with the comment,

"And the train took off with a jerk." I'm sure that the somewhat pompous and patronizing Thomas Dewey didn't particularly relish Reston's remark. But I'm glad he wasn't deterred from making it by the misguided principle that giving offense is to be avoided at all costs. I, for one, chuckled at his neat little pun, and I'm certain a legion of other readers did, too.

President John Kennedy was another person who was adept at concocting superbly indirect and subtle ridicule. On one occasion he described Washington, D. C., as "a combination of Southern efficiency and Northern charm." I'm willing to concede that his remark isn't likely to make anyone very mad. Still, on its face, it ridicules two rather large classes of people—Southerners and Northerners. I'm glad he didn't let the thought that he might offend some hyper-sensitive souls in those two groups keep him from making his remark. I laughed at it and savored with special relish the delicate touch he used in pricking his two targets.

Earlier in this chapter, I described how Goodman Ace had defied the injunction of his lecture bureau manager to avoid telling any off-color jokes. The two he told were only slightly suggestive, but I'm sure his manager would have viewed them as too risqué for a mixed audience. I'm glad Goodman Ace had the gumption to tell them. Had he followed orders, he would have deprived us of two gems of impish naughtiness. Still, I probably wouldn't tell them to that church women's society I mentioned a few pages ago.

Chapter 11
Using the Internet to Find or Develop Jokes
by Richard L. Weaver II

"I don't have a computer at home.
Is the Internet available in book form?"
—Customer

A lthough the comment on the previous page from a customer comes from a web site labeled "Misunderstandings about the Internet," you can be absolutely certain that if the Internet were available in book form that a significant portion of the book would be devoted to humor. The Internet—the connection of computers around the world into a huge global network—is the world's largest repository of humor ever. Some evidence for this lies in the number of web pages the search engine Google retrieves for each of the following general headings: Internet Humor = 13,000,000; Humor on the Internet = 12,800,000; Internet Jokes = 5,060,000; Jokes about the Internet = 4,460,000; Best Jokes of the Internet = 2,780,000; and the largest, broadest categories of all Jokes = 14,300,000 and humor = 41,600,000. When the words "Internet Humor" are entered into the search window of amazon.com—the Internet bookstore—43,770 results are produced. (July 29, 2005)

An Internet Study of Humor

Dr. Richard Wiseman, of the University of Hertfordshire, in collaboration with the British Association for the Advancement of Science, conducted a scientific experiment in 2002 to discover the world's funniest joke. I offer the results as a guide for future studies of humor using the Internet and, too, for what the scientists uncovered. In the experiment, conducted in Great Britain, people around the world were invited to judge jokes on an Internet site as well as contribute their own. The invitation to submit jokes attracted more than 40,000 entries, and the site received almost two million ratings—based strictly on the number of people visiting the web site. This is the joke Wiseman's research revealed as the world's funniest:

Two hunters are out in the woods when one of them collapses. He doesn't seem to be breathing and his eyes are glazed. The other man pulls out his cell phone and calls emergency services.

He gasps to the operator: "My friend is dead! What can I do?" The operator in a calm, soothing voice replies: "Take it easy. I can help. First, let's make sure he's dead."

There is a silence, then a shot is heard.

Back on the phone, the hunter says, "Okay, now what?"

Although many of the jokes submitted received higher ratings from certain groups of people, it was the one above that had real universal appeal.

The following joke ranked as the immediate runner-up to the world's funniest joke:

A patient says, "Doctor, last night I made a Freudian slip. I was having dinner with my mother-in-law and wanted to say: 'Could you please pass the butter?' But instead I said: 'You silly cow, you have completely ruined my life.'"

The third choice in the contest reads like this:

A man and a friend are playing golf one day. One of the guys is about to chip onto the green when he sees a long funeral procession on the road next to the course. He stops in mid-swing, takes off his golf cap, closes his eyes, and bows down in prayer. His friend says: "Wow! That is the most thoughtful and touching thing I have ever seen. You are truly a kind man."

The other man then replies: "Yeah, well, we were married 35 years."

Following the rule of three explained earlier in this book, the three jokes above should end my examples of the world's funniest jokes; however, the following fourth- and fifth-place winners so touched my funny bone, that I had to include them as well:

TEXAN: "Where are you from?"

HARVARD GRAD: "I come from a place where we do not end our sentences with prepositions."

TEXAN: "OK — where are you from, jackass?"

A woman gets on a bus with her baby. The bus driver says: "That's the ugliest baby I've ever seen."

The woman goes to the rear of the bus and sits down, fuming. She says to a man next to her: "That driver just insulted me!"

The man says: "You go right up there and tell him off. Go ahead, I'll hold your monkey for you."

The study did not stop, however, at just discovering the world's funniest jokes. The experiment revealed there were wide humor differences between nations. People logging onto the LaughLab web site were invited to rate jokes using a "Giggleometer." This is simply a five-point scale ranging from "not very funny" to "very funny." What it revealed, however, was that people from different parts of the world have fundamentally different senses of humor.

Germans, for example, not renowned for their sense of humor, found just about everything funny. This may explain why the Germans came first on Wiseman's table of funniness. They simply have no strong preferences and so tend to find a wide spectrum of jokes funny. Although they did not express a strong preference for any type of joke, the top joke selected by Germans was this one:

A general noticed one of his soldiers behaving oddly. The

soldier would pick up any piece of paper he found, frown and say: "That's not it" and put it down again. This went on for some time, until the general arranged to have the soldier psychologically tested. The psychologist concluded that the soldier was deranged, and wrote out his discharge from the army. The soldier picked it up, smiled, and said: "That's it."

I mentioned Wiseman's table of funniness in the previous paragraph. He asked everyone participating in LaughLab to tell the scientists which country they were from. They then analyzed the data from the ten countries that rated the highest number of jokes and came up with a "league table" list of countries, in the order of how funny they found the jokes: Germany ranked first, as noted above, then France, Denmark, UK, Australia, The Republic of Ireland, Belgium, USA, New Zealand, and Canada.

Many European countries, such as France, Denmark, and Belgium, displayed a penchant for off-beat surreal humor, such as:

An Alsatian went to a telegram office, took out a blank form and wrote: "Woof. Woof. Woof. Woof. Woof. Woof. Woof. Woof. Woof."

The clerk examined the paper and politely told the dog: "There are only nine words here. You could send another 'Woof' for the same price."

"But," the dog replied, "that would make no sense at all."

These European countries also enjoyed jokes that involved making light of topics that often make us feel anxious, such as death, illness, and marriage. The immediate or first runner-up to world's funniest joke about the Freudian slip, "You silly cow, you have completely ruined my life," is a good example of that kind of humor.

Many jokes submitted to LaughLab contained references to animals, and jokes mentioning ducks were considered particularly funny. The following is the top joke in Belgium, and is a good example of how ducks seemed to capture the imagination:

Why do ducks have webbed feet?
To stamp out fires.
Why do elephants have flat feet?
To stamp out burning ducks.

The researchers concluded that ducks are the funniest comedy animals. They could not determine whether it was because of their beaks, their webbed feet, or their odd shape. But, the implication for these researchers was clear: if you are going to tell a joke involving an animal, make it a duck. The success of the AFLAC commercials, which use a duck as their primary focal point and means for drawing a humorous response from viewers, provides proof that jokes mentioning ducks are particularly funny. Also, recall from an earlier chapter that words having a "k" in them seem to be inherently funny most of the time. In many cases it is just the right combination of elements that makes a word or phrase funny.

You may wonder how LaughLab obtained as many Internet responses as it did. How did the researchers publicize the study? Dave Barry, the well-known humorist whose columns are syndicated in many American newspapers, devoted an entire column to LaughLab in January, 2002. At the end of his column he urged readers to submit jokes that simply ended with the punch line: "There's a weasel chomping on my privates." It served as productive publicity; within just a few days, LaughLab received over 1500 "weasel chomping" jokes. The following weasel joke scored very highly in the USA and almost became the funniest joke in America:

At the parade, the Colonel noticed something unusual going on and asked the Major: "Major Barry, what the devil's wrong with Sergeant Jones' platoon? They seem to be all twitching and jumping about."

"Well sir," says Major Barry after a moment of observation. "There seems to be a weasel chomping on his privates."

What a great example, here, of course, of a play on words with the change from one's personal "private parts" to privates in the military.

Which joke became the top American joke? It was the third choice in the search for the world's funniest joke—the one that occurred on the golf course when a funeral procession occurs on the road next to the course and ends with the man replying, "Yeah, well we were married 35 years."

When we think about the important role a feeling of superiority has in making people laugh, it is not surprising that jokes which make a person look stupid or are made to look stupid by another person are highly preferred, especially by Americans and Canadians. The Texan and Harvard graduate joke that ends "Okay—where are you from, jackass?" is a good example.

Another finding of the Wiseman study was that people living in different regions of the same country have different tastes in humor. Consider Great Britain. The following was the top joke in England:

Two weasels are sitting on a bar stool. One starts to insult the other one. He screams, "I slept with your mother!" The bar gets quiet as everyone listens to see what the other weasel will do. The first again yells, "I SLEPT WITH YOUR MOTHER!"

The other says, "Go home dad you're drunk."

The following was the top joke in Wales:

A turtle was walking down an alley in New York when he was mugged by a gang of snails. A police detective came to investigate and asked the turtle if he could explain what happened. The turtle looked at the detective with a confused look on his face and replied, "I don't know, it all happened so fast."

As I was about to read the top joke in Scotland, I thought for certain, in keeping with the format of the two previous jokes, that it would revolve around an animal. I was delightfully surprised that it did not. Bus drivers and airline pilots, especially, might identify with this joke. It reads as follows:

I want to die peacefully in my sleep like my grandfather. Not screaming in terror like his passengers.

Finally, the top joke in Northern Ireland:

A doctor says to his patient, "I have bad news, and worse news."

"Oh dear, what's the bad news?" asks the patient.

The doctor replies, "You only have 24 hours to live."

"That's terrible," said the patient. "How can the news possibly be worse?"

The doctor replies, "I've been trying to contact you since yesterday."

One can speculate that people in different regions of the U.S. also differ in their taste for humor—Southerners and Northerners for example.

There were three other findings of the Wiseman study that confirm major points made earlier in this book. The first is that he discovered that respondents laugh at jokes for different reasons. Some jokes induce a feeling of satisfaction because they make us feel superior to the target of the joke. Others make us laugh because they surprise us or cause us to sense an incongruity. Wiseman also found that people recognize the profound effect that humor can have on health.

The second interesting finding resulted from a LaughLab computer analysis of the data. It revealed that jokes containing 103 words were thought to be especially funny. The winning "hunters" joke was 102 words long—what the researchers discovered was almost the perfect length for a joke.

Earlier in the book joke length was discussed, and the recommendation was that the best jokes are crisp and sudden. Although 103 words does not appear to be crisp and sudden there may be two explanations, either or both of which might explain this discrepancy. First, it could be that the conclusion that the best jokes are 103 words could be sample specific—that is, a result of the jokes used in this study only. Second, it could be the difference between oral and written jokes. Oral jokes may indeed be brief whereas written ones may be longer, just as the length of spoken sentences tend to be shorter than the length of written ones. People tend to speak using short sentences.

A third intriguing finding of the Internet study was that researchers actually found the date and time when people found a joke to be the funniest. It was the 7th of October at 6:03 p.m. This confirms what was said earlier in this book—namely that it is easier to get audiences to laugh in the afternoon rather than the morning, and often people tend to be even more relaxed, comfortable, and ready to listen and respond to a good joke in the early evening. Why the 7th of October is a good time for humor is somewhat baffling, however. Could it be that October is a funny month because Halloween occurs at its end when people laugh a lot at grotesque costumes and masks? Just a thought.

Finding Jokes

Resources of the Internet. It is likely that almost any joke that has ever been told can be found in some joke archive—a place where jokes are stored—somewhere on the Internet. Too bad there isn't a centralized organizational system, but that problem is one from which the entire World Wide Web suffers. The following are just a few of the joke archives available online arranged here alphabetically by topic:

Adult Jokes	Gambling Jokes	Political Jokes
Animal Jokes	Irish Jokes	Radical Jokes
Arthritis Jokes	Jewish Humor	Random Jokes
Bad Jokes	Jokes of the Day	Recreational Humor
Bathroom Jokes	Late Night Jokes	Sick/Twisted Jokes
Cancer Jokes	Lawyer Jokes	Wildlife, Biology,
Science,	Managed Care Jokes	and Environmental
Clean Jokes	Oxymoron Humor	Jokes
Dumb Blond Jokes		

When you are looking for a joke that fits a particular need—for a speech, an introduction, an article, etc.—the Internet is a wonderful resource.
At Yahoo! Entertainment Directory <http://dir.yahoo.com/entertainment /humor/jokes/> there were 22 categories listed as well as the 10 most

popular web sites for finding humor. In addition the Yahoo! web site included an alphabetical listing of 120 additional sites for humor and jokes.

Most of the joke sites on the Internet offer some combination of categories that will cover animals, blondes, computers, drunks/bars, dumb people, education, gender, holidays, kids, lawyers, lists, medical, miscellaneous, political, red neck, relationships, religions, sex related, sports, work places, and yo mama jokes (those intended to insult the other person's mother: "Yo mama so fat, when she turns around, people give her a welcome back party," or "yo mama so poor she ate cereal with a fork to save milk."). This list of topics is but a sampling because each site covers a different set of topics, and each set of topics differs from any other. There is no such thing as a standard. Often there will be a daily joke presented, funny cartoons, funny videos, funny audio, and funny downloads as well— that is, games, stories, and puzzles that can be copied from a remote computer "down" to your own. At a number of sites, users are allowed to search for humor by keyword, by topic, or even by date.

There are specialty web sites as well such as workjoke.com where there are 50 different categories of jokes organized by professions such as programmers, chemists, accountants, managers, consultants, bankers, journalists, stockbrokers, judges, actuaries, zookeepers, policemen, farmers, and more than 35 others. There is another site for science jokes, too, a web site containing more than 2500 scientific jokes in the fields of mathematics, physics, chemistry, biology, and earth science. At still another web address <http://www.mit.ed/people/jcb/jokes/> there is a section simply called "Instrument Jokes" where there are hundreds of jokes separated into sections entitled strings, woodwind, brass, percussion, and vocal. There are folk/rock/popular music jokes and a category called "general," which covered conductors, musicians, and variations on a theme as well. The following are two examples from the violin category:

What's the difference between a violin and a fiddle? A fiddle is fun to listen to.

How do you tell the difference between a violinist and a dog? The dog knows when to stop scratching.

At Jokes2000.com they have a link to "Cream of the Crop" jokes where 219 jokes are provided. These jokes are rated one-through-three stars; however, in examining all 219 jokes, not one had a single star, and not one had three stars. The obvious question becomes, why rate each of them if they are all two-star jokes? Sometimes Internet entries can be puzzling.

The following is an example of one of the 219, two-star jokes:

An Illinois man left the snowballed streets of Chicago for a vacation in Florida.   His wife was on a business trip and was planning to meet him there the next day. When he reached his hotel, he decided to send his wife a quick e-mail message.

Unable to find the scrap of paper on which he had written her e-mail address, he did his best to type it from memory. Unfortunately, he missed one letter, and his message was directed instead to an elderly preacher's wife whose husband had passed away only the day before. When the grieving widow checked her e-mail, she took one look at the monitor, let out a piercing scream, and fell to the floor dead.

At the sound, her family rushed into the room and saw this note on the screen:

> Dearest Wife,
> Just got checked in.   Everything prepared for your arrival tomorrow.
> Your Loving Husband.
> P.S. Sure is hot down here.

Accessing Internet Resources. Now that you have some idea about how many jokes are available on the Internet, how do you access them? There are at least four different ways to obtain jokes via the Internet: e-mail, getting a joke-a-day, using categories and using blogs or weblogs. The first two have jokes come to your personal computer whereas the final two require the use of a search engine—a program such as Google used to search for things on the Web—the central repository of humanity's information in the 21st century.

Receiving E-mail Humor is the most common form of joke distribution and receipt on the Internet. E-mail involves electronic messages sent via the Internet. Friends simply forward jokes they receive from others because the process is so simple: remove the sender's address, add any number of addresses you want from your own address book—or everyone in your address book, as some people do—and click "send." Simple. The joke is on its way.

There may be a way to increase the volume of jokes you receive via e-mail. When some people send jokes to you they leave the e-mail address or addresses on the e-mail which indicates the person or people from whom they received the joke. Some jokes may have five or ten "forwards." By examining those e-mail addresses, you may discover that a number of the forwards come from just one source or from very few sources. Because you now have the address or addresses of those sending jokes to the person who sent them to you, simply contact that person or persons and ask them to put you in their address book. If they are willing, the number of jokes you receive should increase dramatically. This method eliminates some of the "middle people"—those who screen the jokes they forward or who send just a sampling of the ones they receive.

One friend—a professor at a small eastern college—defended his screening, saying, "I simply didn't forward any material I thought might be offensive." When I intervened and began receiving e-mails from one of that professor's primary sources—without screening—it was quickly evident why the material was screened. Much of it could be classified as rude, coarse, and vulgar, and much was in very bad taste. But, that is the nature of the Internet. It is open, uncensored, and democratic. If one's goal is to discover jokes that are crude, coarse, vulgar, and in very bad taste, the Internet has a plethora of available web sites that should fully satisfy such an appetite. Like a large city that has its theaters and expensive restaurants, but also has its ghettos and unsavory sections, the Internet is a diverse and varied resource.

Many people, of course, would consider reading much of the humorous information circulated via e-mail a waste of time. Several people in my Internet address book specifically asked not to have any jokes forwarded to them and, certainly, their request was honored. As a writer, however, I was looking for humor I could use in my other writing and in my speeches as well; thus, the Internet became a valuable, important, and necessary supplement, even though I had to sift through a great deal of chaff to discover only a few golden kernels of grain. For example, from a list of over 50 "daffy-nitions" at one web address, very few could be used. These few examples had some potential usability: "An adult is a person who has stopped growing at both ends and is now growing in the middle," "A committee is a body that keeps minutes and wastes hours," "An egotist is someone who is usually me-deep in conversation," "A gossip is a person who will never tell a lie if the truth will do more damage," and "Tomorrow is one of the greatest labor-saving devices of today." But, look at the amount of sorting necessary to find those five out of 50 provided.

Getting a Joke-a-Day at your own Internet (e-mail) address is a second way of getting jokes. A number of web sites make it possible to have jokes sent directly to your e-mail mailbox. They require you to fill out a form at their web site, but the rest is simple: The jokes arrive daily without interruption. There is a way, however, to avoid having them clutter your normal, everyday e-mail mailbox. If you secure a second mailbox—for

example, a free one from <http://www.hotmail.com> —you can use it for such purposes. I have found that having an extra box is useful, too, for receiving advertising, business notices, or other information I do not want clogging my primary mailbox. This is the mailbox, too where you can have your jokes sent. If you do not access them on a daily basis, this secondary mailbox offers a place for them to accumulate. There are a number of "joke-a-day" web sites:
<http://www.ajokeaday.com>, <http://www.funny.co.uk/jokeaday.phtml>, and <http://www.joes.com/home/joke/> Entering "Joke-a-day" into the Google search engine will yield 382,000 web sites, many that offer this service for free. You may think a-joke-a-day may dilute the quality of the jokes you receive; however, a couple of representative examples clearly prove otherwise:

A man consults a therapist and states, "Doc, I'm suicidal. What should I do?"

The doctor replies, "Pay in advance."

A man at the airline counter tells the rep, "I'd like this bag to go to Berlin, this one to California, and this one to London."

The rep says, "I'm sorry sir. We can't do that."

The man replied: "Nonsense. That is what you did last time I flew with you."

It is hard to believe that in the time the Internet has existed, this much humorous information could have become available, but it is clear that at the very time the Internet began, the use of the medium to distribute and store humorous material was seen as not just accommodating but highly beneficial and desirable as well. Obviously, the two have grown in harmony, exponentially, ever since.

Using Categories to Obtain Humor is another way to get Internet jokes. It involves using categories such as puns or lightbulb jokes. Enter these categories into a search engine like "Google" to get examples. When you write "Lightbulb Jokes" into the search window of Google (using quotation marks), you get 295,000 web sites. The first, with the title "Definitive Collection of Lightbulb Jokes So Far Known," will produce, if printed out, close to 50 single-spaced typed pages of lightbulb jokes. Can you imagine thousands of jokes based on the lightbulb framework such as: "How many cops does it take to screw in a light bulb? None. It turned itself in?" or "How many lawyers does it take to screw in a lightbulb? How many can you afford?"

There are other categories that can be used to access Internet humor. Entering the names of comedians can lead to a vast array of humorous material. Entering the words Yogi Berra jokes produced 19,700 web sites, Jerry Seinfeld jokes yielded 74,500, Steven Wright jokes had 279,000, and Henny Youngman jokes had 14,400. Mention an event, add the word "jokes," and any search engine will guide you to a wealth of humor. The country is at war somewhere in the world? Name the country (Iraq, Afghanistan, Saudi Arabia, etc.) where the U.S. currently finds itself, add the word "jokes," and readers have yet another search-engine entry point.

The joke archives, of course, are an effective beginning point for finding joke categories. However, if readers are looking for humor connected with specific professions, those professions (like doctors, lawyers, nurses, salesmen, teachers, engineers, or any others) can be entered into a search engine. Doctor jokes had 1,290,000 web pages, lawyer jokes had 850,000, nurse jokes, 989,000, salesman jokes, 209,000, teacher jokes yielded 1,210,000 web pages, and engineer jokes, 780,000, There are so many web pages, so many joke warehouses, so many sources of humor, and so many different ways of accessing it all that it would be impossible in a single lifetime to access them all.

Entering "engineer jokes" in quotation marks into Google produced 16,900 web sites. Going to the first site listed, and choosing from the first of several jokes produced, yielded a joke that will be understood by those familiar with the computer instruction following the installation of any new software or other new feature: "Turn the computer off, turn it on again, and allow it to reboot."

There are four engineers traveling in a car; a mechanical engineer, a chemical engineer, and electrical engineer, and a computer engineer.

The car breaks down.

"Sounds to me as if the pistons have seized. We'll have to strip down the engine before we can get the car working again," says the mechanical engineer.

"Well," says the chemical engineer, "it sounded to me as if the fuel might be contaminated. I think we should clear out the fuel system."

"I thought it might be a grounding problem," says the electrical engineer," or maybe a faulty plug lead."

They all turn to the computer engineer who has said nothing and say, "Well, what do you think?"

"Ummm—perhaps if we all get out of the car and get back in again, it will work this time?"

A second choice at the same web site offered another engineering joke I found amusing, although slightly risqué:

> Three engineering students were gathered together discussing the possible designers of the human body. One said, "It was a mechanical engineer. Just look at all the joints." Another said, "No, it was an electrical engineer. The nervous system has many thousands of electrical connections." The last one said, "Actually it was a civil engineer. Who else would run a toxic waste pipeline through a recreational area?"

Using Blogs or Weblogs to obtain humor means entering another person's personal web site. Blogs or weblogs are a feature of the Internet that many computer users have put to their own private use. A personal, Internet file is known as a blog or weblog. It is simply your own web site that is updated frequently with links, commentary, and anything else—including jokes, humorous stories, cartoons, and links to particular web sites if the user so chooses. Many Internet users have used blogs or weblogs to create humor files. New items go on top, and other items flow down the page. These blogs can be humor journals, personal joke files, and they can range across a universe of topics or any range of joke categories or comedians—whatever choices suit the blog-maker's current interests. The blog form is unique to the Web, and it can be highly addictive.

For those interested in establishing a blog, enter the word into any search engine and a wide variety of host sites will be generated, any of which will be willing to accept your business and show you exactly how easy it is to establish a blog. The word blogs entered into the Google search engine generated 75,000,000 web sites, and the word weblogs produced 25,200,000. This offers some indication of how popular they are on the World Wide Web. More specifically, the words humor blogs generated 3,830,000 web sites, joke blogs 1,980,000, and joke weblogs 620,000. The advantage for those who want to find jokes on the Internet is that blogs can be accessed by anyone who has access to the Internet.

Developing Jokes

Previous chapters have described a process for arriving at a comic idea and developing from it a fully formed original joke. You will recall that it involves identifying such elements as the expressed and inferred ideas and using the effects—self satisfaction, surprise, and recognition of an incongruity—that will trigger laughter. The Internet also can be used to get the creative juices flowing.

<u>Brainstorming</u>.   One use of the Internet is for brainstorming—the process of coming up with as many ideas as possible without the interference of judgment or evaluation.   Whether you are looking for a springboard for a joke, an expressed idea, or an inferred idea, just entering keywords into a search engine will generate web sites containing titles, short explanations, and thousands of related words.

Let's say you will be giving a convention address about conventions, and you want to be humorous.   Think first of as many ideas related to conventions as you can: speakers, meetings, evaluations, discussions, speeches, lectures, luncheons, conventions, leaders, addresses, lights, ice breakers, officers, audiences, breakfasts, conferences, guests, elections, competitions, books, tapes, topics, lights, rooms, conversations, and venues, might be a few of the topics that come to mind.   If you are short of ideas, you can find additional possibilities by entering the word "conventions" into the Google search engine, then examining some of the web sites that result.   Now, to each of these topics, add the word jokes and enter the words into the Google search engine.   Here, I have done this for the first eight words and shown some of the items I received in each case:

Speakers: A speaker dies, and when he gets to Heaven, he sees a New York cab driver who has more crowns. He says to an angel, "I don't get it. I devoted my whole life to my audiences."

The angel says, "We reward results. Did your audiences always pay attention when you gave a speech?"

The speaker says, "Once in awhile someone fell asleep."

The angel says, "Right. And when people rode in this guy's taxi, they not only stayed awake, but they usually prayed!"

Meetings: The two biggest problems in this organization is making ends meet and making meetings end.

Evaluations: Whenever this person opens his mouth, it seems, it is only to change whatever foot was previously there.

Discussions: In a group discussion, the question was "What would you do if you had only 4 weeks to live?" The first member of the discussion said, "I would go out and speak to anyone willing to listen, and tell them how to live better lives." All members agreed that would be a good thing to do. The second member of the discussion said, "I would start listening better—learning all I could from others in the time I had left." All members agreed that would be a good thing to do. A third member said, "I would go and live with my mother-in-law." "Go to live with your mother-in-law?" the leader of the group questioned this member. "Yes, I would go and live with my mother-in-law, because that would be the longest 4 weeks of my life."

Speeches: What the speech lacked in interest, it gained in length.

Lectures: The lecture was a success; the audience was a disaster.

Luncheons: At lunch today I called the waiter over and said, "Sir, this coffee tastes like soap." He replied, "No, that must be the tea, sir. The coffee tastes like glue."

Conventions: Large gatherings of people who know not what they do, but do it with abandon and all at the same time. If a camel is a horse put together by a committee, then a convention must be a whale constructed by a minnow.

The jokes, at this point in the development of the speech, need not all be good ones, as is obvious from some of those above. The point is to use the Internet to find them. If you can assemble about 25 or 30 jokes based on the words brainstormed at the outset, then you will have a sufficient number to work from as your base. Your convention address on conventions can then be formed based on the best material you discover—usually about six or seven jokes—in addition to your personal observations, anecdotes, and other related information. When your mind is not operating in the ideal, free-wheeling mode you desire, stimulate it by going to a search engine and entering related words with the word jokes attached just to see what results those words generate.

If your goal is to acquire sample jokes then, as in the extended example above, simply precede *any* word with the word jokes, and you are likely to discover a whole new world of funny material. For the fun of it, I entered "Stupid Jokes" into Google and discovered 1,910,000 web sites. One of the early offerings yielded the following joke that has substituted the word "ur" for "you're" and "your," and in trying to further imitate the language of the poor, even used the word "smoke" as a substitution for the word cigarette:

ur families so poor that when i walked into ur house and stepped on a smoke ur family said "Who turned off the heat?!!?"

Randomly, and with no specific purpose in mind, I entered the words grandpa jokes into Google which yielded 190,000 web sites. And here is a joke produced from one of those web sites that manifests a play on words:

Sitting on grandpa's lap, the little girl says, "Grandpa, can you make a sound like a frog?"

"A sound like a frog? Well, sure grandpa can make a sound like a frog."

The girl says, "Please, please make a sound like a frog."

Perplexed, her grandpa says, "Sweetheart, why do you want me to make a sound like a frog?"

And the little girl says, "Cause grandma said that when you croak, we're going to Disneyland!"

The point here is the ease of using the Internet to discover jokes on any topic desired. Such an approach would be useful when developing a speech or discovering a point in the speech where a relevant humorous break might be appropriate. Relevance, of course, is a key quality that should be present whenever a joke is selected for a speech or other writing.

Switching. With the exception of simply finding jokes that you can share with others, the Internet is likely to be one of the best sources for jokes that can be switched. As explained in Chapter 7, "Finding Your Way to a Joke," switching is defined as finding a good joke, making some changes in it, and presenting it as your own. Some have labeled this feature "portability"—jokes that can be transported to fit a number of situations. The following is a joke found in an online joke archive, but, as you read it, notice the overall format of the joke and how easy it would be to switch the joke to another situation:

A graduate student, a post-doctoral student, and a professor are walking through a city park when they find an antique oil lamp. They rub it, and a Genie comes out in a puff of smoke. The Genie says, "I usually only grant three wishes, so I'll give each of you just one."

"Me first! Me first!" says the graduate student. "I want to be in the Bahamas, driving a speedboat with a gorgeous woman who sunbathes topless." Poof! He's gone.

"Me next! Me next!" says the post-doctoral student. "I want to be in Hawaii, relaxing on the beach with a professional hula dancer on one side and a Mai Tai on the other." Poof! He's gone.

"You're next," the Genie says to the professor.

The professor says, "I want those guys back in the lab after lunch."

When you switch a joke, as explained in Chapter 7, you put it into new surroundings, supply new characters, or add an original twist of your own. Pretend, for example, you must give a speech in a business setting. You could switch the above joke to an employee, a supervisor, and a vice president or president of the company. You could even give each individual the name of specific people within your business, and further, you could give them wishes that correspond to their precise hobbies or recreational pursuits. Different situations could include a secondary school, a doctor's office, lawyer's group, a hospital, or any environment where people are held to some kind of schedule.

Here is another example. Because the format is simple, notice how easily the joke can be switched. Switch it to a setting and circumstance with which you are familiar.

> An angel suddenly appears at a faculty meeting and tells the dean of the college that in return for his unselfish and exemplary behavior, he will be given his choice of infinite wealth, wisdom, or beauty. Without hesitating, the dean selects infinite wisdom
>
> "Done!" says the angel, and disappears in a cloud of smoke and a bolt of lightning.
>
> Now, all heads turn toward the dean who sits surrounded by a faint halo of light.
>
> At length, one of his colleagues whispers, "Say something."
>
> The dean looks at them and says, "I should have taken the money."

Switching jokes is not only a way to come up with jokes specific to situations that are immediate and personal, but it is also an easy way to develop jokes. Look, for example, at the possibilities for this joke called "The Exam":

> A college student in a philosophy class was taking his first examination.
>
> On the paper there was a single line which simply said: "Is this a question?" –Discuss.
>
> After a short time he wrote: "If that is a question, then this is an answer."
>
> The student received an "A" on the exam.

This prompted an immediate response, which is, once again, a switch, but a switch that creates a joke specific to another discipline (Speech Communication), that can be easily understood by anyone:

> A college student was in a speech class taking her first examination.
>
> On the paper there was a single line which simply said: "Is this feedback?"
>
> –Discuss.
>
> After a short time she wrote: "No. But this is."
>
> The student received an "A" on the exam.

Using Frameworks or Patterns. Frameworks or patterns, as noted in Chapter 7, are often easy to switch simply because they follow a prescribed format. In addition, there are so many samples of formula-driven jokes on the Internet that it is easy to obtain examples. Knock-knock jokes have 702,000 hits at Google; lightbulb jokes received 295,000 hits, Yo Mama (Your Momma) jokes had 295,000 web sites, Little Willy jokes produced 167,000 web sites, Tom Swifty jokes netted 4,340, redneck jokes had 1,130,000, Why did the chicken cross the road? supplied 854,000, puns produced 730,000, limerick jokes received 83,500, and limericks without the word jokes following it produced 752,000. The final framework, limericks, produced this gem:

> A flea and a fly in a flue
> Were caught, so what could they do?
> Said the fly, "Let us flee."
> "Let us fly," said the flea.
> So they flew through a flaw in the flue.

At this web site
<http://volweb.utk.edu'Schools/bedford/harrisms/limerick.htm>
—the same one where the above limerick was discovered—they even explain how to compose limericks.

Giving Credit Where Credit Is Due

The concept of authorship with regard to Internet humor is a difficult issue. An example will make this clear. During the 1980s the well-known "You have two cows" joke circulated widely in typewritten form. Originally, the joke was used in Economics 101 classes to describe how the government and bureaucracy would interfere with one's quiet enjoyment of one's cows. It seems to have first appeared on the Internet in 1993 with the simple descriptions of communism, capitalism, and socialism—the specific examples used in basic-economics classes:

> Communism: You have two cows. The government seizes both and provides you with milk.

> Capitalism: You have two cows. You sell one, buy a bull, and build a herd of cows.

> Socialism: You have two cows. The government takes one and gives it to your neighbor.

Soon after the "You have two cows" joke appeared on the Internet, however, it evolved into satires of various political, cultural, social, and philosophical systems and theories. Eventually, virtually anything came to be usable as "cow joke fodder":

Conservatism: You have two cows. You freeze the milk, embalm the cows and charge people to look at them.

Feminism: You have two cows. They get married and adopt a veal calf.

Idealism: You have two cows. You get married and your partner milks them.

Indian Corporation: You have two cows. You worship them.

Mexican Corporation: You think you have two cows, but you don't know what a cow looks like. You take a nap.

Japanese Corporation: You have two cows. You redesign them so they are one tenth the size of an ordinary cow and produce twenty times the milk.

Attempting to attribute authorship becomes impossible, and the jokes quickly become a publicly owned resource simply because no one can validly claim legitimate ownership—especially after they became a part of the international development of the World Wide Web. The jokes are still circulated today. They are translated and quoted on many web sites, in dozens of versions, and new definitions are added every year. When the words "You have two cows" are entered into the Google search engine, 6,990,000 web sites are produced, revealing the phenomenal growth experienced by this genre of jokes.

Even when the originator of the humor is credited, often it makes no difference because the proper, original source of the humor is quickly, easily, and often quite deliberately deleted. It is as if once a joke is written and circulated it becomes part of the public domain. Henceforth, nobody cares about giving proper credit—even though they *should* care. For example, one of those people who forwards me humor, never adds a source of any kind. From the material received from this person, I cannot even tell where he received it, because he deletes the addresses of all previous forwards. Although people may know where they received a specific piece of information—the e-mail address and name of the sender—they seldom know the original source of the humor.

Another person who forwards humor to my e-mail mailbox, on the other hand, may include two, three, or even more previous e-mail addresses attached to the entry. Actually, it's easier to do it this way; deleting the forwards takes a few minutes. These may be people in the chain of forwards. Clearly, they are not necessarily—and most likely never—the proper, original sources of the humor.

I often wonder who is it who creates all these jokes? Do these joke makers care that they are seldom if ever credited for their material? Neither of these questions can be, or ever will be, answered. Perhaps a joke maker's pleasure comes from the joy of seeing his or her joke returned or archived. With respect to the credit on many of the stories that appear on the Internet, many, if they appear at all, relate to an Internet-joke warehouse, the web-editor of which requests humor from readers and simply catalogs the humor upon receipt. The web-editor neither claims credit for the joke nor authorship. One web-editor explained his site this way: "Most of the material here is just that. Comedy and stories from friends who got it from friends who have no clue where it originally came from."

There is an interesting byproduct of this "credit problem." The Internet is truly a democratic vehicle that represents social equality at its finest. Often, it is difficult to know the origination of a joke, as previously noted, because on the Internet they come from comedians, newspapers, magazines, speeches, television, movies, as well as friends and family members. What this means, however, is that the Internet offers an opportunity for neophyte, untested, joke makers to test their mettle. The Internet is a vehicle for the creation, publication, and distribution of jokes, and, thus, exposure. Because the demand for laughs is never-ceasing, what better way for beginners to test their ability?

The real problem regarding giving credit for jokes occurs when speakers plan to use them publicly or when authors intend to include them in material that will be published. When credit is given along with the jokes found on the Internet, then speakers and authors can track down the originator of the humor and gain the appropriate permission to use them. As noted in Chapter 7, if we know who the author of a joke is, it would be a graceful note to mention the name. When credit is not given, the best advice is to be careful. When in doubt, of course, it is best to select material that is *clearly* in the public domain, but this, we admit, is often very difficult to determine. Just because a joke is circulated with no authorship attached does not automatically mean the joke is in the public domain, even though this is likely to be the assumption. And, as further noted in Chapter 7, even when an author and a joke are connected, we can't always be sure the attribution is correct. All of these elements complicate the problem of giving credit, but they do not make it impossible in every instance.

Bibliography

Allen, Fred. (1956). *Much Ado About Me*. Boston: Little Brown.

Allen, Fred. (1954). *Treadmill to Oblivion*. Boston: Little Brown.

Allen, Steve. (1956). *The Funny Men*. New York: Simon and Schuster.

Allen, Steve. (1987). *How to be Funny*. New York: McGraw-Hill.

Allen, Steve. (1993). *Make 'Em Laugh*. New York: Prometheus Books.

Belzer, Richard. (1988). *How to be a Stand-Up Comic*. New York: Villard Books.

Berle, Milton. (1989). *Milton Berle's Private Joke File*. New York: Crown Publishers.

Bier, Jesse. (1968). *The Rise and Fall of American Humor*. New York: Holt, Rinehart and Winston.

Cerf, Bennett, ed. (1954). *An Encyclopedia of Modern American Humor*. Garden City, NY: Doubleday.

Copeland, Lewis, and Faye Copeland, eds. (1940). *10,000 Jokes, Toasts and Stories*. Garden City, NY: Halcyon House.

Davis, Robertson, ed. (1981). *The Penguin Stephen Leacock*. New York: Penguin Books.

Dundes, Alan. (1987). *Cracking Jokes: Studies of Sick Humor Cycles and Stereotypes*. Berkeley, CA: Ten Speed Press.

Eastman, Max.(1937). *Enjoyment of Laughter*. New York: Simon and Schuster.

Eastman, Max. (1922). *The Sense of Humor*. New York: Charles Scribners. Republished, New York: Octagon Books, 1972.

Franken, Al. (1996). *Rush Limbaugh is a Big Fat Idiot and Other Observations*. New York: Delacorte Press.

Gilliat, Penelope. (1990). *To Wit*. New York: Charles Scribners.

Green, Lila. (1994). *Making Sense of Humor: How to Add Joy to Your Life*. Manchester, CT: KIT (Knowledge, Ideas, & Trends, Inc.).

Gruner, Charles R. (1978). *Understanding Laughter: The Workings of Wit and Humor*. Chicago, IL: Nelson-Hall.

Harmon, Jim. (1970). *The Great Radio Comedians*. Garden City, NY: Doubleday.

Helitzer, Melvin. (1987). *Comedy Writing Secrets*. Cincinnati, OH: Writer's Digest Books.

Holland, Norman, N. (1982). *Laughing: A Psychology of Humor*. Ithaca, NY: Cornell University Press.

Jenkins, Henry. (1993). *What Made Pistachio Nuts?: Early Sound Comedy and the*

Vaudeville Aesthetic. New York: Columbus University Press.

Josepberg, Milt. (1987). *Comedy Writing for Television and Hollywood.* New York: Harper Collins.

Kachuba, John B. (Ed.) (2001). *How to Write Funny: Add Humor to Every Kind of Writing.* Cincinnati, OH: Writer's Digest Books.

Kant, Immanuel. (1790). (J. H. Barnard, trans. (1972)). *Critique of Judgment.* New York: Hafner.

Kaplan, Justin. (1966). *Mr. Clemens and Mark Twain.* New York: Simon and Schuster.

Kinney, Harrison. (1995). *James Thurber: His Life and Times.* New York: Henry Holt.

Koestler, Arthur. (1964). *Act of Creation.* New York: Macmillan.

Kusher, Malcolm. (1990). *Light Touch: How to Use Humor for Business Success.* New York: Simon and Schuster.

Lax, Eric. (1977). *On Being Funny: Woody Allen and Comedy.* New York: Manor Books.

Leacock, Stephen. (1935). *Humor: Its Theory and Technique.* New York: Dodd Mead.

Leamer, Laurence. (1989). *King of the Night: The Life of Johnny Carson.* New York: William Morrow.

McGhee, Paul E. (1979). *Humor: Its Origin and Development.* San Francisco: W. H. Freeman.

Maltin, Leonard. (1978). *The Great Movie Comedians.* New York: Crown Publishers.

[No author]. (no date). "Misunderstandings about the Internet." *Slinkycity.com—Jokes, Pranks, Games & Humor.* Retrieved September 26, 2004, from http://www.slinkycity.com/internet-mistakes.html.

Mulkay, Michael. (1988). *On Humour: Its Nature and Place in Modern Society.* Oxford, England: Basil Blackwell.

Neider, Charles, ed. (1961). *The Complete Humorous Sketches and Tales of Mark Twain.* Garden City, NY: Doubleday.

Paar, Jack, with John Reddy. (1959). *I Kid You Not.* Boston: Little Brown.

Paine, Albert Bigelow. (1912). *Mark Twain: A Biography.* New York: Harper and Brothers.

Paul, William. (1994). *Laughing Screaming: Modern Hollywood Horror and Comedy.* New York: Columbia University Press.

Paulos, John Allen. (1980). *Mathematics and Humor.* Chicago: University of Chicago Press.

Perret, Gene. (1990). *Comedy Writing Step by Step.* Hollywood: Samuel French.

Perret, Gene. (1982). *How to Write and Sell Your Sense of Humor.* Cincinnati: Writer's Digest.

Perret, Gene. (1993). *Successful Stand-Up Comedy.* Hollywood: Samuel French.

Powell, Chris, and George E. C. Paton, eds. (1988). *Humor in Society: Resistance and Control.* London, England: Macmillan Press.

Provine, Robert R. (2000). *Laughter: A Scientific Investigation.* New York: Viking.

Radowitz, John von. (2002, October 3). "World's funniest joke no laughing matter!" *icWales (The national website of Wales).* Retrieved September 26, 2004, from http://icwales.icnetwork.co.uk/0100news/0600uk/page.cfm?method=full&objectid =12251019.

Rapp, Albert. (1951). *The Origins of Wit and Humor.* New York: E. P. Dutton.

Redfern, Walter. (1984). *Puns.* New York: Basil Blackwell.

Rosten, Leo. (1994). *Carnival of Wit.* New York: E. P. Dutton.

Schopenhauer, Arthur. (1819). (B. Haldane and J. Kemp, trans. (1907)). *The World as Will and Idea.* London: Kegan Paul, French, Trabner and Company.

Schreiber, Brad. (2003). *What Are You Laughing At? How to Write Funny Screenplays, Stories, & More.* Studio, City, CA: Michael Wiese Productions.

Shalit, Gene, ed. (1987). *Laughing Matters: A Celebration of American Humor.* Garden City, NY: Doubleday.

Sikov, Ed. (1994). *Laughing Hysterically: American Screen Comedy of the 1950s.* New York: Columbia University Press.

Taylor, Robert. (1989). *Fred Allen: His Life and Wit.* Boston: Little Brown.

Thurber, James. (1945). *The Thurber Carnival.* New York: Harper and Row.

Untermeyer, Louis, ed. (1946). *A Treasury of Laughter.* New York: Simon and Schuster.

Wertheim, Alfred. (1979). *Radio Comedy.* New York: Oxford University Press.

White, E. B., and Katherine S. White, eds. (1941). *A Subtreasury of American Humor.* New York: Coward-McCann.

Wilde, Larry. (1976). *How the Great Comedy Writers Create Laughter.* Chicago: Nelson-Hall.

Wiseman, Richard. (no date). *LaughLab.co.uk/* Retrieved September 26, 2004, from http://www.laughlab.co.

[No author]. (2002, October 3). "World's funniest joke revealed." *NewScientist.com.* Retrieved September 26, 2004, from http://www.newscientist.com/news/news.jsp?id=ns99992876.

A

B

Printed in the United States
68360LVS00007B/12